**Women Across
Continents**

FEMINIST COMPARATIVE S
POLICY

Boc

04

Women Across Continents

FEMINIST COMPARATIVE SOCIAL POLICY

Lena Dominelli

Professor of Social Administration
University of Sheffield

HARVESTER
WHEATSHEAF

NEW YORK   LONDON   TORONTO   SYDNEY   TOKYO   SINGAPORE

First published 1991 by
Harvester Wheatsheaf
66 Wood Lane End, Hemel Hempstead
Hertfordshire HP2 4RG
A division of
Simon & Schuster International Group

© Lena Dominelli, 1991

Typeset in 10 on 12 pt Bembo
by Photoprint, Torquay

Printed and bound in Great Britain by
BPCC Wheatons Ltd, Exeter

British Library Cataloguing in Publication Data

Dominelli, Lena
Women across continents: feminist comparative social
policy.
1. Social policies
I. Title
361.61

ISBN 0-7450-0336-2
ISBN 0-7450-0939-5 pbk

1 2 3 4 5   95 94 93 92 91

To
Assunta, Raffaela and Giuseppina
for their strength in getting on with their lives
whatever governments do or say

Contents

Acknowledgements

The welfare state has had a substantial impact on the lives and welfare of women. Not all of this has been beneficial. Women have both gained and lost through its interventions. But academic analyses outside of feminist discourse have seldom commented on the specific experience women have had of welfare state provisions and the labour they have undertaken both within it and on its behalf. Feminist analyses have focused primarily on the experience of women within single countries rather than presenting extensive comparative analyses. Thus comparative social administration students are left with the task of making the connections between developments in one country and those taking place in another and trying to formulate explanations which can deal adequately with both the diversity and similarities among welfare states. The immensity of such a project is daunting enough to discourage individuals from even attempting it. However, such work becomes less threatening if one is being encouraged to undertake it and supported in doing so by countless others.

I wish to express my gratitude to the generations of Warwick University students taking social policy for the intellectual stimulation they have given me in this subject. Additionally, I wish to thank the readers of my drafts for their help and insights. In particular, I would like to mention Kelly Maier, Paul Stubbs and David Howe. Rita Thodos deserves my special thanks for undertaking the tedious typing task. Finally, I must highlight the contribution made to the care of my young son by my mother, father, sister Maria, and husband David, for without the easing of this responsibility, it would have been impossible for my mind and time to be freed for the enormous commitment writing such a book requires. It is at such points that the contradictions between being a mother and a worker are at their most acute and I felt I was living the contradictory experience of the welfare state explored in this book.

1

Introduction

CONVERGENCE BETWEEN CAPITALIST AND SOCIALIST MODELS OF WELFARE

The welfare state has been heralded as a measure providing for the well-being of its citizens by redistributing income to the have-nots, reducing individual insecurity during financial crises, and endorsing egalitarian relationships (Crosland, 1956; Titmuss, 1968; Heclo, 1974; George and Manning, 1980; Lenin, 1965; Deacon, 1983; T. Marshall, 1965). However, these aspirations remain unrealised. The capitalist welfare state has neither redistributed income (Offe, 1984) nor promoted equality and dignity between and among workers and claimants (Bolger *et al.*, 1981). Coverage and access to its provisions has been patchy, leading to a differentiated user experience. Key dimensions against which differentiation occurs are those of class (Offe, 1984), 'race' (Mama, 1989), and gender (Pascall, 1986; Dale and Foster, 1986). Middle class people receive more welfare benefits because they know how to demand them (Field, 1989; Glazer, 1988). In the socialist world, Communist Party bureaucrats and state employees have greater access to superior welfare resources (George and Manning, 1980; Bonavia, 1982). White people in capitalist countries are more likely to seek its resources because they are not subjected to racist barriers in doing so (Dominelli, 1988a; Mama, 1989; MacPherson, 1982). Men have greater access to insurance-based provisions than women because eligibility rules have been drafted with men's career patterns in mind (Pascall, 1986). Moreover, welfare resources in both capitalist and socialist countries are concentrated in urban areas, thereby disadvantaging people living in rural areas (Heclo, 1974; George and Manning, 1980; Deacon, 1983; Bonavia, 1982; Silver, 1976; Andors, 1983).

Working class people have contributed proportionately more of their income to the creation and maintenance of the welfare state than their middle class counterparts in Britain, the United States, Canada and Sweden (Fry, 1969). Yet, the middle classes have succeeded in making better use of its facilities, whether it be health care, education, income maintenance, day-care or other positive provision in the personal social services. Black working class people's access to positive welfare resources is less than white people's. However, they are disproportionately represented in penal institutions (Home Office, 1986). Working class people are also found at the lower echelons of the welfare state labour hierarchy, doing back-breaking physical work while middle class people are involved in its managerial structures (Sidel, 1986). The welfare state labour force is also racially structured with white people at its apex and black people at the bottom. Additionally, the division of labour follows gender segregation with women at the lower reaches.

Black authors, for example, Carby (1982), Gilroy (1982, 1987), Lorde (1984) and Sivanandan (1976), have been indicting the capitalist welfare state for failing to meet their needs and exploiting their labour for some time. White academicians have been slow in following their lead. Analyses focusing on the impact racism has on welfare theory, policies and practice by white authors remain the exception, for example Gordon (1985), Williams (1987, 1989), Stubbs (1985) and Dominelli (1979, 1988a).

Developing an adequate understanding of the racism enshrined in welfare provisions requires analysts to consider the implications of: the world economy on welfare services (Sivanandan, 1976; Rose and Rose, 1982; Barratt Brown, 1985; Nove, 1983; Mandel, 1986); the exclusion of black people from access to positive welfare resources (Carby, 1982; Gilroy, 1982, 1987; Dominelli, 1988a); the over-representation of black people in its punitive elements (Mama, 1989; Tipler, 1986; Dominelli, 1983); use of black people's labour to finance welfare provisions on the cheap (Moraga and Azaldua, 1981; Prescod-Roberts and Steele, 1980; Hooks, 1984; Bryan et al., 1985; Sivanandan, 1976); and the detrimental impact of policies on black families (Mama, 1989; Dominelli, 1988a; Bryan et al., 1985). The constraints imposed by multinational companies and international financial organisations on the development of social policies conducive to all people's welfare require further clarification and elucidation. Examining these has revealed that the development of welfare states in the Third World countries has been severely curtailed by the constraints of loan repayments on debts owed to Western international financiers (Hayter, 1981). Western countries have also felt the restraints of international finance capital. In Britain, for example, the massive welfare programme including institutional provisions for childcare funded through the taxation system anticipated by the Wilson government of the mid-1970s was halted by the public expenditure cuts imposed by the International Monetary Fund. While this limited women's access to day-care resources, this restriction was more serious for black women who have a higher rate of involvement in the labour market when their children are small (Bruegel, 1989; Mama, 1989; Sidel, 1986). In the United States, Reagan substantially cut welfare spending as part of a programme aimed at containing the budgetary deficit. These have disproportionately affected the poor who are primarily women and black people (Sidel, 1986).

Women have a contradictory relationship with the welfare state. The welfare state provides women claimants and women workers with opportunities – benefits and jobs respectively – through which they can achieve a measure of financial autonomy (McIntosh, 1978). This is a mixed blessing for it has fostered women's dependence on the state for financial resources in the form of jobs when employed by it, and income support when unwaged. It has contributed directly to women's oppression by reinforcing their subordinate position within the family (Wilson, 1977), legitimating their dependent status *vis-à-vis* their menfolk (Land, 1976; Land and Ward, 1986; Pascall, 1986), the rules and regulations governing eligibility to benefits, and ghettoising women workers in the low pay echelons of its labour hierarchy (J. Armstrong, 1985; Howe, 1986; Coyle, 1989). These features make sexism an integral feature of the organisation of the welfare state. Examining power relations between men and women and the role of the welfare state in their perpetuation, modification and elimination is a feature central to feminist analyses. Comparative social administration literature rarely explores this relationship. However, the impact of welfare policies on women is a major theme in this book.

Analyses focusing on social divisions have revealed the classism, sexism and racism which both permeate and emanate from welfare relationships (Mama, 1989; Dominelli, 1990). These have generated controversy and exposed the inadequacy of conceptualising the welfare state as a neutral entity operating from a value free power base. Welfare relationships cover the whole gamut of interactions between service providers and users and include issues of participation in the creation and running of services, access, quality, social control, delivery, funding and the relationship between private and public spheres in social life. Thus, a full analysis of the welfare state encompasses microlevel policies and provisions, employment practices, and macrolevel policies, economics and ideology.

The welfare state is in crisis in both capitalist and socialist countries

(Mishra, 1984, Offe, 1984; Oyen, 1986). Financially, it cannot meet its promises as social security, health, education, and housing costs escalate. But the crisis is not merely fiscal. The quality of services provided under its auspices is also being questioned. Claimants have been frustrated by its remote, bureaucratic and alienating influence and have challenged it (Bailey and Brake, 1975). Workers have also begun to back their demands for better quality care by taking industrial action, for example, health workers in Britain and the United States, social workers in Britain (Joyce et al., 1987), the Pro-Democracy Movement in China. The welfare state's failure to realise its objectives has embroiled all segments of the political spectrum in debates about its nature and future. These have included arguments for: dismantling it on economic and moral grounds by the Right (Murray, 1984; Glazer, 1988), broadening the range of providers from the Centre (Hadley and Hatch, 1981), and creating market socialism from the Left (Nove, 1983). As we enter the 1990s, it seems the welfare state has fallen into disrepute. Both capitalist and socialist countries are re-examining their commitment to state funded, organised and delivered welfare. Reconsidering the founding premises of the welfare state demands the resolution of the following issues: client dissatisfaction with the inaccessibility of welfare services; stigmatised responses meted out to service users; government bureaucrats' and welfare professionals' failure to maintain and enhance the quality of services in a climate of fiscal austerity; demoralised welfare professionals whose autonomous decision-making powers and control over their work have been whittled away by the proletarianisation of their jobs; the welfare state's failure to reduce social inequality and social divisions; and the inability of neo-conservative welfare proposals to make good deficiencies in existing welfare provisions.

This book will consider the ways in which the distinctive welfare states of the United States, Canada, Britain, Sweden, Soviet Union and China have responded to these crises and draw out the similarities and differences between them from an anti-racist feminist perspective, that is, paying particular attention to their specific impact on women and black people. Comparisons have to be treated with caution as the bases of statistical compilations used in each country and the provisions covered vary substantially. In many areas, statistical data is unavailable. However, we can use what exists to gain impressions of the relative weighting given to welfare expenditures in each country. Hence, the book will focus largely on qualitative materials in seeking to understand the nature of the welfare state developed in each country and its impact on women's lives.

A BRIEF OUTLINE OF THE POLITICAL AND ECONOMIC CONTEXTS OF THE COUNTRIES UNDER STUDY

The countries under study have varied political and economic systems ranging from industrialised western capitalist democracies to an industrialising Third World socialist country. A thumbnail sketch of their political and economic layouts is provided below. The United States is a federal representative democracy in which individual states have jurisdiction over welfare matters. The government consists of an executive arm headed by the President, a legislative arm consisting of the House of Representatives and Senate, and the judiciary – the Supreme Court responsible for interpreting the Constitution. A system of checks and balances in which each division of government is separate from and controls the others is in operation. The two main parties vying for power are the Democratic Party and Republican Party. The President, elected every four years on a collegiate basis, can only hold office for a maximum of two terms. A president elected from one party may find the majority in the House and Senate is from the opposite party. Also the political majority in each legislature can vary. America's market economy exerts a strong influence on the allocation of power and resources. Ideologically, it is an open society in which individual upward mobility is the outcome of hard work. All 'races' and 'immigrants' are expected to assimilate into the dominant white Anglo-Saxon protestant culture and fit into its vast 'melting pot'. Under the Constitution, Americans are free and equal under the law.

Canada's political system is also a federal representative democracy in which the provinces are primarily responsible for welfare matters. It has a bicameral parliament with an elected House of Commons and an appointed Senate (due for reform). Its history and traditions are different from America, not least because it repatriated its Constitution, including a Charter of Rights and Freedoms from Britain in 1982. The country is a constitutional monarchy with a government headed by a Prime Minister who is normally a member of the largest party in the House. The Supreme Court of Canada has the task of interpreting the Constitution, the Charter and the 1977 Bill of Rights. While the economy is a market-based one in which foreign investment particularly from the United States, Britain and Japan looms large, there is a substantial public sector which has become vulnerable under the 1989 Free Trade Deal between Canada and the United States. Ideologically, Canada follows Anglo-Saxon culture and history, but is constitutionally obliged to recognise the equal status of Quebec and its French culture. Canada is a bilingual country which does not subscribe to the 'melting pot' thesis. Rather, ethnic cultures and languages are protected by a state fostering ethno-cultural diversity. This theory is often breached in practice and the Meech Lake Accord, if it had been ratified, promised to strengthen Quebec's 'distinctive society' status. Its ratification was ultimately blocked by the serious objections raised by New Brunswick, Manitoba and Newfoundland. The failure to reach agreement on the status of Quebec is a longstanding one giving rise to separatist political factions favouring the creation of an independent Quebec state. Political leadership in each province may differ from that provided federally. Canada is also an open society in which individuals can be upwardly mobile and groups can organise collectively to influence the political system.

Britain is a liberal parliamentary democracy. Although it provided the initial model for both Canada and the United States, it is substantially different. Made up of separate countries – England, Scotland, Wales and Northern Ireland – Britain has a unitary state which delegates powers to local authorities. It has an unwritten constitution and no Bill of Rights, giving the central state a key role in enacting legislation and determining the powers of the local state. The British parliament is bicameral with an elected House of Commons and a largely hereditary House of Lords. The Queen is head of state but the government is run by a Prime Minister who normally leads the largest party in the Commons. The House of Lords also acts as the final Court of Appeal, although British citizens have access to the European Court. Britain has a mixed economy with large private and public sectors. Ideologically, Anglo-Saxon culture and traditions are dominant, although black people have succeeded in retaining many of their customs and traditions despite white British attempts at assimilation.

Sweden is a constitutional monarchy in which a system of proportional representation is used to allocate seats in the Riksdag (Parliament). The government is headed by a Prime Minister who comes from the majority party in the Riksdag. Except for a break between 1976 and 1982, the Social Democratic Party (SAP) has been ruling since 1932. Sweden differs from the other three western democracies in that business interests, the trade union movement and the state, sit together in tripartite committees to consider social policy. Social democratic consensus politics are the main vehicles for handling social conflict. Sweden operates a market economy tempered by a large public sector primarily concerned with the allocation of welfare resources.

The Soviet Union is made up of theoretically independent republics. Until recently, the Soviet Union was governed through a Politburo headed by the Communist Party Secretary and the Premier. This has recently changed as the processes unleashed by *peristroika* and *glasnost* reshape Soviet society. It is now governed by a President and Parliament. These changes can potentially diminish the direct power exercised by the Party. The Soviet Union was the world's first proclaimed communist state. Officially, it deems itself socialist in a transitional stage to communism. Debates over the nature of the Soviet state abound, but the economy is largely a state dominated one in which central planning determines the allocation of power and resources. Its command economy is easing under *peristroika* and market oriented initiatives are being encouraged. Ideologically, the Soviet union is socialist. Its unity is being questioned as internal divisions and ethnic rivalries are currently coming to the fore. The Soviet Union's stranglehold over the Eastern Bloc has also been ruptured.

China's Communist Party, under the leadership of the Secretary, is the key organ of government. Its authority is being challenged in Tibet, and although crushed, by the Pro-Democracy Movement in China itself. The economy is a predominantly rural command economy with substantial central state planning guiding decentralised local operations.

COMPARATIVE ANALYSES OF THE WELFARE STATE: THE ABSENCE OF GENDER FROM ACADEMIC DISCOURSE

The welfare state has been created as governments assumed roles traditionally fulfilled through the family and charitable institutions (Glazer, 1988). However, the state has been selective about the areas in which it has intervened and the extent to which it has done so. Income maintenance, the personal social services, housing, education and health are the major fields falling into the ambit of the 'welfare state'. Definitions of the welfare state are diverse and problematic because modern states are complex entities in which virtually every aspect of socio-political and economic life is subjected to some form of governmental control. Briggs (1961) concentrates on the role of the welfare state in varying the impact of market forces:

> A 'welfare state' is a state in which organised power is deliberately used . . . to modify the play of market forces . . . first, by guaranteeing individuals and families a minimum income irrespective of the market value of their work or their property; second, by narrowing the extent of insecurity by enabling individuals and families to meet certain 'social contingencies' (for example, sickness, old age, and unemployment) which

lead otherwise to individual and family crises; and third, by ensuring that all citizens without distinction of status or class are offered the best standard available in relation to a certain agreed range of social services. (Briggs, 1961, p. 228)

This definition is inadequate in several respects. It fails to encompass welfare services outside the market. These include those which are provided by charitable institutions for political and ideological reasons, for example, religious welfare institutions, and voluntary organisations such as the Elizabeth Fry Society. But more importantly from a feminist perspective, it excludes welfare services provided free by women in the domestic economy as part of their 'labour of love' (Graham, 1983). Moreover, gender and racial inequality in welfare provisions and among welfare workers are ignored. Other social divisions such as class, age and disability are absent from this analysis which also fails to grapple effectively with claimant perspectives and their evaluation of the quality of services provided. Furthermore, it ignores the role of the market in setting benefit levels. Income support schemes safeguarding individual and family finances during hard times have been calculated so as not to undermine the low waged sector of the economy and to enforce labour discipline in both capitalist and socialist countries (see Piven and Cloward, 1972; Ginsburg, 1979; George and Manning, 1980). Finally, Briggs' (1961) definition underrates the significance of a dimension highlighted earlier by Titmuss and Abel-Smith (1956), namely, that 'social welfare' is only one mechanism whereby the state distributes benefits. Although not usually classified as welfare, tax breaks, tax exemptions, subsidies, grants and loans, are also redistributive measures. Only these benefit the monied middle and upper classes (Titmuss and Abel-Smith, 1956) and can be substantially more than the amounts expended on what is traditionally understood to be the welfare state. For example, in Canada, the National Council of Welfare dubbed these financial transfers the 'hidden welfare system' and estimated them to be equivalent to the federal budget deficit (National Council of Welfare (NCW, 1979a)). In Britain, Lawson's 1988 budget tax cuts benefited the top 5 per cent of the population to the tune of £4 billion. Reagan's 1981 budget benefited investors rather than welfare claimants (Glazer, 1988).

A feminist definition of the welfare state takes account of social welfare relationships in both public and private spheres (Gordon, 1977) including fiscal transfers occurring through the tax system. It acknowledges that these two domains are indivisibly interconnected and that activities in one arena have significant implications for those taking place in the other (Prescod-Roberts and Steele, 1980). In other words, feminist analyses reject the dualism characterising classical analyses in which economic policy and social policy, the private sphere and the public one are deemed to operate independently of each other. Treating these worlds as unconnected to each other enables non-feminist theorists to ignore the contribution the domestic economy makes to sustaining and reproducing accepted public welfare relationships, and the impact economic policies have on social policies. In feminist analyses, the welfare state comprises of those public and domestic relationships which take as their primary objectives the well-being of people. This draws in the contributions women make to welfare relationships in both waged and unwaged capacities.

The connections between public and private policies explored through feminist analyses show that classical theories of the welfare state need to be broadened if the true costs of welfare provisions to society are to be ascertained and the unacknowledged work contributed by women through their 'labour of love' noted on the balance sheet. Moreover, feminism's commitment to egalitarianism means that *all people have a right to welfare*, regardless of their status. They acquire this right by virtue of their existence – no other qualifying criterion is necessary. Therefore, residency requirements, contributions schedules, and citizenship status are unnecessary. There is no division between the 'deserving' and the 'undeserving', which must be enforced because all are eligible. But as people have rights, they also have obligations. As members of society, people meet these through the work they do, whether waged or unwaged.

Comparative analysis draws on single state analyses of welfare for its theoretical discourse and descriptive contents in *explaining and giving an account of similarities and differences between countries* with varying socioeconomic and political systems. Comparative analysis, like single state analysis, is marked by controversy over competing explanations of the welfare state. In particular, these involve: the nature of the relationship between the individual and the state; the significance attached to economic and political forces; the impact of industrialisation and its relationship to the 'social division of welfare' (Titmuss, 1958); the impact of demographic factors; the role of the domestic economy in welfare provisions (Land, 1976); and the influence of ideology (Taylor-Gooby and Dale, 1981).

Drawing on single state sources means that comparative analyses suffer from the deficiencies inherent in these, while attempting to overcome them. Foremost among the problems which must be transcended are: the tendency to treat nation states as autonomous entities without reference to international economic and communication forces which shrink the world into one global village; the capacity to ignore inequality expressed through 'race', gender, class, and other social divisions; and the difficulties of finding common bench marks from which to compare developments. Industrialisation and urbanisation are key factors in the development of the welfare state. Many initiatives against poverty and public health measures in Britain and the United States, for example, were linked to the expansion of the market (Stedman Jones, 1971; Glazer, 1988). Although modernisation is a key theme in the development of the welfare state, we cannot assume that every state will follow the same path as the one before it, or that there is a unilinear development which is applicable to all states (MacPherson, 1982; Frank, 1981). As we shall see, the development of the welfare state immediately after the Bolshevik Revolution in the Soviet Union and during the Great Leap Forward in China did not follow Western patterns.

Questions regarding the values endorsed by the welfare state, its priorities in distributing resources, its clientele, its workforce, the role of the state itself, and the explanations for state intervention in welfare have been answered differently by different theorists. I shall classify their theories according to their views on the role of the state in mediating welfare relationships and eliminating class, race and gender inequality. I divide current analyses along a continuum ranging from anti-collectivist to collectivist options. The polarities encompassed by this continuum are private provisions individuals supply through domestic resources or purchase in the market at one extreme and publicly funded services available to all at the point of need at the other. This division places theories concerned with eliminating public resources in favour of individual ones at the anti-collectivist end of the spectrum. Theories favouring redistributive public provisions aiming to transform social relations in keeping with egalitarian objectives and principles are at the collectivist end. In between lie theories concerned with modifying the status quo through piecemeal engineering and modest reforms. This classification differs slightly from previous attempts which have varied from early initiatives considering the effects of the welfare state in mitigating inequality (see Wedderburn, 1965; Titmuss, 1974) to later ones examining ideological perspectives (see Taylor-Gooby and Dale, 1981), or social divisions such as class, race and gender (see Williams, 1989).

On the anti-collectivist end of the spectrum are residual forms of welfare emphasising individual and familial responsibility in providing for one's well-being. The role of the government in this schema is minimal – only safety net provisions for very narrow categories of the 'deserving' poor are permissible (see Glazer, 1988; Murray, 1984). Otherwise, people falling on hard times will have to look to charity, local government institutions, kinship and neighbourhood networks. The old Elizabethan Poor Law view of welfare was founded on this theoretical perspective. Its modern equivalents have been apparent in Thatcherite and Reaganite approaches. Politically, these have been intensely conservative, with change introduced from the top, usually to ward off threats from progressive grassroots forces which have been labelled dangerous for having created a welfare state encouraging dependence among employable individuals and destroying traditional values such as hard work and family responsibility. Key architects of welfare provisions have relied on residual models to limit state involvement, for example, Bismarck, the founder of the German welfare state. Modern architects include Hayek (1949) and Friedman (1962) whose monetarist philosophies have been crucial in halting the advance of collective provisions in Britain and the United States. This perspective takes no cognisance of gender or race based inequality. Women belong in the home being cushioned from hardship by the domestic net provided by men's foresight and hard work. Meanwhile women are expected to toil unceasingly for the welfare of others. Black people are told to rely on the labour market instead of drawing welfare (Glazer, 1988; Murray, 1984). This approach also blames individuals for their plight and pathologises their failure.

Collectivist theories have a publicly funded welfare state as the centre piece of their analysis. However, there is substantial variation between them regarding the role of the state, political structures, economic exigencies, social divisions, consumer participation, ideology, and culture. Collectivist theories can be subdivided into reformist approaches and revolutionary ones. Reformist perspectives have a partial commitment to redistributing welfare resources. However, this redistribution is often within the same class of claimants, for example, within the working class – from the poor to the more poor, whether it be women, or black people. Welfare resources come from insurance based contributions for non-stigmatised provisions, and a non-contributory system for those escaping either the insurance or domestic net. There is no commitment to transforming society, merely to ironing out its wrinkles at minimal cost to the Exchequer – for example, Britain's welfare state (Kincaid, 1973), and America's 'New Deal' (Leuchtenburg, 1968). Reformist approaches are gender and race blind. Significant variations exist within this approach and the boundaries between variants are often blurred. However, functionalism is a common theme. Welfare provisions are considered necessary in modern society to help individuals deal with hardships caused by the processes of industrialisation (Wilensky and Lebaux, 1965). While some reformist theories blame the hapless victim for their unfortunate circumstances, some theorists seek structural causes. Reformist approaches include traditional social administration, functionalist theories, convergence theories, pluralist theories, and non-Marxist materialist theories.

Revolutionary approaches include Marxist, feminist, and black perspectives. While there are several schools of thought within each of these, they all aim to transform existing social relations. The key differences between them concern their analysis of class, gender, and 'race' based inequality, the relationships and interactions between each of these social divisions, and how these can be handled in practice. Marxist approaches have until recently paid scant attention to gender (Marchant and Wearing, 1986; Dominelli and McLeod, 1989), and 'race' (Mama, 1989). Focusing largely on class, Marxists have argued that eliminating economic inequality will eradicate racial and gender oppression. Unity of people in struggle and a presumed similarity of experience have been a strength and a weakness of this perspective. It has ignored the more restricted access women and black people have to welfare resources and neglected their contribution to struggles establishing welfare states.

Anti-racist and black perspectives have acknowledged the significance of imperialist hegemony and class in racial oppression. They have had less to say about gender oppression. Feminist perspectives share a commitment to ending gender inequality and developing forms of practice reflecting this. Although their positions on 'race' and class have varied, most feminists now accept a patriarchal capitalism. White feminists have recently begun to tackle racism, while black feminists have incorporated gender, 'race' and class in their analyses for some time (see Lorde, 1984; Davis, 1981). In this book, I attempt to follow their lead.

The schema I have adopted in classifying theories in social policy is the following:

1. Anti-collectivist theories
   (a) Residual approaches
       (i) The 'great man' in history theories, e.g. Bismarck as the
           founder of West Germany's welfare state, Beveridge as the
           architect of Britain's post-war welfare state (Pascall, 1986).
       (ii) Monetarist welfare approaches, e.g. Friedman (1962).
2. Collectivist theories
   (a) Reformist approaches
       (i) Empirical social administration, e.g. Pinker (1979).
       (ii) Functionalist theories, e.g. Parsons (1954).
       (iii) Convergence theories, e.g. Rimlinger (1971).
       (iv) Pluralist theories, e.g. Hadley and Hatch (1981).
       (v) Social democratic, e.g. Mishra (1977).
       (vi) Fabian socialist, e.g. Titmuss and Abel-Smith (1956),
            Townsend (1979).

(vii) Non-Marxist materialist theories, e.g. Walker (1984).
(b) Revolutionary approaches
  (i) Marxist materialist theories, e.g. Gough (1979).
  (ii) Black perspectives, e.g. Gilroy (1987).
  (iii) Feminist theories, e.g. Pascall (1986), Bryan et al. (1985).

As we shall discover, except for feminist versions, a recognition of the importance of gender in the development of welfare services and determining individual eligibility to them is virtually absent from these accounts.

Anti-collectivist approaches

Residual approaches

THE 'GREAT MAN' THEORIES

The view that history is created by 'great men' has been a major factor in writing out women's contribution to social development. Women's role in struggling for certain welfare policies and provisions has not been noted. This has meant that, for example, in Britain, feminists' efforts in securing the acceptance of family allowances paid to women as a universal benefit has been ignored until these have been highlighted in feminist literature. Dale and Foster (1986) reveal how the implementation of these provisions was curtailed by men opposing them for fear these would reduce men's wages – wages which were expected to cover the needs of their families not just themselves. Thus, an appreciation of the importance of overcoming opposition from men and the organised labour movement is essential in fully comprehending the limitations of family allowances (now child benefits) in securing the financial well-being of British children. Equally, black people's struggles to have children living overseas eligible for child benefit has also been overlooked (Plummer, 1978). Organised male workers' opposition to family allowances because these would reduce men's wages inhibited the development of family allowances in Canada (Strong-Boag, 1979). Male trade unionists in the United States have rejected family allowances on similar grounds. The United States is the major western country lacking such provisions (Glazer, 1988).

Similarly, the divergent interests of men and women have inhibited developments favouring women and children in socialist countries. For example, gains in women's reproductive rights and sexuality during the Bolshevik Revolution were withdrawn when men feared emancipating women through specific policies would divide the working class, despite assurances from feminists including Kollantai to the contrary (Kollantai, 1971). The obstruction of family reforms in China in the 1950s by landless men peasant farmers wanting to prove their manhood by becoming breadwinners who farmed land for themselves is essential in understanding the ensuing trade-offs between land reforms and women's liberation (Johnson, 1983). Ignoring women's involvement in the creation of the welfare state has meant non-feminist academics have failed to consider the implications of the conflict of interests between men and women in the formation of the welfare state and accessibility of its various provisions.

MONETARIST WELFARE THEORIES

Monetarist theories of welfare have emphasised the significance of freedom of choice through individual action exercised in the market place. There is minimal room for state intervention. As Thatcher in Britain and Reagan in America have demonstrated, at best state services are limited to safety net provisions for the most needy of the 'deserving' groups in society. Reducing the dependency of claimants on state income support (Dominelli, 1988b; Glazer, 1988; Leuchtenburg, 1989) by targeting employable men and women including those heading single parent families for more restricted access to benefits while channelling limited state funds more effectively towards more 'deserving' claimants, for example, children and older people (Glazer, 1988; Murray, 1984), characterise this approach.

Monetarist welfare theorists take some cognisance of 'race' and gender when identifying groups which have become over-reliant on state provisions, for example, black women on Aid for Families and Dependent Children in America, to argue strongly that these be denied state resources and provide for themselves by selling their labour (Glazer, 1988; Murray, 1984). Theorists like Glazer (1988) and Murray (1984) claim that by granting single parent families unstigmatised resources, the welfare state has encouraged the destruction of traditional moral values and increased rates of crime and family breakdown. The New Right blames women and black people deriving their livelihood through welfare for the fragmentation of the moral order.

Collectivist theories

Reformist approaches

CLASSICAL SOCIAL ADMINISTRATION

Classical social administration has responded slowly to the anti-racist feminist challenge, taking little notice of the needs of welfare consumers and those excluded from specific benefits. It has failed to account for the gendered impact of the welfare state on women as contributors to schemes, beneficiaries of schemes, employees of the welfare state and negotiators for services accruing to other family members, particularly children and older people. Women's relationship to the welfare state as contributors to schemes has been undermined by their assumed dependent status within the family which has allowed women either to pay lower contributions for fewer benefits, for example the 'married women's contribution' in Britain, or to pay the same contributions as men, but without access to full benefits, for example pensions in Britain where women are denied widowers pensions. Insurance schemes based on men's working careers and designed with men in mind are ill-equipped to handle women's access to and receipt of benefits because their working patterns are substantially different (Pascall, 1986). White women having employment breaks to care for children and older relatives lose out on receiving benefits and contributing towards future benefits during this period. They also have lower incomes which handicap their supplementing basic state provisions through earnings related additions and purchasing additional benefits in the market. Black women who are sole breadwinners for their families are unlikely to have career breaks when their children are small (Mama, 1989; Bruegel, 1986). Their employment on the lowest rungs of the labour hierarchy with more limited opportunities than white women makes it difficult for them to augment basic state provisions privately.

The invisibility of women in the welfare state has enabled the patriarchal underpinnings of welfare and the contribution women make to welfare services through their waged and their domestic labour to remain masked in classical comparative analyses (for examples, see Heidenheimer *et al.*, 1983; Rimlinger, 1971; Mishra, 1977). The predominance of 'convergence theories' in the literature partly accounts for this. Emphasising industrialisation has downgraded the roles ideology, patriarchy, imperialism and the domestic economy have played in the formation of specific welfare states.

Moreover, classical social administration plays down the significance of conflict and endorses pluralistic or social democratic solutions to social problems. These have resolved neither the conflict between competing demands for financial and personnel resources nor the fiscal crisis. Marxists have identified the crisis as one of accumulation and legitimacy (Gough, 1979). Feminists have argued that the crisis is broader than this because it involves the maintenance of social relations in both public and private spheres, including the squandering of valuable social resources in unproductive defence spending (Davis, 1989). Both capitalist and socialist societies siphon substantial funds for defence purposes, thereby limiting the range of options governments have in choosing between financing welfare or warfare. Two letters only mark the distinction between them, but the difference these make to the standard of living the average person enjoys in both capitalist and socialist countries is considerable. Prioritising defence strategies has reduced public expenditure in Britain, the United States and Canada, producing swingeing cuts in housing, education, health care and the personal social services with massive increases in defence and law and order expenditure (for example see Glazer, 1988). Sweden has curtailed welfare expenditures to finance defence commitments. Under the openness of *perestroika*, the Soviet Union has revealed the limitations the arms race with the United States has imposed on welfare expenditure. China has also had to channel resources towards defence, especially during the Korean War, border 'skirmishes' and ideological struggles with the Soviet Union, indigenous uprisings in Tibet and Vietnam.

Classical social administration remains patriarchal in conception and unable to explain either the continued subordination of women in socialist societies or the 'crisis' in welfare currently raging in both capitalist and socialist countries. Its responses to such criticisms have been unconvincing because they continue to neglect patriarchy and simply replace the exaggeration of economic constraints with an over-emphasis on political ones (see Mishra, 1984).

FUNCTIONALIST THEORIES

Functionalist theories of welfare focus on the usefulness of the welfare state in maintaining social stability by providing contingency benefits for people. Both convergence theories and Marxist theories contain elements of functionalism. Non-Marxist functionalist analyses of welfare owe much to the writings of Parsons (1954) and Merton (1976). Focusing on social stability, functionalism endorses a conservative philosophy favouring the status quo and a gender segregated division of labour. In it, men uphold 'instrumentalist' values occupying the public domain of work, resource allocation and decision-making while women maintain the 'expressive' or caring and nurturing capacities essential in the domestic sphere.

This division of responsibilities has become incorporated in popular ideology as the 'natural' division of work between men and women and reflected in the organisation of the welfare state (Wilson, 1977). As a result, women have been considered obvious subjects for the caring roles located within the personal social services, health system and educational establishments. Although waged, these activities are considered extensions of work women normally undertake at home, using their natural aptitude and training. Women with minimal formal training have become the cooks, cleaners and physical carers for those receiving the ministrations of the welfare state. Women with formal qualifications are employed mainly as basic grade social workers, nurses, and primary school teachers. Men have collared the managerial jobs allocating resources over the vast empires constituting the welfare state (Howe, 1986; Coyle and Skinner, 1988). Without the labour of women, particularly low paid black women, the welfare state would not have been possible, let alone be maintained (Mama, 1989). In Britain, for example, the health service relies heavily on black women for its cleaners and lowest paid nurses (Bryan et al., 1985). The situation is paralleled in the United States where a racially structured labour force also exists (Sidel, 1986).

Functionalist theorists have ignored the fact that women's labour, purchased at minimal cost to state exchequers, has facilitated the creation of a welfare state and enabled it to continue providing public welfare services despite rising costs. Throughout the fiscal crises engendered by the global economic recessions of the 1970s and 1980s, welfare provisions have been maintained by exploiting women's labour. Women have borne the brunt of the redundancies occasioned by cost-cutting initiatives. Black women at the bottom of the welfare state labour hierarchy have been at the knife edge of public expenditure cuts.

CONVERGENCE THEORIES

Closely linked to functionalist theories, convergence theorists (see Wilensky, 1975; Rimlinger, 1971) consider the welfare state a desirable working apparatus which absorbs the casualties of both capitalist and socialist systems. Industrial development and economic exigencies exert pressures dictating which provisions will be available and push welfare provisions in both capitalist and socialist societies in similar directions despite their different starting points (Kerr, 1962; Rimlinger, 1971). Although capitalist societies begin by having the bulk of their welfare services available for individual purchase through the market and social-ist societies have theirs provided by the state, both will move towards each other and eventually complete their development with a mixture of private market provisions and state supported insurance services with institutional forms dominating. A mixed economy of welfare will prevail as the driving forces of industrialisation, the endorsement of political philosophies of the centre ground, a growing consensus around welfare and the elimination of poverty gain currency (Kerr, 1962; Rimlinger, 1971).

Capitalism will become more socialised through benign state intervention because pressure groups such as trade unions offer countervailing forms of power to the state. Moreover, managers will replace owners and pursue interests based on managerial rather than entrepreneurial imperatives. Politically, the context of the Cold War has lent ideological respectability to convergence theorists by underlining the importance of a healthy workforce for industrial development and economic growth. Convergence theorists hold that capitalism is capable of providing sufficient economic growth to finance welfare provisions. But they caution the wise use of welfare state aid rather than unlimited public expenditure riding on the back of unparalleled economic growth. Additionally, the state can support institutionalised provisions through economies of scale.

Convergence theorists are having difficulty maintaining the validity of their position. Countries are not developing welfare services which approximate one another's. There are more differences in welfare services between countries than similarities between them (Glazer, 1988). Factors other than industrialisation have been shown to affect the development of welfare provisions. These include political organisations and forces, ideological practices, and cultural traditions (Glazer, 1988). Convergence theorists have ignored the adaptability of the capitalist system in accommodating challenges to its hegemony and neutralising potential threats. For example, trade unions have failed to protect workers' interests at local, national and international levels in the face of increasing work rhythms, rising unemployment and the relocation of multinational firms from developed countries to developing ones.

Convergence theorists have paid scant attention to gender in either service provision or employment. Women's contribution to maintain crisis-ridden welfare states through their unpaid domestic and low paid waged labour has been disregarded; as has the assumption of women's dependent status in determining their eligibility to benefits (Pascall, 1986). Convergence theorists have failed to acknowledge the subordination of black people who staff the welfare state's least desirable jobs and have more restricted access to benefits than white people. For example, the exclusion of black children living overseas from British child benefit (Gordon and Newnham, 1985) and lower pensions accrued through their lower earning potential (Dominelli, 1988a).

PLURALIST THEORIES

Pluralist theories of welfare arose in response to critiques highlighting the bureaucratic, insensitive and unresponsive features of state services in capitalist societies (Deacon, 1985). They promote the idea that the free market and state planning can coexist in one welfare state. Pluralism is founded on the liberal philosophy that individuals have a responsibility to look after the welfare needs of themselves and their dependents and that the body politic has a duty to mitigate economic duress caused by circumstances outside an individual's control such as illness, structural unemployment, old age and death. Collective initiatives reducing inequalities arising from income differentials are endorsed, but these do not have to emanate from the state. Welfare services can be obtained through the statutory, voluntary, commercial or informal household sectors (Hadley and Hatch, 1981). For this reason, pluralist theories can support conservative forms of welfare, including those favouring market provisions popularised under the aegis of the 'Radical Right' epitomised by Thatcherism and Reaganism (Beresford and Croft, 1984).

Reliance on the voluntary sector has enabled pluralist theoreticians to support services calling for increased consumer control by democratising, restructuring and redefining services. Their theoretical position adopts a piecemeal approach to change and misses the connection between the possibilities for change open to voluntary organisations and the constraints imposed upon them by their reliance on state funding to survive (Beresford and Croft, 1984; Dominelli and McLeod, 1989). They also ignore the limitations of the market in providing welfare resources only for monied people. Inequality of access to and poor quality control mechanisms over the marketplace can deleteriously affect people's welfare. The transformation of services is not possible within a pluralist framework; a diversification of sources for welfare provision is.

Pluralist theorists argue the voluntary sector's influence should be extended through community alternatives (see Wolfenden, 1979; Hatch and Mocroft, 1983). However, pluralist advocates do not cost the input made by women's unpaid labour, thereby not acknowledging the burden shunted onto women as the main providers of caring labour in both the voluntary sector and the community (Finch, 1984; Finch and Groves, 1983). They have also neglected the substitution effect coming from replacing women's paid labour with their unpaid labour. As state services previously hiring women become privatised, they shed redundant women workers (Coyle, 1984). Redundant women are then available as a pool of unwaged workers who can undertake unpaid voluntary work (Coussins and Coote, 1981). Their contribution is over and above that provided by women who have either always worked in the domestic arena or undertaken voluntary work on top of their waged work. Welfare pluralists neglect the impact of government intervention in increasing or decreasing the caring burden shouldered by women. Nor do they address gender inequality in the caring sphere. They do not reveal that the bulk of caring work is currently undertaken by women with either no or limited state support in the privacy of the home. This holds for socialist (Scott, 1976), social democratic (Wistrand, 1981) and capitalist societies (Finch and Groves, 1983).

SOCIAL DEMOCRATIC THEORIES
Social democratic theorists, for example Mishra (1984), share much with pluralist theorists. The main difference is that social democrats envisage

a more central role for state-based redistributive welfare than the pluralists. Mishra (1984) posits Sweden as the *model welfare state* for others to emulate. This perspective also says little about inequality derived from social divisions other than class.

FABIAN SOCIALISM

Fabian socialists incorporate class analyses in their understanding of welfare states to a greater degree than social democrats. They view the welfare state as compensating for the dysfunctionality of capitalism by grafting social responsibility, subject to economic exigencies, onto capitalist states. They promote state welfare provisions to further equality, fraternity and altruism. Fabian socialists' vision of welfare has become anathema to claimants who experience its bureaucratic, alienating and stigmatising reality. Fabian socialists' demand for universal services ignores the discrimination women and black people experience in the welfare arena, blinding this perspective to gender and 'race' based inequality. Without altering their conceptual framework, some Fabian socialists are beginning to face this deficiency in their data collection. For example, Townsend's (1979) analysis of poverty in Britain highlights income differentials between men and women.

Revolutionary theories

MARXIST THEORIES

Marxist materialist theories examine the structure of the welfare state including the ideas informing it, for ideas constitute ideology and reflect a set of materialist relationships (Leonard, 1984). In the west, Marxist analyses consider the welfare state part of the capitalist state, functional for the bourgeoisie, and primarily about social control (CDP, 1977; Walker and Beaumont, 1985; Corrigan and Leonard, 1978). The welfare

NON-MARXIST MATERIALIST THEORIES

Non-Marxist materialist theories examine systems and structures either without overtly considering their implications for either capital accumulation or the reproduction of labour power, for example, Pincus and Minahan (1973); or, by asserting the importance of social policy and the democratic process as vehicles for change, for example, Walker (1984). Their version of the welfare state can be less statist, more libertarian and humanitarian than that proposed by Fabians. The compatibility of economic priorities with social ones is possible through consumer-led social planning. Provisions would be universal and decentralised so that more account of social divisions could be taken than in centrally controlled systems.

veneer of support peels away during economic crises when the requirements of capital accumulation supersede those of providing for workers'
welfare (Offe, 1984). Gough (1979) and Ginsburg (1979) provide a less
deterministic analysis by arguing the welfare state has been tempered by
class struggles carried out by the labour movement in establishing a state
administered 'social wage' to defray the costs of reproducing workers'
labour power.

Marxists in socialist societies have been preoccupied with the capacity
of the economy to support industrial development and a welfare infrastructure in the transitional period between capitalism and communism.
Normally identified as socialist, the welfare state is considered an
instrument through which the proletarian vanguard ensures welfare
services are distributed among those needing them. The state, in the
absence of the market, is the vehicle through which redistribution takes
place. Theoretically, the principle guiding welfare allocations would be
work done (Deacon, 1983). Only during the communistic stage would
each receive according to need (Lenin, 1965).

Marxist materialist analyses have handled gender issues poorly. They
have highlighted the contradictions a country's economic and political
structures engender in welfare provisions, but have failed to surmount
their preoccupation with the welfare needs of waged workers and
develop models of welfare responsive to the demands of the unwaged.
This has facilitated Marxists' uncritical acceptance of welfare provisions
and employment practices in 'socialist' countries such as China and the
Soviet Union (Dominelli and McLeod, 1989). The 'Radical Right' in
Britain and America has taken the initiative on welfare reform away
from the 'Left' by pointing to the negative impact of state organised
socialist welfare (Loney, 1986; Glazer, 1988).

Marxist materialist theorists have also dealt inadequately with 'race'
and the impact of racism in welfare state services and employment
practices (Williams, 1987, 1989). Orthodox Marxists take class as the
overriding determinant of social organisation and change (Lenin, 1965).
Racism and sexism are expected to disappear with the formation of
socialism. However, the experience of socialist countries such as China
and the Soviet Union have demonstrated that gender inequality persists
despite state ownership of the means of production being enshrined in
the economy (see Scott, 1976; Molyneaux, 1985). Racism has also
continued under these regimes, as is revealed by the struggles for ethnic
autonomy by Jews, Armenians and Ukrainians in the Soviet Union, and
Tibetans in China.

BLACK PERSPECTIVES

The failure of white Marxists to incorporate 'race' and racism in their accounts of the welfare state has been central to critiques informed by a black perspective. Black people expressed concern over the subordination of their needs to those of class when white people demanded unity in the class struggle at the expense of the specific working class experience of black people (Sivanandan, 1976; Gilroy, 1987). Their works have emphasised the importance of collectivist provisions taking account of social divisions which cut across class lines (Bryan et al., 1985) and the different starting points black people and white people have when approaching the system. Without taking these into account, universal provisions are colourblind, exclude black people and reinforce racism. To establish egalitarian welfare relations, black perspectives place race on an equal footing with other social divisions and challenge the residential and citizenship requirements for eligibility to state welfare (Mama, 1989; Bryan et al., 1985). They have also highlighted how essential their labour and resources in both Third World countries and the West were in creating state welfare, especially in Britain and America (Bryan et al., 1985; Mama, 1989; Lorde, 1984), and sustaining it during the financial crises of recent decades (Bryan et al., 1985; Mama, 1989).

FEMINIST THEORIES

The politics of welfare have ensured that people's welfare in the countries being studied has improved to some extent, but not in relative terms. Poverty among women, particularly in old age and when raising children, has increased and given rise to the concept of the 'feminisation of poverty', amongst Western feminists (see Scott, 1984; Stallard et al., 1983; Eichler, 1983). Feminist analyses have begun influencing welfare debates. Feminists have gone beyond considering the welfare state as merely part of 'a peace formula between labour and capital' (as in Offe, 1984), by conceptualising it as part of a generalised crisis of power in society, but focusing specifically on the gendered organisation of social relations and ideological hegemony. Besides focusing on state services, feminist analyses cover the whole network of social and economic relationships linked to welfare provisions including economic relations, patriarchal family relations, and adherence to the 'Cold War' ideology sustaining warfare states.

With few exceptions (for example, Scott, 1976), feminist analyses to date either are primarily an examination of welfare provisions in one country (see Pascall, 1986; Andors, 1983; Sidel, 1986), or focus on a comparative analysis of one aspect of social policy like family policy and child care (see Adams and Winston, 1980). Feminist studies of welfare states in capitalist, socialist and social democratic countries are absent. This book, based on an anti-racist feminist perspective, contributes towards filling this gap.

Feminist theories follow a variety of approaches ranging from liberal bourgeois to radical separatist (Banks, 1981; Adamson et al., 1988) providing a richly diverse feminist practice. However, all feminists examine gender relations as socially constructed unequal power relationships giving rise to male supremacy and women's subordination. Relationships in white, two parent Western families assume women's dependency on male breadwinners (McIntosh, 1978). The Chinese family straddles several generations, but patriarchal relations endorsing male supremacy are still the norm (Lang, 1946; Chan et al., 1984). The subordination of women seems to be universal, though its form varies over time and in different societies (Hooks, 1984). At the heart of women's relationship with capitalist welfare states is the assumption women depend on a male breadwinner for their economic well-being (Wilson, 1977). It controls women's access to welfare provisions and defines the possibilities of their employment within the welfare workforce (Pascall, 1986). In socialist states, women's labour is crucial to the development process, but subordination features strongly in women's lives as men achieve liberation at their expense (Stacey, 1983).

More recently, feminists have developed analyses and modes of practice engaging with the multiplicity of oppressions impacting simultaneously on individuals' lives and avoided ranking these on a scale determining the point at which they are dismantled (Bryan et al., 1985; Mama, 1989; Williams, 1989; Dominelli and McLeod, 1989). Feminists have paid particular attention to class, race, age, disability and sexual orientation and demonstrated the variety of ways through which these heighten women's oppression and make their subordinate status more complex and onerous than initially realised.

Feminist analyses emphasise the social construction of relationships between men and women. Radical feminists basing their understanding of women's oppression on women's fertility and childbearing capabilities describe how men wield power over women and further their own interests by controlling women's reproductive powers (Firestone, 1970). Although this theory has a biological dimension, the way biology is socially mediated accounts for women's oppression. For radical feminists, the welfare state reinforces women's position as subordinate beings and foists upon them the duties and obligations of motherhood and nurturers of others. These relationships are usually detrimental to women, making the welfare state a site for feminist social action. Women's interests are furthered by creating separate alternative resources for women. Lesbian women have played key roles in struggles over women's reproductive rights and exposed the prevalence of homophobia in the welfare state. Homophobia guides state reaction to them as employees, depriving them of jobs if they make public their sexuality, and denying them the opportunity to raise their own children when custody is contested by heterosexual fathers (Hanscombe and Forster, 1982).

Socialist feminists wishing to assert the social basis of their analyses and avoid painting men as villains have engaged with capitalism as a system oppressing men and women (Davis, 1989). Gender relations are mediated by a patriarchal capitalist state in which women's oppression benefits men. The welfare state maintains male supremacy and reinforces women's subordination by focusing on women's roles as mothers, wives, low paid and unpaid carers of dependent elders and children and excluding men from caring relationships. Even men employed in caring professions, for example, social work, quickly leave the caring frontline to ascend the managerial ladder (Walton, 1975).

Liberal feminists have emphasised the importance of women gaining equal opportunities alongside men to work in and enjoy the provisions of the welfare state. They have allied with men when struggling to improve women's position at work, for example equal pay, eliminating sexual harassment (Dale and Foster, 1986).

Black feminists have highlighted racism as an endemic feature of the welfare state (Mama, 1989; Bryan et al., 1985). Black women are at the receiving end of the poorest provisions (Guru, 1987), used as guinea pigs by pharmaceutical companies in both the West and the Third World (Bryan et al., 1985; Malek, 1985), and paid the lowest wages (Mama, 1989). They have emphasised the importance of feminists recognising the substantially different experiences black women have of state welfare compared to white women because they are subjected to racism and sexism (Lorde, 1984; Bryan et al., 1985; Malek, 1985; Mama, 1989).

Women with disability have highlighted the welfare state's failure to deal adequately with their specific plight (Campling, 1981). Services geared to their specific needs are rarely available and employment within its structures is difficult. More recently, they have exposed the disablist attitude the state and feminists have taken on abortion issues. With mental and physical handicap as acceptable grounds for abortion, the message of being expendable is clear. The present welfare state patholo-gises those with disabilities while forcing them to cater for their own needs.

Women are the largest group of workers in capitalist welfare states where a gendered and racially structured division of labour exists (Armstrong, 1984; Coyle, 1984; Sidel, 1986). Women workers are also central to the socialist welfare states of China and the Soviet Union. Like their Western counterparts, they are located at the bottom of the labour hierarchy (Sidel, 1972; Andors, 1983; Mamanova, 1984). Opportunities for part-time employment in the welfare sector have attracted women with childcare responsibilities, wifely duties and the care of older people because these enable them to undertake unpaid domestic labour and paid waged work.

Classified as being essentially about caring, welfare state jobs are considered 'naturally' women's jobs and attract lower rates of pay. This is particularly true in the health, education, and personal social services where white men occupy the higher echelons controlling research, personnel and financial resources while women fill the posts having direct contact with service users. In Western health care, white men dominate the prestigious research and surgical specialisms, black men assume the consultancy roles in the less desirable field of geriatric and psychiatric care (Littlewood and Lipsedge, 1982; Sidel, 1986). White women are located in the higher ranks of the nursing profession while black women provide the domiciliary services. In the personal social services of the Western countries studied, fieldworkers and residential workers are female and the managers male. The increased penetration of social work by men has led to the masculinisation of social work, an upsurgence of instrumentalist male values, and an attendant rise in salaries. At the same time, women have experienced increasing control of their labour by male managers in areas which were once women's realms, for example, childcare work, and the proletarianisation of their occupation as their professional autonomy has been whittled away (Howe, 1986; Dominelli, 1990). In socialist China and the Soviet Union, men are also found primarily in the top decision-making echelons while women form the majority of the lower level cadres and those doing caring work (Andors, 1983; Mamanova, 1984).

An anti-racist feminist analysis of welfare has much to offer comparative social administration. Formed as a critique of other collectivist analyses, an anti-racist feminist approach draws on the strengths of these. It challenges comparative social administration's cosy assumption of the undifferentiated impact of social policy on people's lives, and reveals that improving people's welfare is not the sole aim of policymakers. They are also concerned with maintaining labour discipline (Ginsburg, 1979), reducing welfare expenditures, limiting individual dependency on the welfare state (Glazer, 1988), and reinforcing familialist norms and values (Glazer, 1988). The imposition of the work ethics and labour discipline has occurred largely through income maintenance policies and the reinforcement of patriarchal conjugality via the 'family wage' which enshrines the two parent, breadwinning, man-nurturing, dependent woman in regulations governing access to welfare resources in the West (McIntosh, 1978) and the extended family in the East (Andors, 1983; Stacey, 1983). Family policy has also been manipulated to both encourage and discourage population growth, depending on the economy's need for it, for example, encouraging it in the Soviet Union after the Second World War and in Britain after the First; discouraging it in China since the mid-1970s. Demographic considerations are now assuming a greater role in policies affecting senior citizens and birth control. Enhancing the power of professionals with technological expertise and their control over service provisions, especially those covering health care, education and the personal social services have been subsidiary aims of social policy (Perry et al., 1979).

Besides conceding the importance of both national and international political and economic constraints in developing welfare provisions, feminist analyses place demographic shifts, ideology, the power contained within personal relationships, particularly those within the family, and women's unpaid work in the home into the political arena of welfare policy and practice. They also emphasise the importance of providing consumers with a welfare state which is participatory, and overcome the traditional divisions between economic and social policy. Moreover, anti-racist feminists have provided prefigurative models of welfare which reflect all these principles in their practice, for example women's resource centres, refuges, well-women clinics, and rape crisis centres (Dominelli, 1990).

This book examines the welfare state in the predominantly capitalist market economies of the United States, Canada, and Britain, the social democratic mixed economy of Sweden, and state planned socialist economies of the USSR and China in the three major policy areas – income maintenance (Chapter 2), family policy (Chapter 3), and health care (Chapter 4) from an anti-racist feminist perspective. In choosing these countries, I shall be exploring the differences and similarities in women's experience of the welfare state in countries which have sought to provide for the well-being of their citizens through 'free market' capitalist, mixed economy social democratic and 'socialist' forms of welfare organisation. I highlight the processes whereby the welfare state came into being; the principal decision-makers, points of convergence and divergence, and neglected aspects of welfare. I shall also consider the extent to which provisions have promoted the welfare of women, and by extension that of children and men. By the end of the book (Chapter 5), I shall have identified the distinctiveness of anti-racist feminist analysis, and drawn on current feminist and black activist welfare practices pointing towards the development of non-oppressive welfare policy and practice meeting human needs rather than economic and political exigencies.

2

Income maintenance

A FORM OF SOCIAL CONTROL AND LABOUR DISCIPLINE

Poverty is a spectre haunting individuals without a regular source of income or working for low wages. Affecting large proportions of the population in all the countries being studied, governments have sought to address poverty through welfare state provisions such as income maintenance during times of hardship. Operating through a variety of programmes, income maintenance systems take two main forms – social security and social assistance. The former is usually contributory and insurance based; the latter is means-tested and non-contributory. By providing assistance to individuals in need, income maintenance systems theoretically involve some measure of redistribution. Redistribution makes income support contradict market ideology as beneficiaries receive aid without paying for it. Having the insurance principle as an integral element of benefit provision, strengthens the influence of the market. But, social insurance modifies market ideology for government subsidies rather than actuarial considerations finance the system and the contribution record is determined by social policy rather than market criteria (Armitage, 1988).

From a feminist perspective, Armitage's position underestimates the impact the market has in determining social policy. Social insurance based schemes follow market imperatives in that risks primarily affecting women are not covered. There are no social insurance provisions for unwaged homemakers when they fall sick; lose their jobs through separation, divorce and children leaving home; adopt unconventional lifestyles; and reach old age. Feminists (e.g. Coote, 1981) and others (e.g. Walker, 1984) have lamented the subordination of social policy to economic policy. Cameron (1989) has placed the responsibility for the welfare state's failure to meet people's needs squarely on the shoulders of financial and industrial capital which has set the agenda on welfare provisions by controlling resources and government policy on an international scale.

Income maintenance systems can be either universal, applying to all irrespective of need, or selective. However, other criteria of eligibility imposed on universal schemes can exclude people. For example, residence requirements denying black people benefits make such systems profoundly racist. Excluding black children living overseas from child benefit when their parents live in Britain, work and pay taxes, including national insurance contributions illustrates this (Plummer, 1978). Governments and neo-conservatives in the West are increasingly challenging universal provisions in favour of selective targeting because they regard universal schemes received by everyone regardless of need as inefficient (Armitage, 1988). Proponents of this view reject the resolution of this problem through non-selective means such as income tax transfers because they abhor circulating money through high income earners' pockets twice (Armitage, 1988; Glazer, 1988). Their arguments are untenable and selective. Money is intended to circulate frequently. Governments and neo-conservatives have not hesitated to circulate money twice when taxing unemployment benefits. Governments are in the business of making money constantly enter, exit and re-enter people's pockets through various forms of direct and indirect taxation and social insurance premiums.

The main universal programme under neo-conservative attack is family allowances. To feminists, spurious arguments about circulation camouflage neo-conservatives' real concern which is that these programmes give women access to an income independent of men and without stigma. Being preoccupied with reasserting male dominance and privilege, neo-conservatives prefer to have women submit to degrading means-tested provisions than recoup universal benefits through income taxes which would affect mainly men earning high incomes. Moreover, family allowances are for children. These should not be seen as the property of either men or women. Targeting them with means-tested selective criteria reinforces the principle of aggregation and assumed dependency of women and children on 'family', that is, men's resources.

Social security and social assistance have a gendered impact giving men and women a different experience of their provisions. Women tend to be concentrated in the social assistance arena because they constitute a larger proportion than men of the unwaged, single parents and older people (Phillipson, 1982). Non-contributory social assistance schemes are steeped in notions of residual welfare. Women having recourse to these provisions are stigmatised and branded failures (Brook and Davis, 1985).

Women's dependent status within the family and subordinate position in waged work disadvantages them in insurance based social security schemes. As family members, unwaged women are deemed dependent on men and have a dependant's access to insurance based schemes to which their male partners have contributed. The assumption of women's economic dependency is questionable for both black and white women. The male-headed breadwinner family is a declining species in the West and does not form the major family type in Canada (Eichler, 1983), Britain (Segal, 1987), the United States (Sidel, 1986) or Sweden (Wistrand, 1981). Female-headed single parent families form a large proportion of the population in the European part of the Soviet Union. The picture is less clear in the Asiatic part. In China patriarchal social relations are the norm, but family income is pooled. Western families are increasingly relying on women's income as a necessary part of family finances. The same is true of China as families struggle to improve their standard of living (Croll, 1983). Soviet women also contribute substantially to their families' financial resources. Low wages and blocked employment opportunities for black men in the West have meant that black women have been major contributors to family incomes for some time (Hill, 1972; Mama, 1989). The barring of black men from employment opportunities has forced black women into the main breadwinner role (Mama, 1989). Both social security and social assistance have a racist impact as black people are more likely to be excluded from them. Meeting contributions criteria and residence requirements is problematic for black people who are discriminated against in the labour market. The discretionary element in schemes often serves to deny them benefit.

Social policy assumes that family members share their incomes equally and aggregates it on that basis. Taking equality in the distribution of family resources and the justness of aggregation for granted is problematic for women as it does not reflect reality. Income is unequally distributed within the family (Pahl, 1980). Men get the lion's share while women and children make do with very little. Unlike men, women do not automatically get a share of the family income for personal use. Moreover, aggregation presupposes economies of scale when two people live together and benefits for couples are calculated on this basis. No allowances are made for the higher expenses women incur in caring for themselves as women, for example, sanitary towels. Within households, women subordinate their needs to ensure that men and children receive the bulk of whatever housekeeping resources are available. The distribution of living space in the home is unequal. Men have first call on spare capacity as their needs for privacy and rest are assumed to be greater than women's. Women have no space to call their own. The home is women's workplace, but is seen as belonging to everyone in terms of its use.

Women share the kitchen, bathroom, living room with everyone else. Even their bedroom is shared. Aggregation reinforces the unequal distribution of resources already taking place in the family and has a deleterious impact on women's welfare. The unequal distribution of family resources means women have to make do with substantially less than their share of financial, physical and emotional resources. Aggregation is the norm in both capitalist and socialist countries.

Economic insecurity often follows major breaks in earning capacity despite income maintenance systems' role in preventing excessive drops in income following unemployment, sickness, relationship breakdown, old age and death of the income earner for surviving dependants. Instead of providing for the financial well-being of individuals and their dependants, income maintenance systems in both capitalist and socialist countries have at best managed to keep them above the bread-line. Responsibility for the failure of income maintenance schemes to meet their objectives has been laid at various doors. Pluralists in the West have blamed the Treasury for releasing inadequate funds (Kincaid, 1973). Non-Marxist materialists have pointed the finger at the use of the income maintenance system to enforce labour discipline (Piven and Cloward, 1972). Marxists have argued that the system's ability to meet its obligations to people is distorted by giving the needs of capital accumulation precedence over people's needs (Gough, 1979). Feminists have added its failure to make enhancing people's welfare its major aim (Dominelli and McLeod, 1989).

Labour discipline is a concept referring to the social control of workers through the organisation of both access to social security benefits and the determination of benefit levels (Ginsburg, 1979; Piven and Cloward, 1972). To receive social security benefits, people have to meet certain criteria of eligibility. These usually involve their having worked for the requisite contribution period, paid the necessary contributions, and actively seeking the means for securing their livelihood. Eligibility is geared to keeping workers in the labour market earning their own living (Piven and Cloward, 1972). Coverage is for a stipulated period at predetermined levels based on a variety of criteria which can include special needs, type of risk being covered, and the number of dependants. Benefit levels are also set so that they do not impinge on employers' ability to attract workers to low paid jobs. Thus, Marxists argue that labour discipline ensures that workers stay in their jobs because their eligibility to benefits is strictly controlled by the state, geared to keeping them at work and reinforces the low wage structure of the economy (Ginsburg, 1979). It is about the social control of one class by another. Social control in the income maintenance system is not only relevant to class, it also applies to gender and 'race'. For women, the income maintenance system perpetuates women's dependent status by treating the household as the unit for calculating entitlements. Although the majority of households in the United States, Britain, Canada, Sweden, and the Soviet Union (figures not available for China) are not composed of heterosexual couples with dependent children, men are fallaciously assumed to be 'heading' the household. Women-headed households with dependent children and single person households are categories rising steadily and increasing their share of household distribution tables. In addition, though less true for working class and black women, women's career patterns are often interrupted by taking time off to care for children and dependent older relatives, thereby reducing their ability to meet eligibility requirements. Women's lower earnings over a lifetime, particularly if they are black and working class, entitle them to lower benefit levels than men in a similar occupation. Women's different employment patterns disadvantage women as claimants, but income maintenance systems are blind to this fact (Pascall, 1986). In both capitalist and socialist countries, insurance based income maintenance systems relying on contributions from waged work discriminate against women who lack paid employment and cannot make the contributions giving them access to social security provisions. For feminists, this situation is deplorable for it negates the value of women's domestic labour in freeing men to engage in more prestigious paid labour, ensuring the daily survival of people and providing society's next generation.

From a feminist perspective, existing income maintenance systems are problematic for they neither treat women as equal to men, nor do they meet women's need for an independent income. An income maintenance system meeting women's needs as women and following feminist principles would:

1. Be universal in the sense of being available to everyone regardless of their marital status; employment status (waged or unwaged); racial origins; sexual orientation; age; residential status; citizenship status.

2. Be individually allocated rather than aggregated. This would also mean children having a right to a guaranteed income as individuals in their own right.

3. Provide a decent standard of living which would be historically determined, and well above the poverty line. This accepts needs as being socially determined and not skewered against human well-being by economic imperatives. Society's top priority would be human welfare. Economic production would be organised with this in mind.

4. Be redistributive from those who have wealth and large incomes to those who do not.

5. Be non-stigmatising in administration and service delivery.

6. Promote egalitarianism – socially, economically, politically and geo-
   graphically.
7. Involve users in determining policy and practice.
8. Eliminate hierarchy based on professionalism – experts would serve
   claimants and facilitate access rather than ration resources, enforce
   labour discipline and disenfranchise claimants by speaking for them.

This chapter examines the income maintenance systems in the United
States, Britain, Canada, Sweden, the Soviet Union, and China and
considers the extent to which social control and enforcing labour
discipline are essential features of their social security systems. Each
country will be examined historically for major shifts in provisions;
moves away from residual concepts of welfare towards institutional ones
or their reversal; and the prevalence of its social control elements and
patriarchal underpinnings. The differences and similarities in women's
experience in capitalist, social democratic and socialist systems will also
be assessed.

INCOME MAINTENANCE POLICIES IN CAPITALIST COUNTRIES

The American income maintenance system

Welfare issues in America are matters of local state jurisdiction. Unlike
Britain, control of welfare is decentralised. As in Canada, the federal
government has to rely on financial inducements and administrative
procedures to coax states into participating in given programmes,
making welfare programmes vulnerable to the economic vicissitudes of
the federal budget and willingness of individual states to embark upon
and sustain particular schemes. Constitutionally, the federal state secured
its breakthrough to intervene in welfare matters in 1913 when the 16th
Amendment to the Constitution authorising a federal income tax provided the financial base from which it could act. Before that, the Colonial
Poor Laws of the seventeenth century accorded local authorities sole
responsibility for relief. The types of relief available were: outdoor relief;
indenture; and institutional care. Until the 1935 Social Security Act
giving outdoor relief enabled poor people to remain in their own homes,
institutional provision in almshouses and indenture prevailed (Sidel,
1986, p. 79).

America has a welfare state which I call a mosaic welfare state. While sharing features characterising the mixed economy welfare state, the mosaic welfare state differs from it in having substantial elements provided through the domestic economy and self-help movements as well as the market and the state. The American welfare state mosaic is made up of the following five elements:

1. Federal government and local state provisions consisting largely of Aid to Families with Dependent Children, Unemployment Insurance, Old Ages Supplementary Income, Medicaid, and Medicare.

2. Private insurance companies providing coverage on a variety of risks for those who can afford the premiums. These are often obtained through workplace schemes as fringe benefits for waged workers belonging to unions.

3. Private charities which plug the gap between market and state provisions for those who are too poor to pay for minimal care.

4. Self-help groups providing models of localised collective care for women and black people.

5. Domestic provisions which include free care provided by women in the home.

Unlike other welfare resources, women's contribution to domestic provisions is not publicly acknowledged although its existence is presumed. They are paid for neither by family members who rely on them directly nor by the state which presupposes they are in place for individuals requiring them throughout their life-cycle, particularly childhood, old age, and illness.

The state funded income maintenance system within this mosaic is made up largely of provisions covering pensions, unemployment insurance as part of a labour market strategy and means-tested benefits for the poor, particularly aid to poor families with dependent children. The system is not redistributive. Rather, it tends to confirm existing income inequalities (Glazer, 1988). The American welfare state mosaic has been formed under a constellation of factors which often operate in contradictory directions as the state attempts to hold the line in the struggle between the *legitimation* of people's aspirations for a decent life-style and the *accumulation* of social and private wealth. These factors are ideological, economic, political and constitutional.

The dominant ideologies of individualism and familialism emphasise reliance on the private market and domestic provisions rather than collectivist approaches. Taking care of oneself and family has been a persistent theme in American welfare debates (Glazer, 1988) pressing provisions towards the anti-collectivist, residual end of the spectrum. A central plank in these ideologies is that of controlling state intervention so that it does not undermine individuals' capacities for self-reliance and self-sufficiency (Glazer, 1988; Murray, 1984). Popularised as Social Darwinism, this ideological position focuses on the struggle for survival which ensures life for the fittest, and enables the 'fit' to blame the poor for their predicament. Government intervention becomes construed as denial of freedom and a source of pernicious dependency sapping individuals' strength. Consequently, Social Darwinism enforces Poor Law Ideology, endorses a virulent anti-communism, and proposes that only non-collectivist welfare can sustain individuals' freedom.

Economic shifts have affected popular adherence to these ideologies. During the early part of the twentieth century, the destruction of the rural economy following the mechanisation of agriculture, the growth of large corporations beyond public control, and increasingly poor overall economic performance dislocated poor farmers and black people who migrated to cities searching for work. These economic forces proletarianised farming communities squeezed by finance capital into providing wage labourers with limited opportunities for securing their livelihoods. Cyclical recessions coupled with widespread unemployment, especially during the Great Depression when 25 per cent of the workforce ultimately joined the ranks of the unemployed, also caused Americans to re-evaluate their views on government welfare intervention. The inability of charitable relief to cope with such numbers and the increased social unrest among working class people agitating for protection from the ravages of a major economic crisis beyond their control also had a significant impact in shaping public opinion by shifting public perceptions of who bore responsibility for poverty. Too many 'deserving poor' were caught out by economic recession for explanations of workshy or pathological individuals taking advantage of public relief to carry much weight. Social responsibility for poverty became acceptable and legitimated a role for government in relieving poverty caused by losing one's earning capacity through economic upheaval. However, government action was tolerable only insofar as it *did not* undermine individual self-reliance.

THE 'NEW DEAL'

This understanding of American political thought is crucial in comprehending the New Deal promulgated by Franklin Delano Roosevelt, the founder of the modern American welfare state (Conkin, 1968). The 'New Deal' was one of two milestones in the development of publicly funded welfare. The other was the War on Poverty in the 1960s. The New Deal marked major moves away from a private residual model of welfare to a publicly funded insurance one and has been heralded as challenging American *laissez faire* approaches to welfare and laying the foundations of a socialised system (Conkin, 1968). However, this claim should be treated with caution, many old beliefs and customs remained intact. Under the 1935 Social Security Act, individuals contributed to their benefits by working and paying premiums. This practice gave the principle of individual responsibility for welfare provisions legal status. In his bid for the presidency during the 1932 election, Roosevelt attracted big business and farmers by promising to tackle unemployment through economic renewal. He appealed to working class voters by proposing a federal relief system. Having won the election, he implemented the New Deal consisting of legislative acts and executive orders passed between 1933 and 1938. Its key legislative acts tackling the needs of farmers, businesses and unemployed workers were the:

1. National Industrial Recovery Act (NIRA) of 1933.
2. Social Security Act of 1935.
3. National Labour Relations Act (Wagner Act) of 1935.

These measures provided economic stability and enhanced consumer spending controls by guaranteeing prices when these were plunging drastically, reducing uncertainty in the stock market, releasing federal funds for public works, providing employment opportunities, and paying benefits to the unwaged.

The Social Security Act of 1935 responded to Huey Long's organised workers demanding a share of the wealth their labour had produced and Townsendites seeking pensions for older people by creating new areas of federal responsibility in welfare matters. These included the four parts constituting the Social Security Act: contributory Unemployment Insurance, Old Age Insurance collected by a compulsory payroll tax, the means-tested Old Age Assistance Supplemental Income and Aid to Dependent Children.

In drafting the Old Age Insurance plan, Roosevelt opted for a 50–50 split in contributions between workers and employers as in the German model. Now 90 per cent of American workers are covered under Old Age Insurance which includes an earnings related component discriminating against women who form the bulk of the low paid. The majority of middle class male workers supplement Old Age Insurance through private schemes. Although 209 million workers are covered by Old Age Insurance, large numbers of women are not. These include black elders, 10 per cent of whom live on the poverty line. Old Age Assistance Supplemental Income was improved in 1974 when the federal government assumed funding responsibilities. This benefit provides a minimum cash benefit for the older poor and uses financial incentives to encourage states to supplement federal contributions. The 1974 scheme revealed greater numbers of elders living in poverty and doubled the number of Old Age Assistance Supplemental Income claimants to six million. The high numbers of older Americans on supplementary means-tested benefits contrasts with Sweden where the number of elders assisted in this way is low – about 3 per cent.

The Unemployment Insurance promulgated under the 1935 Social Security Act was administered by individual states and called for employer contributions through a payroll tax. Benefits, limited to one third of previous wages, were earnings related and lasted for one year. Farm workers, domestic workers, and casual workers were excluded from coverage, thereby hitting women and black people located primarily in these categories hard. Benefit levels were low so that states could adapt employers' contributions to meet local conditions. This left state jurisdictional boundaries and constitutional responsibilities intact but introduced regional disparities and interstate competition into the scheme as employers moved their firms to states demanding lower contributions. These were located largely in the South where black people already provided cheap labour. In time, this policy has caused serious underfunding of the Unemployment Insurance scheme. Occupational schemes covering unemployment are uncommon. Employers find them too expensive as do trade unions.

The income support offered through the Social Security Act of 1935 did not rupture previous ideological positions and constitutional arrangements, although their boundaries were extended somewhat. The contractual basis of both Unemployment Insurance and Old Age Insurance did not challenge individual responsibility in welfare matters. Low benefit levels neither redistributed wealth nor altered the low wages structure. Benefits excluded farmers, domestic servants and elders when the schemes began. Women were without coverage as domestic servants, elders without a previous employment record, and unwaged homemakers. These features reinforce women's assumed dependent status within the family and endorse minimal state support for women's welfare.

Despite their market orientation, big business and professional interests relinquished some of their opposition to government funded welfare when they realised:

1. Economic dislocation limited individuals' ability to pay.
2. Their interests could be secured by controlling government provisions.
3. Government intervention did not necessarily skew market mechanisms.

Government subsidies cut costs, eased profit margins, maintained incentives to work and upheld the low wages structures. By offering something to both big business and working people, the New Deal was instrumental in maintaining the status quo and controlling working class unrest (Leuchtenburg, 1963).

Notwithstanding the success of the 'New Deal' in containing working class militancy, Roosevelt's opponents, big business and their supporters in Congress expressed concern. They felt Roosevelt's use of leftwingers in promoting New Deal programmes, leftwing support for the National Workers Alliance demand for a permanent right to relief, the escalating costs of relief – $4.8 billion for thirty million people in 1935 – and the spread of 'socialised' welfare, transgressed legitimate boundaries. They launched a powerful offensive to dismantle the 'New Deal'. It included:

1. Challenging its legality in the Supreme Court.
2. Abolishing the tax payments it authorised.
3. Rejecting the 'soak the rich' bill in Congress.
4. Criticising deficit financing in the relief programmes.
5. Campaigning against Social Security Act provisions which Republican and Southern Democrat Senators declared 'the thin edge of the socialist wedge' threatening the American way of life.

Roosevelt responded to this challenge by seeking broader electoral support through the unions and promulgating the third part of the New Deal, the Wagner Act.

The Wagner Act marked a break with previous federal legislation by legitimating trade union activities. It guaranteed collective bargaining rights for unions chosen by the majority of employees, legalised collective action including strikes and boycotts, and initiated a code of fair employment practice. The Wagner Act did not apply to public employees, service workers, agricultural workers and those involved in intrastate commerce. The Wagner Act had limited relevance for waged women located mainly in service industries.

Despite Roosevelt's efforts, the New Deal failed to revive the economy: the construction industry remained depressed; unemployment hovered at around eight million; and consumer spending was down on 1929 levels. These economic realities notwithstanding, Roosevelt won the 1936 election with a 60 per cent majority by promising economic prosperity.

Ignoring his electoral success, big business continued to resist government interference in economic matters through the courts. In 1936, Roosevelt tried to prevent attacks on this flank by asking judges over 70 to retire in the hopes of placing his own men in the Supreme Court. This move backfired and Roosevelt lost prestige for mishandling the issue (Leuchtenburg, 1963). The New Depression exacerbated economic ills. Unemployment increased to eleven million and the stock market fell by 43 per cent. His opponents blamed the New Deal for the New

Depression and Congress retreated from supporting additional welfare initiatives, making Roosevelt increasingly frustrated with domestic affairs.

The 1938 Fair Labour Standards Act forbidding child labour, setting minimum wages and standards marked Roosevelt's last incursion into welfare politics. It appealed to workers in small factories. As before, workers in mining, agriculture, domestic service and retail industry were excluded and women's interests as waged workers not enhanced. Congress continued opposing his welfare proposals and pushed Roosevelt into establishing a 'White House Staff' to support him in his role as president. This institutional provision for the president to surround himself with a group of hand-picked workers remains today.

The New Deal affirms the convergence hypotheses insofar as state intervention on welfare followed economic imperatives and refutes it to the extent that the New Deal straddled well-worn ideological tramlines and responded to political pressures. Roosevelt promoted welfare measures by eliciting support from a wide segment of the population and not significantly challenging the prevailing ideology governing state involvement in welfare matters (Conkin, 1968). The general public backed the New Deal because it was sold to them as a package consistent with traditions of the past: its contributory principle confirmed individual responsibility in caring for one's family; free market and domestic household provisions continued to be the dominant modes of welfare; the labour market and its existing wages structures were not undermined; and it did not redistribute wealth. Small businessmen and farmers were attracted by the economic stability it promised and implemented to a considerable degree through subsidies for their activities. Federal government employees favoured the New Deal because it enabled them to control unemployment. The working class supported it because it promised more jobs. Organised labour endorsed it because it gave them the right to negotiate welfare benefits through collective bargaining. Community activists and the Townsendite pensioners' movement approved of its pension proposals. The New Deal also gained support because Roosevelt dropped controversial proposals like the nationally funded health insurance scheme.

Additionally, Roosevelt's measures controlled social unrest among bankrupt farmers, the working class, and tenants organisations by guaranteeing a minimum income which counteracted economic hardship and misery without centralising production, thereby curtailing the spread of socialism and preventing the formation of a strong leftwing party (Conkin, 1968). It also shifted the burden of the Depression onto the poor.

The gains of the New Deal have not been consolidated because: the absence of a powerful, independent claimants movement reduced the pool of potential supporters; working class organisations were weak; the trade union movement supported occupational welfarism; left activists had been incorporated into the state apparatus thereby weakening the non-parliamentary opposition; and the Democratic Party's ambiguous stance on welfare deprived Roosevelt of internal support for his initiatives. Anti-union sentiments and legislation pushed American unions into economistic positions, using collective bargaining to improve working conditions. For decades, union leaders like Samuel Gompers of the American Federation of Labour rejected union involvement in political issues on ideological grounds. Unions never developed their own party as they did in Britain with Labour. Consequently, welfare provisions, particularly pensions and health became 'fringe' benefits conceded by employers through collective bargaining. In return, union leaders agreed to control rank and file militancy. Women working in the home and in poorly organised workplaces lost out on negotiated fringe benefits in their own right.

Unions were weakened by not developing an effective unified structure like the British Trade Union Congress. Divided along industrial and craft lines, the American Federation of Labour and the Congress for Industrial Organisation were at loggerheads over the best strategies for protecting members' interest. They argued about the nature of union organisation, the roles of unions, direct action, involvement in the political process and equal opportunities. The Congress for Industrial Organisation tried hard to incorporate anti-discrimination measures into its constitution. The lack of similar measures in the American Federation of Labour and the racist and sexist nature of individual unions in both organisations gave short shrift to the interests of women and blacks. Ironically, the American Federation of Labour eventually supported feminist demands for a Mothers Pension early this century to keep women out of the labour market.

The demise of the socialist movement meant that the radical thrust on welfare issues was replaced with a political vacuum. Contrary to popular opinion, America had a visible socialist movement, including Marxists and Communists during the late nineteenth and early twentieth centuries. Although reformist, the Order of the Knights of Labour, Christian Socialists, demanded state intervention on behalf of the able-bodied poor, decent working conditions and pay. Their views were backed by the Socialist Party, the Marxist International Working Men's Association and the Social Democratic Party. To their left and operating along more revolutionary lines including taking direct action were the Industrial Workers of the World or 'Wobblies'. At the peak of socialist activity during the 1912 presidential election, Socialist Party candidate Eugene Deb polled one million votes. He was defeated by Woodrow Wilson who undermined the socialist position through his programme of the New Frontierism which accepted a broad role for the state in welfare matters. This shift in the Democratic Party's position on welfare was also brought about by feminist incursions into electoral politics through the Women's Party (see Irwin, 1971). This change in the Democratic Party's position, the instability of the socialist and feminist movements, the considerable state repression against socialists particularly after the Bolshevik Revolution, and the success of Roosevelt's New Deal sounded the death knell for socialism as a movement enjoying popular support. This has made it easy for Republicans and Democrats to reach a consensus on 'safety net' provisions as the ultimate in state sponsored welfare. This consensus has recently been questioned by Jesse Jackson, former civil rights activist and radical black minister seeking the presidential nomination for the Democratic Party in 1984 and 1988, and the Rainbow Coalition which he heads.

The absence of a viable political party of the Left forced American radicals into pressure group politics through which to pursue welfare issues. The most notable mass movements of this nature were:

1. Those featuring the needs of older people, particularly the Towns-endies in the 1930s and the Gray Panthers in the 1970s.
2. The black civil rights movement running campaigns around deseg-regation in employment, housing, education, transportation and welfare provisions, during the 1960s and early 1970s.
3. The women's movement since the 1960s particularly in relation to equal rights, sexuality, health, and welfare provisions.
4. Community activists organising around welfare in the inner city ghettos during the 1960s and 1970s.
5. Ecological movements of the 1980's

The long-term implications of the New Deal were nonetheless substantial. It laid the basis for a form of 'socialised' welfare by endorsing federal government involvement in mitigating unavoidable hardship for the 'deserving poor', that is the involuntarily unemployed, older people, and children. Its provisions bolstered labour discipline and the low wages structure, thereby reinforcing deterrent models of welfare. It legitimated the 'hidden welfare system' by heavily subsidising private industry. Having provided sufficient welfare measures to 'cool out' discontent, it reduced political debates over poverty. Moreover, the New Deal's support for collective provisions was curtailed by its commitment to personal provisions through contributory insurance schemes which incorporated government welfare expenditures into market mechanisms. This effectively reduced popular support for welfare as right safeguarded by the public purse. Finally, the New Deal encouraged people to think that while poor economic performance can cause social problems, these are temporary distortions in a basically sound system.

Sexism and racism remained unaffected by the New Deal. Aid to Dependent Children reinforced sexism through the 'man about the house' rule and compelled women to accept low paid work. Poverty being a major feature of black people's lives meant they were disproportionately represented amongst Aid to Dependent Children claimants. This and the splitting of black families caused by the 'man about the house' rule forcing black men to leave home so that their families could receive benefit reinforced racism and sexism. Black women were blamed for this state of affairs by dominating their menfolk (see Moynihan, 1965). Except for Roosevelt's legislation banning discrimination in the employment of black people in the defence industry, action picking up on their specific concerns was not forthcoming. The dreams of reformers for a publicly funded comprehensive and non-oppressive welfare state failed to materialise through the New Deal and remain a project for the future.

THE WAR ON POVERTY AND THE WELFARE EXPLOSION

The golden age of the New Deal was replaced with a deterrent model of welfare. The state tightened its discretion and curtailed welfare demand during the 1940s and 1950s. This resulted in a 50 per cent rejection rate for welfare applications. As unemployment declined from their Depression heights hovering around 13 per cent, Americans started believing they had entered the Age of Affluence in which poverty had disappeared. The firmly rooted belief in economic recovery and individuals no longer being prevented from providing for their families by structural economic forces produced a consensus assuming affluence. This consensus suggested America had solved its social problems through economic advancement. Sociologists theorised this as the 'end of ideology' (Bell, 1960). The Cold War ideology endorsed this analysis by focusing on American economic performance, social achievements, and the freedom enjoyed by its people compared to those living under the yoke of socialism. Ironically, this outlook coincided with the most arbitrary limitations on personal expressions of opinion and political activity. Known as the McCarthy period, leftwingers and anyone criticising the status quo were hounded and purged from public office.

The 'rediscovery of poverty' in the late 1950s broke this illusion of affluence. It also became clear that American society had problems other than poverty to handle, although these correlated strongly with it. These included increasing marital and family breakdown, rising juvenile delinquency and serious social unrest, especially among black people (Glazer, 1988; Murray, 1984). Analyses highlighting the 'rediscovery of poverty' exposed the racist and sexist features of poverty and revealed half of the black population was living below the poverty line. Black women at the sharp edge of poverty saw black family income decline from 57 per cent of white family income in 1952 to 53 per cent in 1963. Most of the 8.8 million poor households on public assistance were single mothers with dependent children having access only to stigmatised, differential relief. This situation was defined as unacceptable by both liberals and activists. But it was largely black people, especially black women on welfare, who spearheaded campaigns to resist poverty and remove the stigma attached to welfare claimants (Braeger and Purcell, 1967). These struggles took place under the aegis of the black civil rights movement, community action based on the welfare rights movement, student activism, and the feminist movement. Although they all tackled welfare issues, there were few formal links between them, making their efforts fragmented.

Recognition of these serious social issues prompted calls for state intervention to resolve the crises they engendered. The response, initiated under President Kennedy, peaked under Johnson, who poured substantial federal funds into a variety of projects which came under the umbrella of the War on Poverty. Aimed at increasing economic growth, education, jobs and training, Johnson's War on Poverty was a Great Society strategy against poverty. Launched in 1964, it was based on the following principles and liberalised the deterrent model of welfare by legitimating government aid for people enduring hardship:

1. The diversion of resources to the poor to enable them to help themselves.
2. The involvement of the people through self-help community programmes.
3. The encouragement of liberal interpretations of the discretionary elements in local state provisions.
4. Full employment to bring all poor people into the labour market and create the Great Society.

These principles were consistent with the American belief in individuals helping themselves. The Programme targeted the groups causing most concern – women, black people and youths. The most important publicly funded initiatives encompassed by the War on Poverty were:

1. Mobilization for Youth involving young people in neighbourhood and advocacy work on welfare.
2. The Economic Opportunities Act of 1964 and the Equal Opportunities Act aimed at increasing job prospects for both women and black people. This legislation extended welfare provisions to middle class people.

3. Amendments to the Social Security Act of 1935, including increases in pensions and Aid to Families with Dependent Children (AFDC).
4. Medicare to provide health care for older people.
5. Medicaid making health care available to the poor.

These innovations financed radical organisations; raised the expectations of the poor; made welfare an arena of struggle for women on welfare, black people, feminists, and community activists; legitimated increased take-up in welfare benefits, especially AFDC and Old Age Supplementary Income; and caused a massive rise in federal and state welfare expenditure. For example, pension expenditure exceeded payroll income; AFDC claimants numbered eleven million by 1974. The large number of claimants at higher benefit levels produced what was subsequently called 'the welfare explosion'.

The black civil rights movement demanded an end to racial discrimination in employment, education and housing. It initially pressed for equal opportunities and engaged primarily middle class blacks through the National Association for the Advancement of Coloured People and the Congress on Racial Equality. The failure of both these organisations to attract working class blacks led to demands for a mass movement dealing with the issues relevant to them. The Students National Co-ordinating Committee and Black Panthers were among the prime movers of such demands. Their campaigns involved student and working class activists in strikes, boycotts, mass voter registrations, demonstrations and other forms of direct action, for example, the Freedom Riders, aimed at influencing Democratic Party politicians. They also set up community support networks co-ordinating with trade unions to challenge the quality of services provided, the role of professional welfare workers, and introduce autonomous welfare provisions under black control. Black activists used monies from the Mobilization for Youth and community action programmes to empower black communities, bring a sense of pride in their achievements, and dismantle racism.

Unfortunately, the decline of the black civil rights movement eliminated a powerful force favouring welfare reforms. The demise of black activism can be traced to:

1. The channelling of black activists' political energies into electoral politics.
2. The incorporation of black élites and middle class blacks into mainstream structures.
3. The white backlash against 'affirmative action' and Black Power.
4. The failure of the black civil movement to become a movement of the poor urban black population (Conkin, 1968).

Community action produced a grassroots movement involving significant numbers of women, especially black women. Sexism featured strongly in the movement as men occupied leadership positions while women performed the supporting roles. Nonetheless, the community action movement attacked the stigmatising procedures and inadequate benefit levels bedevilling the system. The National Welfare Rights Organisation was established as a major vehicle for achieving this objective. Viewing information as a source of power, the organisation informed claimants of their existing rights and supported their assertion of them. The strategies its activists used were campaigns to augment the take-up of benefits. They produced 'How to Kits', mounted 'Door-to-Door Knocking Campaigns' and encouraged mass applications for benefits to overwhelm the welfare bureaucracy with unmet demand. This strategy was effective, increasing substantially the numbers on welfare. For example, the AFDC caseload rose by 1.5 million (71 per cent) between December 1964 and February 1969. The impetus of the community action movement was not maintained and the aggressive confrontational 1960s style advocated by Alinsky and his supporters was replaced with more conciliatory approaches during the 1970s, for example, the Arkansas Community Organisation for Reform Now. In the 1980s, community action has failed to mobilise the American populace in substantial numbers.

Student activists also organised around welfare issues in the 1960s, attacking the status quo and rejecting the capitalist materialist values which they felt had destroyed American humanism and morality. Their demands for reform were channelled through various organisations calling for direct action in pursuit of their aims, for example, Students for a Democratic Society, the New Left, the Anti-Vietnam War Movement, and Draft Dodgers. All these questioned the orientation of a society in which one in ten persons in waged work was involved in the war industry and demanded that caring collectivist values replace destructive individualistic ones. Although the resistance student activists offered was significant for a period, the state's counter-attack eventually forced them to retreat.

Women also participated in the students' movement, but found its sexism and authoritarianism intolerable. Women criticised both the New Left and black activists' expressions of 'egalitarianism' for reinforcing sexism by making women become more like men, remain subordinate to their will, and sexually available. Rejecting these definitions of themselves, women forged their own movement. Although the modern feminist movement initially involved women from all classes, 'races' and age groups, it quickly came under the control of white middle class women capturing media attention and alienated other women (Hooks,

1984). Despite its limited representational base, feminism significantly challenged the American way of life. Its greatest impact was the questioning of unequal opportunities in waged work, mindless domesticity, restrictions on women's sexuality and reproductive capacities, (Friedan, 1963), and the lack of health services appropriate to women's needs (Ruzek, 1978). Assuming a universal sisterhood (Morgan, 1970), white feminists highlighted the importance of gender in welfare provisions, exposed how these reinforced women's dependency on men, demanded improvements in the quality of welfare clients' lives (Burden and Gottlieb, 1987), and called for a publicly funded unstigmatised guaranteed minimum income. Black women continued to struggle for improvements in their quality of life and identified the racist nature of white middle class feminist demands (Hooks, 1984; Lorde, 1984). These included citing the family as the site of women's oppression when it was a major source of support for black women in a racist society and calling for abortion on demand when enforced sterilisations and abortions were being foisted on black women by white doctors. Their point was that while women were oppressed as a gender, discrimination on the basis of class and 'race' made the oppression of black women different from that of white women. Hence, sisterhood was not a universal feature which could be assumed. Rather, it had to be created on the basis of struggles acknowledging different experiences among women (Hooks, 1984; Lorde, 1984).

The mass movements described above consolidated and extended provisions originating under the New Deal and initiated major changes in the welfare state of the 1960s through the War on Poverty Programme, legislative changes such as the anti-busing provisions, the Equal Opportunities Act of 1964, and constitutional changes including the liberalisation of abortion in 1973. Having lost their momentum and failed to form a national political organisation, these disparate movements could not sustain these gains during subsequent periods of austerity. Funds black women secured through community organisation were diverted elsewhere and women on Aid for Families with Dependent Children were forced to assume low paid waged work.

THE PERIOD OF CUTS

Cuts, poverty, an increased care burden for women and the flourishing of self-help initiatives replaced the state-sponsored welfare explosion. The cuts began in the late 1960s when the Democrats initiated the Work Incentive Programme to force women with dependent children to leave the welfare rolls by accepting waged work. Such action undermined women's caring role, but was consistent with the idea that individuals should not become reliant on state aid and chimed in with fiscal imperatives curtailing welfare expenditures. The Republicans under Nixon slashed spending on the War on Poverty Programme, channelled money into independent community activities as a further measure in making claimants self-reliant, and rationalised welfare expenditure to reduce costs and increase efficiency. Nixon hoped a guaranteed income administered through a negative income tax would curtail welfare spending. In 1969, he proposed the Family Assistance Plan (FAP) to promote this. This plan promised all families with dependent children a minimum income. Originally a progressive idea endorsed by the Left and feminists, it was undermined by Nixon's overwhelming preoccupation with reducing welfare costs. To save on welfare, income levels under FAP were set very low – $1,600 for a family of four – and targeted 'needy' families to spread limited resources among the greatest number. Except for six Southern States, the levels were below those provided under AFDC, making women and children, the major group affected by this plan, bear the brunt of public expenditure cuts. The reduction in benefits was not aimed solely at saving money. It also forced claimants to accept low paid jobs and cease claiming welfare. These elements enforcing labour discipline and deterrent welfare endeared FAP to conservative politicians who expected it to help the working poor. Feminists and leftwingers campaigning to eliminate welfare stigma and the horrific encounters between claimants and welfare bureaucrats supported FAP for its administrative simplicity – completing a tax return. The National Welfare Rights Organisation, worried about the proposed low benefit levels, launched the ZAP FAP Campaign of mass protests and sit-ins to improve income levels. This strategy backfired because conservatives and liberals in Senate formed an unholy alliance to defeat FAP in 1970 (Burke and Burke, 1976). The combined opposition, coupled with taxpayers' revolts against higher taxes to finance welfare, changed Nixon's mind. At the end of this fiasco, women and children were the losers.

Women and children lost benefits in 1971 when Nixon introduced measures striking 21 per cent of claimants from AFDC rolls and reducing benefit levels for a further 28 per cent. The National Welfare Rights Organisation protested these cuts through Operation Nevada, and the Children's March to Washington, DC. Additionally, the National Welfare Rights Organisation joined forces with others in the 'Poor People's Conference' denouncing these cuts at the Democratic Party Convention in 1972. The Poor People's Conference obtained the Democratic's support for a $4,000 guaranteed minimum income. Nixon retaliated by attacking 'welfare scroungers' whom he claimed his political opponents supported. His subsequent defeat of McGovern in the 1972 Presidential election destroyed the two Party 'consensus' on welfare and halted further bids to increase the income of the welfare poor. Despite these cuts and the government's failure to upgrade benefits in line with inflation, public expenditure as a proportion of Gross National Product (GNP) went up from 10.6 per cent in 1960 to 20.1 per cent in 1975.

By the end of Nixon's period of office, support for welfare improvements had dwindled. There are seven main reasons why the welfare explosion came to an end. These included the following economic, ideological and political factors:

1. Declining economic performance limiting federal welfare funds.
2. Demands for welfare outstripping available resources.
3. Political and economic pressures disengaging the federal government's commitments to welfare. Politically, the states were asserting their autonomy on welfare issues. Economically, deficit financing became unsustainable.
4. Declining grassroots activism removing a powerful source of pressure on policymakers.
5. The backlash of the white Moral Majority reinforcing traditional white heterosexual family values and highlighting discontent among white working class men who felt women and black people had gained at their expense.
6. Consumer discontent undermining existing provisions by attacking them for being degrading, bureaucratic, irrelevant and/or dangerous without proposing alternatives.
7. Abuse of the system, decried by both opponents of state welfare and its advocates. The Moral Majority focused on claimants cheating to gain access to benefits. The Left criticised the enormous profits insurance companies and hospital suppliers made out of existing welfare provisions, and professionals' concern to protect their jobs and incomes rather than further claimants' interests.

The Democrats' victory in the 1976 Presidential election following Nixon's Watergate debacle did not herald a better future for welfare recipients. Carter proposed cuts in his 1978/79 budget. He saved $609 million in 1980 by phasing out benefits for post-secondary school children and limiting minimum benefits for newly retired people to their previous earnings, thus cutting the link between benefits and contributions. Moreover, he cut disability pensions in 1980 despite opposition from his own administration. These cuts enabled Carter to maintain commitments to Old Age Supplementary Income whose costs were escalating beyond control. Keeping this benefit afloat also required the diversion of funds from Medicare. Carter did, however, establish a commission to evaluate financing social security through general taxation. This initiative was cut short when he lost the 1980 election to Reagan.

Political and economic pressures compelled Carter to cut welfare. Expenditure on programmes exceeded the income generated for them. Costs increased as new programmes, especially health care and the Food Programme, needed funding. Furthermore, demographic changes produced a growing number of older people requiring assistance, marital breakdown left more single parent families relying on AFDC, and the economic recession raised the number of unemployed people needing support. Women featured significantly in these changes. The growing popularity of the tax revolt movement following the success of Proposition 13 in prosperous California made increasing welfare expenditure politically undesirable. Tax cuts, demands for government efficiency, and 'no support for scroungers' became the orders of the day.

Reagan won the 1980 election by promising to restore economic prosperity, control public spending, roll back the welfare state, and give individuals freedom and choice. His first budget proposed massive cuts in welfare providing safety net provisions for the *most* needy, reversed the 'New Deal' framework of federal funding for welfare programmes by providing cash limited block – grants and devolved responsibility for welfare funding more resolutely onto the states. Tax cuts benefiting the rich made the tax system regressive and ensured the burden of financing *all* state expenditure fell on the poorest 60 per cent of the population (Davis, 1989). The overall impact of Reagan's policy on welfare meant that half of the people living below the acknowledged poverty line of $8,400 for a family of four did not receive state aid.

Reagan's attack on welfare was important for assailing *both* the *principle* of welfare and its *costs*, despite a 28 per cent reduction in these. While penalising the poor, his moves were advantageous to the rich. Through his intervention, those with an annual income of below $10,000 lost $16.83 billion between 1983 and 1985, while those with an annual income above $80,000 gained $55.6 billion. Women, especially black women, forming the bulk of the poor, suffered most. Overall, Reagan succeeded in saving welfare money; restructuring social attitudes through popularising disciplinary ideologies; endorsing the view that welfare is not the state's responsibility, but the individual's; encouraging charities and voluntary organisations to foster self-reliance; keeping families together by forcing them to care for their members; and installing the social policy of the 'New Right' on a firmer basis. Reagan succeeded in increasing women's dependency on men. Additionally, cuts in the welfare state resulted in lost jobs in the welfare sector, affecting women disproportionately.

Opposition to Reagan's cuts was severely weakened by: the demise of the civil and welfare rights movement; a timid and defensive labour movement; and the demoralisation of welfare recipients. Piven and Cloward (1985) argue the picture is not so bleak, for elements countering Reaganism exist. These are: a young, new electorate, the American tradition of protest, especially evident in the feminist movement, the 'Redistribute America' movement, black activism, and finally the persistent demand for economic protection as long as unemployment, currently 9 per cent, remained high. Michael Dukakis', victory over Jesse Jackson in the Democratic bid for the presidency, and Bush's accession to Reagan's throne have dented the Piven and Cloward hypothesis substantially.

Self-help initiatives have not challenged the existing distribution of welfare resources, although they have provided alternatives to the private commercial provisions favoured by Reagan, and emphasised consumer control and collective sharing of welfare costs. The major identifiable self-help groups have been: black people supporting community initiatives, the feminist movement making available highly personalised health provisions for women; alternative medicine; environmentalists; and communal living collectives. The main problems with self-help provisions are that these are supported by a limited number of people and do not challenge the mosaic welfare system, they are part of it. Besides, these initiatives rely on the group's own resources and small sums procured for their survival from charities and states and leave the unequal distribution of power and resources intact.

IN CONCLUSION

The federal government's initial financial commitments to welfare, especially AFDC, Medicaid, Medicare, was open-ended. Increased demands for services and a declining revenue base called a halt to these. Limitations on spending were achieved through:

1. Block-grants such as Nixon's curbs on community development and renewal.
2. Cuts like Carter's moves on AFDC payments for post-secondary school students.
3. Abolition, for example, Reagan eliminating lump sum death benefits.

A move towards a guaranteed minimum income was defeated under Nixon, the proposals for a national comprehensive health insurance were dropped under Carter, substantial feminist gains fostering women's reproductive rights were destroyed during the Reagan Administration, and the continuing fiscal crisis remains an obstacle to improved welfare provisions. Moreover, Reagan established a discourse on welfare legitimating the withdrawal of state power over people's lives. This neatly reinforced petty bourgeois ideology and possessive individualism emphasising self-reliance and freedom to look after oneself. In addition, the Reagan era has been instrumental in reasserting traditional morality and nuclear family virtues (Glazer, 1988). The AIDS scare has helped this process.

The presence of a mosaic welfare state runs counter to the expectations of convergence theorists' suggestion that a social insurance based model giving federal and local state benefits more prominence in mitigating poverty would become the norm in America. Since the early 1970s state provisions in the United States have been rolled back in terms of the groups covered, levels of entitlements and range of available provisions while the sums of money involved increased (Glazer, 1988). Meanwhile the state has actively intervened to foster the growth of private insurance based welfare through market and domestic provisions. This has restructured the American mosaic welfare state in line with free market and residual concepts of welfare. The residual welfare state is buttressed by private insurance for the upper and middle classes, a state based minimum safety net for the most 'deserving' poor among blacks, elders, and women with children, and domestic provisions for everyone else. Despite rising demands for welfare services among the young un-employed, black people, woman-headed single parent families, single men, single women and older people, the future for an expanded publicly funded welfare state in America is bleak (Glazer, 1988).

American welfare developments suggest convergence theorists may have correctly identified the importance of economic factors since the government's fiscal position has been crucial in undermining public provisions in the American welfare mosaic. But economic issues are not the whole story. Welfare cuts have been undertaken in the name of financial exigencies while Reagan presided over the largest ever American budgetary deficit and defence budget, making political and ideological factors highly significant. Reagan wanted more federal money to go into defence despite its scaling unprecedented heights. Political priorities were re-aligned as Reagan intensified the ideological attack on individuals by demanding they be revitalised and cease depending on state aid. The family, especially women, bore the brunt of poverty and women physically having the caring burden deposited firmly on their shoulders. The countervailing tendencies offering some comfort amidst this gloom include the feminist movement, especially its self-help groups which have established prefigurative forms of collective welfare provisions, black activists pushing back boundaries within the 'normal channels', for example Jesse Jackson, the Rainbow Coalition, and community activists fighting environmental issues.

The Canadian income maintenance system

Since its inception in 1870, the Canadian state has had to respond to the effects of French, British and American imperialism as well as carve out an identity of its own. The wholesale destruction of indigenous forms of welfare already in place among its native Indian and Inuit people is an issue which the state has yet to address adequately. Canadians have drawn lessons from both British and American experiences of welfare and responded to the demands of their French Canadian activists – Quebeckers, trade unionists, feminists and Native populations to create a distinctly Canadian welfare state.

Our understanding of Canadian welfare developments is further complicated by Canada's federal status. Its constitution, initially drawn up by the British as the British North America Act of 1867, left the division of powers concerning welfare ambiguously differentiated between the federal government and each of the ten provinces. The federal government held most of the taxation and revenue raising powers while provincial governments were responsible for welfare provisions. This division of power has given each province considerable autonomy and legislative authority in matters concerning the personal social services, social security and health. Consequently, each province has its own system, though the basic funding is a combination of federal and provincial inputs. Through its funding, the federal government has been able to insist on minimal requirements as part of its strategy of maintaining a 'national' system. In practice this has meant the transferability of financial credits or entitlements from the federal government to provincial ones. At the time of writing this whole arrangement is under threat unless the discord surrounding the Meech Lake Accord is successfully resolved. Federal–provincial jurisdictional disputes, therefore, continue to feature centrally in Canadian politics.

Individual responsibility and Elizabethan Poor Law ideology have been continuous threads in Canadian welfare provisions and debates. These have been tempered by the notions of collectively provided, universal, non-means tested provisions which also feature significantly in them (Guest, 1986). Until the First World War, individuals seeking assistance had to rely on either their own resources, the extended family, the private market if they could afford it, or charitable agencies including those which were funded by the municipality. Public relief at this time was primarily the responsibility of the under-resourced local authority and grossly inadequate. Individuals receiving relief were highly stigmatised.

Armitage (1988, pp. 156–8) argues that the Canadian income maintenance system is made up of cash programmes, goods and services programmes, employment related measures, fiscal measures, occupational welfare measures, enforced dependency measures and the work of private agencies in food banks, shelters and soup kitchens. Most discussions focus on cash programmes including Old Age Security, Guaranteed Income Supplement, Family and Youth Allowances, Child Tax Credit, Canada/Quebec Pension Plan, Unemployment Insurance, Workers' Compensation (with Provincial Assistance Plans) and Assistance for Native Peoples. Among other provisions, goods and services programmes cover Medicare, education, and housing subsidies. Employment related measures include minimum wage legislation and regional economic expansion programmes. Enforced dependency measures affect mainly women and children, and focus largely on the Unmarried Mothers Act, and maintenance orders (Armitage, 1988). Fiscal measures encompass tax credits and a variety of tax exemptions primarily taken up by high income earners. Occupational welfare measures are generally employer provided and are enjoyed mainly by higher income earners, or men (NCW, 1989). These include company cars, expense accounts, pensions, medical and dental coverage. Occupational welfare schemes in the private sector are not treated as income, despite a recommendation that these be taxed by the Royal Commission on Taxation, the 1981 MacEachen Budget, and 1987 Wilson Budget. Occupational schemes are likely to be encouraged through further tax incentives. For example, in 1989, Mulroney's government raised deductions for registered retirement savings plans while ignoring reform of the Canada Pension Plan.

The taxation system can be used as a powerful instrument of social policy. In Canada, as in Britain, the burden of taxation falls disproportionately on low income earners and can catch them in a poverty trap through the taxation of benefits and low incomes. Canada's taxation system remains regressive, despite the progressive effects of tax credits because cutting marginal tax rates has reduced the taxes paid by high income earners. This tendency is exacerbated by increased sales and excise taxes affecting people at the point of consumption and hitting people on low incomes most. Women, as the majority group in this position, bear an unfair proportion of the tax burden (NCW, 1989). Wilson's proposed Goods and Services Tax of 9 per cent will accentuate this trend by drawing commodities previously exempt from tax into its net. The poverty lobby and the 1962 Royal Commission on Taxation (the Carter Commission) have highlighted the importance of reducing the tax burden for low income groups and recommended equity in the treatment of income, regardless of its source. Some of its suggestions became adopted in the Benson tax proposals of 1969 and foreshadowed legislative changes enacted in 1971 for implementation in 1972. If the relationship between taxation, poverty and redistribution were resolved in favour of low income groups, women would be the main beneficiaries.

Institutional forms of income maintenance

SUPPORT FOR THE WAGED WORKFORCE

The earliest form of state financed social security providing benefits as a right was the Workmen's Compensation Act (WCA) of 1914. Each province promulgated its own Act, causing substantial variations in benefit levels between regions (Armitage, 1988). Ontario's Workmen's Compensation Act was considered the model for subsequent demands for universalistic, non-means tested provisions. The Act's coverage was limited since it encompassed only male industrial workers. The large rural population and women workers remained unprotected from loss of income incurred through workplace accidents. Other forms of income loss remained unaffected by this legislation. The sexist bias in this legislation is also evident in the title which reflects the view that only men are engaged in waged work and carry the responsibility of providing for their families. Workers' compensation is funded through employers' contributions calculated according to employee accident records.

As in America, further progress on state funded income support occurred during the Great Depression of the 1930s when unprecedented numbers of unemployed people exposed the inadequacy of municipal relief. Despite the low level of benefits, a municipality's resources including those of the charitable agencies proved incapable of meeting the heavy demands made on their funds. Unemployed people on relief organised to fight for adequate federally financed benefits. The Great Trek of relief workers marching 3,000 miles from Vancouver to Ottawa was led by the Relief Camp Workers' Union in 1935. The 'Trekkers' are as important to Canadian working class history as the Jarrow Hunger Marchers are to British workers.

Working class demands for systematic government welfare intervention curbing the impact of unemployment and economic instability during the 1930s continued amidst rising social disorder. Their agitation and the efforts of the 'Trekkers' eventually led the federal government to formulate the Employment and Social Insurance Act of 1935. Although it excluded one third of the workforce, much of it female, it was hailed as a milestone in Canadian social security history for the benefits it promised. This Act was never implemented because Ontario challenged its legality. The British Privy Council declared it unconstitutional in 1937 because 'property and civil rights' were deemed matters of provincial jurisdiction. This action succeeded in delaying the implementation of a federally funded unemployment insurance scheme until the Second World War. A watered down version of the 1935 proposals was passed as the Unemployment Insurance Act of 1940, after a constitutional amendment allowing the federal government to finance the scheme received British government approval. The National Employment Service established in 1941 had a strategy of getting people off welfare and into employment. Meanwhile, the constitutional questions about the distribution of legislative powers posed by the aborted legislation and its relevance to the issues facing the country caused the government to appoint the Royal Commission on Dominion–Provincial Relations (the Rowell–Sirois Commission) to study them.

The Rowell–Sirois Commission, reporting in 1940, argued for national standards enforced by the federal government to equalise social services between the different parts of the country. These became subject to further discussion and meetings. The crunch point came in 1945 when federal–provincial agreement on welfare issues was negotiated during the Dominion–Provincial Conference on Reconstruction. This followed the agenda set up by the 'Green Book' proposals (*Proposals of the Government of Canada*, 1945) seeking to establish general conditions for high employment and income policies following national minimum standards.

Federal–provincial disputes form a delicate thread running through Canadian social policy. Challenges to the status quo led to a complete review of the Canadian Constitution on welfare in 1968. Proposals tabled by the federal government in 1969 failed to satisfy Quebec which was seeking to gain full political autonomy and led to a further conference in Victoria in 1971. Although the agreements reached there strengthened provincial control, Quebec remained unconvinced that other provinces would accept its continued right to protect French culture. Its scepticism is being borne out by premiers who oppose the Meech Lake Accord because granting Quebec 'distinct society status' will give it too much power, limit federal powers to spend money in areas of exclusive provincial jurisdiction and undermine the federal government's ability to use cost-sharing programmes in setting 'national' standards.

Under the 1956 Unemployment Insurance Act, the federal government met half of the provincial social assistance payments to the unemployed. A major revision to this Act took place in 1970 when it was expanded to cover all wage and salary earners, increase benefit levels and extend the period for which benefit could be obtained. The minimum contribution period to qualify for benefit was also reduced. But most importantly from women's point of view was the inclusion of maternity benefits within its scope for the first time. Unwaged women, however, were still not covered for benefits, including maternity pay. The 1970 Act also introduced sickness benefits. Both sickness and maternity benefits were payable for fifteen weeks. However, Unemployment Insurance benefits were not paid to workers with a continuous employment record of less than eight weeks. This discriminated against casual workers and those employed only for short periods. Many of these were women whose family responsibilities precluded them from assuming full-time employment. The value of benefits has deteriorated since 1974 when benefit levels brought a wage-earner and two dependants to the poverty line. In 1985, benefit levels could only achieve this for a wage-earner and one dependant (Armitage, 1988, p. 176). Moreover, the long-term unemployed, (those unemployed for longer than one year) lose entitlement to benefit. This regulation penalises women who take time off to raise children, and enforces their dependence on either male partners, the extended family, friends, or means-tested assistance, and indicates how the system presupposes a male working pattern.

Ideological struggles over the appropriateness of providing able-bodied people with unemployment insurance and the extent to which unemployment benefits contribute to the problems they are intended to solve produced a stream of demands for restructuring unemployment insurance during the 1980s. The MacDonald Commission Report and Forget Commission Report argued that unemployment insurance discouraged people from seeking work, tampered with the labour market and exacerbated unemployment levels. Their recommendations suggested strengthening the insurance basis of unemployment benefits, making these less of an income transfer mechanism and equalising regional disparities through other means. Additionally, the De Grandpre Report had proposed turning labour market expenditures away from income maintenance towards retraining and employment.

The federal government did not adopt these suggestions directly. However, it introduced the Canadian Jobs Strategy in 1985 to respond to these criticisms. This strategy provides retraining and employment programmes for the long-term unemployed and those on social assistance. Funds have been diverted to the Canadian Jobs Strategy from the Canada Assistance Plan and savings made by cutting Unemployment Insurance benefit. A crucial weakness in the Canadian Jobs Strategy is that people are being trained for non-existent jobs. Also training is being provided by the private sector, which is making profits out of public resources but is not accountable for the nature of the services being delivered. This strategy is similar to that being adopted in Britain by the Manpower Services Commission, now the National Training Commission. An employment strategy is also followed in Sweden where skills and jobs are more closely matched and a political commitment to full employment underwrites it. Several Canadian provinces, for example, British Columbia, have introduced 'Workfare' type schemes compelling the unemployed to work for their benefit and have enforced the 'actively seeking work' requirement for eligibility with disastrous consequences for single parent women (*The Vancouver Sun*, 1989). Wilson's 1989 budget proposed shifting the full financial costs of the scheme onto employers and employees and reducing Unemployment Insurance benefits. In 1989, the unemployment insurance scheme played a key role in maintaining labour discipline among Canadian claimants.

The concern with reinforcing work incentives means that changes in minimum wages legislation need to be examined alongside social security provisions. A major shift accompanying a reduction in minimum wage levels has been the presumption of two incomes in a family rather than one as was the case in the early 1970s. Policies formulated on the assumption of two-earner families operate to the detriment of women who are mainly located in minimum wage occupations and form the bulk of single parent families. They also contribute to a reduction in income maintenance benefit levels by ensuring these are pegged so as not to undercut minimum and other wages (Armitage, 1988). The Working Paper on Social Security (1973) made clear the expectation that all adults will work when it argued that social security: 'must contain incentives to work and a greater emphasis on the need to get people who are on social aid back to work.'

SUPPORT FOR CHILDREN

A devastating effect of the First World War on the Canadian population was the creation of large numbers of widows with children. These combined with high numbers of woman-headed one-parent families, produced a substantial group of people living in poverty. Concern over the economic hardship these two groups experienced, anxieties about the devastating impact of poverty on children's lives, and forceful lobbying on this issue by trade unionists and feminists produced strong support for the Mothers Pension Movement (Strong-Boag, 1979). The Mothers Pension Movement demanded non-stigmatised incomes for women and children as of right. These demands became reality when legislation was passed in some provinces. Manitoba began the process in 1916. Ontario and British Columbia followed in the 1920s. Mothers Pensions, however, were only for morally upright women. In its inception and implementation, Mothers Pensions reinforced women's traditional role as mothers and women with moral standing. Its success was short-lived, for after ten years, the business community and professional groups opposing Mothers Pensions secured 'cuts' in benefits. In British Columbia, the opposition demanded obligatory social work intervention as a condition of receipt of benefit and the conversion of the pension from a right to a form of public assistance (Guest, 1986). Its success turned the pension into an allowance embedded in socially controlling women. Under the caseworkers' surveillance, women's adherence to the appropriate middle class standards was closely monitored and bourgeois notions of femininity reinforced (Strong-Boag, 1979). Following the scrutiny of women claimants' lifestyle, only cases satisfying the social caseworker of leading a suitably righteous life were accepted.

Popular and professional concern over the destitution among Canadian workers following the Second World War refuelled debate over the necessity of adequate state funded social security provisions available to all in need as a right. In 1943, the Canadian equivalent of the Beveridge Report, the Marsh Report, was published. The Marsh Report came out of the House of Commons Advisory Committee on Post-War Reconstruction. It laid the foundations for many of the post-war developments in the Canadian welfare state though the Report was never implemented as envisaged (Armitage, 1988). Marsh suggested a comprehensive income maintenance system including universal medical care, pensions, unemployment insurance and employment protection for the disabled.

Poverty continued to devastate families with children as inadequate nutrition, poor sanitation facilities and a high infant mortality rate exacted their toll. In 1944, the federal government introduced the Family Allowances Act to offset poverty by increasing the spending power of families. This provided the first universal welfare payments in Canada. Aggregating family incomes underwrote family allowances and disguised the impact of poverty on women and children. Additionally, making family allowances available endorses the government's claim of catering for their specific needs. Family Allowances continue to be a major element of family income support.

The level of benefits paid in family allowances varies from province to province, thereby intensifying regional disparities. A child tax credit of $384 per year was introduced to provide extra income for low income families in 1977. Combined with family allowances, this averages $750 per year in federal support per child, and is well below the $3,000 the government believes is necessary to maintain a child at the poverty line. Family poverty has not been reduced by the existence of such programmes which assume the presence of other earnings or incomes to take children out of poverty. Neo-conservative resistance to the universal nature of family allowances and fiscal exigencies have undermined this demogrant. Strong support for it among a variety of groups including women and feminists has prevented the government from eliminating it. However, as with British child benefits, it has not been adjusted to keep pace with inflation and is making a diminishing contribution to 'family' resources. Further creeping erosion in the value of the family benefits package of family allowances, child tax credit, tax exemptions for dependent children and tax deductions for childcare expenses occurred in 1985 through partial de-indexation and the clawback of the family allowances element which will become fully operational in 1991. These changes will have a major impact in reducing state finances for families, including poor ones. Family allowances institutionalise dependency within the family and buttress familial ideology rather than mitigate the effects of poverty on women and children. The low levels of benefits ($31 per child per month in 1985, after which provinces have tended to freeze growth in this area) render tokenistic even the idea that these provide women with an income independent of men. Additionally, it would be hard to argue that these sums encourage women to have more children. Canadian Family Allowances are not pronatalist, despite a decreasing birth rate. Nor do they support children's rights and their access to an independent income.

OLDER PEOPLE

The Old Age Assistance Act (OAA) of 1927 was the first federal–provincial cost-shared programme whereby provinces administered the programme and recouped 40 per cent of their expenditure from the federal government. Initially, it provided only a means-tested allowance for older Canadians. Increasing poverty among the aged and their being considered a deserving group led to agitation for improved provisions for them. Income maintenance structures for older people were extended in the 1950s and 1960s as the government set about ensuring sufficient income support for keeping them out of poverty and led to universal rather than means-tested Old Age Security payments at age 70 being enacted in 1951. Also, the Old Age Assistance Act was revised in 1951 to cover people aged between 65 and 70. A comprehensive series of reforms introduced in the 1960s produced a contributory pension scheme called the Canada Pension Plan/Quebec Pension Plan (CPP/QPP), a lowering of the age qualification for the universal federally funded Old Age Security pension (OAS) and a Guaranteed Income Supplement (GIS). Introduced in 1966, the latter supplemented elders' incomes on a means-tested basis to prevent older people falling below the poverty line. While important, these measures only tackled the problem of poverty for some. Women whose work is confined to that of homemaker cannot contribute directly to CPP/QPP and obtain benefits in their own right. Moreover, those lacking either a tax deductible private contributory scheme or the CPP/QPP and relying solely on OAS and GIS are experiencing a long-term drop in their income despite the federal government's stated objectives to the contrary. Armitage (1988, p. 173) declares the 'total value of these minimum benefits is further behind the poverty lines now than it was in 1974'.

The Canada Assistance Plan of 1967 was an anti-poverty measure extending federal cost-sharing in provincial programmes. It aimed at 'lessening, removing, and preventing the causes of poverty'. Consolidating previous cost-sharing arrangements, it meant the federal government provided 50 per cent of the costs of welfare services. Despite the bleak scenario for older people, particularly women on their own who are totally reliant on state support, the incremental increases in income maintenance like the Guaranteed Income Supplement, the Spouses Allowance and the CPP/QPP, substantially reduced the number of older Canadians living in poverty in the mid-1980s (NCW, 1989b).

Unfortunately, this position is being eroded. Provincial governments started clawing back index-linked money from claimants in a bid to reduce expenditures on older people. Additionally, the federal government attempted to partially de-index Old Age Security as a cost-cutting measure in 1985. A massive national protest halted this plan until the 1989 budget. Then, the finance minister introduced a clawback for Old Age Security. Though initially affecting only 4.3 per cent of the older population because the clawback does not go into effect until the $50,000 threshold is reached, this will alter over time. The National Council of Welfare (1989) argues that the partial indexing of this threshold will cause it to drop in value so that 'today's 35 year old, middle income earner will receive a considerably reduced Old Age Security Payment on retirement' (NCW, 1989b). These measures can be seen as taking action to limit public expenditure on pensions when older people become a significant proportion of the population in the twenty-first century. Most of these will be women.

POVERTY

Poverty has been a major issue which the Canadian income maintenance system has sought to address. The special Senate Committee on Poverty (the Croll Committee) reporting in 1971 revealed extensive poverty among women-headed single parent families. Its Majority Report recommended a uniform guaranteed annual income administered by the federal government through a negative income tax delivered on an income-tested or selective basis. The Minority Report proposed a more generous guaranteed annual income but implemented through demogrants.

Income security for Canadians issued in 1973 suggested replacing family allowances with the Family Income Security Plan which would introduce a means-tested guaranteed income supporting children and families. This was not implemented, though the family allowances system was changed.

Pressure from the parliamentary opposition, especially the New Democratic Party, forced the minority Liberal government to act on the matter of the guaranteed income. It released *The working paper on social security in Canada* (the 'Orange Paper') in 1973 to initiate a review of social security and examine: income support – a guaranteed annual income for those unable to work; income supplementation – a work incentive programme for those able to work; a 'fair and just relationship' between minimum wages, support and supplementation; provincial variation; and federal–provincial consensus. Additionally, family allowances and the Canada Pension Plan/Quebec Pension Plan were highlighted for reform.

The Orange Paper proposed five strategies for the creation of an effective social security system. These included:

1. An employment strategy to create training opportunities equipping people with the skills for working rather than relying on social assistance. The community employment programme providing socially useful work for the long-term unemployed constituted part of this strategy.

2. Targeting social insurance provisions on the temporarily unemployed or retired and continuing to supplement incomes where necessary. Income supplementation was deemed highly appropriate for the working poor.

3. Increases in family allowances.

4. A guaranteed income for those with insufficient finances and unable or not expected to work. These provisions covered women heading single parent families, and those on Old Age Security and emergency relief programmes.

5. The continued funding of social services. Mindful of federal–provincial jurisdiction disputes, the 'Orange Paper' suggested provinces set the levels for family allowances, supplements, and income guarantees within minimum standards established by the federal government.

The review process established working parties to hammer out provisions covering income maintenance, social services and the employment strategy. Agreement on income maintenance proposals was reached at working party and ministerial levels in April 1975. Their proposed guaranteed income scheme with one component of income support for those 'unable to work or for whom employment cannot be found' and another of income supplementation with 'built in work incentives' for the working poor, drew fine distinctions between the 'deserving' and the 'less deserving' poor. However, the financial implications of the proposal were substantial. It was scuppered by the full cabinet endorsing it in principle, but making it await future resourcing. The failure of the two levels of government to agree on the way forward in the social security review led the federal government to unilateral action through the tax system. In 1978, it introduced the Refundable Child Tax Credit Programme on its own initiative. This became effective in 1979.

The issue was picked up again in 1985 by the Royal Commission on the Economic Union and Development Prospects for Canada (the MacDonald Commission). The MacDonald Report highlighted the need for a better income maintenance system to facilitate the social and economic adjustments following the implementation of the Free Trade Agreement with the United States. The fear is that Free Trade will cause a significant deterioration in Canadian social programmes, especially income maintenance and social services (Drover *et al.*, 1988). This is expected to take place through the continued dismantling of welfare provisions, especially in unemployment insurance benefits and health care as economic priorities of cutting subsidies to welfare services and maintaining international competitiveness take precedence over social needs. Privatised services provided either through the market or subcontracted out through the public sector will replace state welfare provisions (Drover *et al.*, 1988). However, the scene for these changes was set before the advent of Free Trade.

The 1980s have seen an erosion in welfare provisions either through dramatic direct cuts like those taking place in British Columbia in 1983 and Saskatchewan in 1987, attrition by adjusting budgets below the level of inflation, or increases in real costs. Despite cutbacks in welfare provisions hitting able-bodied claimants particularly hard, expenditures on social security have continued to rise as in Britain and America without covering real increases in the costs of providing services stemming from growing demands for services and inflation. In 1984–5, Canada spent $61.6 billion on social security (MacDonald, 1985, p. 772). However, Canada's position on the international league table is that of a moderate provider. It devoted 4.6 per cent of GDP to income maintenance in 1985, compared to 11.8 per cent for Sweden, 7.4 per cent for Britain and 7.4 per cent for the United States (Armitage, 1988, p. 190).

Poverty in Canada follows the pattern prevalent in Britain and America. It is located largely among women, particularly single parent families, older women, and black and Native women. During the past fifteen years, the government has responded to feminist demands for a guaranteed income for all by targeting families through the safety net provided by the Guaranteed Income Support, the Canada Assistance Plan, the restructuring of family allowances, and implementing a negative income tax in some provinces. These measures fall short of feminist aspirations. Also, benefit levels are low for those covered. Pensions continue to be aggregated for couples, so women lose out here too. Additionally, some provinces clawback federal pension increases tied to the consumer price index through the contributions they make to Guaranteed Income Support. However, women gained the right to claim pension credits from former spouses as part of their divorce settlement in 1978.

Except for social security provisions such as pensions and family allowances cognisant of women in their roles as wives and mothers, feminist agitation has failed to secure specific recognition of women's needs in Canada's welfare state. This has happened despite a lengthy investigation on the position of women conducted by a Royal Commission on the Status of Women. Its *Report on the status of women*, published in 1970, presented a comprehensive statement on the underprivileged status and discrimination experienced by Canadian women. The Report's failure to contribute significantly to improvements in women's position is attributable to the lack of political commitment on this score, public expenditure cuts, a faltering economy, and the weakness of the women's movement.

IN CONCLUSION

Welfare provisions in the 1980s have been marked by instability as the Canadian welfare state has struggled to maintain the gains of the 1970s. Like its British counterpart, many provisions are falling under the government's public expenditure cuts at both provincial and federal level. Family allowances and unemployment insurance are two areas which have been hard hit by financial restraints.

As Canada enters the 1990s, social policy in general, and income maintenance in particular, will have to respond to business pressures arising from the business community's fear that a substantial welfare state will undermine its competitiveness in the international market by making Canadian goods more expensive. Its hand in reducing the 'social wage' and high wages has been strengthened by the Free Trade Agreement which has enabled Canadian firms to relocate in Mexico, exploit the unorganised labour force lacking welfare rights in special zones set aside for foreign investment and dramatically reduce labour costs. Business interests already have strong representational and lobbying power in Parliament to ensure that they play a crucial role in setting the welfare agenda.

Countervailing forces to capital determining the direction followed in social policy are the women's movement, Native People's movement and black people now settling in Canada. Immigration policy in Canada has been used to recruit Third World people to power its economic development and compensate for its declining birth rate. They are organising to protect their interests and tackling sexism and racism in the process. Moreover, as those in countervailing movements experience the highest levels of poverty because of their disadvantaged position in the labour market, defending, extending and transforming the welfare state so that it meets their needs has become an important element in their struggle for equality. Direct community action and legal suits have become fundamental strategies in the assertion of their rights. The Charter of Rights and Freedoms has been instrumental in taking welfare concerns to the highest court in the land, giving the Canadian Supreme Court an important role in formulating social policy, for example, questioning mandatory retirement (Tindale, 1988); men's rights to parental leave. Ironically, these cases have been brought by men who have argued that their rights have been infringed because they could not choose what they wanted to do with their lives.

Convergence in developments taking place in the United States, Britain and Canada, follows the line of governments promoting private market and domestic provisions at the expense of public measures including safety net provisions and foisting the burden of compensating for reduced public amenities onto women as carers. Although economic factors in the form of fiscal crises engendered by escalating costs in welfare provisions, larger budget deficits, demographic changes, and increasing demand for services are important, the reasons for this convergence are more than economic. Though not as powerfully entrenched as Reaganism in America or Thatcherism in Britain, the New Right under Brian Mulroney has successfully attacked the notion of publicly funded provisions based on pooling risks between the unwaged drawing benefits and the waged paying taxes for them. His success has been possible as a result of weakened popular activism among the Left, trade unionists, black people, Native people, and women. However, it has been thwarted by parliamentary opposition orchestrated by the New Democratic Party, continued activism among women's groups, trade unionists, black people, and Native people, and legal challenges through the Charter.

The British income maintenance system

Britain has two elements to its income maintenance system: a non-means tested insurance based component funded through contributions from employers and employees, and a non-contributory means-tested one. Benefits in the social insurance system are universal and not means-tested. They provide protection against economic risks without stigma to those in waged work. Marshall (1965) called this the citizenship model of welfare. It assumes equity on the basis of a worker's contribution record. As not everyone in society is engaged in waged work, for example, young people, older people, and young mothers, it embodies conservative and individuating notions of self-support and family responsibility which reinforce dependency on a waged worker facilitating access to insurance related benefits. It also ignores the lower earning power of women and black people who receive less in benefits than white men. By catering for the needs of better off and more effectively organised workers, the social insurance system reinforces sexism and racism. It also binds male workers to the state through a contract which takes social security out of the political arena.

The contributory National Insurance System of social security contains an inbuilt bias against those who are not free to enter the labour market. These are mainly women caring for children or older relatives at home. The exclusion of women from national insurance schemes by their lack of waged work makes them the major beneficiaries of means-tested social assistance schemes. Income Support, previously known as national assistance and then supplementary benefit, is the most important of these.

The British social assistance system is a residual safety net one with considerable stigma attached to those drawing on its services (Ginsburg, 1979) operating as a remote bureaucracy outside consumer control. It provides assistance following a means test. Eligibility is according to householder status and the aggregation of the income of family members and cohabitees. It makes non-breadwinners dependants of breadwinners and penalises women, youths, and black people whose family structures differ from the white heterosexual nuclear one, thereby exercising social control over family forms. Needs are bureaucratically determined and shaped by governmental concern not to make benefit levels high as this would discourage individuals from being thrifty, acquiring savings and accepting low waged work. Benefits rates are consistent with maintaining labour discipline (Ginsburg, 1979).

Maintaining labour discipline enables the social security system to reproduce capital–labour relations and control both waged workers and unwaged ones. This includes reproducing and maintaining the reserve army of labour, not undermining low wage rates by keeping benefits low (Ginsburg, 1979) and enforcing work incentives by having low benefits and 'genuinely seeking work' a condition of relief. Both men and women applying for unemployment benefit sign 'availability for work' tests and submit to interviews by the Rehabilitation Officer who can refer them to the Restart Programme for training. Similar controls were exercised previously through the 'four week rule'. Time limits on eligibility for insurance based benefits also reinforce labour discipline. Making men responsible for the economic welfare of their dependants increases their willingness to work and operates as a form of psychological coercion (Dominelli, 1986c) and provides benefits for unwaged people on a stigmatised dependent basis, for example, pensions for married women. Additionally, social security disciplines workers by curbing their militancy, for example, excluding from benefit striking workers or those whose actions have led them to lose their job (the old six week rule, now the twenty-six week rule). Piven and Cloward (1972) suggest benefits are increased during industrial unrest and cut during periods of stability to reinforce work discipline. Even in the Soviet Union, social security was used as a tool of labour control. The Commissar of Labour told the British TUC in 1932: 'We shall handle social insurance as a weapon to attach workers to their enterprises and strike hard at loafers, malingerers and disorganisers of work' (quoted in George and Manning, 1980). Social security is a significant element of public expenditure. The British government spends social security monies as follows: 74 per cent on National Insurance benefits, 15 per cent on supplementary benefits, 5 per cent on child benefits, and 6 per cent on other non-contributory benefits.

Drawing on Income Support subjects women to increased stigma and state intervention. It highlights their contradictory relationships with the welfare state (Wilson, 1977). It expects women to stay at home caring for others, but if they are on Income Support, it pushes them into low paid work. This is achieved by having women on social assistance pass an 'availability for work' test to prove eligibility for benefit. A crucial question in it relates to arrangements regarding the care of dependent children. Those failing to satisfy the officer investigating the claim are denied benefit. Given women are primarily responsible for the care of children, the test has a greater impact on them than men. Asking women to submit to an 'availability for work' test also negates the work women do in the home nurturing other people, and categorises it as non-work. The welfare state's failure to provide unwaged women carers with an unstigmatised income and encourage men to assume full caring roles keeps women in subordinate and dependent positions in the family (McIntosh, 1978; Land, 1975).

The state's relationship to women is one of increasing their social control and giving individual men greater power over them. Feminists back publicly funded institutional services over family provisions to move women away from having directly dependent relationships with men. For such dependency gives men personal control over women's behaviour and makes women feel personally obligated to them. Although women may become dependent on the welfare state for financial resources, the impersonal dependency this engenders is preferable to private ones locking them in unsatisfactory personal relationships with men (Binney et al., 1981). Institutional provisions can guarantee women's freedom to choose their lifestyles in a way which is not possible when relying directly on men.

THE IDEOLOGICAL BASIS OF THE BRITISH SOCIAL SECURITY SYSTEM

The struggle for an income maintenance system covering all risks and available to all when needed came together in demands the British Left, labour movement and feminist movement made for a comprehensive, publicly funded social security system (Corrigan, 1977). Their ideal became encapsulated in the Beveridge Report which argued for an income support system based on insurable risks which could be undertaken collectively. The view that the welfare state is humane, responsive to need and eliminates poverty performed an invaluable function in shaping British attitudes to social security and controlling their aspirations for its development. However, a close reading of Beveridge reveals that his conception of welfare, predicated on the notion of insurable risks was both racist and sexist (Williams, 1989; Pascall, 1986). Additionally, drawing heavily on full-time work for a substantial proportion of one's life time and responding specifically to the needs of white male workers, fiscal and ideological constraints undermined the establishment of a comprehensive system of income maintenance available to all as needed (Kincaid, 1973).

The bedrock of Beveridge's social security system was the family having an adult man holding a significant position in the labour market, while the adult woman stayed home, providing caring services and unpaid housework. The existence of unpaid housewives obviated much of the state's obligation to provide domestic services. For example, only 5 per cent of elders are cared for by the state (Higgins, 1989), indicating that only in extreme cases where the family cannot, will the welfare state assume responsibility for them. Children are mainly cared for by women at home until they go to school. The state then channels their education into socialising them for entering the workforce by acquiring the skills required by the economy (Offe, 1984; Willis, 1977).

Beveridge assumed men and women live in family units in which men control the money coming in and women depend economically on them. He articulated women's dependency on men in the following terms:

> The attitude of the housewife to gainful employment outside the home is not and should not be the same as the single woman – she has other duties. . . . as mothers [they] have vital work to do in ensuring the adequate continuance of the British race and of British ideals in the world. (Beveridge, 1942, p. 51, para. 114 and p. 53, para. 117)

In practice, the Department of Health and Social Security translated this into the following dictum: 'A husband and wife who live in the same household form a single assessment unit. Only the husband can normally receive benefit' (DHSS, 1982, p. 29). Its interpretation of family life was formally broken in 1983 when the European Court ruled that in failing to observe the European Economic Community directives on equality for women, this practice constituted sex discrimination. This ruling forced the British government to introduce the concept of the 'nominated breadwinner' in which families can choose who adopts this role. Since men earn more than women, men continue to be the majority of those holding the 'nominated breadwinner' position.

The view that women are men's dependants had serious implications for both women's access to social security provisions and the creation of services meeting their specific needs. For white women the system is structured in ways which enforce familialism, for black women, immigration control combines with social security provisions to divide their families (Dominelli, 1988a). Pascall (1986) argues that Beveridge dropped specific provisions for married women in the event of marital breakdown because doing so conflicted with the insurance principle of not provoking situations requiring benefits. In allowing their marriage to fail, women committed a dereliction of duty making them responsible for their fate. In such cases, the state could only provide stigmatised national assistance. Today, this punitive element in women's claims is particularly highlighted when single parent women have their independent status challenged during Special Claims Squad interrogations. The portrayal of black people and foreigners as 'scroungers' has meant that their access to social security is more likely to be denied than allowed (Gordon and Newnham, 1985).

Other ideological dimensions draw on Poor Law ideology dividing claimants into the 'deserving' and the 'undeserving' poor. Social security covers those in waged work when they are ill, unemployed or poor; excludes unwaged women acquiring access through their dependent status and assumes the deserving poor are white British people for black people's dependants are denied benefits when living overseas, and while living in Britain if the male breadwinner goes abroad for long periods.

Britain's income maintenance system is not an income transference system transferring money from the affluent to the needy. Since 1979, £8 billion have been cut from the social security budget. Meanwhile, tax cuts of £4.5 billion have been allowed. Of these, £2 billion went to the richest 5 per cent of the population. Income inequalities in Britain are also evident in after tax figures. The richest 10 per cent of the population have an after tax income of £50 billion, while the poorest 10 per cent have one of £6 billion. The ramifications of this are that income maintenance and taxation need to be considered together to develop a full picture of how the state subsidises the lifestyles of different social groups. The taxation system forms part of the income maintenance system through tax exemptions. These are regressive because they are more valuable to the better off. Tax relief on mortgages, life insurance premiums and private health premiums benefit mainly the upper and middle classes. *Tax relief is therefore, an unstigmatised hidden system of welfare although it is not recognised as such.* Tax relief also aggregates a married couple's income, prioritising the man's income over the woman's, and reinforcing sexism (LWLC, 1979). Lawson's tax reforms giving married women privacy in taxation matters aggregate allowances and promote their transferal from the lower income partner, usually the woman, to the higher income one. Black people maintaining dependants overseas continue to be denied tax relief. Besides highlighting the income maintenance system's function in enforcing the work ethic and labour discipline (Ginsburg, 1979), this discussion reveals its role in: maintaining the stability of white nuclear families (Eichler, 1983); dispersing black families (Bryan *et al.*, 1985) and reinforcing white British cultural identity (Barker, 1981).

The Left has considered women's access to an income independent of men as a positive achievement of social security, albeit at the margins of poverty. The degree of freedom from male dependency that women have acquired through an income guaranteed by the welfare state is an issue for the 'New Right'. It has charged the social security system with aiding women's liberation, undermining family stability and eroding men's power over women by providing extra-familial support for women and children (Glazer, 1988). The 'New Right' aims to control women's freedom to stem the high percentage of marital breakdown and is prepared to restructure state welfare to achieve this. As a leading right wing ideologue says:

When the state provides (social) services there is serious concern that families feel morally justified in abandoning their responsibilities to the state. This is an unhappy situation . . . Society rightly feels that elderly parents and relatives, for example . . . are the responsibility of next of kin to help. (Minford, 1984)

Mystified by referring to the family, this view reinforces the notion that women are responsible for caring. Minford takes his position seriously for he recommends punitive measures against those abrogating familial responsibilities: 'The logical action to take is therefore for such responsibilities to be made legally mandatory . . . . Neglect of these family responsibilities would be actionable by the state . . . to maintain law and order' (Minford, 1984).

The 1980 Social Security Act increased the economic and ideological attack on families on welfare. Deductions of £12 per week to the benefits of strikers' families were authorised on the grounds that family income was aggregated and strikers were getting at least that from union funds. In 1980/81, cuts of 5 per cent in real terms were imposed on the sick, the unemployed and disabled as the Rooker–Wise Amendment was annulled. In January 1982, the earnings related element in unemployment benefit was abolished. This increased reliance on the social assistance system. In 1983, in a bid to reduce the number of civil servants, sick pay was changed to statutory sickness benefit and devolved to employers for the first eight weeks, thereby reducing the number of civil servants, many of whom were women.

The Fowler Review was a monetarist attack on social security. This aimed to increase contributions for fewer benefits, attack supplementary benefits and discretionary awards, eliminate the State Earnings Related Pension Supplement (SERPS) and restructure social security so as to encourage individual self-reliance and reinforce patriarchal ideology. The ideological groundwork had been clarified by Patrick Jenkins when he said: 'I don't think that mothers have the same right to work as fathers. If the good Lord had intended us to have equal rights to go to work, he wouldn't have created men and women.' (Jenkins, 1963)

The Fowler Review followed the popularly dubbed 'No cost no benefit' Review of 1976 initiated by Labour. Fowler intended to reverse gains women made in obtaining an independent income during the 1970s and 1980s and increase men's control of household finances. This followed Howe's warning in 1982 that 'cuts in child benefits were part of a plan to reassert the family as a unit headed by the father'. The proposal to place Family Credit under men's control through the pay packet and withdraw it from families of strikers indicates this. The threat to cut maternity benefits, abolish child benefits; and get rid of SERPS was calculated to exacerbate women and young people's dependency on the 'family', that is, its male breadwinner. Restructuring social security also marked an attempt to stretch expenditure on income maintenance to cover a greater number of people. This was to be achieved by trading the income of one group with another, having a flat rate of income support, aggregating family resources, creating a Social Fund based on loans, establishing premiums for priority groups, eliminating long-term benefit rates for single parent families and the long-term unemployed and reducing housing benefits by compelling claimants, including elders and single parents, to pay 20 per cent of rates and water charges. These measures directly disadvantaged women's access to financial resources through the social security system and did so throughout their life-cycle, thereby worsening women's already inadequate position caused by interrupted earnings, low pay, part-time work, unemployment pay, poverty line pensions, and the lack of retraining facilities aimed specifically at meeting their needs (LSSC, 1986).

Women's poverty was also exacerbated by Thatcher's failure to respond to the demonstrated need for substantial support for women, the terms for eligibility to Social Fund monies, and the abolition of the right of appeal. Paying benefits on a household basis also discriminates against women. Women have to bear the brunt of managing on less money. When Income Support replaced supplementary benefits, only Regulation 30 remained to provide safety net provisions for financially hard-pressed families if risk to health and safety could be proved. Moreover, the Social Fund gives the state a policing role over women's budgeting of family finances. Single parents using the Social Fund face increasing social work intervention and surveillance without the provision of new resources. Fowler sought to encourage people to find *private solutions* to the problem of ensuring their income, including forcing men to remain in or seek work; making women provide caring in the family to save money on welfare expenses and achieve some measure of personal economic security; compelling black people to satisfy their needs through community provisions.

Fowler's attempts to bolster men's control of women was not a new initiative. The social security system had already endorsed male control through the 'liable relatives clause' forcing men to support their families and sponsoring of black people's dependent relatives. Sponsorship is impossible for those on Income Support because those emigrating cannot have 'recourse to public funds' without breaching their conditions of entry and committing a criminal offence (Gordon, 1985).

Underlying the New Right's concern that women have acquired too much freedom via state welfare is its anxiety about men's position, particularly their relevance to family life if their breadwinning role is lost and with it, their control over women and children.

To a great extent poverty and unemployment, and even the largely psychological conditions of 'unemployability' are chiefly reflections of family deterioration . . . . Nothing is so destructive to all these male values as the growing, imperious recognition that when all is said and done his wife and children can do better without him. The man has the gradually sinking feeling that his role of provider, the definitive male activity from the primal days of the hunt through the industrial revolution and on into modern life, has been largely seized from him; he has been cuckolded by the compassionate state. (Gilder, 1982, p. 118)

The New Right's response to these worries has been to restrict women's access to income maintenance through the 1986 Social Security Act. When this came into effect, many of Fowler's proposals reached the statute book. Although Fowler's proposed shift of Family Income Supplement to Family Credit coming through the wage packet was defeated through organised lobbying by feminist and anti-poverty groups such as the Child Poverty Action Group, Fowler made explicit his view that men's wage packet was more important than women's. He stated: 'The disincentives to work and self-help are exacerbated by the way that Child Benefit and Family Income Supplement are paid normally to the wife, so that wage earners may not be fully aware of the total income their family is receiving.'

The measures through which the 1986 Social Security Act limits women's financial independence include:

1. Eroding the value of child benefit by freezing it for several years.
2. Abolishing single payments for floor coverings, furniture, thereby constraining women leaving violent men.
3. Cutting maternity benefits.
4. Reducing widows' benefits.
5. Cutting earnings related pension supplements affecting women, already handicapped with smaller pensions, more than men.
6. The deleterious impact of cutting housing benefit on single parent families headed mainly by women.
7. The lack of additional support for single parent families, supported primarily by women.
8. Introducing the Social Fund which increased poverty through the repayment of loans and affected women more than men because they are responsible for managing household resources.
9. Withdrawing the right of appeal formerly successfully used by women claimants.

The irony is that marital breakdown, low wages in their working lives, and low pensions in old age make women the largest group of recipients on social assistance. However, the social security system fails to keep women out of poverty because benefit levels in both the insurance based and means-tested schemes are low. Moreover, the National Insurance system is predicated on male working patterns which makes it difficult for women to acquire sufficient contributions to escape charitable safety net provisions. Poverty, a scourge primarily afflicting women (Scott, 1984), forces them into relying on state benefits.

WOMEN, SEXISM AND THE BRITISH SOCIAL SECURITY SYSTEM

Women have a contradictory relationship with the social security system and welfare state. Elements favouring women's liberation include:

1. The provision of an income independent from men.
2. The adoption of some socialisation functions, for example, education.
3. The provision of employment opportunities for women in low paid service work.

Aspects contributing towards women's oppression are those:

1. Reinforcing women's dependency on men in family relationships.
2. Reinforcing women's caring responsibilities through policies such as community care and their role in the personal social services.
3. Redistributing resources between different groups of women and within the working class.

Social security provisions are excluded from the Sex Discrimination Act of 1975, making sexism in access to and receipt of benefits beyond legal challenge. Social security provisions have institutionalised sexism by assuming that women are dependent on and have the same career patterns as men, thereby ignoring women's position in the labour market where low wages, interrupted career patterns and part-time employment disadvantage their contributions record. Women's low earnings and poor contribution record make them liable to lower benefits and heighten their vulnerability to means-tested benefits. Social security provisions reinforcing women's dependent status as unpaid domestic workers dependent on men include: employment status defining access to benefits; aggregating family income through the cohabitation rule; deducting maintenance payments from women's supplementary benefits while men receive tax relief on it; granting one-parent additions only to women holding jobs and not cohabiting; denying women's claims to unemployment benefit and sickness pay for unemployed partners unless they are incapable of working; and the 'availability test' for mothers claiming unemployment benefit.

Patrick Jenkins as Secretary of State for Health and Social Security maintained that: 'Motherhood is the most important form of social work'. Such views reinforce familial ideology placing women in the home caring for others. By glorifying motherhood as a private activity undertaken in isolation at home and enforcing women's dependency on men, social security reinforces the idea of fatherhood as a financial activity undertaken in the public sphere. Its assumption of the nuclear heterosexual monogamous family belies the diversity of family forms found in reality. Only 8 per cent of all family units in Britain, and 17 per cent of those with dependent children conform to this norm. Ten per cent of families are single parent families. Moreover, by 1978, 51 per cent of mothers with dependent children worked for wages. The male 'family wage' was a myth for if women did not go out to work, family poverty would quadruple. Unemployment, the prospects of part-time work and low pay have also challenged men's position as breadwinners and increasingly forced women to become a family's major earner.

Institutional sexism has disadvantaged women receiving lower pensions than men. Low wages prevents their competing in the market for private occupational schemes. Overcoming their disadvantaged position requires substantial increases in the basic pension. Until 1977, married women had access to the married women's option enabling them to pay lower National Insurance contributions in exchange for limited benefits through their husbands. Married women paying full National Insurance premiums are still not entitled to the same benefits as men, for example, sickness benefits, unemployment insurance and pensions disallow women claiming their partners as dependants. Also, married women have been excluded from claiming: Invalidity Care Allowance (until 1987); Householder Non-Contributory Invalidity Pension (until it became the Severe Disablement Allowance); and supplementary benefits in their own name until 1983. The continued application of the 'cohabitation rule' and aggregation of family incomes for both social security and taxation purposes ignores the unequal distribution of income within the family which disadvantages women (Pahl, 1980, 1985).

Provisions reinforcing women's status as low paid workers include pensions, unemployment pay, sick pay and misconduct rules. Women have lower incomes, fewer contributions by retiring five years earlier than men, and interrupted earnings which mean lower pensions. They cannot claim male partners as dependants for pensions. Women receive lower unemployment and sickness benefits because they earn less, work largely part-time, and carry domestic responsibilities. Absence from work for the purposes of caring for sick children can become grounds for self-inflicted dismissal, depriving women of benefits for a qualifying period.

Social security provisions do not deal adequately with women's specific needs during pregnancy. For example, the universal maternity grant of £25 was not updated for many years. It has been replaced with a means-tested grant of £80. This illustrates how the state takes resources from one group of women, allegedly better off, and redistributes them to another group of women who are worse off. This action has enabled the government to avoid redistributing men's income. Maternity benefits, based on national insurance contributions in the relevant tax year, are payable for eighteen weeks. The rates are low and need supplementation. This assumes a woman is relying on a man for additional finances.

Provisions directly available to women include child benefit, a virtually universal benefit disadvantaging black women whose children live abroad. Child benefit is payment for the children and not the woman herself. It is related to neither the costs of living nor bringing up children. Treated as a *man's* income for supplementary benefit purposes, it is deducted from supplementary benefit. Child benefit is currently threatened with abolition in favour of a taxable means-tested benefit. The one parent child benefit addition is a fixed amount regardless of the number of children. It is deducted from supplementary benefit, but not wages. Widows are excluded from receiving it but are paid a widowed mother's allowance even if employed. However, this is withdrawn if they remarry, the assumption being that the new man in her life will provide for her. This allowance may also be abolished. Women with children working more than thirty hours a week became eligible for Family Income Supplement as of November 1983 even if they lived with a man. Half of the claimants for Family Income Supplement were single parent women. Originally introduced in 1971, Family Income Supplement subsidised low wages. It tried dealing with family poverty by drawing single parent women into waged work and supplementing their low wages. Thus, Family Income Supplement, like other supplementation programmes in both Canada and the United States, is a *hidden subsidy to employers*, or a fiscal transfer enacted by the welfare state and benefiting capital, paid for by poorly paid workers and women's unpaid domestic labour which makes up the gap between low pay, Family Income Supplement, and actual family expenses. More importantly for claimants, Family Income Supplement acted as a passport to other entitlements such as optical care, dental care, free school meals. In 1988, Family Credit replaced Family Income Supplement. It can still be paid to women, but it has lost its 'passport to other benefits' function.

Women are also employed by the welfare state in low paid part-time work reproducing the existing sexist division of labour. Women also bear the brunt of public expenditure cuts, cash limits, rate capping and decimation of public sector jobs. This has diminished women's employment opportunities and increased unemployment among them (Coyle, 1984).

The economic recession of the 1970s contributed substantially to the restructuring of the welfare state. Government expenditure could not rise to meet the demand for welfare services coming from increased unemployment; raised expectations regarding income maintenance, housing, health, education and the personal social services; an ageing population; and gains in social security provisions guaranteed by the Rooker-Wise Amendment. The Keynesian way out of the mess, the spending solution, had failed as the International Monetary Fund imposed cuts in Britain's welfare programmes. Labour's response became one of managing capitalism and labour militancy by: cutting education and housing; introducing cash limits; reducing the rate support grant; curbing workers' demands for higher wages through the Social Contract; and controlling claimants by enforcing measures pushing them back to work. These included: reviving the four-week rule causing 37,000 claimants to lose benefits; stepping up interviews with the Unemployment Review Officer to weed out 'malingerers' and those 'neglecting to maintain themselves'; urging stricter interpretations of the discretionary elements in social security; and subsidising low wages through Family Income Supplement, thereby giving claimants access to supplementary finances. These initiatives reduced claimant numbers by 39 per cent.

The Tories cut further public expenditure in housing, education and health while increasing 'law and order' and defence expenditures. In 1982, social security benefits did not keep pace with inflation and rising demand. Social security cuts financed tax reductions for rich people who were expected to create jobs through investments, thereby fostering individual self-reliance. Additionally, public money was diverted to finance the Falklands War. The Thatcherite restructuring of social security marked a break with the post-war consensus on welfare between the Labour and Conservative parties.

RACISM IN THE BRITISH SOCIAL SECURITY SYSTEM

Institutional racism in the British social security system divides black families and excludes black people from having full access to both national insurance benefits and social assistance. This situation arises because social security has become incorporated into the internal immigration control machinery (Gordon and Newnham, 1985). The connection between immigration control and social security stems from the impact of people's immigration status on their access to benefits and the effect claiming has on their immigration status. Certain categories of immigrants are excluded from drawing benefits including income support, council housing, housing benefit, Family Credit, mobility allowances, attendance allowances, government training schemes, the National Health Service, and education because their conditions of entry do not entitle them to 'have recourse to public funds'. They must maintain and house themselves and their dependants without state resources.

The definition of 'having recourse to public funds' changes frequently and has become extremely elastic. The Home Office takes the view that it covers everything except what it chooses to disregard. Exclusion from benefits lasts until a person's immigration status is changed. Requests for a variation of the conditions of entry involves the Home Office ascertaining whether or not the person has used public funds. This form of institutional racism has been formally endorsed through the government's demand for a 'presence test'. The 1985 Green Paper on the Fowler Review clarified its position by stating:

> We are concerned that the present conditions can allow too ready access to help by those who have no recent links with this country. Claimants will, therefore, need to satisfy a presence test; that is, claimants will need to have been present in the country for a set period to qualify for income support.

The categories of people denied income support are the following:

1. Those admitted for a limited period. This includes fiancé(e)s who are also classified as unavailable for work and dependent upon their prospective spouse.
2. Overstayers.
3. Anyone subject to a deportation order.
4. Illegal immigrants. These people can request 'urgent needs' help and risk jeopardising their immigration status when requesting a variation in their conditions of entry.
5. Work permit holders. People holding these cannot claim benefits for having received permission to hold specific jobs with specific employers they are considered unavailable for work.
6. Residents visiting relatives abroad. Those on benefit must inform the Department of Social Security (DSS) of their visit, otherwise they may be charged with fraud. Income Support payments are stopped. Persons not required to sign on may be paid for four weeks on their return or payment can go to the spouse remaining in Britain. Urgent needs payments can be paid if individuals return within twenty-six weeks, but they must demonstrate they have no other means of support. Women intending to claim in their own right if their partner goes abroad must satisfy the 'availability for work' test and have been available for work six months prior to the departure of their spouse. This regulation works against women who remain at home caring for children.
7. People on sponsorship. Persons on Income Support are not allowed to sponsor relatives, including dependants, into Britain. This keeps

families divided. Moreover, since the 1980 Social Security Act tightened sponsorship provisions, failing to maintain sponsored dependants has become a criminal offence leading to deportation.

8. Those failing to speak English. Those who cannot speak English are deemed unavailable for work, and ineligible for income support. A number of black women were refused supplementary benefit on these grounds in 1981 (Gordon, 1985).

Immigration regulations concerning welfare benefits in theory cover everyone. In practice, they are applied largely against black people who find their immigration status checked constantly in their interface with the welfare state. Black people come under closer scrutiny than white people because the word 'immigrant' is associated with them. Moreover, the visibility of their skin colour means that all black people are treated as if they were immigrants whether they are immigrants or not. Double-checking people's immigration status when processing claims allows officials to turn their attention to black people already settled in Britain as the principle of 'universal challenge' is borne primarily by black people whose visibility makes them prime targets for questioning. The 'resid-ence test' discriminates against black people. They travel abroad for long periods for family reasons. These absences are interpreted as breaks in their residence which disqualify them from receiving assistance. Such measures intensify black people's sense of insecurity and the harassment of their communities.

The connection between an applicant's claim for benefits and their immigration status is made by local benefits officers responding to an application by asking claimants to let them examine their passports or referring the matter to the DSS Headquarters. It then consults with the Home Office. Similar links exist between the Home Office and the police immigration units, local authority departments such as education and housing, hospital, and the Inland Revenue (Gordon and Newnham, 1985).

Local benefits officers use a means test and an immigration test in policing welfare. When assessing claimants' eligibility for benefits, officers conduct an immigration status check and a means test covering capital resources held by applicants and their extended families overseas regardless of whether or not the applicant owns them. Skin colour and foreign accents are taken as prima facie indications of a person's immigration status (Gordon and Newnham, 1985). The role of the social security system in reinforcing immigration control began on an experi-mental basis in 1970 when the Department of Health and Social Security (DHSS) asked new applicants for National Insurance numbers for their passports.[1] This became permanent procedure in 1975 and the DHSS formally became involved in immigration control. Other government departments followed suit. In 1976, passports were demanded of black applicants to government training schemes. In 1980, checks were enforced in NHS hospitals to prevent the 'abuse' of the health system by foreigners. The Inland Revenue checks immigration status when receiving requests for tax relief for spouses living overseas. These actions encourage a climate of reporting in which black people are the main suspects facing immigration status checks whenever they contact the welfare state. Strictly speaking, requests for passports are not legal for only immigration officers are entitled to ask for passports. Moreover, they can only do so at the port of entry (Gordon and Newnham, 1985). But benefits can be refused if passports are not produced.

Institutionalised racism would constitute illegal discrimination were it not for the exclusion of specific Acts of Parliament and decisions of ministers from Section 41 of the 1976 Race Relations Act. The links between the different government departments ignore the rules of confidentiality for immigrants. Moreover, the flow of information between government departments keeping track of individual immigrants was computerised in 1979. This fact was kept secret from both Parliament and the Lindop Commission on Data Protection (Gordon and Newnham, 1985). In 1981, a minicomputer in Harmondsworth and the computerisation of the Central Intelligence Index, tied arrival and embarkation details and the conditions of admissions together. This facility will become even more powerful when machine readable passports are issued to everyone. Targeted for 1986, this goal has yet to be implemented.

Companies and government ministers such as Enoch Powell encouraged black people to come to Britain to work during the post-war economic recovery (Gilroy, 1987). Initially, they had access to the welfare state. However, declining economic performance from the 1960s onwards put pressure on the government to cut welfare expenditures. The exclusion of people from eligibility to benefits was one way of achieving this. With regards to black people, this process began with the 1962 Commonwealth Immigration Act which introduced a voucher system to control entry for British subjects and withdrew Commonwealth citizens' permanent right to settle. Besides needing work permits, new Commonwealth entrants could not be joined by their families. The vouchers were for specific jobs with specific employers and could only be varied with the written approval of the Department of Employment. This changed the status of black people from immigrant labour to migrant labour and opened up the possibility of repatriating black people (Sivanandan, 1976).

Additionally, vouchers were more readily given to black professionals such as doctors and nurses who could assume work in the understaffed and under-resourced welfare state. Importing qualified professionals saved the British welfare state resources during their training period and marked an inflow of resources from Third World countries. Meanwhile black people were employed in the lower reaches of the welfare state labour hierarchy. Mama (1989) has argued black people, especially women, have maintained the welfare state through the exploitation of their labour and the resources of their countries of origin.

The work permit system excluded work permit holders from sharing in the 'social wage' by denying them access to welfare rights; facilitating police involvement in internal immigration control; increasing the powers of the executive arm of government in immigration matters while decreasing the willingness of the courts to interfere in executive decisions, including those defining the meaning of 'recourse to public funds'. The restriction of black people's access to the 'social wage' in Britain also applies to welfare benefits on the Continent. The EEC treaty of accession excluded Commonwealth citizens from the definition of British national, thereby ensuring that black people resident in Britain without British citizenship are not entitled to EEC health care and social security provisions.[2]

The 1962 legislation facilitated the extension of immigration control from the point of entry to daily life, that is, an internal form of control designed to reduce workers' militancy and allow for their deportation, as happened to Franco Caprino who organised a strike among workers at Garner's Steak Houses. The 1962 Immigration Act also contributed to defining 'race' as a problem of the numbers of black people entering Britain and suggesting that fewer black people in Britain made for more harmonious race relations (Mullard, 1973). The problem became black people and not the racism white people perpetrated (Mullard, 1973).

The 1971 Immigration Act systematised the control of immigrants by dividing them into *patrials* who had unrestricted entry to Britain by virtue of a 'close connection' with the country and *non-patrials* who had none. The 1971 Act stopped primary immigration and placed the focus on the dependants of people already settled in Britain who constituted the only group of black people who could seek entry. Additionally, all Commonwealth citizens entering Britain after 1973 became subject to deportation. This decision rested with the Home Secretary who had the power to decide whether an individual's presence in Britain was conducive to the public good or not. The police acquired widespread powers of arrest as they undertook 'fishing raids' to capture 'illegal immigrants' suspected of breaching their conditions of admittance. The 1971 Act also contained a retrospective element insofar as those entering Britain clandestinely before 1973 were made liable to deportation. The definition of 'illegal immigrant' was broadened to include those who had entered clandestinely; entered unknowingly on someone else's passport; obtained indefinite leave by deception; overstayed their time period while awaiting a reply to their application for an extension; not declared all the 'relevant information' on their application forms despite the absence of guidance as to what this might be; and married after receiving entry certificates (Gordon and Newnham, 1985).

In 1978, the Tories expressed their radical new philosophy on immigration and racism which aspired to tighter immigration controls to protect the white British way of life (Barker, 1981). Thatcher made it clear that (white) British people did not want to be 'swamped' by an alien culture. The Report of the 1978 Select Committee on Race Relations and Immigration endorsed internal immigration control. It claimed that primary black immigration had ended and that attention could be shifted to identifying dependants, 'illegal immigrants', and people already here. Fascists in the National Front and British Party were pushing for the repatriation of black people. Hawley and Powell demanded a register of dependants and controls on arranged marriages, which they classified as 'marriages of convenience' aimed at subverting immigration controls. Labour's response to these challenges was to affirm the 'numbers game' and claim the issue was under control because black immigration was falling, detected illegal immigration increasing, and deportations rising. These forces coalesced in demanding a new nationality law which was finally promulgated as the 1981 Nationality Act. It increased internal immigration controls.

Both the Fowler Review and 1986 Social Security Act endorse institutionalised racism as is indicated by the 'presence test' required for Income Support and the continued disallowance of claims for overseas dependants. Moreover, cuts in mortgage relief for the unemployed affect black people disproportionately as proportionately more of them become unemployed owner-occupiers. Higher levels of homelessness among black people follow from this. Moreover, discretionary elements of administrators can result in black people being classified as undeserving. Family Credit will reinforce the payment of low wages to black people. Also, cutting FIS related benefits, for example, free school meals, harms black families to a greater extent than white families because of their lower income levels. Furthermore, withdrawing additional payments hurts black families relying on means-tested benefits to a greater extent than white families because special additions addressing their specific needs are lost, for example, diet additions for those with sickle-cell anaemia (LSSC, 1986).

RACISM, BLACK PEOPLE AND NATIONAL INSURANCE BENEFITS

Access to national insurance benefits depends on individuals' contribution record, their meeting residence requirements and their immigration status. Regardless of their contribution record, claims for unemployment benefit and pensions from work permit holders can be construed as having 'recourse to public funds', if the Home Office exercises its discretion to define it so (Manchester Law Centre, 1983). Work permit holders are also excluded from benefits having a residence requirement attached to them, for example, the Non-Contributory Invalidity Pension (NCIP), SDA, the old HNCIP, maternity grants, death grants and widows benefit. The maternity grant was payable abroad only if the mother went overseas for treatment and had been resident in Britain six months before giving birth. Although claims for national insurance benefits should not involve liaison with the Home Office, they can do, as Parveen Kahn discovered to her detriment. She was refused child benefit for her child born in Britain although she had left her husband because the Home Office had declared him an 'illegal immigrant'. Her child benefit was resumed following a vociferous public campaign advancing her cause (Gordon and Newnham, 1985).

Child benefit is not payable for children resident abroad. The children must live in Britain, and if they are temporarily absent (not more than twenty-six weeks), they must have received child benefit prior to their absence to continue being eligible. Moreover, parents must have been in Britain for six out of the previous twelve months and pay tax in the relevant tax year. If their absence from Britain is permanent, there is no entitlement. These exclusions follow a long line of measures denying black families access to benefits. For example, family allowances were never paid to dependent children overseas. Tax relief on dependent children started being phased out in 1979 following the introduction of child benefit in 1977 and ended in 1982 (Plummer, 1978). Besides causing hardship, the British regulations ensure that black parents do not receive social recognition for maintaining children abroad. The British position on child benefits also reflects the manipulation of extended family ties.

A black person claiming benefit for maintaining dependent children of relatives in Britain is thought to be abusing the system; a black person requesting money from the Social Fund is assessed on the basis of resources held by the extended family. Despite being excluded from these benefits, black people pay national insurance contributions and taxes on the same basis as white people. Freezing child benefits since 1986 hurts black women as it is the one benefit to which they have universal access, providing the children reside in Britain. The reduction of unemployment benefit for those under 25 will disadvantage black youths more than white youths as they are more likely to be un-employed.

Also, black people will not qualify for full national insurance benefits because their higher unemployment rates deleteriously affect their contribution record. This will mean that cuts in SERPS will affect them disproportionately. Furthermore, they will be unable to mitigate the impact of such measures because purchasing private pensions is more of a dream than a reality for unemployed or low income earners. Welfare state administrators have ignored the low take-up of benefits in black communities. Leaflets explaining changes in social security legislation are not made available in all the relevant languages.

Other problems not addressed by the social security system and perpetuating institutional racism include:

1. Challenging the validity of black people's marriages, and not accept-ing their marriage documents as proof.

2. Not making arrangements for the payment of contributions while black people visit relatives abroad, thereby disrupting their contribu-tion record.

3. Not making arrangements for accepting late claims, especially where language problems and lack of information at the appropriate time have caused the delay.

4. Not allowing upratings on benefits allowable overseas, for example pensions, widows' pensions, widowed mothers' allowance, disable-ment benefit.

5. Not paying benefits such as invalidity care allowance, child benefit, one parent additions to British people while abroad, but paying these in arrears on their return to Britain (or quarterly into a bank account).

Black people living and working in Britain find themselves and their dependants treated differently from white families, simply because their immigration status is queried. The presence test means that black people as legal residents can be denied basic subsistence levels of income and services to which resident British citizens are entitled. Such practices divide black families and exacerbate their experience of racism.

IN CONCLUSION

The British social security system reinforces gender and 'race' oppression and maintains class rule. Hence, it has been attacked by the Left, feminists and black activists for being bureaucratic, remote, sexist, racist, and stigmatising. The 'New Right' has criticised it for encouraging scroungers and lazy people, disrupting family life, taking away family responsibilities, and allowing too much state intervention in people's lives. Claimants are forced to comply with the requirement to 'actively seek' work. This criterion has become more stringently enforced as the long-term unemployed face a barrage of initiatives aimed at equipping them for work. The problem with this approach is that it pathologises the unemployed who are then sent to search for elusive jobs.

'Workfare' is also on the cards as the government attempts to make claimants work for benefits. The procedure of retraining people for work marks the government's shift towards an explicit employment strategy in social security provisions. Also tied into it is the reduction of unemployment insurance benefits through measures reducing the period for which benefits are paid, increasing the length of time unemployment insurance benefit is withheld if claimants are deemed responsible for losing their jobs, and removing benefits from those who refuse 'reasonable offers' of employment.

The vicious attacks on the trade union movement including curbing its powers through a variety of legislative acts (see Hyman, 1989) to reduce overall wage levels, force people into low paid work and decrease the 'social wage' allocated through the welfare state, indicate the whittling away of improvements workers have struggled to achieve by being organised as employers attempt to bring British wages closer to those prevailing in Third World countries where multinational firms are now relocating if British workers fail to accept their terms. The opening up of Eastern Europe to western capital intensifies the downward pressures on wages because the wage rates prevailing there are lower. Mitigating against this trend are the struggles working men and women are waging in the Third World to improve their standard of living by obtaining higher wages and welfare benefits. Eastern Europeans are also likely to defend their 'social wage' and demand increased wages, although they may have to temper the latter in the short term as Lech Walesa suggested Polish people will have to do to encourage western capitalists and governments to invest in Poland when he toured America in 1989. The objectives of increasing international competitiveness by holding down both wages and the growth of welfare expenditures are as relevant to Britain as they are to America and Canada.

Britain's social security system has failed to eradicate poverty and redistribute income from the rich to the poor. Targeting benefits as proposed by the 'New Right' suggests that redistribution will be from the needy to the more needy, thus shifting the burden of poverty among the poor rather than onto the wealthy.

Although Thatcherite policies and ideology favour dismantling and restructuring state welfare in favour of private market solutions, there is increased opposition to such proposals as people become more aware of the implications of this approach to welfare. Though the expression of it may vary, the British income maintenance system shares oppressive features centred on social divisions alongside the American and Canadian one. Moreover, each of these countries exhibits the subordination of social policy to economic imperatives. However, it is not only the business élite who sit on the stage where the welfare drama is being enacted. Claimants are also taking part in it. The future of Britain's welfare state is in the balance. While it mitigates hardship for some, others in need are excluded from its provisions. It is inadequate and must be transformed in egalitarian directions.

INCOME MAINTENANCE POLICIES IN SOCIAL DEMOCRATIC COUNTRIES

The Swedish income maintenance system

The development of the Swedish welfare state has proceeded more smoothly and gradually than in other Western countries for political and economic reasons. Industrial capitalism took over the predominately agrarian Swedish economy between 1870 and 1930. Industrialising much later than other European countries, it was not achieved through the massive upheavals characterising Britain during the enclosures or America during its Civil War. Change occurred on the basis of capital intensive small farming causing pressure for industrial development to rise from below (Wilson, 1979). In the nineteenth century, this process caused shifts in the population as large numbers of peasants were driven off the land and became landless. Poor prospects forced 60 per cent of these to leave Sweden for greener fields in Europe and North America, thereby alleviating pressures on both relief provisions and the land. Unlike Britain, Sweden's industrialisation was telescoped into a short intensive period in which the Swedish industrial indigenous bourgeoisie relied on capital accumulated earlier in small Swedish industries rather than that being held by élite classes, as was true of Britain, or imported from abroad as happened in the British colonies. The Swedish industrial élite was therefore independent of either agrarian or foreign interests and could control industrial developments according to its own needs (Wilson, 1979).

The Swedish Poor Law, revised in the 1830s, was akin to the British Speenhamland system. However, Swedish relief was relatively liberal, for unlike Britain's Poor Law which became increasingly repressive to cope with the strains of high demand for relief, it did not have to deal with massive urban unemployment. Nonetheless, life on the land was hard and poverty was common in Sweden.

On the political level, Sweden retained its absolute monarchy until the early twentieth century. It continues to have the constitutional monarchy established in 1911. Men were granted the right to vote in 1911. The Swedish organised labour movement developed independently and relatively free from the repression that marked labour history in Britain and the United States. This enabled a fairly peaceful relationship to develop between labour and capital. The Swedish trade union movement developed rapidly. By 1909, two years before the achievement of male suffrage, it included 66 per cent of industrial workers. It organised a general strike in 1909, by which time both employers and workers had formed their respective federations. The workers' organisation was called the Lansorganisation. Thus, corporate organisations of both employers and employees were in place before the achievement of universal suffrage. The presence of these corporate organisations representing capital and labour facilitated peaceful industrial relations. Moreover, the Swedish Social Democratic Party (SAP) was formed around this time. Unlike the British working class which organised its movement around its entry into the political arena through universal manhood suffrage, the Swedish working class organised around its trade unions. The trade union movement developed an extensive network of occupational welfare schemes for skilled workers covering unemployment and sickness benefits. Benevolent societies were also privately funded to cover similar risks.

The existence of a sizeable network of trade union run welfare schemes meant that welfare reforms were only slowly initiated by the Swedish state. Before the First World War, the Liberals launched a meagre state pension scheme and a health insurance system based on employee contributions. Welfare matters stagnated until the 1920s as trade unions continued focusing their energies on occupational welfare schemes rather than demanding state welfare. The 1920s and 1930s were marked by intensive political and industrial conflict. Strikes, including the Miners Strike of 1931 when miners were shot in the streets, lockouts, and demonstrations marked relations between capital and labour. Shortlived governments proved unable to effectively resolve these tensions. Control of the situation finally came in the early 1930s when SAP became the largest party in the Riksdag and formed a government in coalition with the Farmers' Party. The stability of its regime is indicated by the fact that SAP has governed continuously from 1932 to the present time, with a brief break of six years when a conservative coalition took the reigns of government following an indecisive election in 1976.

THE SWEDISH WELFARE COMPROMISE: A DEAL BETWEEN CAPITAL AND LABOUR

The abandonment of *laissez-faire* and anti-collectivist approaches to welfare by employers, workers, and the ruling political élite facilitated the establishment of a compromise between labour and capital in reducing conflict over welfare issues, particularly unemployment (Duncan, 1985). The pragmatic and reformist nature of SAP's welfare ideology helped enormously in bringing this about (Peynstone, 1935). This was based on SAP's rejection of Marxism, especially its commitment to nationalisation or the socialisation of the means of production.

The consensual position reached has been referred to by Peynstone (1935) as an 'end of ideology' approach by SAP endorsing state neutrality in the class struggle. Kilturn (1985) maintains Peynstone's view is oversimplistic. SAP did have an ideology, although it withdrew from heavy Marxist dogma. Instead, it adopted a gradual approach towards socialism in which 'Keynesian' economics and state regulation of the economy provided the keys unlocking economic growth. This committed SAP to using the welfare state to put money into the workers' pockets and regenerate the economy by increasing their spending power, much in the same way as Roosevelt did in the United States. Macmillan reluctantly accepted Keynesian economics in restoring the economy of Britain in 1937. Increases in Swedish wealth were assured through taxation and fiscal policies which encouraged economic activities. 'Keynesian' economics were developed in Sweden by Wigforis, the Finance Minister who talked about the role of the welfare state in revitalising the economy and controlling unemployment before Keynes wrote his famous texts.

Wigforis also promoted the idea of state intervention in the labour market to train people and move them about the country in accordance with economic demands. However, his approach to labour mobility was less dictatorial than Stalin's in the Soviet Union at this time. Wigforis used housing allowances to encourage house construction in areas where workers were needed and move workers into them. This approach was fairly successful as unemployment dropped from its peak of 139,000 in 1933 to 9,600 by August 1937. This decline in unemployment was attributable to the public works programmes for the unemployed, increased housing construction, means-tested housing allowances granted on a massive scale to lower income families, and family allowances. It was also influenced by the booms and slumps of the world economy. The regeneration of the global economy through rearmament complemented the interventionist reformist economic policies SAP fostered in Sweden. These policies enabled Swedish workers to weather the 'Great Depression' without the massive social dislocation evident in Britain, Canada and the United States.

Working through the corporatist structure of industrial relations, the trade union organisation, the Lansorganisation, and employers negotiated a national wages agreement which gave employers total managerial freedom to direct labour and control the workforce in return for guaranteeing agreed increases in wages through which employees in firms unable to pay these would be redeployed in expanding ones. The agreement benefited workers in some respects and gave organised labour some say in labour market decisions. It also provided employers with a mobile workforce by compelling workers out of declining industries and into profitable ones. This was rather like the Social Contract agreed between the employers, the TUC and the Callaghan government in Britain in the mid-1970s. The Swedish government was not involved in the 1938 agreement; it was simply a matter between capital and labour. The existence of a state labour market policy facilitating labour mobility was crucial to the success of the agreement which later survived a general strike.

THE PROVISIONS IN SWEDEN'S INCOME MAINTENANCE SYSTEM

The 1930s was a time of modest welfare reforms as financial stringencies kept all levels of benefits low, especially for unwaged dependants of workers, that is, women and children. However, family allowances were a major innovation introduced in 1937 to bolster Sweden's declining birth rate. Influenced by the Myrdals, an influential husband and wife team in academia, SAP adopted family allowances as part of a pronatalist strategy encouraging population growth. During the Second World War, Sweden concentrated on the war effort and suspended improvements on welfare.

The end of the War placed welfare struggles in the frontline of politics. Between 1944 and 1948, serious ideological debates over the future development of SAP ensued as both the gradual road to socialism and the liberal pluralist path were found wanting. Trade unions exerted considerable pressure on SAP to enhance workers' power in industry by going beyond the 1938 agreement which gave employers power to sack workers and dictate events on the shopfloor. Grassroots demands for SAP to become more socialist added fuel to organised labour's demands. These pressures echoed British people's demands for socialist programmes during the 1940s. The Swedes also wanted speedier and more comprehensive welfare reforms. The ensuing power struggle climaxed during the 1948 election when SAP withdrew proposals to nationalise major sections of industry and its more extreme socialisation programmes and heralded Sweden's return to liberal forms of welfare and gradual reforms.

The expansion of welfare services in Sweden occurred during the

1950s and 1960s. It did not redistribute wealth and required high rates of contribution through the taxation system. Family allowances, family policies, provisions for single parent families, and day nurseries were expanded under the aegis of a Labour Market Board encouraging labour retraining and mobility. A national hospital health insurance scheme was promulgated in 1955. A generous earnings related pension scheme was adopted in 1957. Passed by one vote, this legislation indicated the somewhat fragile nature of the consensus on welfare which prevailed. The Right demanded a private system regulated by the state while SAP pushed for government backed earnings related provisions. A referendum on the issue produced a small majority in favour of the government's proposal. The national pensions scheme was introduced in 1959 as a basic flat-rate pension with a supplementary earnings related component. This component is funded through employer contributions while funding for the basic pension comes from central government and employees. The earnings related element worked against women for they formed the bulk of the low income earners. Nonetheless, the Swedish scheme provided a basic social minimum pension with a high level of superannuation. Increases in the basic pension are linked to increases in wages. Also, the pension scheme had a high level of replacement of earnings, for it was pegged at 70–80 per cent of the average wage. As the level of the basic pension is high, some redistribution does occur. Some low income couples can be better off after retirement than before because after tax earnings replacements are high. Moreover, the pension is calculated on the basis of the best fifteen years' earnings. This works in women's favour given their broken career patterns.

The existence of extensive occupational welfare retarded the development of national schemes. As a result, state intervention in key areas of risk such as unemployment took place later than in other Western countries. For example, a national unemployment benefit scheme was not introduced in Sweden until 1974 when high levels of unemployment revealed the gaps in occupational provisions and forced the government to act. During the 1970s, unemployment in Sweden increased from 2 per cent to 5 per cent, most of it being concentrated among young people who were unable to enter the labour market. This highlighted the fact that 24 per cent of the registered unemployed were not insured because trade union schemes dealt primarily with workers already in the workforce. This prompted the state to make unemployment insurance compulsory and include non-unionised workers, though at lower rates. The trade union controlled element was retained until 1979. At that time, the two tier system was replaced by a national scheme funded largely through a payroll tax, or surcharge on employers.

Providing for people in poverty is the responsibility of local authorities in Sweden. The local schemes are highly discretionary. Claims are few, and last for short periods. Benefit levels are low. Unlike Britain, no national guidelines on poverty assist the local states in determining benefit levels, and no concept of welfare rights exists. Like British welfare claimants, people relying on local Swedish state assistance are highly stigmatised for falling into the safety net provided for the uninsured. In the 1970s, poor relief was claimed by 6–7 per cent of Swedes (Wilson, 1979). This marked a substantial increase from the 1950s and 1960s when a buoyant economy provided most Swedes with their livelihood. Unlike the British situation, this form of social assistance is marginal to the Swedish welfare state, for the insurance system takes people out of primary poverty (Wilson, 1979). The Swedish welfare state has therefore played its part in raising the population from the dire poverty besetting it at the turn of the century to a fairly affluent one enjoying the highest life expectancy and lowest infant mortality rates in the West.

The Swedish government spends a considerable proportion of its GNP on state welfare. In 1975, it was 24.8 per cent of government expenditures. This compares to 20.1 per cent being spent by the British government, 15.6 per cent in the United States, and 27.5 per cent in Germany (OECD, 1976). Privately purchased welfare schemes make these figures somewhat misleading as they are excluded from these calculations (Wilson, 1979). Although presented as the model welfare state (Heclo, 1974), Sweden spent less on welfare expenditure than West Germany which represents the most complete capitalist welfare state (Heidenheimer *et al.*, 1983). The proportion of Swedish welfare state finances derived from taxes is high at 52 per cent of GNP. This includes both central government and local government taxation. It compares to 42 per cent in Germany where most of the revenue comes from contributions to the insurance system.

By the early 1970s, the world-wide economic slump had repercussions in Sweden. Industry was suffering from a crisis of profitability and workers were asked to exercise wage restraint. A turn around in some company fortunes became evident in the mid-1970s and initiated discussions about the creation of a more equitable society. The trade union movement came up with wage-earner funds as a way of creaming off excess company profits without resorting to taxation, as opposition to high taxes was already being forcefully expressed (Righter, 1984).

The formation of wage-earner funds became a controversial issue in 1976, and contributed to the defeat of SAP in both the 1976 and 1979 elections. The initial Lansorganisation proposal recommended that workers who had produced handsome profits for companies through wage restraint collectively use excessive company profits to buy shares in that company. These shares would be inalienable, but would give workers the opportunity to elect workers to the company board, produce dividends which workers could use to train themselves in management and eventually take control of the company. Its objectives were to advance equality and industrial democracy, redistribute wealth and affect the basis on which capital accumulation occurred.

Fears that SAP would lose the 1982 elections if the Lansorganisation proposal on wage-earner funds remained in its pure form led to a compromise which was less frightening to capital. The revised scheme proposed that excess profits would be taxed and paid to a regional fund. The fund would belong to all workers in the region and be invested in companies of their choice. Control of the fund would be in the hands of a board originally appointed by the government but eventually elected by workers. The majority of the board would be worker representatives. The purchase of shares in a company would give the workers an option of having half the voting rights up to a ceiling of 20 per cent. Furthermore, the scheme was to run as an experiment until 1990. Workers could hold a maximum of 40 per cent of the funds in any one company. The funds were also expected to yield a return of 3 per cent on their investments. However, even this amended version was vehemently opposed by business who staged a huge demonstration in protest. It also failed to appeal to leftwingers in SAP who argued that the issue of the funds diverted attention from the more urgent task of enhancing public services and achieving a more egalitarian society (Linton, 1985).

IN CONCLUSION

The liberal coalition which took over the government in 1976 was being pressed by workers and their trade unions to initiate positive welfare reforms and employment protection legislation. Employers as well as workers were pressing for relief in their respective tax burdens. Tax revolts threatened the stability of welfare provisions. Yet, welfare users complained that great class inequalities in income and opportunity persisted in Sweden, despite all the attempts of the welfare state to eradicate them. Like the other Western countries, Sweden has great concentrations of wealth and monopoly power in few hands. In the mid-1970s, one Swedish family owned 17 per cent of manufacturing industry. Moreover, seventeen families controlled 38 per cent of manufacturing. Private industry is the power in the land, the public sector is small. Only 25 per cent of Swedish employees work in nationalised industries and welfare services. In Britain, the public sector employs 60 per cent of the workforce. Yet the income distribution and inequalities in incomes in

Britain and Sweden are remarkably similar. In the mid-1970s, the top 20 per cent of households in Sweden held 44.5 per cent of personal disposable income, this compared to their holding 39 per cent in Britain. The bottom 20 per cent of Swedish households had 6.6 per cent of the disposable income, in Britain it was 6.3 per cent. In other words, earnings related welfare benefits worked to the advantage of the middle classes. Finally, Sweden's welfare state does mitigate inequality slightly at the lower end of the social structure, but it has not created an egalitarian society.

INCOME MAINTENANCE POLICIES IN SOCIALIST COUNTRIES

The Soviet income maintenance system

The Soviet Union provides the world's first example of a socialist income maintenance system. Debates about whether or not it really represents a socialist model of social security abound and are shrouded in the controversy about whether or not the Soviet Union is a socialist society (see Lane, 1978). Unlike its counterpart in the West, labour power in the Soviet Union is not a commodity sold in the market place, but is distributed according to a central plan. Arbitrary limits are placed on the extent to which labour can be exploited and how. The Soviet Union lacks markets in major areas of consumption, for example, housing. Prices for goods are centrally determined. Profits form part of the production plan and are aimed at introducing efficiency and compliance among the workforce rather than structuring the economy in particular ways.

State pricing policy follows the principle of setting the price of basic goods below their value or cost of production and luxury goods above it. While such a policy mitigates people's experience of poverty, it makes visible the stratified nature of Soviet society. Party bureaucrats and high earners can afford luxury consumer goods like cars, televisions, fridges, washing machines which ordinary workers cannot. Women, as the low income earners in Soviet society, and those excluded from high office miss out on obtaining these so-called luxuries in their own right, even though they are essential in easing the burden of the work they carry out in the home. The population is stratified, not on the basis of class, but according to a person's employment status. Those accorded the highest prestige and pay are workers in industrial engineering and technology.

The lowest paid workers are located in collective farms. Farm workers receive two-thirds of an industrial worker's wage. However, this differential is decreasing. Wage differentials between the highest paid and the lowest paid dropped from 3.2 in 1965 to 2.12 in 1973. These compare favourably with the West where top managers earn three or four times a skilled worker's wage.

Differences between the living standards of bureaucrats and Party workers approximate those between professionals and manual workers in the West. A major difference, however, is that although there is a managerial élite in the Soviet Union, there is no class deriving its wealth through inheritances as in the West. With full employment, a major social goal which has been largely achieved, there is no unemployed reserve army of labour. Women, who traditionally constitute the major source of easily available reserve labour, were drawn into production early in the industrialisation process, so that today women workers form a larger percentage of the workforce in the Soviet Union than in any other country. Consequently, there is a severe shortage of labour which is contributing to the Soviet accumulation crisis. My view corresponds with Howard's (1988) that the Soviet Union is not a capitalist society, but a command economy in a transitional stage between capitalism and socialism.

Analysing the Soviet social security system is problematic because documentary material on it is inadequate. The literature that is available reveals that social security provisions and legislation are handed down from the higher echelons of the Party and the bureaucratic élite. The contribution the taxation system makes to people's welfare is difficult to gauge. Taxes are lower in the Soviet Union than in most western countries. Lower taxes coupled with low wage differentials have an equalising effect which is complemented by the existing social security provisions. The 'social wage' distributed through welfare services like subsidised housing, free medical care, free education, increases manual workers' annual wage by about 35 per cent. This compares favourably with the West.

THE CONTEXT WITHIN WHICH THE SOVIET SOCIAL SECURITY SYSTEM DEVELOPED

Developments during the first decade of the Russian Revolution can be understood more easily if it is subdivided into three periods. The first part covers what Lenin called a transitional period lasting from October 1917 to May 1918. This followed the bloodless Revolution and was marked by gradual changes as the Bolsheviks awaited imminent revolutions to unfold in Europe, particularly Germany. They anticipated that these events would help develop the Soviet system by bringing it the benefits of industrialised Germany. Trying not to foreclose on the possibilities this presented led the Bolsheviks to dampen spontaneous outbreaks of workers' control and land seizures and reforms. Carr (1966) suggests Bolshevik hegemony during this period did not extend beyond Petrograd and Moscow. Moreover, the Bolsheviks had limited support among striking workers and militant peasants in the Soviets. The number of Red Guards available to tackle the complex task of taming the Russian Empire and controlling its chaos was insufficient. Shortages in human and material resources compelled Lenin to pull the Soviet Union out of the First World War in 1918. This action dismayed the Allies who were further appalled when Lenin ceded the industrialised Ukraine to Germany in the Treaty of Brest–Litovsk. Though his actions were castigated by most observers as 'selling out to the enemy', Lenin felt he had no option but to settle with the Germans if he was to prevent them from overrunning Russia and destroying the Revolution.

The second period was that of war communism. During this time, the Bolsheviks faced a civil war in which the White Army, helped by the Western Allies, was fighting the Red Army. War communism was marked by intense hardship for the people who faced starvation, a mass exodus from the countryside to the cities, and the imposition of strict controls over their economic activities. From June 1918 the Bolsheviks nationalised factories, requisitioned food from the peasants, and forced people into compulsory labour. Meanwhile, they lost control of fertile areas of country and saw the country nearly destroyed by the civil war. Trotsky's military genius rescued the beleaguered Revolution by building the Red Army into a strong force of five million soldiers. Colletti (1970) claims that military exigencies necessitated the development of centralised military power. The Red Army emerged victorious from the civil war in 1920. But until that point, Soviet society sat on the brink of destruction. Large areas of the countryside and a substantial proportion of the population were devastated. The urban population decreased by 35.2 per cent. Moreover, the civil war distorted both welfare and political processes. The utopian welfare policies promulgated by the Bolsheviks contrasted with the misery produced by the civil war. Their actions, including the liberation of familial relationships from enforced unions by making access to divorce easy, were calculated to encourage people to fight for the Bolshevik cause. However, except for divorce, the proposed welfare measures were not implemented.

The third period began with the introduction of the New Economic Policy following peasant revolts over the requisition of food and workers' opposition to tight political control. The policy encouraged economic activity by restoring food markets, denationalising small enterprises, and providing incentives to increase productivity. As a result of these measures the economy reached pre-war production levels for the first time in 1926. Meanwhile, the Party argued over industrial priorities – the pace, rate and processes which should be followed, the diversion of surplus towards capital investment, and the weighting of resources in favour of industry and agriculture. The questions the Bolsheviks were then tackling resemble those exercising Chinese Communist thinking today. The Bolsheviks were divided in their views. The rightwing of the Party and the majority of peasants favoured a gradual approach to change. The leftwing of the Party wanted change introduced quickly through central planning and workers' control. Stalin's removal of Trotsky in 1928 enabled him to pursue the leftwing position to its extreme by forcing the rapid industrialisation of heavy industry, chemicals, armaments, coal, and steel. However, the means of production were socialised at a horrific cost – the destruction of Stalin's opponents. Many peasants, particularly *kulacks* (rich peasants) opposing the confiscation of their lands, were shot as they resisted being driven from their fields. The rural population dropped to 67 per cent. Enforced production on the collective farms meant that by 1938, they accounted for 94 per cent of agricultural output. Meanwhile, Stalin personally supervised the process in Siberia during 1938. Repressive measures made Stalin a formidable foe. However, he also had the support of the Party and the masses behind him. This added to his strength and made it easier for him to destroy his opponents.

The Stalinist period lasted from 1928 to 1956. It focused on harnessing the country's material and human resources to force the collectivisation of agriculture and build a powerful military-industrial base. The industrialisation process ruptured the demographic makeup of the Soviet population. While only 18.4 per cent of the population lived in the industrial areas in 1928, Stalin's measures increased this to 31.6 per cent by 1940, and 48 per cent by 1960. The majority of the Soviet population now lives in urban areas. The brutal pace of industrialisation, the magnitude of the operation, and the hardship caused by this massive shift in labour resources from rural to urban areas can be grasped by examining the numbers of people involved in the move. In 1927, there were fifteen million non-agricultural workers in the Soviet Union. By 1940, it had nearly trebled to forty-one million as the peasants were driven into cities to create a landless urban force.

Stalin's activities also have to be understood within the context of another milestone in Soviet history – the Second World War. Known as the Great Patriotic War, twenty million Soviet people died in it. The Germans also had a high casualty rate in the Eastern Front where 90 per cent of their fatalities took place, making the Second World War seem like a war between the Soviet Union and Germany. As the industrial parts of the Soviet Union and Leningrad fell to the Germans, Stalin became desperate enough to seek a pact with Hitler. Internal emergency measures including the militarisation of labour, the cessation of welfare measures, the glorification of motherhood, and the favouring of patriotism rather than international socialism were also introduced. Stalin's actions split the Comintern, but saved his country. Without the unity forced upon the population through purges, the cult of Stalin and compulsory industrialisation, it is unlikely that the Soviet Union could have fought this war. Hitler's armies reached the suburbs of Moscow before being stopped.

THE EXPERIMENTAL DAYS: SOVIET SOCIAL SECURITY 1917–18

The Soviet income maintenance system was founded on five principles enunciated by Lenin before the October Revolution. His formulation of these drew heavily on the welfare position adopted by the German Social Democratic Party. Though radical for their time because no society had a system based on them, they lack a vision of the future. His five principles were:

1. Coverage of all cases of incapacity.
2. Universal provisions covering both workers and their dependants.
3. Benefits based on full earnings.
4. Employers and the state rather than workers bearing the costs of the scheme.
5. Local administration of the scheme carried out on a uniform territorial basis under the control of the insured workers (George and Manning, 1980).

George and Manning (1980) suggest only the principle of excluding employers either individually or collectively from administering the system is distinctly socialist and anti-capitalist. Looking at these principles from a feminist perspective, I would go further and argue that even this is not particularly socialist or anti-capitalist since women working in the home are excluded from either participating in the scheme or determining how it is run. Women as workers would carry wage based inequalities with their benefits. Unwaged working women would be covered only as dependants of working men. Thus, instead of guaranteeing them an income in their own right through either an insurance system acknowledging the social contribution women provide through their domestic labour or a state funded assistance system, women working in the home only receive benefits through the marriage contract. These criticisms are additional to those mounted from a classical socialist position. These would identify the failure of the scheme to rectify the problems of the low paid who would receive lower benefits because their incomes are lower and the exclusion of workers not considered part of the working class, for example, the peasants. In practice, this ruling affected a large proportion of the Soviet population, 80 per cent of which lived on the land at that time. The failure of classical Marxists to address these issues directly can be traced to their belief that such difficulties would be resolved through the elimination of class inequalities (Offe, 1984).

Introducing a social security system based on Lenin's principles was important ideologically in signalling the nature of the revolutionary changes which would transform Tzarist Russia. Idealistic and experimental as these principles appeared to external observers aware that the Soviet Union lacked the economic infrastructure necessary to produce the surplus financing these provisions, Lenin's social security scheme embodied proletarian aspirations for a greater society. These principles formed a consistent backdrop to social security provisions between 1917 and 1928. In practice, dramatic switches in policy occurred as Soviet society and its welfare state developed.

The social security system based on Lenin's five utopian welfare principles was introduced within five days of the Revolution. It included unemployment benefit, sickness benefit and maternity pay. The introduction of maternity pay in the Soviet Union on 29 December 1917, made it the first country to provide state welfare for pregnant women. Unfortunately, Lenin's ambitious scheme was never fully implemented. Nor did it cover everyone. It was restricted to wage-earners, regardless of the length of their previous employment. Peasants, single women working in the home, and old people were excluded. Unwaged married women were covered as dependants of workers. Though funded by employers, benefits were limited to the average wage of the locality and could not exceed an unemployed worker's previous earnings. Thus, it firmly followed the labour discipline principles of social insurance. Nonetheless, unemployment insurance, sickness benefits and maternity pay were generous for their time. Trade union representatives and representatives of the insured workers administered the scheme.

SOVIET SOCIAL SECURITY UNDER WAR COMMUNISM

During the period of War Communism, social security provisions were more important on paper and in people's minds than in reality. The Civil War forced the Bolsheviks to use social security as a vehicle drawing adherents to their cause. Consequently, social insurance provisions were expanded to cover all groups including the peasantry. Additional benefits covering invalidity, old age, widowhood, and burial costs were added on 31 October 1918. Benefits were calculated on the same basis as previously. The scheme was funded through employers' contributions and assets the state confiscated from private owners. However, the

Income maintenance

precarious economy and limited resources under Bolshevik control impeded the scheme's realisation. Nationalising industries during 1918–21 added further impediments as resources were diverted to sustain these and confiscated goods ceased being a source of bourgeois revenue. Industry now had to produce the wealth financing welfare provisions. The decline in industrial production during this period made this objective unrealisable. Benefits for peasants, artisans and homemakers remained a 'dead letter' (Madison, 1968).

TIGHTENING THE BELT: SOCIAL SECURITY UNDER THE NEW ECONOMIC POLICY 1921–8

Fiscal austerity during the New Economic Policy (NEP) meant only industrial workers were covered for limited risks – sickness benefits and unemployment insurance, though women workers also received maternity pay. Peasants, single women working in the home, and old people were excluded. Unwaged married women were covered only as dependants of workers. Although benefits were generous, industrial workers had to satisfy stringent conditions reinforcing the work ethic and labour discipline. For example, benefit rates for the unemployed were poor and could be refused after four weeks. Those becoming voluntarily unemployed were denied benefit. Moreover, the scheme favoured skilled workers lacking other means of support. Unskilled workers had to have a three year employment record to meet eligibility requirements. This created differentiation among workers. It was extensively developed under Stalin. With improved economic conditions, the scheme expanded to cover eleven million waged workers by 1928, a significant increase from the five and a half million covered in 1924. Old age pensions, payable to women at age 55 and men at 69, were introduced in 1928 for manual workers having a twenty-five year employment record. These provisions were more substantial than those then available in Britain and the United States. The lengthy qualification period excluded women workers taking time off to care for children, or entering the labour force late in life. Low benefit rates for pensions also have serious implications for women who make up three-quarters of older people. Moreover, the lack of private occupational schemes means that a meagre state income cannot be increased, even by those who could afford it. Collective farmers excluded from the system relied on mutual aid provisions for their old, sick and disabled until 1964. This meant rich farms could provide better coverage than poor ones.

THE ASCENDANCY OF INDUSTRIAL PRIORITIES: SOCIAL SECURITY UNDER STALIN 1928–56

Throughout the Stalinist period, the social security system was sub-ordinated to the needs of the economy and adapted to stabilise the rapid industrialisation of industry, promote collectivised agriculture and transform raw peasant recruits into disciplined factory labour (George and Manning, 1980). Stalin's Commissar of Labour revealed its role in maintaining labour discipline when he stated that: 'egalitarianism must be eliminated from social security. We must give the most privileged treatment to the shock workers and those with long service' (Navarro, 1977).

The shock troops were the industrial workers supporting the Soviet Five Year Industrial Plan. The domination of social policy by economic exigencies aimed to: increase the supply of labour; encourage workers to work harder; and give precedence to industrial priorities set by government. The Labour Code was amended in 1927 to make it difficult for workers to shirk work. These measures included dismissal for unauthorised absences from work, and eviction from company housing for industrial misconduct. The abolition of unemployment benefit in 1930 also reinforced labour discipline and compelled able-bodied people to remain working to secure their livelihood even during times of illness when the issuing of medical certificates was tightened up. Trade unions were charged with helping redundant workers secure jobs. From 1931, people needed two years of uninterrupted work with the same employer to be eligible for these benefits. Other benefits were also subjected to the economy's demand for labour. Pensioners were encouraged to remain working by being allowed to retain part of their pension. This was later extended to the whole of their pension in 1938. Pensions, disability benefits and sickness benefits became more rigidly dependent on the worker's contribution record. The need to maximise the number of working people eventually affected maternity benefits. In 1938, coverage was reduced from sixteen weeks to nine. The sixteen week period was not resumed until the 1950s.

The industrial workforce employed in industries central to the Five Year Plan, hazardous jobs or underground was given better social security provisions in the form of higher and more easily obtained benefits, creating differentiation among claimants according to the ascribed value of their labour. Stalin's desire to industrialise rapidly stratified the working class through a division of labour which turned industrial workers into a 'labour aristocracy' while relegating other workers to an inferior status. Women's work in the home was ignored, thereby reinforcing a sexist division of labour classifying 'women's work' as non-work. Stalin's changes made the social security scheme increasingly inegalitarian and discipline oriented.

The administrative basis of the social security system was changed in 1933 when the local government bodies running the scheme were replaced by trade unions. Unfortunately, trade unions had lost their independent status by becoming subordinate partners in the state and

Party apparatus. They were used to ensure that the day-to-day running of the social security system followed the Party's industrial strategy. Economic growth as a result of Stalin's industrial policy enabled the social security system to expand. The numbers covered rose from 10.8 million in 1928 to 31.2 million in 1940 (George and Manning, 1980). It also facilitated the introduction of mothers' subsidies for families with seven or more children in 1936. The main change Stalin introduced in social security provisions during the 1940s was extending family allow-ances in a pronatalist move seeking to stem the declining birth rate. In 1944, lump sum payments were paid to women giving birth to three or more children. The size of the grant increased with each child. Addi-tionally, monthly allowances payable for fourth and subsequent children aged from 1 to 5 were introduced. These payments rose with each qualifying child.

Stalin's radical restructuring of the social security system was a response to the economic crises of the 1930s. Moreover, the basic format of the system formed under his regime remained intact until the 1980s. Although coverage was extended and improved to some extent during the Khrushchev years, the basic risks covered, administrative structures and principles guiding it remained those established by Stalin. The pattern of social security set during the crises of the 1930s lasting until recent times is also evident in capitalist societies. For example, the restructuring of the American social security system essentially created by Roosevelt began under Reagan.

The change of direction initiated by Stalin in the 1930s laid the foundations for future problems. These included the uneven develop-ment of the Soviet Union by concentrating industrialisation in its Western regions. This combined with enforced Russification made racism an integral feature of Soviet development. It also reinforced sexism and racism by according priority to jobs located in industries central to the Five Year Plan. These were dominated by white Russian men, especially at the higher echelons. Sexism was also perpetuated by the regime's lack of attention to the specific needs of women. Their liberation was secondary to the industrialisation process. The main changes which occurred were those facilitating women's entry into production (Molyneaux, 1985).

SOCIAL SECURITY IN THE POST-STALINIST PERIOD

The post-Stalinist period in the Soviet Union has been marked by attempts to develop the consumer economy, erode inequalities that had crept into the system, and widen participation in the regime. A stagnant economy compelled Khrushchev to introduce both economic and social changes when he succeeded Stalin. Denouncing the excesses of Stalin's forced industrialisation during a secret speech to Twentieth Party Congress in 1956, he criticised the cult of Stalin's personality, declared unnecessarily high the costs of the industrialisation process and lamented the mass slaughter of Soviet people liquidated during this period to dissociate himself from the repression and hardship imposed by Stalin's regime.

This stance enabled Khrushchev to relax the heavy control of work exercised through the social security system and extend welfare provisions. This he did primarily by improving benefit levels and providing assistance to the poor. However, the most important changes he introduced affected the economic base of the country. These included decentralising the industrial apparatus and state control of industry to reduce the rigid planning imposed by central direction. Khrushchev hoped these measures would improve economic efficiency and productivity and give more emphasis to the consumer and agricultural sectors.

The need to address these areas was critical. Food, the major consumer good in the Soviet Union, was seriously short. Grain was particularly scarce. The grain deficit was being made up through costly imports which detracted resources from being used to foster economic performance. Productivity in the agricultural sector was low because of serious underinvestment and the presence of a poor and ageing population. These demographic features coupled with industrial policies encouraging people to work in the cities produced a labour shortage in the rural areas. The existence of a social security system which discriminated against agricultural workers exacerbated this situation. Khrushchev had to alter the social security system to bring the agricultural workforce within the scope of its benefits.

Khrushchev introduced three major social security reforms. One repealed the law requiring workers to work for the enterprise to which they had been assigned. This encouraged labour mobility and freed some workers to enter areas of labour shortages in the expanding consumer industry. The second reform took place in 1956 when the pension plan was extended to cover most workers and their dependants. However, dependants' allowances were meagre, for example, widows' pensions were low, married men received only 10 per cent extra to cover their wives. These meagre outlays indicate that women were expected to earn their own pension through waged work. It leaves women engaged primarily in domestic labour out in the cold, particularly if they were single parent women. Also excluded from the pension reform were collective farmers and self-employed workers. Benefit levels in general were increased by up to 100 per cent and made more egalitarian between low paid and higher paid workers. Anomalies were also reduced. Government funds supplemented employers' contributions to social security. These measures added to the cost of the scheme, but they made the system more comprehensive for industrial workers. The third reform affected agricultural collectives. Promulgated in 1964, it became effective in 1965 and brought agricultural workers into the social security system by covering sickness, maternity, and old age. However, their benefits were lower than those of industrial workers, maintaining Stalin's earlier divisions. Financing for these benefits came from the collective farms with a supplementary grant from the state. These changes aimed to revitalise agriculture and break the flow of people from the countryside into the towns.

Despite its shortcomings, social security represented a significant proportion of the government's budget. By 1965, social security as a percentage of government expenditure rose from 4.4 per cent in 1950 to 10.2 per cent. This compared to 6.3 per cent in the United States, 10.5 per cent in Britain, and 13.5 per cent in Sweden. Private welfare provisions in Western countries, particularly in pensions would have increased the overall social spending in these areas. However, since most private pensions in the West are purchased by men, gender inequality is greater. Gender inequality would increase in the Soviet Union if it were to allow such provisions because men also earn more than women.

Khrushchev's reforms reflected a considerable shift away from Stalin's policies on heavy industries like coal, steel, mining, and chemicals and the creation of an élite within the working class. However, the social security system was unable to fulfil the role expected of it. One problem was that increasing benefit levels and extending benefits to previously ineligible segments of the population increased people's spending power and demand for consumer goods. Unfortunately, the Soviet economy was already facing excess demand in consumer durables such as washing machines, fridges, televisions, cars. Adding to these pressures did not ease the situation and left more people dissatisfied. Moreover, unmet demand for consumer durables meant that one sector of the economy which had been left relatively untouched by Soviet industrialisation and modernisation – the domestic economy and the nature of 'women's work' within it – remained within its traditional backbreaking tramlines. The takeoff in consumer good production during the 1960s altered women's situation only marginally.

The moves towards decentralisation and the emphasis on consumer goods led to the formation of regional bodies responsible for economic and social policies as well as appointing factory directors. Some of the Party élite argued that these measures were another form of the New Economic Policy reintroducing market forces into the economy. Khrushchev was unceremoniously removed from office in 1964 because he was unpredictable, had mishandled the Cuban missile crises, and failed to direct national policy towards developing the decentralised consumer economy necessary for further industrial advancement. Khrushchev's industrial reforms continued under the aegis of Kosygin who advocated decreasing centrally set targets in favour of those established by local managers as a way of dealing with economic inefficiency and low growth. This freedom was reigned in when Breshnev gained ascendancy over Kosygin. Maintaining that corruption was becoming a problem engendered by too much local freedom, he advocated more rigid central planning controls. Gorbachev continues the struggle with this conundrum.

No major reforms of social security took place after 1964, though steps have been taken to improve provisions (George and Manning, 1980). These included ameliorating the position of collective farmers and low paid workers. The retirement age for collective farmers was reduced by five years to bring it in line with industrial workers in 1967. Also, in 1970, sickness benefit payments to collective farmers were made almost identical to those of industrial workers. Pensions were similarly drawn into line for them in 1971. The minimum wage was increased. This in turn augmented benefits for low paid workers, many of whom struggle with poverty. Moves to reduce poverty included increasing pension levels and introducing an income tested family allowance scheme in 1974. Also, the length of employment condition for maternity benefits was abolished in 1973. Changes in the qualifying conditions for sickness benefit took place in 1975 so that those with three or more children could receive full earnings irrespective of the length of time in waged work.

The Soviet social security system failed to address the issue of poverty, particularly among families with children, including single parent ones. The family income supplement was introduced in 1974 in response to pressure from Party activists for the government to deal with family poverty and low pay. The introduction of the family income supplement doubled the number of children covered. Expenditure on the family increased five times, but still encompassed only 37 per cent of children under eight. This expenditure illustrates the existence of poverty and low wages on a massive scale in the Soviet Union. Interestingly, dealing with the working poor has also been a problem for capitalist countries. Their response has been similar. For example, Britain introduced its Family Income Supplement scheme to deal with poor working families in 1971. Paying workers wages that are high enough for them to purchase a decent standard of living on their own is one way out of the dilemma presented by the working poor. However, this would require a social security system that was not oriented towards buttressing the low wage economy. Estimates of the extent of poverty vary from 15 to 30 per cent of the population (George and Manning, 1980, p. 62). Poverty in the

Soviet Union also highlights the absence of a comprehensive public assistance scheme like British Income Support providing safety net provisions for those excluded from other benefits.

Industrialisation and the pressures forcing women out to work have meant that 80 per cent of Soviet women are in waged work and form 51 per cent of the workforce. Encouraging women to work was one way in which the Soviet government hoped to deal with family poverty (George and Manning, 1980). However, women's high participation in the labour force has not reduced the large numbers of poor working families. Female poverty is largely the product of women earning only between 60 and 70 per cent of men's wages, despite equal pay legislation. This is because the Soviet workforce follows gender segregation. Women work in lower paid industries and in lower paid jobs in the higher paid industries (McAuley, 1981).

In the absence of a national public assistance scheme, each Soviet republic is responsible for providing assistance to its needy citizens. These come into action only if there is no family available to be legally compelled to take responsibility for them. The risks covered by the national social security scheme are extensive. Although many social security benefits are more generous than Western ones as they can include full earnings, for example, maternity pay, coverage is far from ideal. Moreover, the principle of contributing through one's employment is more central to eligibility in the Soviet system than in Western state systems, making an individual's employment record a key determinant in receiving benefits. This makes the unemployed particularly vulnerable to exclusion from a system lacking unemployment insurance. The Soviet system also rewards workers in difficult and unhealthy occupations such as mining with higher benefit levels. Thus, the Soviet social security system rewards hard labour while private schemes in capitalist countries reward middle class people (George and Manning, 1980).

In both cases, men are the main group being advantaged. In earnings related pension benefits, Soviet levels match 50 per cent of earnings on retirement, comparing favourably with Britain, but not Western Germany. However, the German system, financed through equal state and enterprise contributions, is more inegalitarian since a modified earnings related element for the low paid makes its redistribution of income regressive. Trade unions rather than state bodies implement the Soviet scheme at local level. Moreover, the Soviet social security system is highly bureaucratic and has a strong emphasis on labour discipline rather than people's needs. This detracts from its socialist orientation. The presence of poverty, particularly among women in the Soviet Union, suggests that inequality still persists, even if the differential between different groups of people are not as exaggerated as those prevailing in capitalist societies. Gender is a significant feature of Soviet inegalitarianism. So is 'race' as many of the low paid workers are located in the collective farms in the Asiatic part of the Soviet Union. The current structure of the Soviet social security system perpetuates these inequalities.

IN CONCLUSION

The receipt of social security benefits in the Soviet Union is not based on an individual's contract with the state, but on a status relationship between the individual and the state. This makes the discretionary powers of the trade unions and the social insurance authorities more important. Despite the comprehensive nature of its social security system, significant numbers of Soviet people remain without provisions. This affects those experiencing family breakup, young people without a work record, those having congenital disabilities preventing them from working, those having accidents outside the workplace, alcoholics, and incarcerated young offenders who cannot pay insurance contributions while serving their sentence.

Gorbachev has sought to reform both the economic and political infrastructures of the Soviet Union. Until Gorbachev's reforms of 1989, politics in the Soviet Union favoured an electoral process based on the Communist Party. Gorbachev's reforms provided a parliament having oppositional groupings. Although this has highlighted controversies about the nature of the political and economic tasks facing the Soviet Union, the major forum of debate in which the Soviet public participates is the mass media. This form of communication is particularly relevant to welfare issues such as child care and women's dual career roles. Large numbers of people become involved in these discussions at the local level. Their arguments influence Party policy by being filtered discretely into its higher decision-making echelons. Though partially developed, these informal mechanisms enable the working class to exercise some control over the state, thus fostering allegiance to its activities. Support for regime is high among manual workers (Dott, 1966). The Soviet state, therefore, derives its legitimacy by promoting consensus rather than terror. However, the security police, terror and repression are there for the state to use as necessary. Maintaining this consensus draws heavily on Soviet achievements, for example, successes in the Second World War, the preservation of the industrial achievements of the 1920s and 1930s, and the Party's measures to improve internal democracy, and its attempts to encourage participation in economic affairs by decentralising production (Colletti, 1970). The dictatorship of the Party resting on a tension between the masses and the élite is incomplete. It is currently being channelled by the Party. This tension can break at any moment, as has already happened in Poland, Hungary, Czechoslovakia, East Germany, Bulgaria and Romania.

The welfare state also performs an important function in legitimating the Soviet system by providing a basis for consent and stability. This aspect of the welfare state has become more dominant since the death of Stalin as some achievements of the Revolution come to fruition. The significance of the Soviet welfare state in the ordinary citizen's life is witnessed by Russian émigrés who long for its universalistic social services – education, social security and health care. This suggests that the collective ethos of command economy welfarism is more supportive of individual freedom than welfare capitalism which espouses it in rhetoric while opposing it in practice. Unfortunately, the political processes whereby policy making is conducted are undemocratic as they exclude the Soviet masses from political participation at all levels of society.

Such participation is a precondition of socialist welfare processes, but is absent in the Soviet Union. The birth of the Russian Revolution in a situation of feudal legacies, economic underdevelopment, enormous material scarcity, civil war, and a poorly developed proletariat mitigated against the creation of real socialist structures. Socialist democracy, the abolition of class structures, the elimination of 'race' and gender inequalities and the presence of an efficient industrial system are all necessary for social relations to be transformed. However, it requires more than this if the masses, including women, are not to remain depoliticised and uninvolved in the political processes bringing about such change. It also requires the transformation of personal relations and the domestic division of labour. Social change, therefore, must take place in both the private and public arenas. Whether Gorbachev's reforms will facilitate changes of this nature remains to be seen.

The Chinese income maintenance system

Like the Soviet Union, data on the Chinese social security system is scarce. Income support in China changed from *ad hoc* provisions based on family wealth in the pre-revolutionary days to the 'iron rice bowl' system of communally funded welfare after the revolution. This means that the patriarchal Confucian tradition with its class ridden and gender riven order in which dominance in the welfare arena was accorded to market and domestic provisions was challenged by the strengthening of collective forces endorsing equality between people. This 'iron rice bowl' is now in danger of cracking, as private provisions and the *Responsibility*

System assume the welfare burdens previously borne by community organisations in communes and factories.

The main goal of the Chinese worker today is to secure a factory job because this provides the highest wages, welfare benefits and job security (Bonavia, 1982). Only top scientists, physicians, and senior Communist Party officials have extra fringe benefits and higher salaries. Competition for factory jobs is tough as urban jobs are in short supply, and unemployment in major cities such as Beijing and Shanghai substantial, particularly among the young people who have served their stint in the rural areas, the *xia-xiang* youth. The Chinese government cannot encourage depopulation of the rural areas without risking serious social dislocation and the formation of large slum estates in the cities. The major problem faced by Chinese policy makers has been that of matching economic growth with population growth, a goal that remains elusive.

After the revolution, the Chinese strove to create an income maintenance system which reduced social divisions including those between mental and manual labour, and urban and rural areas. This aim remains to be realised. China's present income maintenance system has three tiers:

1. A state tier taking care of the top scientists, physicians, and senior Party cadres.
2. An urban tier catering for workers in factories and workshops.
3. A rural tier for commune workers.

Income support through the state tier is available only to government employees. It forms the prestige sphere because job security and the fringe benefits attached to it are substantial. However, it excludes the bulk of the population living in rural areas.

The urban tier, located in factories, confers benefits according to the size and resources of the firm. Large factories provide workers with housing, medical schemes, pensions, recreational facilities, schools and childcare resources, although grandparents remain the preferred child care option (Andors, 1983). Trade unions run their own workplace schemes and manage welfare provisions on a factory by factory basis. In the latter, they operate as an arm of management using welfare resources to control members' disruption of production (Howard, 1988). Trade unions were disbanded between 1966 and 1973, and came under Communist Party control in 1977.

Women workers in the cities are often pushed out of factory employment so that men can hold these jobs (Andors, 1983), thus confirming their role as a reserve army of labour. Women are more readily employed in workshops established by neighbourhood organisations or street committees and run collectively by the women who work in them. Workshops created largely by women and relying on their own resources have become important avenues through which potential unemployment is avoided by substantial numbers of women. Approximately 10–20 million women were employed in neighbourhood workshops in 1980. Street committees intervene in the lives of all individuals. Bonavia (1982) claims that these represent socialism at its worst when operating as mechanisms of surveillance or socialism at its best when spreading information about the community and its services, providing contraceptive aids and birth control advice, and caring for older people, families in financial difficulties and teenagers in trouble. Neighbourhood schemes lack state financial support and are responsible for providing the bulk of the welfare services in urban residential areas (Andors, 1983). But because these activities were run by women, they reinforce the view that caring is 'women's work'.

Rural welfare schemes received their greatest impetus during the Great Leap Forward with the creation of communes owned by the peasants rather than the state. Communes were mainly established during 1958 to develop agriculture while the state concentrated on industry and atomic power. During the Great Leap Forward, the Chinese Communist Party took the conscious decision of limiting the growth of urban areas, developing rural areas and investing in labour intensive production. Its policy towards women became one of transforming household chores into social labour and freeing women to enter the production process. Communes had to finance their own medical and welfare schemes and run their own accounts. Communes were also entitled to trade on equal terms with state owned sectors of the economy, particularly urban industry, urban services, government, and the armed forces. The commune obtained funds for its welfare projects through the factories and workshops it owned and operated. Poor communes had less resources to devote to income maintenance than richer ones. However, the state did not intervene to equalise their resources (Andors, 1983).

There were 50,000 communes at the peak of their development, each differing in size. Communes were composed of a production brigade and a production team. Production brigades varied in size but were responsible for maintaining welfare facilities, junior schools, culture and the people's militia. A production team, consisting of one or more villages, was remote from the commune, but it was responsible for providing senior schools and operating clinics. The commune paid workers in workpoints which were accumulated to provide welfare services. Workpoints operated along sexist lines as women received fewer points than men although they were often doing the same work

(Andors, 1983; Croll, 1983). Except for a brief period, aggregation was the basis of the payment system with the head of the family receiving all the workpoints accrued by its members and distributing them. The commune rarely gave food or financial aid to poor families – although it could provide them with direct grants – because the extended family was expected to intervene with support. Older people get direct grants including a funeral grant if there is no surviving family.

The system enforces both labour discipline and family responsibility. Better workers subsidise poorer workers as hard-pressed families can borrow from the commune until their next harvest. The levelling of income between different members of the commune has been considered a disincentive to work, reducing a commune's ability to extract as much as possible out of its lands (Chan et al., 1984). The commune welfare system was dubbed an 'iron rice bowl' system by Liu Zi-zhen who considered this a superior aspect of the socialist system for reducing unemployment and providing total job security. It is the security provided by the 'iron rice bowl' system which is being threatened by the Responsibility System currently being fostered in China.

The major impact of the commune on women's labour was two-fold. It drew large numbers of women into production work by allowing 'women to substitute for men' in technically more simple though physically arduous tasks, thereby freeing men to undertake technically more sophisticated and skilled work in heavier industry and new industries such as the atomic industry (Andors, 1983). And, it made consumption a site of production by socialising domestic work through the creation of a service industry made up of mess halls, kindergartens, nurseries, laundries, tailoring, food processing and repair shops, and attracting women with the traditional skills these were based on to work in them. These measures enabled women to contribute substantially to family incomes, making the two-earner couple within an extended family network a reality in China. They also reinforced women's subordinate position in the labour force and maintained a gender segregated division of labour. In the Chinese experience, drawing women into production reinforced rather than challenged their traditional role albeit the context had altered (Andors, 1983). It made women shoulder the dual career burden for they remained primarily responsible for whatever caring work remained to be tackled at home.

Important dimensions shaping the development of the Chinese income support system are: sexism in that women are assigned fewer workpoints for their work than men – seven or eight compared to eleven or twelve; few differentials in pay, including between administrative and skilled labour; significant variations between urban and rural areas; extended family responsibility for the welfare of members; and a shortage of urban jobs restricting the mobility of labour. As payments of benefits is based on one's earnings, inequality in the workplace is also reflected in these.

Concerned about the egalitarian trends fostered by the communes and their implications for production, Deng Xiao Ping and Liu Shao Chi published the *60 Articles* to guide commune administration and clarify the rights of the production team in 1962. The measures these advised improved production until the 'chaos' of the Cultural Revolution halted it. The Cultural Revolution aimed to reduce income inequality while increasing people's motivation to work for the greater good.

Mao countered Deng's attacks on the 'iron rice bowl' welfare system with the Dazhai Concept. Dazhai was a commune in Shaanxi where Chen Yong Gui promoted terracing of hillsides, equalising income and increasing production. Chen was promoted to the Politburo in recognition of his efforts in 1973 but was sacked in 1979.

The success of Dazhai notwithstanding, the Communist Party introduced further changes which were considered a negation of the principles of collective ownership and income equalisation in the early 1970s. These led to a distribution of income according to the labour performed, and production teams losing control over funds, goods, labour power and management. In 1975, continued difficulties in increasing productivity levels resulted in the decision to mechanise all farms by 1980. In 1979, this move was repudiated by Hua Guo Fung who raised grain prices instead. Meanwhile, peasant dissatisfaction with stagnant living standards gave increased support to splitting production teams into family units which having met their collective obligations, could engage in forms of production augmenting their private income (Howard, 1988).

The erosion of the commune system was exacerbated through changes introduced in 1979 by Deng. Deng Xiao Ping aimed to increase peasant income through the Four Modernisations: agriculture, science and technology, industry and the military and the Responsibility System which permitted the use of private plots to increase production of light consumer durables and agricultural products. Rewards would be based on an individual's work effort. Goods and produce from these plots could be sold on the free market where all surplus products are exchanged. Women are the key to the cultivation of private plots and development of sidelines through which families maximise their cash incomes (Croll, 1983). To help the process, the rural fairs abolished under the Cultural Revolution were reopened and bonus incentive schemes initiated. Investment of capital in state farms was encouraged. Commune workers were paid wages, not workpoints. This strategy could lead to increased inequality within the commune itself.

This package of changes contributed inflationary pressures to the economy and failed to tackle the major problem of modernising agriculture to produce the surplus necessary for industrialisation. The costs of doing this are prohibitive since modernising agriculture requires twice the gross national product China has at its disposal. Its rapidly expanding population means that unless population size is controlled, the Chinese people can only eke out their survival. Class differences add to the complexity of this situation. Poor peasants in the Peasants Association expressed concern over Deng's failure to control rich peasants and support poor peasants. But instead of having the matters dealt with, the Peasants Association lost its political functions including monitoring change and stopping embezzlement. In 1981, the new system of farming received official blessing, despite opposition from Maoist cadres, the armed forces, and Party officers who called these measures rural capitalism. From their point-of-view, Deng's changes were not rural collectivism as poor families would lose out unless they had the capital to hire their own livestock and tractors.

The needs of the economy have been crucial to the development of the income maintenance system in China. In the immediate period after the Revolution, its focus was on the nation's commitment to shift endemic poverty, famine, illiteracy and disease. This was to be achieved by developing a system of income maintenance which combined state intervention with citizen participation.

A NEW BEGINNING: THE YENAN MODEL OF WELFARE IN THE EARLY DAYS OF THE REVOLUTION
The income maintenance system introduced by the Communist Party after its victory in 1949 became known as the Yenan Model of Welfare (Brugger, 1981a). Its approach contrasted sharply with the pre-revolutionary system in which the market and informal networks determined which welfare services were available. Originally developed in Yenan in Shaanxi Province in 1946–7, it was applied throughout the country. It combined mass participation and consciousness raising in welfare matters with land reforms favouring the peasantry. It was based on the following five principles:

1. Serving the people (altruism).
2. Using internal resources (self-reliance).
3. Individuals having responsibility to help their families, peers, and neighbours (self-help).
4. Problem solving by the community (community organisation).
5. Decentralised organisation, funding and delivery of services (local orientation and decision-making).

These principles were designed to make the best use of existing resources, especially in land, housing and labour, making economic considerations central to the system. Besides strengthening the local area through its drive for self-sufficiency, the system attempted to provide opportunities for women to participate fully in economic development by changing their position in the family and allowing them to play a greater role in local state affairs. Consequently, women were drawn into local level organisations responsible for welfare matters. Though this reinforced women's involvement in 'women's work', it moved women into the public arena (Andors, 1983). By 1951, 10 per cent of local activists whose job it was to assess the welfare needs of individuals and families were women (Croll, 1978).

The Yenan Model ultimately failed to meet the nation's aspirations because it could not produce food and goods quickly enough for a rapidly rising population. Its ability to respond to the challenges placed before it was also restricted by its reliance on Soviet advisers who were often unsympathetic to the needs and aspirations of the local populace. These withdrew when Mao Tse Tung severed relations with the Soviet Union in 1960. The Yenan Model also suffered from the diversion of scarce economic resources to fight the Korean War. It also locked women into the caring jobs which they had always undertaken and bolstered sexism. Mao decided to tackle the problems at the local level through the *Three Antis Movement* to fight corruption, bureaucracy and waste. Free discussions on improving China's economic performance to release surplus for welfare developments were fostered through the first *100 Flowers Bloom* debates.

In 1951, legislative measures enabled the central state to intervene and cover the welfare rights of state employees through the Labour Insurance Regulations. These also provided maternity pay for women workers. By 1953, cuts in social development took place as funds were diverted away from women and welfare matters to economic concerns. The first Five Year Plan and the Stalinisation of the economy in the form of unification and centralisation got under way. Women's interests and those involving social policy were subordinated to economic considerations (Molyneaux, 1985; Croll, 1978; Andors, 1983).

WELFARE PROVISIONS UNDER THE GREAT LEAP FORWARD

In 1956, the *Five Guarantees Scheme* was promulgated to protect the livelihood of rural elders. Its provisions included food, clothing, housing, medical care, and burials guaranteed by the brigade. From 1958 to 1961, the Great Leap Forward caused a major shift in welfare policy as the family lost many of its functions, including those as the provider of economic and social security for individuals. These obligations were assumed by the local state via the commune. The communes were responsible for all social services, nursery, education, health and housing needs. Communes were also required to deal with the needs imposed by natural disasters and accumulate welfare funds through their productive activities. This placed social policy developments in direct conflict with economic ones for the use of scarce capital resources.

Communes drew on women's labour to develop their welfare services and make their transition from a sphere of private consumption to socialised production. There was no single process followed in the development of the communes, with substantial variations between the processes developed in urban and rural areas. Although many urban communes failed to survive the Great Leap Forward, the street committees and welfare services they created did, largely through women's continued involvement in them as opportunities for women to work in the non-service sector dwindled (Stacey, 1983).

Collectivised welfare and social services featured largely in urban communes by 1960, after the political, educational and ideological groundwork necessary for their legitimation and the mobilisation of the masses had been laid during 1958 and 1959. Mess halls, childcare facilities and neighbourhood service centres, some of which had been built earlier, began to be used extensively in 1960 when women came out of their homes to join the paid labour force in unprecedented numbers. The collectivisation of domestic labour hit snags. Inefficiency, poor management and economic scarcity hindered their potential development (Andors, 1983; Croll, 1978). In the communal kitchens low quality meals and poor hygiene resulted from women's lack of experience in preparing food for large numbers.

Women lacked some of the skills necessary for the management of such large enterprises. Accounting and finance were outside the knowledge of poorly educated or illiterate women. The need to develop services on a shoestring meant services were delivered without the basic infrastructure being in place. Childcare centres were organised in spare rooms, hallways and courtyards as purpose-built buildings were absent. In these circumstances, it is not surprising that family forms of care relying on grandmothers and older children remained popular. Working-class women's labour in the collectivised services was used to free other working-class women to take remunerated work, but men remained outside of this movement, limiting their interaction to being consumers of the services provided.

Thus, the traditional division of labour between men and women was not transformed. Instead, women were substituted for men in specific areas of the production process and gender segregation was extended into new areas recruiting women as these became defined as 'women's work' and lost status and pay in the process (Andors, 1983). Although women performed the work involved in the provision of these services, their management, particularly at the higher levels, was undertaken by men (Andors, 1983). This also reinforced the traditional division of labour.

Communes started losing power between 1962 and 1965 when Lui Shao Chi gained economic control and prioritised economic development over matters of reproduction and consumption. He called on the family to resume its traditional functions of caring for its members and wrote *Love, Marriage and the Family* to promote his views. His position endorsed Confucian ideals and legitimated the increased burden women bore as a result of having dual careers – one working for the commune, the other working for the family. The assumption was that as women were only performing their natural role, it was available at no cost to anyone.

The simultaneous expansion of production and welfare services during the Great Leap Forward reinforced the relative inequality between men and women. Despite this, the attempt to move women out of their traditional roles and of being directly accountable to men aroused fierce resistance to these moves (Andors, 1983; Croll, 1978). These so-called 'feudal attitudes' became subject to renewed attack during the Cultural Revolution which aimed to change people's minds as well as their relations of production. The Great Leap Forward demonstrated the impossibility of altering women's subordinate status in society without transforming relations between men and women socially, politically, economically and ideologically in both the workplace and the home. It also revealed that women's position in society becomes a central question when relations of production are changed, even if the issue is far removed from the explicit political agenda, as it was when the Chinese people first embarked on developing the economy through the Great Leap Forward. The link between economic policy and social policy and the need to develop these two areas simultaneously in a way which recognises their interdependence could not have been made clearer (Stacey, 1982; Andors, 1983).

Women's role in the provision of collective welfare services was central. They performed most of the routine caring work associated with service delivery and carried a key responsibility in setting up such services in the first place. Women were expected to make up the shortfall in these through the provision of unpaid welfare work in the home. These activities are rarely aimed at furthering women's interests as women. This is strange because Chinese women have a long history of feminist organising (Croll, 1978; Broyelle, 1977). Feminist activities were much in evidence during the Civil War and during the early days of the Revolution when women's liberation and China's social, political, and economic liberation were considered twin objectives in the creation of a communist society (Croll, 1978). Economic exigencies and the need to ensure the survival of the Revolution in an industrially under-developed country led to the subordination of women's liberation (Johnson, 1983). This was achieved through the incorporation of leading feminists and their organisations into the All China Democratic Women's Federation (Women's Federation) and its being placed under Party tutelage.

This gave the Women's Federation the role of explaining Party policy to women and furthering their development in ways compatible with it. These included gaining women's support for revolutionary goals and objectives and educating them in the benefits of entering social production. Formal equality was legally endorsed and the worst excesses of female abuse under the Confucian ordering of society, for example foot-binding, concubinage, the selling of women, enforced marital unions at an early age, women's exclusion from owning and inheriting property were officially condemned. In the early days of Communist rule, the Women's Federation had the task of raising women's consciousness and bringing them *en masse* into the public arena with socially acceptable responsibilities for them to undertake. These were inevitably defined as making their contribution to the revolution. A direct attack on male privilege would have been too controversial and counter-productive. Men's hostility to women's progress would have been exacerbated (Andors, 1983).

However, the Women's Federation did challenge male prerogative in instances of physical abuse, and supported women in putting an end to it. Public ostracism of the man responsible in 'speak bitterness' meetings was a technique commonly used (Hinton, 1966). Although this handling of the matter raised it as a social issue, it relied on accusations against individual men by individual women. This meant that assaulting women was confirmed as the action of badly behaved men rather than a socially sanctioned method used in controlling women. Thus, it did not challenge the way society organised relationships between men and women or lead to demands for their transformation. As part of the strategy of ameliorating relationships between men and women, the Women's Federation also facilitated women's access to their rights under the Marriage Law of 1950. This included helping women file for divorce, an action which antagonised many men and earned the Women's Federation the title of marriage-wrecker.

During the period of the Great Leap Forward, the Women's Federation played a key role in getting women involved in social production, the collectivisation of domestic labour, the establishment of workshops and street committees, organising and running of women's study groups, and encouraging women to participate in public life.

Thus, the Women's Federation facilitated women's contribution to the goals established by the Party, but in the process it also enabled women to acquire social, political and economic skills which made them more ready to challenge the cultural definition of their role. This brought into the open the tensions between allocating resources to women's liberation and economic development (Andors, 1983). Its demands to have this issue examined led to a polarisation of positions in which feminist demands were seen as damaging to the revolutionary process. Outright conflict was avoided as the Women's Federation soft-pedalled its stance. It finally came to a head during the Cultural Revolution when the Women's Federation was dissolved for dissipating the energies of activists by encouraging them to deal with women's issues as matters outside of class struggle. Before that, the Women's Federation had played a major role in legally mediating disputes among neighbours and trying to resolve them outside of the court process; educating women on matters of birth control and contraceptive aids; encouraging women to marry later and have fewer children; supporting women in meeting the demands of their dual career burdens; and fostering their formal education and involvement in political processes. However, the tensions manifest during the Great Leap Forward became more pressing and the need for full equality for women obvious. Demands for these issues to be addressed were defined as bourgeois deviationism, and the Women's Federation unnecessary as 'class struggle' would ensure the liberation of all, women included. The Women's Federation was closed down in 1967.

The Women's Federation as a national organisation was reactivated in 1973 and again given the task of explaining the Party's economic and demographic policies to women and eliciting their support for their implementation. This meant educating women and getting their agreement to later marriages, practising birth control to have small families and contributing to family income. In the post-Mao era it also involved the Women's Federation in fostering women's initiatives in developing economic sidelines through which family income could be maximised.

WELFARE PROVISIONS DURING THE CULTURAL REVOLUTION

The Cultural Revolution of 1966–8 attempted to reduce inequality and increase the incentive to work. Lui Shao Chi lost power and was branded a bourgeois deviationist. The Red Guard was formed to mobilise youth and introduce changes into Chinese society. Attacking the bureaucracy, the Cultural Revolution reaffirmed the value of collective action. Local organisations like the Local Administration Organisation were replaced by the Revolutionary Committees representing the masses, the Party and the army.

One of the early issues raised during the Cultural Revolution was the matter of wage insecurity and 'harsh economic inequalities borne by some groups in the process of economic development' (Andors, 1983). While women's wage insecurity was not specifically addressed, the grievances of contract labour and the managerial manipulation of factory discretionary and wage funds in the textile mills, brought the issue into the limelight for one group of women workers – contract labourers. Contract labour, being seasonal and part-time, attracted large numbers of women. Payment was usually on a piece-rate and without the welfare benefits that normally accrued to factory workers in permanent posts. These practices threatened the position of regular salaried employees. The situation became more fraught when the Third Five Year Plan restricted the entry of new regular workers into the labour force. Many potential new workers were women graduates whose main avenue to employment now became contract labour with its built-in insecurity. Women organised to get the issue addressed in favour of wage parity for contract workers. Their efforts were unsuccessful and their organisation banned. Given the flexibility with which contract labour could be deployed, it is not surprising that these women's plight was ignored in the face of competing demands for scarce economic resources.

Women's contribution to the development of street based welfare services came under attack during the *January Storm* of 1967 when the cadres of the neighbourhood residents' committees were criticised. Interestingly, millions of women participated in this exercise which was originally aimed at the local Party committees (Andors, 1983). Ironically, neighbourhood residents' committees bore the brunt of an attack on policies they played no part in formulating. The main policies to be found wanting were the *xia-xiang* policy, the lack of employment opportunities for women, the changing role of the family, and women's role within it (Andors, 1983).

The debates of the Cultural Revolution revealed many women supported the family, despite its being a conservative institution (Andors, 1983). These contradictions remained while women both challenged and defended the institution creating these limitations. The *internalisation of patriarchal values among men and women and their social reproduction in the economic, political, and cultural life of Chinese society* was not addressed during the Cultural Revolution, although it aimed to counter 'feudal' ways of thinking and develop the socialist man and woman. Rather, it concentrated on changing people's mental attitudes as if these could be divorced from the material realities in which their lives evolved. Exhortation to a higher morality instead of changing patriarchal institutions became the adopted vehicle for changing people's conceptions of themselves. The opportunity to transform welfare institutions so that they guaranteed people's economic security, complemented production, galvanised workplace and domestic activities along egalitarian lines and re-oriented interpersonal familial relationships in independent directions was lost. Welfare issues remained subordinate to economic ones. And women continued with their socially unequal lives.

Health services were also expanded during the Cultural Revolution to cover ante-natal care and the education system began to challenge hierarchy and élitism. Educational institutions became open to peasants through the elimination of academic admissions criteria and their replacement with political ones. These moves were geared to shifting the mental–manual division among workers and linking theory to practice to reduce economic and social disparities between urban and rural areas rather than address women's welfare directly. Nonetheless, these initiatives enabled women to gain better health services and jobs. In 1969–71, the offensive on the commune system acquired momentum as Lin Piao argued that the family was a unit of consumption with primary responsibility in welfare matters. Women remained the invisible members of the family called upon to provide their free labour. The need to improve productivity in the commune had assumed greater urgency as the population expanded. Returning welfare matters to the bosom of the family enabled the commune to spare more collective resources for economic production rather than providing care for individuals. Population limitation policies became more pressing in 1971 because of the limited resources available for distribution within families.

WELFARE PROVISIONS IN THE POST-MAO PERIOD

The right wing of the Party assumed control after Mao's death and replaced the Local Revolutionary Committee with the Local People's Government. As the commune declined in influence, unemployment became a problem, particularly for youth. Urban youth unemployment was exacerbated by urban youths returning from working in rural areas under the *xia-xiang* policy. However, the presence of food subsidies was used to justify the continued absence of unemployment pay. Also, unemployment insurance has not been made available for fear of encouraging the 'undeserving poor' and undermining the work ethic. Maintaining labour discipline is an important aspect of the Chinese income maintenance system. Education has resumed its earlier hierarchical orientation as expertise has become emphasised in a desperate bid to increase productivity. Hua promoted campaigns to severely limit population growth except among ethnic minorities because it outstripped economic growth. Reducing the birth rate precludes family allowances for children. However, a sophisticated system of welfare rewards like access to housing, is provided for couples adhering to the One-Child Policy of population control. The withdrawal of welfare services is used to penalise non-adherents of this policy.

Problems in developing the Chinese economy emanate from the Stalinisation of its industry (Curtin, 1976). This has led to flagging agricultural production, lack of consumer goods, poor quality products, over-rigid industrial planning, especially in the steel and atomic power industries, excessive bureaucracy and intellectual stagnation. It has also encouraged closer ties with the West as the Chinese seek its technical products and knowledge. Women's labour, particularly that involved in street industries, workshops and sideline production, has been drafted in to produce goods for export to earn foreign exchange to pay for Western expertise while men utilise foreign technology in developing the industrial infrastructure. Unless China solves its economic dilemmas it cannot provide a national income maintenance system covering every-body. It will have to rely on the inadequate local measures currently provided by the commune, the factory and the family, except for safety net provisions recently announced for older people. These include state pensions for women at 55 and men at 60. Deng introduced these provisions as a pragmatic response to China's demographic crisis. Through these initiatives, Deng hoped the state rather than offspring would provide the economic security people seek in old age and would encourage couples to stick to the One-Child Policy. Deng's fears are that without demographic control, hardship among the Chinese will increase and the state will be unable to find the resources necessary for developing welfare provisions. The size of the problem can be measured through the fact that in 1988, one in twelve peasant families lived below the poverty line (Howard, 1988).

The 1981 New Marriage Law reaffirmed the family's role in meeting the welfare needs of its members. Chinese families are continually being asked to shoulder their welfare burden, despite state attempts at providing public welfare institutions to do so. The 'family' really means women caring for children and elders. Andors (1983) sees this situation as inevitable. She argues: 'the family cannot be replaced as the provider of social services in the early stages of development, traditional female roles are reinforced by economic realities, since families with many able-bodied *males* [my emphasis] have greater incomes!' (Andors, 1983, p. 4).

However, the Chinese experience reveals that this pattern is not inevitable. The period of the Great Leap Forward revealed public provisions could replace the family, and a fair allocation of workpoints could undermine the advantage held by male workers. However, this process was aborted before it came to maturity as economic priorities were politically allowed to transcend social ones. When men's opportunities for employment were threatened by declining economic growth, women were encouraged to return to their unpaid domestic work. In other words, men's privileged position was not inevitable, but a socially constructed outcome based on the socially approved subordination of women's interests as women. These so-called inevitable situations arise because society's decision-makers *make a choice* about constructing reality in this particular way. The Chinese experience has demonstrated that income inequality can be reinforced and perpetuated by social and economic developments, and that this inequality can be reproduced in the income maintenance system unless specific steps are taken to counter it. In this context, both class and gender based inequalities need to be tackled simultaneously for an egalitarian social security system to evolve.

IN CONCLUSION

Chinese income maintenance has developed in collectivist directions, although its implementation has been patchy. Inequality persists in so far as workers in the state and industrial sectors have better provisions than those in the agricultural sector. Patriarchal relations have also been reinforced. The patrilineal and patrilocal family still forms the basis of people's social and economic security throughout the life cycle as familial resources are pooled. Women's oppression continues. They are expected to contribute to the creation and maintenance of collective welfare provisions through their involvement in social production and to familial ones through their domestic labour.

CONCLUSIONS

In none of the countries examined did the income maintenance systems achieve equality for all members of the population. In fact, tying social security measures to waged employment exacerbated and reinforced gender inequality. Moreover, their social security systems have fostered objectives other than ensuring the well-being of people. Enforcing the work ethic through social security benefits (Ginsburg, 1979; Heclo, 1974; Curtin, 1976; Piven and Cloward, 1971) has been a major theme for them all, though the context in which it occurred has been different. Capitalist countries have needed to maximise the exploitation of workers to maintain international competitiveness and their profit margins. The socialist countries have exploited workers to accumulate the capital necessary for industrialisation. Only the Soviet Union during the early days of the revolution and China during the Cultural Revolution managed to escape briefly from the constraints of the work ethic. Otherwise, in all the countries covered, social policy has been subordinated to economic exigencies. The needs of capital accumulation, including the development of an industrial infrastructure and a military apparatus in each country, has taken precedence over the welfare needs of the populace.

This has meant that benefits are related to contributions derived from waged work, cover only certain risks, are often miserly in amounts, and available only to specified categories of people for limited periods of time. Within these limits, women and others not engaged in waged work receive either no benefits or only those reliant on their dependent status on a waged male worker. The contribution of domestic labour through the household economy has no place in the formal calculations of either wealth or entitlements. Yet, women are expected to meet the shortfall between family requirements for welfare services and actual state provisions through their unpaid and poorly paid labour. At home, they provide free care services for children, older relatives, and husbands. In social production, they maintain cut price public welfare services through their low wages.

The feminist objectives of breaking the connection between work and income so that all *individuals* receive an income independent of their family situation (Weir and McIntosh, 1982); integrating the responsibilities of work and home to avoid generating the inequalities which stem from the division between home, the workplace and the community (Dominelli and McLeod, 1989); eliminating gender segregation in the division of labour (Armstrong, 1984), and involving men and women in paid and unpaid caring work (Hooks, 1984), remain to be fulfilled in each of these countries. Yet doing so is essential if income maintenance systems are not to perpetuate the very inequalities their establishment is purported to resolve.

NOTES

1. The Department of Health and Social Security (DHSS) was divided into the Department of Health (DoH) and the Department of Social Security (DSS) during 1989. Both of these have maintained their role in internal immigration control.
2. With the expansion of the European Economic Community (EEC) and the integration of the different economies, it is now referred to as the European Community (EC).

3

Family policy

THE REINFORCEMENT OF PATRIARCHAL CONJUGALITY

The family is central to feminist analyses. As the site in which women's subordination develops, it is crucial to our understanding of what happens to women when the state intervenes within its borders. The family as a set of relationships involving men, women and children relating to each other through either social ties or those of consanguinity is a complex network linking individuals in the private arena of the home to the public realm, including waged employment, school and the welfare state. Moreover, there are a variety of relationships which are encompassed by the term 'family'. Among others, these cover single parent families, gay couples, lesbian couples, extended families, joint families, and serial families. The fact that we have to use the term 'family' to describe these relationships indicates the inadequacy of the language we have invented to describe relationships which differ from the 'heterosexual two parents with dependent children' family which is taken as the norm in classical welfare analyses.

Family structures vary considerably from one culture to another, and in times of social flux, from one generation to another in the same culture. Experiences of families are different for black and white people in the West. Whereas white women's experience of families is one mediated by sexism, black women's experience is affected by both sexism and racism (Mama, 1989; Lorde, 1984). White women may find family relationships reinforce their subordinate status as the primary caregivers, but black women find they have to be both primary caregivers and income earners. While family policy may compel all women into greater domesticity by refusing them control over their fertility and enforcing their roles as appendages of their spouses, this affects women differently depending on their class, 'race', age, or sexual orientation. Western white middle class women may have greater access to resources which give them a greater degree of choice than white working class or black or Third World women: for example, having the money to buy childcare services, often from working class, black or Third World women; seeking abortions in other countries if they are refused one in their own or in private clinics if their request is rejected in the public sector. White married women may be refused abortions, but black women are subjected to involuntary sterilisations (Sidel, 1986). White women may find they are forced to relate to their partners when pursuing maintenance payments, but black women see the breakup of their family relationships through racist immigration rules, welfare legislation and employment policies (Gordon and Newnham, 1985; Bryan et al., 1985; Mama, 1989). Black women find their families a source of strength in fighting racism (Hooks, 1984) for family support networks often enable them to resist the daily onslaught of racism in their lives. For them, the family is a site of both oppression and resistance (Carby, 1982; Bryan et al., 1985; Mama, 1989; Hooks, 1984). White working class women have made similar claims.

Traditional definitions of family policy encompass policies having a direct bearing on the fortunes of family members. These include matters relating to birth, marriage, divorce, childcare, sexuality, but exclude those having an indirect impact on family life, for example taxation, housing, education, immigration, and employment (Kamerman and Kahn, 1978). However, the effects of policies having an indirect connection with family life can be so significant in family relationships, for example black people's family life and British immigration policies, that anti-racist feminist analyses include these too.

Countries such as Britain, the United States and Canada have no formally recognised family policy, though there is legislation governing those aspects of family life described above. Nonetheless, I argue that each of these countries has a family policy by default. Most welfare benefits take the heterosexual conjugal nuclear family as the norm in their provisions (Eichler, 1983). Aggregation of family resources and the assumption of their equal distribution within the family follow from this, indicating that patriarchal understandings of family relationships are the guiding principles governing policy formation. The cohabitation rule in Britain, 'the man about the house rule' in the United States, underpin patriarchy. Canada has parallel provisions and cohabiting couples, known as common-law spouses, are treated as married couples in most respects. Even in Sweden, where the division of labour among the sexes has broken down more than in other Western countries, women's position still reflects assumptions about their domestic and dependent status (Wistrand, 1981). In the Soviet Union, despite provisions requiring men to do housework and others encouraging women to develop their careers, women continue to be primarily responsible for the care and nurture of children and dependent relatives. Chinese women, though heavily involved in the waged economy, find their liberation a long way off (Andors, 1983; Croll, 1978). They too are obliged to perform the dual shift – in paid occupations and at home.

The position of women in China and the Soviet Union demonstrates that changing women's waged labour position is an insufficient basis for their liberation (Molyneaux, 1985). Besides becoming extensively involved in public life, women must be released from their dual burden of domestic and waged labour. And men must become extensively involved in caring for others. Family policy can become a major mechanism through which such change is effected if women's liberation rather than their economically dependent status on a male breadwinner is taken as its starting point. Doing so would ensure that childcare provisions become a matter of collective rather than private concern for both women and men and that women have control over their own bodies rather than being expected to breed children for nationalistic and militaristic purposes or to fill shortages in the labour market. Achieving such changes requires women to organise both autonomously as women and in mixed organisations. It also necessitates governments taking up ideological and political issues with the same tenacity they display over economic ones.

The state also plays a vital role in family life through its control of the income maintenance system and taxation. The taxation system tends to aggregate family resources, thus reinforcing their unequal distribution within the family, and women's dependent position within it. Tax relief also favours the higher income earner, usually the man. By making financial resources either through social assistance or family allowances, or both, available to women, the state has a potentially liberating impact by reducing women's direct dependency on the men with whom they form personal relationships. However, that same state reinforces women's dependency on men by forcing them to seek maintenance from the fathers of their children, even in cases where the women concerned oppose this, or where the men cannot afford to pay.

This chapter examines family policies in America, Canada, Britain, Sweden, the Soviet Union, and China, and considers the extent to which family policies further the interests of women as women. This means looking at the way in which the state intervenes in their lives to affect both the work they undertake in the home and that which they perform in the labour market.

FAMILY POLICIES IN CAPITALIST COUNTRIES

American family policy

Academics such as Kamerman and Kahn (1978) argue there is no family policy in America. However, they admit that there are 'family relevant' policies having an impact on the family, for example education and housing. I argue against this view and suggest that while there is no systematic or formally acknowledged family policy, there are a number of federal and local state initiatives which operate on the assumption that American society is made up of white, middle-class heterosexual nuclear families, and, as Sidel (1986) reveals, establish women firmly in the position of being dependent on family obligations and networks for legitimating their social role and providing their economic security.

American family policy is based on the presumption that the two parent family with an economically active father and non-economically active mother and children predominates. It also assumes that parents provide for children and children look after parents. This familialist ideology limits fathering to a financial transaction instead of a caring relationship sustained through social interaction between fathers and children. It also discriminates against women and forms the basis of the sexism permeating family policy. Familialist ideology also discriminates against other family forms and stigmatises them for being 'abnormal', that is, deviating from the prescribed norm (Sidel, 1986). Family forms deviating from the norm are deemed pathological and incapable of fulfilling their responsibilities, especially towards children. This pejorative labelling can apply to families simply because they are poor. These may find their children taken away from them because they are considered unable to provide the 'correct' socialisation (Sidel, 1986).

Yet, the two parent family is not the norm. Declining fertility rates mean many couples have no children, and when they do, have fewer of them. The largest American household type is the one person household: 14–32 year olds and retired people who form 20 per cent of all households. The growing number of female headed single parent families has meant that one in eight families (7.2 million in 1975) fall into this category. The proportion of women heading single parent families is higher among black people. Also, the rising divorce rate is increasing the proportion of single parent women. In 1975, divorces reached one million per year. While relationship breakup has freed men of parental responsibilities, it has reinforced them for women in straitened financial circumstances and with fewer emotional supports. Weitzman (1985), reveals that women's and children's income drops by 73 per cent after divorce while the man's rises by 42 per cent. Although some men withhold maintenance payments for children as part of a power struggle with their former partners, the inadequacy of the male wage prevents fathers from supporting children from a previous relationship when they embark on another. Their new found freedom makes it easier for men to form other relationships, while heavier parental responsibilities severely curtail women's options. The postponement of marriage to later years has also resulted in a declining number of marriages, down to two million per year in 1975.

Inadequate male wages and unemployment among men have forced women to join the paid labour force. Moreover, women have a 'dual career', a domestic one and another in waged labour. Waged work frees women from relying on male breadwinners. In 1975, 40 per cent of women were in waged work, and 52 per cent of them had children. In that year, poverty was the lot of the twenty-six million Americans living in families with an annual income under $5,000. This figure would be higher if women did not work. The situation is even more dire for black women. They have to go out to work because 46 per cent of black men of working age are unemployed (Yu, 1984). However, women earn only 65 per cent of men's wages, so poverty is a greater risk for women than for men even when they are working (Doless et al., 1987).

Sexism in American family policy operates through three elements:

1. Social control operating through women's nurturing role. Women are expected to provide free caring to their families: a role which pushes them into the reserve army of labour doing low paid work.
2. Women's dependency. Men have the main breadwinner and property holder roles, thereby encouraging women's dependency on men.
3. Income aggregation. The income of married and cohabiting couples is aggregated to reinforce dependency and obligations among 'family' members.

Family policy initiatives through which the state plays a major part in controlling women, circumscribing their behaviour and locking them firmly within 'the' family are:

1. Provisions regarding women's fertility and sexuality.
2. Aid to Families with Dependent Children (AFDC).
3. Day-care provisions.
4. Provisions for older people.

These initiatives are familialist because they reinforce women's role as nurturer and men's role as provider. Asserting men's role as provider has become a hot political issue with regards to maintenance payments for children. Aggregating family income means that men and the state tend to treat child maintenance as women's income. The American state, like its British and Canadian counterparts, has taken steps to enforce court ordered maintenance orders. A law enacted in 1984 authorised withholding wages for maintenance payments from 1 October 1985. The state's motives in this area are to reduce welfare expenditures to single parent families by compelling fathers to provide for their children. This strategy is not in women's best interests for it forces them to have contact with men they want out of their lives. Despite more draconian measures, maintenance orders remain notoriously difficult to enforce. In 1989, a desperate federal government undermined civil liberties and privacy by checking the personnel records of 11.6 million people on the federal payroll against a national list of 2.1 million parents defaulting on child support payments. This computer cross-matching came up with 64,000 'hits' – but only by bending a federal privacy law (Calamai, 1989).

American insistence on the privacy of the family and the state's non-interventionist role in its affairs has had major implications for women. One is keeping women's dependent position hidden, thereby mystifying their subordination. Another is exacerbating women's dependency by ensuring that women: are the major group affected by poverty; bear the burden of the public expenditure cuts in welfare; and hold responsibility for the care of others, especially children, older relatives, and male partners. Also, there are strong links between welfare provisions and the taxation system. Men benefit from the assumption that income is equally distributed among family members. Privacy is evoked to ensure that people do not ask questions to discover its veracity. The state is selective in exercising its options over family privacy. The welfare state has not resisted prying into 'private' family affairs and investigates every aspect of poor women's lives if they require social assistance. AFDC's 'man about the house rule' was central to enforcing the state's definition of 'morality' and dependency on men among women claimants. But 'privacy' is respected when it comes to police refusal to protect women from abusive partners (Gordon, 1977). Abused children fare no better. Fear of invading family privacy keeps them locked in abusive relationships (Armstrong, 1988).

Like the cohabitation rule in Britain, the 'man about the house' rule furthers sexism within American family policy. The presence of a man forces women into dependency. However, women face a contradiction here. Since 1950 when women received an income for children and themselves when the man was not there, women have had an income under their own control via the state, and thus potentially 'liberating' for them.

Additionally, women's employment in the welfare state is gendered and racially structured. Waged work in the welfare state offers neither black nor white women a liberating experience, although it provides them with financial independence through the wage (Sidel, 1986). But this is limited as their wages are low. Moreover, caring responsibilities remain all theirs. Women welfare workers also intervene to control other women and enforce conformity and domesticity upon them, for example social workers.

There are five major avenues through which American family policy reinforces racism and works to the detriment of black people:

1. Poverty is three times more likely to affect black people than white. The 'man about the house' rule has been levied most often against black families excluding them from benefit despite high unemployment rates in black communities and substantially increased the number of black women heading single parent families in poverty.

2. Overtly racist ideologies being brought to bear on black families. AFDC's eligibility tests of 'moral fitness' and 'suitable homes' have been applied more harshly against black people who were deemed more immoral and feckless than whites.

3. The one year residency requirement for AFDC operates against the interests of black people migrating to the North and West searching for work.

4. Overtly racist practices have deprived black people of benefits legitimately theirs. For example, black people were given lower benefit levels than whites because white administrators believed black people would misuse unearned money. Also, AFDC was withdrawn from black recipients in the South when white farmers and landowners wanted black workers to harvest their cotton for low wages.

5. Racist fears about black people's fertility led to birth control, sterilisation and abortions being forced upon black women (Champagne and Harpham, 1984).

I will now examine how family policies reinforce women's subordinate position by examining the specific provisions regarding women's fertility and sexuality, AFDC, day-care, and older people.

CONTROL OF WOMEN'S FERTILITY AND SEXUALITY

Although motherhood is strongly supported by American ideology, supportive state provisions are lacking. For example, there are no family allowances in the United States. American women have difficulty obtaining medical insurance coverage for pregnancy. Women got the right to have sick-leave benefits to give birth in 1978. This concession is problematic as pregnancy is not an illness, but a 'normal' event for women (Savage and Leighton, 1986). Additionally, maternity leave remains unacknowledged in welfare provisions.

Women's fertility has also been strictly controlled. The Comstock Law prevented the transportation of contraceptives across state lines until 1965. Only married women could legally obtain contraceptives until 1972. Birth control was a private matter until 1965 when family planning was approved for welfare clients; provisions were enacted in 1967. Abortion became legally available in some states in 1973 following the Supreme Court decision in *Roe v. Wade*. Attempts to undermine this decision have been a feature of the political landscape since then. The Hyde Amendment passed by Congress in 1977 has made it possible for women to be refused Medicaid payments reimbursing them for abortions. By 1985, only fourteen states and the District of Columbia had not exercised this option. This has led to an increase in backstreet abortions and unwanted pregnancies being carried full-term by poor women (Sidel, 1986). Reagan's budgetary cuts severely curtailed family planning expenditure reducing it from $183.4 million in 1981 to $124 million in 1982 (Sidel, 1986). Only modest increases have occurred since then.

These cuts bolstered the New Right's attempts to reinforce traditional nuclear family morality and seriously set back feminist gains in women's reproductive rights for low income women most reliant on state provisions. Teenagers' access to contraceptive devices was threatened in 1983 when Reagan demanded medical authorities notify parents when their children received such aids. This resembled the Gillick ruling in Britain in 1985. Reagan's proposal was withdrawn after widespread protest. Preventing women from having access to abortion and contraceptive devices applied mainly to white women. Black women were often forced to have unwanted abortions and sterilisation as part of a eugenicist and racist concern with restricting their fertility. Enforced sterilisation affected mainly poor black women on welfare receiving medical care in publicly funded hospitals (Sidel, 1986), and gave institutional respectability to racist practices. Sterilisation abuse was made a public issue by the Committee to End Sterilisation Abuse which demanded a halt to it in America and world-wide as American aid was financing compulsory sterilisation programmes in the Third World (Sidel, 1986; Davis, 1989).

Following the recent defeat of the Equal Rights Amendment, the acceptability of sex-role stereotyping and the curtailment of women's independent rights has increased. Consequently, the ideological attack on women's reproductive rights has reached unprecedented heights. Through the efforts of conservative women like Phyllis Schlafly (Ruth, 1989), the New Right has whittled away hard won feminist gains in this arena. Feminism itself has become a dirty word associated with women over-reaching themselves and bringing havoc and destruction upon the family. The New Right claims women have won too much freedom and it is time to draw in the reins. Extreme rightwingers have resorted to physical intimidation including shooting women and blockading clinics as well as legal coercion to compel women to carry unwanted foetuses, making controlling women's reproductive capacities a battleground for this ideological struggle.

The New Right has scored another victory in the recent Webster decision giving local states the power to impose conditions on legally available abortions. The seriousness of the New Right attack has galvanised Pro-Choice women who have sought to make abortion an election issue by asking all candidates to state their position on it. Pro-Choice women also demonstrated in Washington, DC in November 1989 to keep the issue on the political agenda. Their activities have already influenced the outcome of several state elections. Meanwhile, Pennsylvania, a staunch anti-abortion state, was among the first to approve restrictions on abortions following the US Supreme Court decision authorising this on 3 July 1989. Tougher measures enacted on 14 November 1989 required spousal notification of abortion, a twenty-four hour waiting period before an abortion could be performed and a twenty-four week limit unless the mother would be injured by going ahead with the pregnancy. Sadly for women wishing to make their own decisions in this matter, pro-abortion advocates failed to amend this legislation (Reuter, 1989).

The debate over women's reproductive rights has also fractured the Left. Some leftwingers calling themselves the Pro-Family Left have created organisations to promote their views, for example Friends of Families. These groups have channelled their energies into arguing for state support for the traditional white heterosexual, two-parent family, on the grounds that public provisions, such as parental leave, would stop the family being an oppressive private institution (Lerner, Zoloth and Riles, 1982). This position has been strongly criticised by white feminists for reinforcing the sexist division of labour and endorsing the view that family issues are private matters (Epstein and Ellis, 1983). The position adopted by the Pro-Family Left ignores the diversity of family forms and reinforces the deviant labelling of 'families' other than white heterosexual nuclear ones.

STATE AID TO FAMILIES WITH DEPENDENT CHILDREN

Aid to Families with Dependent Children (AFDC) was not the first programme to help poor families. The Mother's Pension Movement sought public aid for women with children to reduce child poverty and prevent children going into institutional care. However, this movement was unable to overcome opposition demands that public money should neither go to unworthy women, nor relieve fathers of their responsibility to financially support their children. Consequently, states enacting Mother's Pensions were influenced by these criteria and inserted a strong element of social control aimed at ensuring conformity with dominant behavioural norms into the programme. Illinois was first to authorise Mother's Pensions in 1911. By 1913, twenty other states had followed suit. The movement peaked in 1921 when forty states had similar schemes (Costin and Rapp, 1984). Widows, considered a worthy group, made up 82 per cent of the recipients of Mother's Pensions. Of these, 96 per cent were white, the racial group considered the most worthy. Unmarried mothers were castigated and weeded out on the grounds of undeservability as they were thought unfit to raise children (Costin and Rapp, 1984).

The AFDC programme has become the euphemism for welfare (Sidel, 1986). Initially launched under Title IV of the Social Security Act in 1938, it was called Aid to Dependent Children and covered primarily children of widowed women and legitimated their position as the deserving poor. Its concern with controlling women to ensure they behaved in 'acceptable' ways was part of its initial remit. At that time, 61 per cent of claimants were widows. In 1950, Congress added a caretaker grant and renamed the programme, Aid to Families with Dependent Children (AFDC). This enabled adults to be included, but only the one living with the children, usually the mother. Even unemployed fathers were excluded. The 'man about the house rule' prevented couples from claiming AFDC, regardless of their income or employment status, forcing men, especially black men, to leave their families (Sidel, 1986). Campaigns led by women, particularly black activists, attacked this rule for its disruptive influence on family life. Consequently, the rule was relaxed slightly in 1962 to enable unemployed fathers to remain with families claiming AFDC. However, there still are thirty-eight states disallowing AFDC benefits to two parent households. Despite these changes, the ideology of the man providing financial security for 'his' family shines through. The state only steps in when this breaks down for reasons outside of the man's control.

In 1980, there were 3.8 million families or eleven million people on AFDC. Of these, seven million were children, half of whom were under 8 years of age. Separation and divorce and the subsequent decline in family income account for 45 per cent of children on AFDC (Sidel, 1986). Child poverty is therefore a serious issue in America. AFDC cost $12.46 billion, or 1 per cent of the federal budget and stood as the largest public assistance programme. Providing assistance to one family in fifteen, it covered only the very needy – mainly single parent families headed by women. These made up 80 per cent of those on AFDC (Sidel,

1986). The fact that it is mainly women single parent families relying on such assistance reflects women's position as the poorest group in American society. Moreover, poverty afflicts black women to a disproportionately greater extent than white women. In 1980, 51.8 per cent of AFDC families were white, 43.7 per cent were black, 1.4 per cent were American Indians. Notwithstanding their recourse to AFDC, 54 per cent of female headed single parents were in low-paying, low status, part-time jobs. Single parent women are pushed into waged work because benefit levels are so low. Thus, AFDC bolsters the American low wages structure. Women's wages are also low because family commitments prevent their working full-time. This contributes to the difference in median earnings between men and women. In 1975, women earned $7,500 compared with men's $12,760.

Additionally, benefit levels vary considerably between different states. For example, benefits for a family in Mississippi were $60 compared with $433 in Oregon. This meant benefit levels were inequitable, but also not based on need. As the 10th Amendment to the American Constitution makes family matters a state responsibility, benefit rates are set locally in accordance with the local labour market and wage demands. Challenges to this situation can only occur through the Supreme Court via the 14th Amendment. AFDC's requirements encourage migration and relationship instability – a point Reagan used to his advantage in cutting welfare expenditure. Instead of seeking structural causes such as low benefit levels, inadequate childcare provisions, poor people's reliance on the low wages sector of the labour market for work, and the 'man about the house' rule for the problems experienced by families on AFDC, Reagan and the 'New Right' argued that AFDC discouraged claimants from working and increased their dependency on the welfare state (Glazer, 1988). Reagan's solution to the problem was to reinforce work discipline by cutting benefit levels and restricting entitlement conditions, thereby trying to support the 'normal', that is white middle class heterosexual nuclear, families.

The Reagan administration targeted AFDC, already serving the needy, for cuts aimed at ensuring only the *most* needy received benefits. The Omnibus Budget Reconciliation Act reduced the $7 billion federal AFDC budget by $1 billion. This was matched by a further cut of $1 billion off the state budgets. Combined with other cost-cutting measures, this led to dramatic reductions in the number of welfare claimants. For example, in Massachusetts, the AFDC caseload dropped from 124,000 in 1980 to 92,000 by 1982. The numbers had been projected to increase to 140,000 in 1983. Nationally, 750,000 families were thought to have lost AFDC benefits (Sidel, 1986, p. 86). The situation got worse as a further $85 million was slashed off the federal budget in 1983 through the Tax Equity and Fiscal Responsibility Act of 1982. These cuts were being instituted at the same time that family poverty, particularly among women headed single-parent families was rising (Sidel, 1986) and exacerbated child poverty.

Besides the financial cuts on AFDC budgets, the Reagan administration introduced a series of mandatory and optional measures intended to further restrict the numbers on the AFDC rolls. The mandatory measures introduced during 1982 included: lowering the level of eligibility; changing the calculations concerning the income of working parents; including a step-parent's income in eligibility calculations whether this income went to the child or not; refusing AFDC assistance to first time pregnant women until their sixth month of pregnancy; tightening the eligibility regulations for 18 to 21 year olds; and calculating payment on a retroactive basis. The optional measures came into operation in 1981 and enabled states to include the value of food stamps and housing subsidies in determining eligibility and benefit levels; require AFDC recipients to accept jobs in 'Workfare' programmes; and create other work programmes for claimants. These changes seriously aggravated the position of the working poor and the unemployed; tied AFDC more strongly into supporting labour discipline and low wages; reinforced the stigmatised nature of the programme; and denied previous AFDC claimants access to other benefits including Medicaid, food stamps; and punished women and children – the major victims of poverty (Sidel, 1986).

Reagan's changes caused the number of poor families receiving AFDC to drop from 88 per cent in 1979 to 62.9 per cent in 1983. The position of poor children was more grave for while 83.6 per cent of them received AFDC in 1973, only 53.3 per cent did so by 1983. AFDC has a limited impact on mitigating poverty among its recipients. In 1983, only 4 per cent of poor families crossed the poverty threshold after receiving AFDC monies (CDB, 1984). Moreover, the relative position of those on AFDC has worsened. While AFDC previously covered 63 per cent of the poverty threshold for a family of four, this had dropped to 43 per cent by 1985 (Sidel, 1986). AFDC does not provide sufficient funds for families to meet basic needs. Many poor families survive only by drawing on a network of relatives and friends who can help them extend their meagre resources. Often these supportive networks are themselves stretched to the limit as they exist within a community that is itself materially poor (Stack, 1975).

Aid to Families with Dependent Children directly controls women by monitoring their mothering capacities. This role was strengthened in 1956 when poor families had to accept casework intervention for eligibility to AFDC. Besides increasing the state's surveillance of and interference in poor women's lives, the caseworker felt obliged to enforce nuclear family morality. Women had to prove their conduct constituted 'moral behaviour' and their homes 'suitably run' for their cases to be considered sympathetically. 'Illicit liaisons' provided grounds for refusing aid. 'Race' and class were important factors in the exercise of this control. The belief in the privacy of the family applied mainly to middle class families and 'respectable' working class families who did not have recourse to state aid. Poor women asking for assistance found this principle invariably breached as every aspect of their lives was investig-ated in detail. Racism was also a factor in so far as black people were disproportionately represented among the poor and AFDC recipients. In addition, black life-styles were more likely to be considered 'abnormal' for not meeting middle class standards. The 'man about the house rule' and the 'illicit liaisons' criteria were applied more stringently against black women living on their own.

These punitive aspects of AFDC were liberalised as part of the 'welfare explosion', when claimants demanded the 'right to welfare'. However, this 'right' did not extend to families of the working poor, for unlike Britain's Family Income Supplement (now Family Credit), working fathers were not entitled to AFDC. Nonetheless, liberalising AFDC trebled the number of recipients between 1960 and 1973. The 'New Right' maintained this increase signalled the abuse of the system by people too lazy to work and provide for themselves. They had become dependent on the system. Duncan (1984) found claims about welfare dependency exaggerated for although 25 per cent of Americans rely on social assistance at some point in their lives, this was mainly a temporary state in overcoming a crisis and gaining a 'new foothold in security' usually in the form of employment or marriage. Others used the welfare system to supplement low wages. Only 4.4 per cent of all Americans or 20 per cent of those on welfare, were chronically dependent on the system (Duncan, 1984, p. 91).

The backlash to liberalisation came as conservatives tried to stop this alleged 'abuse'. In 1967, the Work Incentive Programme forced AFDC recipients, mainly women, to work for their keep by providing them with training, day care facilities and low paid jobs. Claimants could lose their benefits if they refused 'suitable work' as defined by the state. The Work Incentive Programme was an early form of 'Workfare' which failed to provide either adequate training or childcare provisions, thereby suggesting that women's proper role was in the family looking after the children while men worked to support them. Additionally, the jobs available to women through the programme failed to transcend racial and gender discrimination. Women were given low paid, part-time work with little prospect of either career advancement or getting out of poverty. Nixon's Family Assistance Plan aimed to draw working poor fathers into the welfare net, reduce family breakdown for the 'working' poor and encourage all able-bodied claimants to obtain work. His plans, had they succeeded, would have shifted the benefit system in favour of *white men* (Sidel, 1986).

A further attempt to liberalise AFDC by increasing coverage to include two parent families was defeated in 1971. In 1976, Ford tightened the eligibility rules to cut down the numbers on AFDC. Carter hoped to carry this further through the Programme for Better Jobs which sought to tighten labour discipline by forcing as many AFDC claimants as possible to work, and keep families together by allowing two parent families to claim benefit. The Programme for Better Jobs also suggested a national uniform minimum payment and was opposed by conservative politicians. Progressive people rejected it as a measure seeking to reform welfare without eliminating poverty. Congress turned it down.

The ground for undermining AFDC had been laid long before Reagan, though he hastened to build on it. In 1981, Reagan tried placating rightwing middle class opinion by limiting welfare to the *truly needy* by compelling all 'fit persons' to work. Only women with children under 6 were exempted. He also encouraged states to develop stigmatised 'Workfare' programmes whereby people were discouraged from claiming and repaying benefits if they did. By 1982–3, Reagan's cuts included slashing training provisions under the Work Incentive Programme. Reagan wanted to repeal AFDC as a federal programme and let states choose whether or not to continue it. However, this proposal was rejected. Nevertheless, Reagan successfully resisted income guarantees for the poor whom he insisted should work for their assistance. Aid, he maintained, should only be available as a *temporary* safety-net to prevent working people from providing for non-working people, or 'scroungers' as he saw them on a permanent basis. Reagan adopted this line because although benefit levels for those on AFDC were below the poverty line, they provided 'welfare mothers' with higher incomes than that earned by women working in poorly paid jobs. Arguing in these terms enabled Reaganites to define the problem needing to be addressed as one of 'high' benefits, not low wages or individuals' *right to welfare* to maximise their development and growth.

The American government generally resists involvement in day care provisions. However, the federal government has been instrumental in providing day care initiatives for children in response to:

1. Poverty in urban areas.

2. National emergencies, for example the Second World War.
3. The need to ensure the 'acceptable' socialisation of children.

American day care provisions were initially provided by churches, settlement houses and voluntary agencies as a service to the poor. The first day nursery opened in New York City in 1854 and was called the Nursery for Children of Poor Women. These public nurseries served 'problem families' and prevented poor children from being taken into care (Sidel, 1986, p. 118). Their formation on this basis gave rise to the stigmatised view of public provisions which continues today. Nursery schools were created by middle class parents to provide children with an 'early education experience' and to give mothers leisure time (Sidel, 1986, p. 118). These established another sector of day care present today, but without the stigma attached to government sponsored facilities. The first major state intervention occurred in the 1930s when Roosevelt provided 40,000 day care places under the New Deal. Staffed by people drawn from the relief rolls, these provided high quality care. The Community Facilities (Lanham) Act of 1941 provided for 1.5 million publicly funded places for women working in the munitions factories during the Second World War as part of a strategy of encouraging women into waged work (Adams and Winston, 1980). Yet even this effort met only 40 per cent of need (Sidel, 1986). These facilities were closed after the war when men resumed their roles in the labour force. Women were encouraged to remain at home despite evidence showing that increasing numbers of families required women's wages.

Concern that poor parents neither worked nor prepared their children adequately for school prompted the government to define day care as a public child welfare service under the Social Security Act of 1962. This ensured that day care remained identified as a service for poor families with social problems. In 1967, day care was tied to the Work Incentive Programme, reinforcing its status as a welfare measure. The state covered 75 per cent of the childcare costs borne by women on the programme if they accepted jobs or training opportunities. By 1970, 638,000 places had received such funding. In the late 1960s, the government also initiated 'Headstart', a programme providing disadvant-aged poor black children with educational opportunities and day care. Though educational in their orientation, 'Headstart's' 400,000 places were stigmatised by being for poor blacks and signalled the patholo-gising of black families' childrearing capacities. The government's interest in ensuring poor parents did not fight shy of the work ethic was evident in both 'Headstart' and the Work Incentive Programme.

These measures provided insufficient facilities. More than one million extra places were necessary to meet demand from AFDC pre-school children alone. Ironically, public day care centres provided higher quality care than private ones because the government regulated and enforced standards through licensing and local state registration procedures (Adams and Winston, 1980). However, conservative politicians aiming to cut state subsidies for childcare argued that public facilities were too expensive for the government to maintain. In 1971, Nixon vetoed the Comprehensive Child Care Act on these grounds. Yet, he was willing to support tax relief for day care, a benefit enjoyed by wealthy parents, through the 1976 Tax Reform Act. Public day care provisions continued being severely cut under Reagan. For example, the largest federal day care programme under Title xx of the Social Security Act was cut by 21 per cent between 1980 and 1983 resulting in fewer public provisions by 1983 (Sidel, 1986). These cuts primarily affected poor families headed by women who 'work out of economic necessity' (CDB, 1985) and the working poor who lost out when eligibility requirements were tightened. The quality of day care was reduced when Reagan's 1985 budget cut federal monies for training day care staff. Private companies are moving into the day care arena with workplace provisions. This development may exacerbate the divide between stigmatised public provisions and high quality private ones available to those working for wealthier firms. Yet, unless free, unstigmatised, high quality day care meeting the needs of working people and children becomes publicly available, women cannot climb out of poverty through waged labour.

PROVISIONS FOR OLDER WOMEN

Women predominate among senior citizens. But few provisions are available to them: 60 per cent of older women and 80 per cent of older men live with and are cared for by their families, especially women relatives (Doress and Siegal, 1987). Carers of older women are a particularly exploited group. They can be women with paid employment commitments and families of their own to look after with little state support (Sidel, 1986). A significant proportion of older people (15 per cent), especially women and black people, live below the poverty line. On a gender basis, 15.6 per cent of older women are poor compared to 8.6 per cent of older men. Also, 34.8 per cent of older black women are poor. Pensions acquired through social security legislation are below the poverty line. Yet, 90 per cent of older women rely on them (Doress and Siegal, 1987).

Social security pensions based on one's employment record reinforce gender inequality. This disadvantages women who interrupt their waged employment to care for children and elder relatives, and reinforces income inequality already present in the low wages women earn in paid work. Women earning substantially less than their husbands may find that they receive higher benefits as dependants of spouses than in their own right. If they elect dependency status, they lose all claims to their own pension (Doress and Siegal, 1987). Private pension schemes for those who can afford them, also reflect women's disadvantaged position in the labour market. Private pensions purchased by women are lower than men's because of their lower earnings. Private schemes also assume women are dependent on men who will provide for them on retirement and after their death. But benefits are not paid to women if their partners die before reaching retirement age (Sidel, 1986). Only 20 per cent of women received dependant's pensions. This situation was improved somewhat by the 1984 Retirement Equity Act, a law which also prevented men from electing to exclude women from receiving a dependant's pension. Age based inequalities exist despite the Age Discrimination in Employment Act enacted in 1967 and the abolition of mandatory retirement in 1986 (Doress and Siegal, 1987).

Older people have formed pressure groups to secure government intervention in their favour. The Townsendites mobilised older people in the 1930s and succeeded in having pensions included in the 'New Deal'. The Gray Panthers, organised by Maggie Kuhn in the 1970s, successfully challenged legally fixed retirement ages. In 1974, the government enacted the uniform minimum cash benefit in the Supplemental Security Income Programme as a means-tested supplementary income for old disabled people. Its implementation doubled the number of recipients, 75 per cent of which are women. Medicare was also introduced to cater for the health needs of older people. Medicare covers only 44 per cent of their health costs (Sidel, 1986). Older women make up the difference by economising on heat and food, which creates additional health problems. All these programmes have been seriously affected by public expenditure cuts. Older people remain a socially isolated group whose care remains firmly within the family – another example of family policy by default.

America's demographic crisis is relevant to the care of older people whose increasing numbers the government fears will impose an intolerable financial burden on public resources. It has sought to limit its liability in financing their care by encouraging people to purchase private pension schemes and be looked after in the community, thereby defining elders as a problem to be shifted elsewhere. This stance attacks their dignity as human beings with full rights and devalues them. The government does not include the care women already provide freely in the nation's ledgers. Yet, this is where the bulk of the care occurs. Its stance also fails to deal with the issue of those whose earnings prohibit their buying schemes in the market. Women, black people, and the unwaged are most affected by this. Phillipson (1982) argues that elders are discriminated against in capitalist societies because they are not engaged in social production. Nett (1982) maintains gender itself is a significant factor in ageism – women are considered unproductive whatever they do. Women forming the majority of older people provides the rationale for their shabby treatment. Their failure to provide for themselves is taken as proof of their inadequacy not of their low income as wage-earners or their dependent status in the family. Viewing women as inadequate also deprecates women's role in challenging popular misconceptions of themselves as they have done by organising in the Gray Panthers and Older Women's League. Additionally, demography can strengthen women's power of mobilisation through the substantial electoral influence and purchasing power they hold.

IN CONCLUSION

Family policy exists in the United States. Its impact varies according to the type of family encountered and operates to the detriment of family forms not conforming to the white heterosexual nuclear one. Women fare badly throughout their lifecycle as poverty is more likely to structure their lives than men's. However, social policy does not address this issue. Some welfare policies, for example AFDC, contribute directly towards it by providing benefits which force women to either enter low waged employment or depend on men. The quality of family life may also be adversely affected by inappropriate family policies. AFDC, the absence of day care and inadequate provisions for older people all play a role in diminishing the quality of interpersonal relationships. Men lose out the opportunity to develop full fathering roles; women lose their right to self-development; children are commodities whose futures are determined by those on whom they directly depend; and older people have enforced dependency foisted upon them. Changing this state of affairs requires the development of policies which place children, women and men first.

Canadian family policy

Canada does not have a formal family policy. Like Britain and the United States, it has one made up of *ad hoc* measures having an important impact on families and their members. Canadian family policy has been shaped by a number of economic, ideological, political, and constitutional factors. Income inequality, a major feature of the Canadian social landscape, foists financial difficulties on working class men and women. The bottom 20 per cent of the population earns 4 per cent of Canadian income while the top 20 per cent receives 42 per cent of it. Men do not earn enough money to provide families with a decent standard of living, making two earner families necessary to guarantee a reasonable lifestyle. In 1975, 9 per cent of Canadian families were poor. Had women not worked, this figure would have risen to 14 per cent. Women located on the bottom rungs of the labour hierarchy earn approximately one-third to one-half less income than men (Armstrong, 1984).

Women's earnings alone are generally unable to sustain a comfortable standard of living for their dependants. Consequently, women headed single parent families constitute a large proportion of the working poor. Older women and women with children constitute the poorest social groups. Low family incomes compel women to work. In 1981, 54 per cent of women with children under 16 worked. Despite their entry into the labour market in significant numbers, the sexist division of labour remains intact (Armstrong, 1984). Waged working women continue doing most of the housework, making the 'dual career' burden familiar to Canadian women. State finances have an important economic bearing on the development of income support for families with children. The vicissitudes of the economy have both advanced this cause and detracted from it. Family allowances in Canada were introduced during a period of relative economic prosperity. Cuts were introduced in a package of austerity measures.

On the ideological level, the white heterosexual nuclear family is dominant and provides the standard by which all other family forms are judged. Family forms not complying with this stereotype are viewed negatively (Eichler, 1983). The aggregation of family resources is taken for granted, thereby disadvantaging women and children whose shares of family resources are substantially lower than men's. The two parent family is less dominant than familialist ideology suggests. Divorce is high, affecting one in three marriages, although remarriage levels are also high. Until the 1968 Divorce Act, a woman's domicile was that of her husband. If he deserted her and did not leave a forwarding address, the woman would be unable to file for divorce. The 1968 Divorce Act also changed the grounds for divorce to marital breakdown having a three year waiting period or desertion requiring a five year interregnum. Additionally, the Canadian birth rate is falling, as women, particularly white women, have smaller families. The government has sought to alleviate this through immigration policies. Third World women have been drafted in to solve Canada's depopulation crisis.

STATE AID FOR CHILDREN

Politically, the feminist movement was important in initiating policies benefiting women and children. The Mothers Pension movement was an early example of this. The rapid growth of female headed single parent families in the form of war widows left by men who died in the First

World War highlighted family poverty and gave feminist demands for a Mothers Pension new meaning. The physical loss of the family breadwinner justified the classification of these women as 'deserving' poor, and facilitated public acceptance of their receiving a state allowance as a right.

The Mothers Pension Movement incorporated feminist concerns between 1910 and 1920 (see Strong-Boag, 1979). It established pensions, not allowances, as a right for women caring for dependent children. It also provided an institutionally guaranteed payment to women without other sources of income, eliminated their stigmatised treatment as clients, broke the direct economic link of dependency on the children's father, and gave social recognition to the work women did as carers (Strong-Boag, 1979). Predicated on women's mothering role, Mothers Pensions reaffirmed the sexual division of labour in which women nurture others. Mothers Pensions were introduced on a patchy basis across the country over a period of years, for example Manitoba in 1916, British Columbia in 1920. Economic exigencies and political forces drove the state into withdrawing this particular form of assistance to women. As the Mothers Pension Movement lost impetus, public hostility and government spending cuts during the Great Depression ended it.

Resistance to Mothers Pensions was generated in a variety of quarters opposing women's unfettered access to state funds – business interests, the organised labour movement, and social work professionals. In 1929, the Trades and Labour Congress pitted men's interests against those of women and children by demanding the abolition of Mothers Pensions on the grounds that men should be providing for their families (Strong-Boag, 1979). Social workers led by Charlotte Whitton opposed unstigmatised state aid to women and demanded that provisions did not undermine the morality of the patriarchal family (Guest, 1980). Whitton suggested casework to ensure women claimants followed righteous paths. And, as the logic of the market reasserted itself, stigmatised provisions replaced Mothers Pension, marginalising once again the value of women's contribution in caring for children.

Feminists continued agitating in favour of women's freedom from financial dependency on men by demanding family allowances. Low wage rates for men and women supported their arguments that inadequate wages caused family poverty. Pronatalists favoured feminists' stance because they thought family allowances could potentially stem Canada's declining birth rate. However, the Canadian Trades and Labour Congress came out against family allowances in 1929 because it feared employers would reduce wage rates by including these in their wage calculations. Family allowances were ideologically suspect in different quarters. For the Congress, they undermined the 'family wage'. For black people, they furthered eugenist aims and objectives. Ultimately, family allowances reinforced women's role as children's prime caregivers.

The Marsh Report of 1942, a milestone in Canadian welfare history, recommended the development of family allowances based on the number of dependent children. Concerned with eliminating family poverty caused by family size, this suggestion did not challenge patriarchy. It continued to assume the dependency of women and children within a male-headed household. Family allowances endorsed the aggregation of family incomes and reinforced women's position as carers within the family. Opposition to Marsh's proposals was considerable. The male dominated trade union movement voiced anew its fears that family allowances would reduce male wages by being incorporated into family income. Social workers rejected these proposals because they could undermine family stability. However, public concern over high infant mortality rates and poor nutritional standards among the working poor coupled with parliamentary pressure on behalf of the poor through the Co-operative Commonwealth Federation forced the government to act. The government finally agreed to fund families with children through family allowances because this targeted help on those needing it.

The Liberal government passed the Family Allowances Act of 1944. Allowances were granted on a sliding scale which decreased after the fourth child. Benefits were low. This suggests the scheme was more window dressing than a substantial attempt at reducing poverty for families with dependent children. French Canadians criticised its racial implications because they constituted the group most affected by the provisions penalising larger families. The organised working class opposition to family allowances seemed vindicated for employers continued paying low wages on the grounds that families were now receiving the extra income they required. The major significance of family allowances was that it introduced the first universal welfare programme in Canada and required a substantial financial input from the federal government. This made recipients claimants, not suppliants. Moreover, family allowances were paid to women, thereby giving women an income independent from their male partners. But, this was an income received by women in their role as mothers. It was for their children, not for themselves. Thus, it reinforced a sexist division of labour in which women were the primary caregivers. And, it continued to deny women an income acknowledging the work they were doing at home.

The popularity of family allowances was indicated by the high rate of take up – 92 per cent of children under 16 were covered by 1946. In 1964, family allowances were extended to include 18 year olds. This recognised the longer period of dependency youths have if they continue their education and contributed to families supporting their 'adult' children in staying out of the labour market.

Despite such intervention, the Report of the Royal Commission on the Status of Women in Canada in 1970 and the Croll Report of 1971, highlighted increased poverty among women and children. By 1975, child poverty had reached critical levels – 69.1 per cent of children were poor. Declining earnings for women heading single parent families meant they achieved about 52 per cent of family incomes. However, the largest group of poor women were located in husband–wife families (Strong-Boag, 1979, p. 24).

Although the showpiece of universal provisions, attacks on family allowances during the 1970s undermined their universality. The Left criticised family allowances for advantaging middle class families by providing an untaxed component to their income. The Right demanded the curbing of government expenditure on universal provisions and the targeting of benefits on those in greatest need. Feminists called for financial independence for women through a guaranteed income for all individuals except single people under 40. The government's response to these critiques was to restructure family allowances towards residual forms of welfare by relating them to family income, taxing them, and making them more attractive to the working poor through a proposal called the Family Income Security Plan. This proposal was never implemented thanks to parliamentary opposition by the New Democratic Party (formerly the Co-operative Commonwealth Federation) and the return of a minority Liberal government in the 1972 election. The 1973 Family Allowances Act replacing the Family Income Security Plan made family allowances taxable and gave provincial governments flexibility in setting benefit levels. This arrangement suited Quebec because it provided scope for adapting family allowances to protect the interests of French Canadians.

The taxable nature of Family Allowances was mitigated by tax exemptions available for children. Tax exemptions, claimed by the highest income earner in the family, the man having access to better paid occupations in the labour market, operated more in men's favour than women's. Also, the 1973 Act made provisions for maintaining the value of family allowances during an inflationary period by index-linking them. It also extended coverage to 'adult' children of 25 if they continued in full-time education, thus recognising the prolonged dependency of young people on their parents. Paying family allowances directly to mothers, meant 'adult' children did not have direct access to an income which was ostensibly theirs. Calling children's allowances family allowances and paying them to mothers mystifies the dependent position women and children occupy in the family. Additionally, this enables the government to dodge the question of whether family allowances are part of family policy or income support. Their being a form of income support is undermined by the low levels of benefits for children.

At this point, state aid to families took the form of: family allowances available to all women and taxable, costing the exchequer $2 billion a year; a refundable child tax credit paid to poor mothers ($238 per child in 1981); a tax exemption for a dependent child, usually benefiting men earning high incomes, costing the Treasury $9 billion a year; and the childcare deduction for working mothers. The redistributive effect of family allowances was limited. Men who did not perform the caring work received more in tax exemptions than women received on behalf of their children through family allowances. Further reforms aimed to terminate full indexation in January 1983 and introduce partial indexation. The child tax credit would remain fully indexed and $50 per family added in 1983 to compensate low income families for reductions in family allowances. The tax exemption remained untouched. This reform failed to achieve its aims. Quebec and Manitoba refused to pass on the full tax credit to recipients, depriving over half a million low income families of it (Johnson, 1985).

In 1985, family allowances were partially de-indexed as part of a further round of cuts. More recently, they have also been made subject to clawback which is to be introduced gradually and completed by 1991. These two changes will quietly erode benefits. However, changes to the family benefits system may become more controversial if the threat to end the universal basis of family allowances is confirmed.

DAY CARE PROVISIONS

Day care provisions in Canada are inadequate and reflect the ideology that childcare is primarily a private issue handled within the family and women's incomes are secondary to family prosperity. As in America, the government has intervened to provide publicly funded day care when the needs of the nation have required it and to help children of the very poor. For example, the federal government funded day care services during the First World War when a labour shortage compelled women to work. These facilities were closed down with alacrity when men returned from the War, particularly in Ontario and Quebec. However, feminist protests in Ontario forced some to reopen. Government funding for day care was resumed in 1967 under the Canada Assistance Plan, to provide facilities under the welfare system for the very poor. These provisions were stigmatised. They were cut during the austerity measures of the

1970s. Rich people benefited through the 'hidden welfare' system with income tax deductions for childcare expenses. In 1981, 47.8 per cent of children under five were cared for by their parents, usually the mother; 22.3 per cent went to nursery schools and kindergartens, 5.8 per cent attended day care centres, 18.6 per cent were cared for in childminders' homes. The care of children takes place primarily in the private realm, by women working in isolation from each other. After school provisions for school age children follow a similar pattern: 70.9 per cent are looked after by their parents, usually the mother, 16.1 per cent are left on their own and 13.0 per cent are supervised by others.

Feminists have continually challenged this state of affairs. For example, the Coalition for Better Day Care in Ontario demanded free, publicly funded day care through the education department to avoid stigmatising social services provisions. In 1979, Action Day Care informed the government day care issues were the concern of *all* working people. It was supported by the New Democratic Party, the teachers' federation, and service sector unions in the Ontario Federation of Labour. In 1980, Saskatchewan's provincial government highlighted the scarcity of publicly funded day care provisions and revealed 93 per cent of the children in the province requiring day care could not have places. Nationally, the Department of Health and Welfare fuelled concerns being expressed by others by stating 50 per cent of day care centres provided poor quality care. These tactics had a limited impact on federal ministers.

Continued pressure from the parliamentary opposition, the childcare lobby, and feminist groups, forced the federal government to propose the National Child Care Strategy in 1988. However, the implementation of the Canada Child Care Act was halted by the 1988 federal election. Fiscal austerity prevented it being funded through the 1989 budget. This proposal indicated an important role for the private sector provisions. The government was prepared to finance this development through tax exemptions for parents and subsidies on operating costs for providers. Non-profit agencies and public facilities would be eligible for capital grants as well. Provisions under the Canada Child Care Act lacked the open-ended cost-sharing arrangements available under the Canada Assistance Plan. The proposed legislation had a variable formula benefiting poorer provinces. While giving the programme flexibility, this variability would have made it difficult for the federal government to enforce national standards, control quality, monitor facilities and their operation, and impose penalties on recalcitrant provinces and those with sloppy standards.

On these grounds, Banting (1989) suggests the Canada Child Care Act was more 'an intergovernmental transfer than an instrument of federal program design' and was in keeping with the federal government's intention of withdrawing from national welfare initiatives and giving provinces some of the powers envisaged in Meech Lake. In the process, regional disparities would have been exacerbated and market forces given a greater say. In refusing to implement the more universal aspects of the Canada Child Care Act, the government was prepared to finance affluent people's privileges in exercising choice through the market. Although public day care continues to be an area neglected by government, private providers are showing interest in the profits which can be made by providing places for working women. More and more mothers going out to work increases demands for facilities. However, the ability of women to fund other people's livelihood from their already inadequate income will limit the extent to which they can purchase private day care. Moreover, since the responsibility for securing it, paying for it and supervising its quality is theirs, day care reinforces women's subordinate status *vis-à-vis* the family and the welfare state.

CONTROLLING WOMEN'S SEXUALITY

Canadian women's reproductive rights are fragile. Provisions for pregnant working women are limited. Maternity pay is provided by the Unemployment Insurance Commission. Coverage is for sixteen weeks, but not on full wages. Moreover, women can lose their job, benefits and seniority during this time if their leave is prolonged. Motherhood is a risky business for women with controversy raging around their rights, those of the foetus and their male partners. Women's right to control their fertility remains to be won. Abortion was a criminal offence until 1969, when amendments to the Criminal Code authorised abortions for health reasons. A committee controlled by the hospital board and assisted by doctors determined eligibility to abortions. These committees ensured that health reasons were strictly defined, making abortions difficult to obtain, especially in the Maritime provinces. Moreover, a hospital committee's decisions could hinge on the power wielded by a few anti-choice individuals on the hospital board. For example, in 1989, a hospital committee in Richmond, British Columbia was refusing to let women use hospital facilities for abortions. Such actions are strongly endorsed by LIFE organisations. Additionally, LIFE supporters have taken the law into their own hands, defying injunctions against their behaviour, as has happened in Vancouver where LIFE supporters have flouted the law and picketed abortion clinics to prevent women having abortions. Men like Jean Tremblay are using the courts to control the birth process and women's actions by obtaining injunctions denying particular women abortions.

Meanwhile, the feminist Coalition for Reproductive Rights has been supporting women's rights to decide what happens to their bodies. Doctors backing women like Henry Morgentaler have risked all. His Quebec clinic was raided by the police for performing therapeutic abortions. His case was taken to the Supreme Court which eventually ruled in his favour and threw out the Criminal Code restrictions on abortions in 1988, leaving a legal vacuum on this issue. This action prompted Nova Scotia to enact legislation prohibiting abortions in free standing clinics. Morgentaler is currently facing court charges in Nova Scotia for having defied this legislation. On another front, in Quebec, Chantal Daigle was prevented from having an abortion in 1989 by an injunction obtained by her boyfriend, Guy Tremblay. The injunction was finally quashed when the Supreme Court declared neither foetus nor father have rights over a woman's body. Meanwhile, Daigle had to get her abortion in the United States and run the risk of facing contempt of court proceedings had Tremblay pressed these. The Mulroney government has agreed to enact legislation to clarify the law. Its proposals threaten to make doctors performing therapeutic abortions face criminal charges and fine women by encompassing abortions under the Criminal Code. This latter point is an improvement for women in that previous provisions also made them liable to criminal charges. But it places control over women's fertility in the hands of the medical profession. The proposed legislation is being strongly resisted by Pro-Choice feminist groups and their supporters.

The battle for control of women's sexuality reveals women's subordinate status in the family and in the patient-doctor relationship. Men and the medical profession hold the key to women's access to contraceptive and birth control resources.

PROVISIONS FOR OLDER WOMEN

Poverty, afflicting a quarter of older Canadians (NCW, 1989b), hits women primarily. For example, 66 per cent of widows are poor. Women who spend their lives caring for others without pay do not get the opportunity to make pension provisions for their old age through either the state system or the market. Women working in low paid jobs lack funding to save for their future. Provisions made for women as dependants are crucial to their survival in old age.

The first major cost-shared programme between the federal and provincial governments was the Old Age Pension Act of 1927 providing universal benefits for Canadian citizens over 70, and means-tested assistance for those aged 65-9. This was followed by the Old Age Security Act (OAS) in 1962 which provided a universal, flat-rate pension at age 65 for all those meeting a ten year residency requirement. Old Age Pensions were restructured following public demands for a guaranteed minimum for retired people when the Canada/Quebec Pension Plan was introduced in 1965. Quebec was given scope to deal with the specific needs of French Canadians. The Canada Pension Plan unified retirement, disability, survivor pensions and death benefits in one social insurance package. The plan was contributory, therefore wage related. Replacing income up to 25 per cent of earnings up to the average wage, the Canada Pension Plan requires supplementation to keep people out of poverty. Doing this through private pensions is an option only few women and black people can exercise.

In 1966, the state intervened through a needs-tested supplement based on *family incomes*, the Guaranteed Income Supplement (GIS). Coupled with the Old Age Security Act, it provided additional state assistance for needy older people. In 1989, 47 per cent of Canadians on Old Age Security received GIS payments. Single people, particularly single women, are most likely to need these. In 1988, 79 per cent of GIS claimants were women, reflecting their lower income levels. GIS enabled federal and provincial governments to share the costs of providing supplemental income for older Canadians on the poverty line. But it did not succeed in eliminating poverty from the lives of older people, particularly those living in cities (NCW, 1989b). GIS has provided a mechanism whereby some provinces, for example British Columbia, can clawback provincial income when federal contributions to Old Age Security pensions increase through indexation because provincial supplements hit a ceiling on total income for GIS claimants. Some pension is discounted before the clawback rule is applied to encourage individuals to be responsible for their own maintenance. Clawbacks happen regularly as cost of living increases limited to 2 per cent per year are built into GIS provisions. A Spouse Allowance intended to bring a couple's income up to OAS/GIS levels was introduced in 1975 for those aged 60 to 64 whose spouses were on Old Age Security pensions, and receiving GIS. In 1979, payment of the Spouse Allowance was continued after the death of a spouse on Old Age Security. In 1985, widowers became eligible. Single people, separated and divorced people remain excluded.

A residency qualification introduced in 1977 disadvantages Canadians who have spent an appreciable portion of their adult lives elsewhere and primarily affects people immigrating as adults, thereby excluding them from full benefits and reinforcing racism. The universality of the Old Age Security pensions is being threatened by federal 'clawback' provisions announced in the 1989 budget affecting those with incomes beyond $50,000. The Canada Pension Plan covers 92 per cent of Canadian workers. However, housewives, casual employees, family workers and migrant workers remain excluded. The exclusion of housewives combined with the lower proportion of women in the paid workforce has resulted in proportionately fewer women than men receiving pensions from the Canada Pension Plan. Women's pensions are lower because their earnings are lower than men's (NCW, 1989b). Women also do badly on survivor pensions as benefits reached only 60 per cent of a spouse's pension up to a maximum of $4005 a year in 1989. However, a childrearing 'dropout' clause was recently added to the Canada Pension Plan to enable women (and men undertaking this work) to exclude childrearing time up to the child's seventh birthday from their calculation of life-time earnings.

These additional provisions have failed to camouflage the main weakness of the system: state pensions are set at levels which are too low to take older people out of poverty. This theme has been persistently articulated by the poverty lobby and the National Council of Welfare. Low public pensions are useful in the context of private pensions because 46 per cent of workers have been pushed into buying additional benefits through the market. Private pension plans flourish, but women and black people are not the main purchasers. Private sector workers, particularly women in poorly paid part-time work, are badly covered by occupational pensions. Proposed legislation may change this picture if pension plans open up to include part-time workers. Registered Retirement Savings Plans are particularly attractive to higher income earners who can take advantage of tax exemptions. Men are the main subscribers to Registered Retirement Savings Plans, outnumbering women by two to one (NCW, 1989b). The limits on such investments have risen constantly since 1984.

The Left and feminists have criticised the Canada Pension Plan/ Quebec Pension Plan for being sexist and regressive. It is regressive because a low upper limit is placed on contributions, sexist because women's lower earnings are reflected in lower benefit levels, racist because migrant workers cannot provide for their unwaged future while employed. In 1977, the government responded to these criticisms by raising the ceiling for contributions to the Plan and introducing pension splitting for divorcing couples requesting it. Unfortunately, few women apply for this right. Pension splitting was the outcome of feminist pressure on the government to provide a pension for non-earners and recognises women's role in and contribution to family life. Pension splitting means that pension credits acquired by spouses during marriage can be split equally on dissolution of the union, enabling divorced women to claim their share of their husband's pension contributions for the period of the marriage. Claims must be lodged within three years of divorce. Only 1 per cent of *decrees nisi* have included such claims. While giving women access to resources to which they have contributed by staying at home looking after the family, pension splitting still reinforces women's position as men's dependants and does not recognise women's work in the home independent of men's earnings. Moreover, pension splitting is not possible following divorce even though women may be penalised financially by staying home to look after the young children of the marriage.

IN CONCLUSION

Canadian family policy exists insofar as the concept of a white heterosexual nuclear family underpins much of social policy. Aggregation is central to benefit allocation involving couples, even though some of this, for example credit splitting of pensions, has a progressive dimension in that it acknowledges women's contribution to a man's career during their marriage. However, inequality is structured into welfare provisions for women throughout their life cycle because they either are excluded from waged work by their domestic responsibilities or work in low paid jobs. This means they are more likely than men to spend their life in poverty providing care for others. The social control of women features strongly in family policy, but is particularly evident in matters involving women's reproductive rights.

British family policy

Britain, too, lacks an explicit family policy. Attempts to formally focus on family policy were evident during the early years of the Thatcher regime when the Family Policy Unit was formed. However, the hostility its controversial proposals aroused ensured that it was quietly dropped. Nonetheless, an implicit family policy largely promoting white heterosexual nuclear families at the expense of other family forms and women's full social development is evident in Britain's post-war social policy (Segal, 1984). British social policy presupposes a subordinate position for women and has developed welfare provisions in keeping with this.

FAMILIALIST AND NATIONALIST IDEOLOGIES SHAPE THE BRITISH WELFARE STATE

The themes of 'Family' and 'Nation' were central to the formation of the British welfare state in 1945 (Williams, 1989). Beveridge's proposals, imbued with patriarchal notions of heterosexual motherhood and white family life, became lynchpins maintaining the 'British Race' and 'British Values' (Beveridge, 1942), making familialism and nationalism central planks of post-war British social policy. The 'New Right' has couched these concepts in cultural terms to reassert the superiority of the white British way of life and reimpose traditional familial norms it believed undermined by the liberalisation and amoralism of the 1960s (Thatcher, 1990).

The British welfare state represents a partnership between the family and the state providing for people's well-being. However, the partnership is unequal, for the state has the power to either make available or withhold public resources from families and pass legislation having a considerable impact upon them. Families can influence state policies by organising pressure groups promoting their interests. Feminist groups, child poverty groups, and neo-conservative groups have actively pursued this course. Besides making available welfare services, and mediating relationships between the family and other public institutions, the welfare state is expected to provide the national unity which had earlier been based upon the colonisation of the Third World (Williams, 1989).

The post-war British welfare state idealised motherhood and house-work without providing the resources necessary for women to perform the task this entailed (Dale and Taylor-Gooby, 1985). The exclusion of women's needs from the political domain reinforced their position as isolated individuals whose primary focus was the home and left them economically dependent on men if they lacked their own income. State support through family allowances was pegged at unrealistically low levels given the finances required for women to stay home and provide children with adequate material, emotional and intellectual care. The communal laundries, nurseries and restaurants demanded by feminists failed to materialise. Women's specific health needs as women were denied. For example, Bevin refused to make birth control devices available under the newly created national health service on the grounds that men would oppose such moves (Cohen P., 1985). Women's access to council housing was restricted by their being dependent on men. They were excluded if single and childless, and if married were not generally co-tenants alongside husbands. This usually became problematic when women left violent partners. Until the 1977 Housing (Homeless Persons) Act, battered women did not receive priority treatment in acquiring council houses of their own. Sadly, the passage of this Act did not prevent local authorities such as Slough defining women as having made themselves intentionally homeless by provoking the violence they experienced (National Women's Aid Federation (NWAF), 1980). Additionally, women could not borrow money for mortgages without a male guarantor until the mid-1970s. This disadvantaged female earners, single parent families and older women. Women's dependency excluded them from the nation and confirmed men's interests as having national importance.

However, the welfare state relied on women's and black people's contribution to its existence in the form of low paid welfare work (Coyle and Skinner, 1988; Mama, 1989) and unpaid goods and services necessary for the family to survive in a context in which the state met only specified insurable risks (Beveridge, 1942). The state's lack of support for women, despite its dependence on their labour, indicates its disinterest in meeting the needs of women as either carers or workers. Black people were expected to contribute to creating the welfare state and subsequently developing it by providing trained immigrant labour to fill welfare jobs (Mama, 1989) and provide wealth through imperialist exploitation (Carby, 1982). Women and black people became scapegoated when the welfare state failed to produce its anticipated results. Women's liberation was blamed for declining social cohesion and breaking up the traditional family unit (Glazer, 1988). Black people were held responsible for shortages in employment, education, housing and social services (Murray, 1984; Glazer, 1988).

The relationships between women, black people and the state mystified structural inequalities caused by the underfinancing of the welfare state, its predication on sexist and racist values, the impact of international economic forces on its development and reliance on a sexually and racially stratified division of labour and facilitated the neglect of such issues. Holding women and black people responsible for society's well-being and welfare provisions increased sexist and racist attacks upon them for failing to meet their obligations.

The New Right has ignored much of the reality in the relationship between the welfare state, social policy and families by problematising departures from white heterosexual nuclear family norms and claiming these required additional or new resources and legislation to deal with them. Black families were singled out as having inappropriate family lives, cultures, aspirations, and languages (Bryan et al., 1985; Dominelli, 1988a). Black families entered declining working class areas where the infrastructure including housing and education was poor. However, the inadequate operation of black families was held responsible for the structural inequality within which their lives are elaborated (see Scruton, 1980; Seidel, 1986). The position of black women is pivotal to white people pathologising black families. Asian women are blamed for being passive and locked into their household; Afro-Caribbean women for going out to work (Carby, 1982; Bryan et al., 1985; Mama, 1989). A higher proportion of black women than white women work full-time: 42 per cent of West Indian women, 25 per cent of Asian women, and 23 per cent of white women work full-time (Barrett and McIntosh, 1985). White women are more likely to work part-time. The figures are 17 per cent for white women, 14 per cent for West Indian women, and 5 per cent for Asian women (Barrett and McIntosh, 1985). The use of black women as cheap labour to staff welfare services and finance its provisions has meant that black women have been servicing the needs of white families (Carby, 1982). Much of this work is heavy, boring and routinised with black women having little or no control over their work processes, rates of pay or working conditions.

Black women's sexuality is also problematised. Promiscuity is considered a danger for young Afro-Caribbean women. White social workers define them as being 'in moral danger' for being sexually active and believe their views vindicated when they become single-parent families. They see young Asian women as trying to get out of their allegedly unwanted 'arranged marriages' (Ahmed, 1978). Such views devalue black people's familial relationships and endorse policies discriminating against them. Trivialising black people's familial relationships is evident in immigration law. The banning of male fiancés and husbands from joining their British fiancées and wives in 1979, for example, divided black families and signalled that black family bonds were unimportant to Britain's ruling élite. These regulations were only altered after the European Court ruled them discriminatory on gender, but not racial grounds. This ruling did not liberalise access for black people. The British government simply had the immigration rules apply to both men and women. This became a neat way of saying discrimination is not discrimination if men and women, black and white, are equally prevented from enjoying 'family' life.

A further element in the lack of recognition of black family forms, is their being denied material support from the welfare state. For example, council housing is not easily available to black families entering Britain because they are disqualified through residency requirements defining emigration as intentional homelessness (*The Guardian*, 1987), and excluded from the Housing (Homeless Persons) Act, 1977. Black families' access to welfare resources became tighter when the 1980 Social Security Act made eligibility dependant on immigration status and prevented sponsored dependants of black people living in Britain from having 'recourse to public funds' (Gordon and Newnham, 1985). Black families were being denied access to the provisions they had helped create and maintain (Mama, 1989).

'Race' has been substantially excluded from classical social administration analyses. Studies examining gender relevant issues in family policy usually omitted 'race'. For example, Titmuss (1958) considered population control, demographic changes, childbearing, older people, and female dependence. While germane to women's interests, his studies idealised the private sphere in which women were the carers; ignored the role of violence in family life and its use by men to control both women and children; and failed to appreciate the value of the work women undertook in the family to bolster the economy (Pascall, 1986). In other words, his model of the family was one in keeping with white male supremacist values enshrined within the welfare state.

The welfare state has drawn on idealised conceptions of white British heterosexual nuclear family to:

1. Buttress the nationalistic and chauvinistic dimensions of imperialism (Bland, 1985).

2. Promote 'racism' by locking the welfare state into immigration control (Gordon, 1985).

3. Define and supervise women's performance of their duties as mothers and wives through the income maintenance system, personal social services and health care system (Wilson, 1977; Hale, 1983).

4. Define and control women's reproductive powers (Bryan et al., 1985).

5. Deny lesbian women's 'family' relationships (Hanscombe and Forster, 1982).

6. Reinforce the marginalisation and exploitation of black people and women's waged work in its role as a major employer (Mama, 1989; Howe, 1986).

The social security system has been drawn into the ambit of family policy by reinforcing nuclear family domestic arrangements or creating them where they do not exist, for example single parent women having friendly relationships with men, through the aggregation of family resources and the enforcement of the cohabitation rule. Both these have been challenged by feminists and claimants, who are arguing for an independent income for each individual and individual taxation. However, victory in establishing women's equality is elusive. The family remains the assessment unit.

In Britain as in America and Canada, the privacy of the family is considered of paramount importance. Yet, its privacy is easily invaded for poor families subjected to social work intervention. Family privacy is not so easily penetrated to protect women from violent partners (Binney et al., 1981; Mama, 1989). Also, black families are denied privacy. For example, immigration officials claim the right to pry into the most intimate details of black families' lives, including their births, marriages, relationships with extended family relatives (CRE, 1985). Even black women's personal body privacy has been denied through virginity tests conducted as part of immigration control to prove the marital status of black women seeking admission to Britain. The denial of human rights in this act is highly sexist and racist.

The family has an important, though contradictory relationship to the British welfare state. On the one hand, the welfare state has supplanted the family in the provision of services formerly its responsibility, for example education, council housing, and statutory social services, thus relieving women of *some* of their obligations. On the other hand, state initiatives have buttressed the traditional heterosexual nuclear family, for example family allowances, the taxation system's married man's allowance, and social security's cohabitation rule. Welfare state professionals, particularly social workers, have played an important role in reinforcing notions of domesticity and femininity (Wilson, 1977, Dominelli and McLeod, 1989). This has meant giving primacy to the mother–child relationship and arguing à la Bowlby, that its continuity is essential to the child's development. While the verity of this position has been challenged by many professionals (Rutter, 1981), feminist social workers (Hale, 1983; Marchant and Wearing, 1986), and black women (Mama, 1989), it continues to shape much of British social work practice.

The welfare state has given women access to their own earned income by employing them. But, it has done so by marginalising women's labour in all respects and reinforcing a sexist and racist division of labour. The welfare state has played an ambivalent part in British women's struggles for emancipation.

FAMILY POVERTY AFFECTS WOMEN AND CHILDREN PRIMARILY

Beveridge assumed most married women would not undertake waged work and would be provided for by their husbands. This became a 'fact' guiding his construction of welfare provisions for women. Additionally, his understanding of universal provision meant treating everyone alike, irrespective of their specific needs, family circumstances and racial status. He also assumed the numbers of unsupported mothers would remain minimal and require no special provisions (Pascall, 1986). However, single parents constitute one of the largest groups on social assistance because insurance provisions have failed to address their needs, and benefit levels are low (Ginsburg, 1979). By 1983, 60 per cent of lone parents lived on supplementary benefits or had incomes just above them (Glendinning and Millar, 1987). Poverty among these claimants is high, giving rise to the concept of the 'feminisation of poverty'. Means-tested assistance has become increasingly important. In 1984, eight million people relied on such benefits, a rise of 77 per cent since 1978 (Piachaud, 1987). Women heavily represented among these claimants include: women caring for older relatives or dependent children without pay, lone women with children whether or not in paid employment, women pensioners living alone, and women in low income households (Townsend, 1986). Poverty, unemployment and low pay reinforce gender and racial inequality. Additionally, rising divorce rates have increased the number of women headed single parent families to 90 per cent (Haskey, 1982) and reduced the proportion of heterosexual nuclear families. In 1961, nuclear families constituted 38 per cent of all households; the figure for 1982 was 29 per cent (Watson, 1987, p. 131).

Women are set to continue being single parents for the foreseeable future for they initiate seven out of ten divorces (Social Trends, 1984). Moreover, the number of children born outside wedlock has been increasing. In 1980, 11.8 per cent of births were to unmarried women choosing to raise their children themselves (Haskey, 1982). However, the rise in single parent families is being tempered by the increasing number of remarriages, a trend evident since the Divorce Reform Act came into effect in 1972 (Haskey, 1982). Thus, divorced women's children may spend some time in a single parent family, but they will eventually form part of a new heterosexual family unit (Haskey, 1983). Women's willingness to undertake parenting on their own has worried the 'New Right' for fear it will undermine Britain's social fabric. Their opinion holds weight in powerful legal circles, for the Law Commission's Family Law Reform bill 'sets out to make it almost impossible for women to raise children without men' (Pollock and Sutton, 1989, p. 134). Pollock and Sutton (1989) claim this response favours the movement for father's rights by extending male power and privilege rather than seeking to establish egalitarian familial relationships. They believe its reforms will assert the rights of unmarried fathers over those of the mother, and increase the number of contested custody cases.

The advance of father's rights at the expense of women's forms part of a backlash against gains women have acquired in their struggle for equality. Father's rights advocates have redefined attempts to place women on equal footing with men as efforts granting women advantages over men (Crean, 1988). Presenting a travesty of women's reality, the father's rights movement has successfully undermined women's position while advancing theirs. Reducing men's obligations regarding alimony and maintenance payments through the Matrimonial and Family Proceedings Act of 1984 by restricting women's access to their former husband's financial support provides a classic example of this. This legislation ignores men's track record in reneging on both alimony and maintenance payments; the disadvantages women caring for children face in (re)entering the labour market; and the contribution women make to men's employment prospects by absenting themselves from work during the marriage (Segal, 1987). However, it penalises women daring to reject their relationship with a man.

The advent of no-fault divorce has enabled women to leave unsatisfactory marriages more easily without adequately providing for their material welfare. Women who have sacrificed their careers for their families found themselves looking after children on minimal resources, relying on the state to provide them with the maintenance men failed to pay because their incomes could not support two families. The introduction of further changes to the divorce laws in the late 1980s simply confirmed earlier trends. Women were having to fend for themselves in a tough economic climate while being seriously disadvantaged in terms of competing successfully in the labour market. From a feminist perspective, neither men nor women should be personally dependent on each other for financial support. Their economic well-being should be guaranteed collectively by a society to which they contribute both paid and unpaid work and taxes.

The issue of parenting raises the question of the appropriate roles for men and women. Feminists have rejected definitions of parenting which subordinate women and restrict their activities and interests solely to this task. It stunts the development of women and children and limits the fathering role largely to that of economic provider. Redefining fathering in ways which reinforce women's subordination is not suitable either (Pollock and Sutton, 1989). Conceptualising parenting as a private responsibility which can be shared by men and women is inadequate because it excludes single parent families without another adult to share parenting. Nor can parenting be defined in terms of families lacking fathers, for besides denying women choice in the lifestyle they wish to adopt, it can reinforce the view that women cannot make it on their own. Or, as Pollock and Sutton, (1989, p. 137) express it: 'Posing fatherlessness as the problem, then presenting men as the solution, serves only to perpetuate political inequality for women and children.'

Parenting has to be conceptualised as a social responsibility in which men and women play an equal part. Achieving this requires the tackling of inequality in both workplace and domestic relations. Sharing responsibilities is only adequate to a point. Having men become involved in 'helping' women with childcare does not establish equality between the sexes. As feminists have pointed out, simply having men involved in domestic work does not mean they lose their 'male dominant privileges' (Segal, 1987; Pollock and Sutton, 1989). As helpers, men are very selective about their participation in childcare and housework. The messy, low status jobs remain with women, indicating that men have the power to choose to do housework or not while women have none. Moreover, men do not undertake an equal share of it. Heterosexual couples fully involved in paid work have women doing a disproportionate share of the housework – over thirty hours per week compared to men's four. The majority of mothers with children are in paid work, Women's exposing the reality underpinning the male family wage. Women's incomes now form a substantial part of the family's financial resources and prevent many families from falling into poverty. Without women's earnings, family poverty in Britain would quadruple. Women's position in the labour market improved slightly when the Equal Pay Act of 1970 and the Sex Discrimination Act of 1975 were passed following extensive campaigns by the feminist and labour movements. These legislative changes have exacerbated rather than challenged women's subordinate status. Employers have circumvented these Acts and women's position at work deteriorated (Coyle and Skinner, 1988). Women's wages have decreased from 73 per cent of men's wages in 1973 to 67 per cent in the mid-1980s (Segal, 1987). Paid work does not necessarily allow women to escape the clutches of poverty. It may make them part of the working poor as women have to accept part-time jobs fitting into their domestic routine and are segregated in the low paid sector of the labour market (Huws, 1985). This trend is unlikely to alter without action countering it since almost every *new* job created in Britain during the 1980s was a low-paid part-time one for women (Segal, 1987).

SOCIAL POLICIES EARMARKED FOR FAMILIES

Historically, policies directly affecting families have trodden a fine line of not usurping the family's primary responsibility of providing for its members. Consequently, state financial aid has been too little rather than too much, for example family allowances. This objective has facilitated the creation of policy initiatives such as low benefit levels, means-tested provisions, and 'availability for work tests' forcing men and women to work for low wages in appalling conditions to provide for their children. Policy has reinforced women's domesticity and men's role as economic provider whether or not circumstances warrant it. This strategy has created a network of provisions which fail to meet the complexity and diversity of families' needs. The view that women would remain at home reigned uppermost in the drafting of the Liberal reform programmes on unemployment pay, sickness benefit, and old age pensions enacted between 1906 and 1914. Predicated on men's working careers, they provided few resources for women except in their capacities as men's dependants. Despite this tendency to deny women an independent income, the Women's Co-operative Guild successfully campaigned to have maternity benefit included in the 1911 National Insurance Act and for payment to be made to the woman (Davin, 1978).

The main issues women including feminists addressed in the early part of this century were the ill health of their children and themselves, the inadequacy of the 'family wage' and the failure of men to distribute income within the family. These concerns prompted women to mount campaigns for infant health centres, ante-natal clinics, birth control advice and aids, family allowances paid to women and maternity benefits. Their demands, consistent with women's roles as mothers and wives, aimed to secure the means for performing their tasks more appropriately and led to the promulgation of the Maternity and Child Welfare Act of 1918. Its measures reinforced women's dependency in the family and followed from the existing organisation of production and definition of women's place in the family (Rowbotham, 1973).

Social policies during the 1920s and 1930s sought to exclude women, particularly married women, from unemployment benefit and jobs. The state was busy keeping women out of public life and enforcing female domesticity. Infant welfare centres and schools where women and girls respectively were compelled to take up domestic instruction pursued the state's interest in this regard.

The 'genuinely seeking work test' barring married women workers from having access to unemployment benefit was introduced in 1921 (Deacon, 1976, 1977). The National Unemployed Workers Movement failed to question 'the genuinely seeking work test' because it intended to keep married women out of the labour market thereby eliminating their competing with men for scarce jobs (Deacon, 1977). A household means test introduced in 1922, became more stringent in the 1930s, causing hardship and discontent (Ginsburg, 1979). Meanwhile, married persons with a working partner and 'aliens' were refused benefit as sexism and racism became instruments for rationing resources. The collapse of the 1926 General Strike revealed the powerlessness of the trade union movement and prompted the Conservative government to tighten means testing and 'the genuinely seeking work test'. Although working class interests would have been better served by uniting the cause of men and women at this point, the National Unemployed Workers Movement and TUC continued campaigning against means testing as it affected men and ignored the 'genuinely seeking work test' which discriminated against women.

Matters deteriorated further for women when the Anomalies Act of 1931 replaced 'the genuinely seeking work test'. This Act declared women ceasing paid employment 'retired' and ineligible for unemployment benefit. Cuts in health insurance benefits to married women followed in 1932 as the government moved to reduce the number of women claiming health insurance benefit. Local resistance to such intervention was common and prompted the national government to replace local democratic control with centralised bureaucratic control. This action effectively stemmed the supervision of means testing and poor relief by claimant oriented local authorities like Poplar, London (Ginsburg, 1979). Centralising unemployment and other insurance benefits created bureaucratic structures which increased the powerlessness felt by individual claimants. However, this issue was not addressed until the women's movement of the 1960s and 1970s challenged state bureaucracy (Segal, 1987). The 'genuinely seeking work test' has its modern equivalent in the 1982 'availability for work test' which discriminates against women having primary responsibility for child-care.

Feminists have differed in their approach to and demands of the welfare state. Liberal feminists have drawn on notions of motherhood and marriage to justify women's access to greater welfare resources, for example family allowances. Radical feminists challenged Beveridge's relegation of women to dependency within its provisions. For example, the Women's Freedom League demanded women's independent status in income maintenance schemes (Abbot and Bompas, 1943). This right has yet to be conceded by the British welfare state. The fragmentation of feminist energies enabled the state to select those elements it would endorse. Thus, by 1939, most women were included within the scope of national insurance, but it lacked a specifically feminist orientation (Dale and Foster, 1986). Family allowances were introduced in 1945 after a campaign that had begun with Eleanor Rathbone and the Family Endowment Society in 1917. Opposed by the male trade union movement because these would cut men's wages, the issue divided men and women. Consequently, when family allowances were finally implemented, they redistributed money in favour of capital rather than labour. Women and children had lost out (Dale and Foster, 1986).

Although feminists had succeeded in getting family allowances paid to the mother, they were introduced not to further women's interests, but through the government's determination to tackle inflation and increase the birth rate. First children were excluded from a flat-rate benefit of five shillings a week. In 1972, the Tories planned to phase out family allowances and child benefit, payable to dependent children living in England, was introduced in 1977. Black children living abroad were not covered, reflecting state disregard for the living arrangements black people had created, often in response to racist immigration laws preventing their bringing families into Britain (see Sivanandan, 1976; Bryan et al., 1985). In the 1980s, child benefit came under neo-conservative attack for undermining patriarchy by giving women access to an independent income and being available to high income women who 'do not need it'. Feminists and popular support of this demogrant so far has prevented its abolition, though not its destruction by attrition.

Neo-conservatives have attacked other provisions ostensibly support-ing families because they fear the independence women have gained through welfare state provisions in their own right. Despite substantial opposition from feminists, trade unionists and the poverty lobby, benefits for women have been eroded by subsequent Tory legislation. These have included: worsening maternity provisions contained in the 1975 Employment Protection Act for part-time workers by making them work longer for a particular employer before becoming eligible for maternity benefits; eroding benefits through the 1986 Social Security Act by abolishing the universal maternity grant for a means-tested £80 targeted on the most needy women. Aside from the fact that this sum would be swallowed up by the purchase of a crib, leaving no money for purchasing other necessities for a newborn, the government's solution has bypassed men and withdrawn resources from one group of women for allocation to those deemed financially more 'deserving'.

The loss of universal provisions can be construed as an attack on women earning their own income and the independence this gives them. It is also telling women their income must be shared with their children. Moreover, it pits women against each other on the basis of their different class based material interests. A less divisive way of handling the maternity grant issue and fostered by feminists was raising the universal grant to a realistic level, making it available to all women as of right, and addressing the matter of income differentials among recipients through taxation. This position acknowledged the social contribution women make in having children regardless of their family form, indicated society accepted collective responsibility for newborn children's welfare, ensured both men and women earning sufficient incomes paid for it and facilitated virtually complete take-up of the benefit. The low take-up rate of means-tested benefits (40 per cent of eligible claimants do not claim) portends a bleak future for mothers. Black women's prospects under the new regulations will deteriorate, partly because racism makes the discretionary element in means-tested benefits work to their disadvantage and partly because many will be deterred from applying by either not being informed of the existence of a means-tested maternity grant, or not wanting to submit to a racist investigation (see Bryan *et al.*, 1985).

CONTROL OF WOMEN'S SEXUALITY

Women's access to contraceptive devices and abortion was tightly controlled by the state until recently. In the sense that women still do not have the right to control their own fertility, the situation has not changed substantially. Contraceptive devices became freely available to adult women regardless of their marital status through the National Health Service in the mid-1970s, when family planning services expanded considerably. However, patriarchal protocol remains strong and unmarried women are addressed as 'Mrs' when they enter their local family planning clinic. Provisions for teenage women are still precarious. In 1985, Victoria Gillick challenged existing arrangements by demanding parents be involved in doctors' decisions to supply young women with contraceptives. A ruling in her favour asserted the supremacy of parental rights. This was overturned on appeal after an outcry from the British Medical Association on the grounds of the damage this ruling would inflict on the confidential doctor–patient relationship. Young women have yet to win the right to decide for themselves whether or not they wish to become sexually active.

Abortion was a criminal offence, unless performed to save a woman's life until the 1967 Abortion Act allowed abortions for social and psychological reasons as well as medical ones. This change followed intensive feminist campaigning highlighting the dangers poor women faced in being subjected to backstreet abortions; the lack of power women had in deciding what should happen to their bodies, and the importance of ensuring that all children were wanted (Greenwood and Young, 1976). However, the decision of whether or not abortions would be performed rested with doctors. Access to NHS provisions has varied throughout the country because facilities are unavailable, doctors refuse to perform abortions, and doctors respond to women differently according to their class, race and marital status.

Doctors' views on the suitability of a woman to be a mother determine the position they adopt in individual cases (Aitken-Swan, 1977; O'Sullivan, 1975). 'Feckless', poor, single or black women are given sterilisation along with abortion as a package; respectable, young white married women are compelled to go to term and 'give up their unwanted babies for adoption' (O'Sullivan, 1975; Aitken-Swan, 1977). Black women have been subjected to additional abuse through the injection of Depro Provera without their consent as doctors aware of the risks they were imposing on them (Berer, 1984) exercised their power to decide which women made 'fit and proper mothers' (Dale and Foster, 1986). The limited victory women acquired in their struggle for fertility rights through the 1967 Abortion Act is vulnerable. Governments have allowed private members bills to challenge its provisions and make women's access to abortion tougher. Initiatives taken by MPs White, Corrie, Beynon, Powell and Alton have been successfully thwarted through a combination of campaigns, petitions and parliamentary filibusters organised by feminists, trade unionists, and Pro-Choice members of parliament. The battle for control of women's reproductive rights is on-going. British anti-abortionists have also now begun obstructing women's entry to buildings where abortions take place as has happened in Canada and America.

Interestingly, neo-conservatives maintain that the liberality of current laws on contraception and abortion have contributed to the decline in family values. Pollock and Sutton (1989) argue the Law Commission has endorsed neo-conservative views by noting the availability of contraception and abortion, blaming women for wanting to raise 'illegitimate' children without men and attempting to curtail women's independence by extending unmarried men's right as fathers.

STATE INTERVENTION AND DAY CARE

The state has intervened in British families on a number of levels. Ideologically, it has reinforced women's position as carers in the home rather than as workers in the wage labour market. As Lord Spens put it: 'Married women should leave paid work to men and stay at home . . . I am not saying they should not be occupied, just that they should not compete in the market for paid jobs' (Spens, 1979). This view has been supported through a series of measures including the cohabitation rule, aggregation of married couples' incomes, child benefit, maternity allowances, and day care provisions. Aggregation has denied women's rights as individuals whilst protecting men's. Pascall (1986, p. 9) points out: 'If women, too, claim rights as individuals (as they have often done) it offers a threat to the fabric of interdependence on which men's rights depend'.

Dale and Foster (1986, p. 111) suggest ideology has defined the 'role of the family in relation to the state rather than the mother–child relationship' by focusing on women's activities as mothers, wives and carers. It has reinforced the white heterosexual nuclear family while labelling other forms deviations from this norm (Mama, 1989). While family policy has reinforced domesticity in white families, its racism has divided black ones. Black women have had to leave their children and go out to work because racism has reduced employment opportunities for black men (Mama, 1989) making high quality childcare essential for black children, but the state has failed to provide it in the form and numbers required.

Tying women to domesticity has saved the state considerable sums of money in services which it has not had to provide (Dale and Foster, 1986) and enabled it to deploy women as a reserve army of labour responding to economic requirements. During the Second World War, women were encouraged to become gainfully employed and ensure the supply of labour for the war effort. The state provided free state nurseries in substantial numbers and communal dining facilities to enable women to work (Dale and Foster, 1986). These services were withdrawn when soldiers were demobbed and demanded their jobs back. Politicians, trade unionists and members of the public shared the view that women's place was at home consuming goods produced by others. Many people worried that family breakup and juvenile crime would increase if women refused to go home to care for children. So, barring feminist criticism, married women were removed from the workforce with little disruption.

In the 1950s, people's fears fed off Bowlby's theories of 'maternal deprivation'. Women forced into waged work to nurture their families under extremely difficult emotional and physical conditions were made to feel guilty. White women participating in part-time work were considered inadequate mothers. Black women in full-time work were labelled failed mothers while black men were castigated for neglecting their familial obligations. Images of 'latchkey children' and the temptations for them to go astray abounded in the popular media, heightening women's guilt for entering the labour market. These enabled the authorities to pathologise and blame women for the ills of modern family life.

Women's place in the home has been used to block the development of publicly funded childcare except in cases of dire need threatening the physical and emotional well-being of children. Since the Plowden Report of 1967, nursery schools have become an educational responsibility used in combating educational deprivation (Dale and Foster, 1986). However, it is tied to the school day and is of limited usefulness to working mothers. Many children attend part-time, but nursery provisions are reasonably good. Day care run by social services departments is geared primarily to the needs of single parent families where social workers fear child abuse or neglect. Thus, as in America and Canada, these provisions are a stigmatised and scarce resource instead of facilities easing the task of raising children and enabling parents to lead full lives. In 1976, there were 16.3 official daycare places per thousand children under five. Most parents, undertaking waged work, therefore rely on registered and unregistered childminders to care for their children (Dale and Foster, 1986). Childminders are poorly paid and care for other people's children while doing their housework and looking after their own children. They also happen to be women, as are the majority of workers in nursery schools and day care centres. Government neglect of this area emanates from the view that childrearing is a private responsibility, not a collectively shared enterprise.

The bourgeois family has created childhood with enforced dependency. Social policy has extended children's period of dependency. Prolonging the school leaving age, removing householder status from the under twenty-fives unless they are married couples with children, and compelling parents to finance the education of their adult children, exemplify this. Besides failing parents by not providing the resources they need to undertake this work, the state's strategy of privatising welfare resources presupposes parents will assume these responsibilities without state aid. Such policies confirm existing inequalities because high income parents can purchase the services their children need, while low income parents cannot.

Most older people in Britain are women living on limited resources, making old age a time of dependency and economic insecurity. Reinharz (1989) maintains that: 'facets of the social-economic structure interweave to deprive the elderly (sic) of status, power and control over their own lives' (Reinharz, 1989, p. 225). The isolation, loneliness and lack of companionship older women experience suggests reality for older people is infinitely more complex than focusing on economic insecurity implies. Gender does make a difference to that reality. Older men are more likely to be valued than older women. Older single men have more resources at their disposal than single women, whether this is incomes, home helps or other state support systems. Older women's incomes are lower than older men's (Townsend, 1979) because men accrue higher pensions through higher earnings and women without adequate insurance provisions rely on means-tested social assistance.

The growing proportion of older people has produced a demographic crisis for government policy analysts pondering how their greater demands for pensions, healthcare and personal social services will be financed. Their answer is 'community care', a policy drawing heavily upon women's unpaid domestic labour (Finch, 1984). More women are looking after older dependent relatives than children (Hunt, 1978). The majority of older people are already being cared for by women relatives in the privacy of their homes with little, if any, state support (Higgins, 1989). The estimated value of care women provide for frail older people at home is £3.7 billion compared with £928 million the state spends on personal social services for the over seventy-fives (Family Policy Studies Centre, 1984). 'Community care' has shunted the responsibility of caring for older relatives previously in state care onto women. Feminist demands in handling this issue have varied. The Rights of Women proposes a system of Home Responsibility Payments to those providing care (ROW, 1979). Other feminists have suggested payments for those requiring care.

Black women have discharged the care of black elders with virtually no state provided day centres, respite care, or old people's homes (Bhalla and Blakemore, 1981). Black elders are less likely to receive state pensions than white elders: 54 per cent of Asian elders and 17 per cent of Afro-Caribbean elders are without state pensions compared to 6 per cent of white Europeans (Bhalla and Blakemore, 1981). Their pensions also tend to be lower: 32 per cent of Asian elders receive partial pensions. Thus, black elders suffer ageism as well as racism. Sex discrimination against women is additional to this.

IN CONCLUSION

Conservative governments under Thatcher in the 1980s wiped out some of women's earlier gains. Women's rights as workers have been particularly undermined as part of their strategy of bolstering familialism and retaining women as an easily exploited workforce. These policies assume women have another income they can draw on – their husband's.

Changes in the 1986 Social Security Act pushed women into either financial dependency on men or into low paid waged work, making it harder for women to lead family lives independent of men. Coupled with attacks on the trade union movement including those public sector unions trying to improve women workers' low pay, these measures have exacerbated women's and black people's oppression and weakened their resistance to them. Finally, the government's community care policies have also intensified the burden women carry at home by forcing them to assume the care of those neglected by the state (Finch, 1984).

For the New Right, the values of good citizenship – law and order, morality – upheld by the family coincide with the virtues of a strong state (Glazer, 1988). Therefore, the family must be strengthened institutionally to socialise citizens into accepting hierarchical relations, obeying authority and demonstrating loyalty (Levitas, 1986b). Under Thatcher, the central state increased its power and control over the local state, families, and individuals. The state's intervention in families contradicts the 'New Right's' espousal of greater freedom for families to choose services from the marketplace rather than relying on the state. Its attacks on local democracy through the abolition of the Greater London Council and metropolitan counties, its financial control of local authority expenditures with rate-capping and the community charge have undermined the power of local representatives. The Criminal Justice and Police Evidence Bill have reduced individuals' freedom, power, and rights when suspected of crimes or placed under arrest. Both family law and criminal law are being used to enforce family obligations. Parents, financially responsible for the prolonged dependency of their children, are being compelled into accepting responsibility when their children commit criminal offences.

Current developments in British family policy, particularly the reprivatisation of welfare services for older people and children, the introduction of private market principles into state welfare, the shift in welfare services from care to control, the shunting of domestic and caring responsibilities onto women's shoulders, women's increased financial responsibility to their families, the rise in the number of women wage earners, and the state's increasing reliance on voluntarism and self-help for the provision of social services has made women's role in the family more onerous than ever. Yet, this catalogue of developments in the Thatcherite era is not formally acknowledged family policy. But its coherent impact on women's lives is no less than if it had been formulated in those terms.

FAMILY POLICIES IN SOCIAL DEMOCRATIC COUNTRIES

Swedish family policy

Swedish family policy has carried two main themes. The first provided families with more spending power, that is, improved its capacity to consume. The other increased the birth rate, or facilitated its ability to reproduce. The first theme was dominant during the 1930s and early post-war period when family policy reflected a Keynesian approach to the economy. Welfare transfer payments were used to encourage consumption. The policy also expanded welfare state activities which in turn extended economic ones. Bolstering the birth rate reinforced pronatalist ideologies. Both themes were measures endorsing traditional family structures by locating women firmly within the family and influenced women in their role as mothers rather than women in their own right.

During the 1930s, Kamerman and Kahn (1978) estimate 10 per cent of married women worked for wages. Incomplete records suggest this underestimates their actual involvement. But high male unemployment discourages women from working. After the Second World War, a labour shortage and changed outlook encouraged women to work. And in a dramatic change, women have become a central part of the waged workforce. By the late 1960s, 70 per cent of married Swedish women worked either full- or part-time, making the dual career family more of a norm in Sweden than in Britain. By the mid-1980s this had reached 80 per cent (Sidel, 1986). Their wage levels as a proportion of men's are relatively high at 80 per cent. Family policy currently focuses on meeting the needs of waged working women. Family policy presupposes a dual career model of family life, making waged work the primary function of the family, while reproduction is secondary. Equality for Swedish women has meant doubling their labour burden. This has been incorporated into formal policy. Meanwhile, the Swedish birth rate continues to decline.

PRONATALIST INITIATIVES

The low birth rate was the first major family policy issue addressed by the Swedish government. Falling steadily since the middle of the eighteenth century, it stood at fourteen births per thousand population in the 1930s. This was alarmingly low even if account were taken of the impact of industrialisation and economic recession. The government introduced a universal lump sum maternity allowance for all mothers to improve this position. This benefit was not insurance based and covered basic items required by a newborn baby. In paying this lump sum to mothers, the Liberals argued public assistance should be granted to those taking great personal risks to assure the continuation of society by giving birth, making the move pronatalist. But the government was also carefully giving the impression that it was not undermining traditional family ideals. This universal lump sum maternity payment continued to be the basic maternity allowance until the 1970s. The amount given increased during the post-war period and contrasted sharply with the small maternity allowance Beveridge introduced later in Britain.

The Swedish state introduced cash advances to single parents in the early 1930s. Under this scheme, single and divorced mothers received cash advances set above the level of subsistence on their child support payments where fathers failed to pay maintenance. The fathers were required to repay these monies. The state also provided women receiving inadequate maintenance payments with a 'supplementary allowance' above subsistence levels. Men were not obliged to pay this off. The election of the Swedish Social Democratic Party (SAP) in 1932 meant family policies followed earlier objectives, for example pronatalist family policies, the lump sum maternity payment and the cash advances. The only criterion of eligibility set was motherhood. The birth rate continued declining despite these measures, so a royal commission was established in 1935 to investigate population growth. Britain created one in 1949. The Population Commission reported that matters were serious as the Swedish population was not replacing itself.

PROTECTION FOR WORKING MOTHERS

The Swedish Social Democratic Party was subjected to considerable trade union pressure to improve the position of waged women through the introduction of employment protection for mothers. Legislation followed. In 1939, it became illegal for women to be dismissed from their jobs for either getting married or becoming pregnant. Moreover, women's employers were required to keep jobs open until women returned to work, within a stipulated time limit. Following these measures, the Swedish birth rate increased slightly. Legislation protecting working mothers was unusual given the low numbers, lower even than Britain, of women in registered waged work at the time. Its significance stemmed from its forward looking and universalistic nature rather than the level of security it provided. Employment protection legislation for working mothers was not passed in Britain until 1974 under Foot's Employment Protection Act.

Limited reforms became the catchword after the Second World War. Cash levels in existing schemes were improved. In 1955, statutory maternity leave on six months' full pay was made compulsory. Employers paid for this provision. In contrast, British statutory maternity leave for insured women lasted for six weeks until the middle of the 1970s. The rediscovery of poverty among Swedish single-parent families in the 1960s led to family reforms. One of these was family housing allowances made available in 1969. Redevelopment schemes in the 1960s produced publicly subsidised high rise flats for families. However, people could afford neither to buy nor to rent them. Dealing with this embarrassing problem prompted the Swedish government to provide means-tested housing allowances to encourage people to live in the otherwise empty flats. The extent of poverty prevalent in Sweden is revealed by the take-up of this benefit. Over 50 per cent of Swedish families receive means-tested housing assistance.

Housing benefit in Britain performs a similar function of reducing housing costs for people on low incomes. Housing allowances in Sweden vary according to the number of children in the family and whether or not the family is a single parent one, integrating these closely with income maintenance and family policies. Ironically, they help families acquire access to unsuitable housing, that is, high rise flats for people with children. Other reforms included raising the profile on employment protection for working women and the introduction of universal family allowances giving every family a child maintenance grant in 1974. This allowance was an annual tax free grant of $500 for each child under 16. It replaced child tax allowances, eliminating a regressive fiscal policy benefiting men as higher income earners for a universal one under women's control. However, giving women this money has not altered inegalitarian family relationships.

The Swedish situation is comparable to Britain's after 1977 when feminist supported child benefits were introduced and child tax allowances discarded. The amount of support paid to children in both countries is approximately 4 per cent of average male earnings, an ungenerous provision for children. In 1982, a supplementary children's allowance payable for the third and subsequent child was made available to large Swedish families. The amount of the supplementary allowance increased for the fourth and subsequent children. The number of large families in Sweden is very small and confined largely to the middle class. Easily available contraceptives and the liberalisation of abortion in the 1950s, made small families viable options for working class people. Over 50 per cent of families had only one child in 1970 (Wilson, 1979). The comparable figure in Britain is 2.4 per cent. Consequently, poverty associated with large poor families has disappeared.

Maternity leave became parental leave in 1974. This provided every mother giving birth access to a nine month allowance which could be used by either parent, depending on who had custody of the child after its birth. If custody was shared, $160 a month was given to the parent who was not working before the birth. If both were working, the allowance was increased to compensate for this. Parental leave is now available at 90 per cent pay for either parent for nine months after the birth of the child. A further three months may be taken with a low payment of thirty-seven kroners a day. When parental leave was first implemented in 1976, few fathers took advantage of this provision. Gradually, their take-up has increased. A major drawback to men taking up the parental leave option is women's lower wage rates. Averaging 80 per cent of men's, women's lower wages are a major disincentive to men taking parental leave. Swedish families have been reluctant to give up the higher wage at the point that their expenses rise dramatically.

A further problem with Swedish parental leave provisions is that aggregation remains central to them. It is assumed that parents will share the time and resources between them. But why should one parent have to forego leave if the other parent also wants it? This suggests that retaining parents' labour in the waged economy has precedence over fostering the quality of life parents enjoy as parents when they both share in rearing their offspring. Also, it presupposes the presence of two parents. Fathers also have a ten day parents allowance at the time of birth to help mothers and newborn babies. In 1977, parents were granted eighteen days' paid leave to care for sick children. Now they have sixty days. This leave can be taken by either parent, and varies according to number of children in the family.

A more controversial measure introduced in 1979 was legislation guaranteeing working parents the right to reduce their working day to six hours until the youngest child finishes the first year in school without losing their job. Unfortunately, parents exercising this option only get paid for the thirty hours they actually work. The trade union movement opposed this measure for not paying workers a full working day, in essence asking parents to take a payout. Instead, trade unions demanded socialised childcare on a twenty-four hour basis to make it easier for working parents to combine work with childcare. Neither of these options is suitable from a feminist perspective because they both place the onus for childcare on the family. So while these measures might encourage some fathers to participate in childcare, they reinforce the private nature of domestic labour. Additionally, the parental leave package assumes there is a male partner with whom the women can share these benefits. This may not be the case. Single parent families may be neither cohabiting nor relating to the children's fathers.

Meanwhile, the birth rate has dipped to twelve live births per thousand people, a figure lower than the one causing so much concern in the 1930s. The falling birth rate has meant that Sweden's post-war boom has relied heavily on immigrant labour. In 1966, 5 per cent of the population had immigrant status. Most immigrants came from Finland. Like the Irish in Britain, they face discrimination in welfare provisions through restricted eligibility to benefits. There are considerable tensions around Sweden's use of immigrant labour followed by demands for immigration control.

These tensions led industry to tap the labour of married women and single parent families. One family in four is a one parent family. This proportion is much higher than the figure of one in ten in Britain (Finer, 1974, p. 12). Swedish single parent families may include unmarried couples as cohabitation rules form no part of the welfare state structure. The demand for their labour has increased the acceptability of and state support for one parent families. In 1978, besides family allowances, single parents received a guaranteed maintenance allowance of $800 per child under 18. Finer recommended special payments for single parents in Britain, but this recommendation has not yet been implemented. In Sweden, single parent families are viewed more favourably and the state plays a greater role in assisting them reduce the poverty entailed in financing children on one or no income. Thus, single parents receive extra housing allowances and help in finding work. This assistance has increased the proportion of single parent women joining the labour force, but assuming waged work on top of family responsibilities increases the dual career burden for women, and reinforces women's domesticity. In Britain, lower levels of state assistance in housing, day care and finances have discouraged half of single-parent women from taking waged work. Fewer divorced and widowed women have done so.

CONTROL OF WOMEN'S SEXUALITY

Another post-war reform in family policy involved abortion (Adams and

Winston, 1980). Legislation governing women's fertility had been changed in 1938 as part of a package dealing with contraception. Despite its natalist concerns at the time, Sweden repealed the 1910 anti-contraception law forbidding the distribution of either contraceptives or information about them. Under the 1938 legislation, a Board of Health authorised abortions on strict medical grounds. Before that, abortions were only possible if the mother's life was endangered. In 1963, abortions were permissible in cases of foetal injury. The widening of the grounds for abortion in Sweden followed those then being established by the Bourne case in Britain. During the 1960s, shocking reports about back-street abortions, Swedish women going to Poland for their abortions, and unwanted pregnancies causing family breakdown caused Swedish people to rethink their position on the issue. The thalidomide scandal widened the grounds for abortion to cover socio-medical reasons. In 1965, a Family Commission began investigating the matter. It reported in 1971 when the number of legal and illegal abortions were rising and women were putting pressure on doctors to make abortions more accessible to them. The law of 1975 gave women free abortion virtually on demand up to eighteen weeks. Though the decision is theirs, women have to consult a doctor before the twelfth week. From twelve to eighteen weeks women must also consult a social worker, but neither professional can refuse women an abortion. After that, a Board of Health decides the matter on the basis of a social worker's recommendation. Legalising abortions has not increased the number of abortions per-formed. It has only made them legal. However, Swedish abortion levels are higher than British ones. In 1976, a new sterilisation act went into effect making sterilisation a family planning option. A woman also makes this decision after consulting a doctor or social worker.

DAY CARE PROVISIONS

Day care provisions in Sweden are not impressive. By 1980, existing day centres provided places for only 30 per cent of children under 6 (Sidel, 1986). Parents provided care for 43 per cent of pre-school children (Dalheim Debate, 1979). Children start school at age 7 rather than 4 as in Britain. Day care provisions in Sweden have concentrated on nurseries for children over 3 years. These have tended to meet the needs of working mothers, unlike the British situation where nurseries have limited hours which fit uneasily with the working day. The expansion of Swedish day care for those over 3 occurred in the 1970s when the costs of private childminding were climbing, and large numbers of childminders were unsupervised. Swedish parents of children under 3 have not had their needs met. Underprovision is massive. Only 50 per cent of working mothers with children under 3 have official places either in a day care centre or with a private childminder. The debate about whether family policy should encourage women to stay home and mind the children or go out to work continues. The reforms introduced by the Liberal coalition government of the 1970s encourage domesticity and familial forms of childcare at the expense of collective provisions.

Day care costs are high. In 1981, pre-school care was estimated at $5,000 per child (Sidel, 1986). Places are subsidised by both central government and the municipality, while parents pay fees based on income. Children with special needs receive their pre-school place free. Children whose first language is not Swedish have priority placing in pre-school facilities and can learn their own language on a voluntary basis. The quality of care is high as children are encouraged to be creative.

IN CONCLUSION

Swedish family policy is concerned with pronatalist issues, encouraging women to enter and stay in waged work, and reinforcing traditional private family forms of childcare. Family allowances have encouraged family building and childrearing. These changes have been encouraged about through a consensual politics in which problems are investigated, and the solutions suggested taken on board in some fashion. The women's movement has been incorporated into the structures of SAP and the trade union movement, diminishing its force outside this framework (Adams and Winston, 1980). Women's independence is assumed achievable through their more egalitarian involvement in waged work. This has meant that women's wages are higher as a proportion of men's than their sisters in other Western countries, but their domestic burden has not been eased, despite state attempts to lessen the yoke of patriarchy in the home by encouraging men to engage in childcare.

Ironically, family policies in Sweden have responded to alterations in family structures, for example one-child households and single-parent families, but the ensuing changes have not substantially dented traditional domesticity. They have reinforced the dual career family and the burden women carry when they become responsible for doing both domestic and waged work. Moreover, moves fostering equality for women have strengthened men's rights in that men are now given inducements to become involved in childcare without improving women's position. Although Swedish family structures give more credence to women as breadwinners, achieving equality for women has also eluded the Swedes (Wistrand, 1981).

FAMILY POLICIES IN SOCIALIST COUNTRIES

Soviet family policy

Family policies have been significant in developing the Soviet welfare state and overtly shaping Soviet women and men's lives. As in Sweden, family policy in the Soviet Union illustrates systematic state intervention in the private lives of individuals, particularly in marriage, birth control, public day care, and family income maintenance. Policy shifts reveal the centrality of economic exigencies in mitigating women's status as a reserve army of labour given a chronic labour shortage throughout the Soviet Union's existence. This situation is contradictory for women for while they have been liberated to join the waged workforce, this has not emancipated women (Mamanova, 1984). Rather, it has reinforced their oppression. Women occupy the poorest paid and lowest status jobs in the waged labour force. Meanwhile, their domestic responsibilities have remained virtually unaffected. They are under the yoke of the dual career burden as are their sisters in Western countries. This outcome follows the state's use of family policy to subordinate women's liberation to the demands of industrial growth (Molyneaux, 1985), and failure to directly tackle men's relatively privileged position. That is, the extent to which women's oppression bolsters male supremacy was neither acknowledged nor targeted for social change. Male success at work drew on women's lack of it in the workplace and home. Thus, the Russian Revolution has been carried by sacrifices women have made (Mamanova, 1984).

Idealism and a commitment to social equality permeated Bolshevik thinking during the early days of the Revolution and made women's liberation seem achievable. In classical Marxist tradition, it was believed that the main measure women needed for liberation was economic – their entry into social production; other aspects of women's oppression were expected to wither away once this took place (Lenin, 1965). Moves to employ women were quickly implemented. In practice, family disintegration, the desertion of women and children by husbands and fathers, the absence of socialised provisions to help men and women perform domestic chores, and a lack of understanding of the nature of women's liberation and how it could be achieved contributed to the failure of the Revolution to meet its commitments to women. Nonetheless, there were some real gains attending measures introduced shortly after the Revolution. These included women's right to vote, the most advanced divorce and civil marriage laws in the world, voluntary marital unions, the abolition of distinctions between legitimate and illegitimate children, the guaranteeing of women's employment rights, equal pay for equal work (at least on paper), and the best maternity leave provisions in any country at the time. Abortion on demand was granted in 1920. But it was not intended to contribute to the liberation of women. It was a practical step taken to stem the high back-street abortion rate and the damage abortion inflicted on Soviet women's health and the economy by depriving it of labour power.

Many of the early Bolshevik gains for women were reversed during the Stalinist period when Stalin rejected the gradual introduction of communism, and in his hurry to industrialise the country, subordinated women's personal fulfilment to economic growth (Heitlinger, 1979). In the process, family policy became a mechanism through which inequality between men and women was extended and women's domesticity reinforced. Early in his reign, Stalin abolished the Women's Section of the Party, abrogated women's right to abortion, and made divorce difficult. The family was charged with acting as society's primary socialising unit and marriage became an emotional necessity for women (Mamanova, 1984).

Since Stalin's death, women's liberation has remained uneasily balanced between the economy's need for women's waged work and public concern about the declining birth rate in the predominantly white European industrial areas. The provision of nurseries and maternity leave supports women in waged work and maintains the nuclear family form. The reinstatement of abortion rights and easier divorce fits less closely with economic requirements. As neither of these measures was inspired by a desire to give women control over their lives as women, they cannot be interpreted as aiming to liberate women. Divorce has been particularly contradictory for women. Freeing them from unsatisfactory relationships with men, it has increased their childcare burden and emotional isolation. Issues around women's sexuality have lain dormant since Kollantai's days. Contraceptive aids including the pill, IUDs, and condoms are hard to obtain. The presence of such problems confirms a deep-seated antagonism against women's control of their lives (Kollantai, 1977). Kollantai had experienced male colleagues' resistance when she sought to encourage alternative family forms.

Such attitudes are not easily identified with the socialist aim of encouraging individual freedom and fulfilment. They mirror more closely anti-feminist ideologies prevalent in the West. Moreover, Soviet economic progress is discredited by the experience of women receiving few consumer durables to lighten their domestic burden. Millett (1972) describes the persistence of the sexist division of labour, the dependent status of women in the family, the heavy burden of domestic labour, and the psychological power of patriarchy as a tragedy for Soviet women.

She claims Trotsky's analysis contributed to the distortion of women's interests in the Revolution as did his failure to support Kollantai's position on women's liberation in her arguments with Lenin. As Trotsky emphasises women's social rights, not their reproductive rights, lack of power in the home, or patriarchy more generally, Millett's arguments are firm. The insurmountable obstacles posed by Soviet men's failure to grasp these aspects of women's reality makes Millett conclude the oppression of women is inevitable, and women's liberation under socialism impossible.

Her pessimistic conclusion appears unsustainable. The position of Soviet women in the 1930s has to be understood in the context of the Soviet experience of introducing change against impossible economic odds, tensions between men and women in the Party, the exclusion of women from powerful positions within the state apparatus, the impact of the Civil War and the ensuing scarcity in labour power and material resources. The Bolsheviks' inability to deliver the promises enshrined in their early legislation is also part of a wider failure of Marxism – its inability to deal adequately with gender divisions in both the workplace and the domestic sphere (Saunders, 1988). Engels (1972) and Lenin's (1965) theories about women, the family and their liberation through women's entry into waged work and the socialisation of domestic labour as the key precondition for liberating women fail to address the psychological aspects of women's oppression and sexuality (Millett, 1972). Also, Marxism ignores personal and sexual politics and with it the unequal power relations existing within the family and which work to the detriment of women and children. Relations between the sexes are assumed to be transformed by the abolition of private property, the establishment of formal equal rights and the libertarian tone of their legislation (Kollantai, 1971). Stalin adopted this formal position to argue women had achieved liberation by the 1930s as socialism in one country had been established and women had entered the workforce across a range of industrial categories.

Traditional attitudes towards Soviet women proved difficult to combat. In the absence of both ideological and material conditions supporting women's liberation, patriarchal attitudes had a real hold on men's and women's thinking (Mamanova, 1984). The tensions of family insecurity, large numbers of orphans and prostitutes added to these obstacles, making the liberation of women problematic. Meanwhile, the lack of resources to make communal kitchens, laundry and housing a success discredited moves to transform the private family.

The promotion of women's liberation by Alexandra Kollantai during her period as the first Commissar for Social Welfare facilitated the passage of Utopian family policy in the early days of the Revolution.

Kollantai had direct experience of working with the working class women's movement over demands for suffrage, free marriage, decent working conditions and proper housing. Struggling to establish women's rights within the Party, she highlighted women's significant contribution to the 1905 and 1917 Revolutions. Writing simply to enable women to educate themselves and embrace the Revolution, she dealt with practical measures through which the Party could support alternative living arrangements for women, experiments on communal living, and the libertarian legislation being promulgated. During the early 1920s, her writings emphasised a new morality and sexuality to foster equality and permeate personal and public arenas. Aware of women's changing sexual relationships and emerging consciousness, she was a woman before her time. Her male comrades, including Lenin and Trotsky, saw the family as a private sphere which the state could influence through legislation promoting women's social rights. However, they opposed state intervention in men's interpersonal relationships with women.

Trotsky reflected on Kollantai's arguments during exile and became aware of limitations in the Bolsheviks' position on the family (Trotsky, 1973). Writing an attack on Stalin, Trotsky suggests the problem emanated from the Bolsheviks' traditional view of family relationships, men's failure to grasp the significance of women's demands, the lack of accepted alternatives to the family; the obstacles and lack of resources impeding the socialisation of domestic labour. The poverty of women's lives under tough conditions were discounted. Women were expected to make the sacrifices necessary for the social advancement of the nation. The interconnections between women's liberation, the private sphere, and public world of production is essential in understanding Soviet family policy.

CONTROL OF WOMEN'S SEXUALITY

Kollantai's efforts in the early days of the Revolution succeeded in making sexuality an issue needing attention. The desire to free people from coercive personal relationships led to the easy availability of divorce, eroded the legal responsibilities family members had for each other, loosened parental obligations in maintaining children, eliminated the distinction between 'illegitimate' and 'legitimate' children, decriminalised bigamy, incest, adultery and homosexuality, and legalised abortion.

Abortion was first legalised in 1920 to the regret of Lenin and other leading Bolshevik men. Lenin accepted its legalisation as an expedient response to the high number of illegal abortions rather than its contribution to women's liberation. During the Civil War, women had resorted to dangerous, illegal abortions which killed 4 per cent of them. Defining it as an unavoidable evil, Lenin consented to abortion as a health measure necessary to save women's lives. In adopting this position, Lenin rejected both the women's liberation arguments and those of the Party's neo-Malthusian contingent. The Neo-Malthusians were a natalist element concerned about the failure of the birth rate to replace European Russians. Interestingly, similar neo-Malthusian concerns were popular in the United States at the time where the 'race suicide' being practised by white middle class women's rejection of motherhood was deplored and control of the high birth rate among working class blacks sought.

While both birth control and abortion were formally on the Soviet statute books, their availability was limited by the low level of hospital provisions and the chaos of the period of war communism. Contraceptives were hard to procure because the health service lacked a comprehensive birth control programme. Male working class hostility to birth control formed an important backdrop to Soviet policy on contraception and abortion. By the early 1930s a strong anti-abortion campaign existed. In 1936, abortion was declared illegal except for extremely strict medical reasons (Trotsky, 1973). Stalin's propaganda on the issue emphasised women's duty in embracing socialist motherhood and the birth of a child with joy. Moreover, Stalin demanded women having illegal abortions should be imprisoned, although it was acknowledged that working class women with less access to contraceptives would be disproportionately affected by such legislation. His proposal was discussed in the press where considerable opposition was expressed despite Stalin's repressive regime. However, this resistance did not deter the Central Committee from making this law.

As in Sweden, Stalin's family policy measures of the 1930s were pronatalist. They were also racist for trying to increase the birth rate among white European Russians while controlling the high birth rates in the Asiatic republics. However, Stalin was not pronatalist in the sense of introducing high family allowances and easily accessible nurseries to encourage women to have more children. He sought to strengthen the family ideologically rather than raise expectations that the Soviet welfare state could provide practical support which would detract resources from his industrialisation effort. The family had to become the primary social institution able to look after itself. Reinforcing family stability through ideology, marriage and limited welfare state provisions were significant aspects of this approach (Mamanova, 1984). Anti-feminist propaganda complemented Stalin's goal of achieving socialism in one country. Arguing this latter objective had been realised, Stalin declared women had no need for separate organisations defending their interests and closed down the Party's Women's Section, the *zhenotdel* (Rosenburg, 1989).

Abortion was relegalised in 1955 for pragmatic reasons. Similarly expediency motivated David Steel to push the 1967 Abortion Act through the British parliament when the scandal of high numbers of back-street abortions pricked the British public's consciousness. Franklin (1978) reckons 67 per cent of Soviet women who have been pregnant have had abortions. Of these, 49 per cent have had three or more. Abortions were also more common among working women. Cohen (1980) suggests their numbers could reach 80 per cent. These figures are much higher than Britain's, but lower than New York State's. The Soviets currently allow abortion on demand up to twelve weeks following an examination by women doctors. After twelve weeks, strict medical criteria are applied. Abortions, performed only in hospital, are still officially disapproved of, though accepted as a necessary evil. This position has enabled the Party to avoid taking responsibility for effectively organising the provision, dissemination, and quality of contraceptives and supporting women's reproductive rights. Women's lives have been endangered unnecessarily because abortions have become a backstop for inadequate contraceptive measures (Mamanova, 1984). A woman's right to choose is not Party policy. Formally, it endorses the view that women bearing children are fulfilling their natural desires and obligations to society. Stemming the declining Soviet birth rate has restricted state support for women's right to choose, but increasing the birth rate by outlawing abortion had been fiercely rejected on pragmatic rather than ideological grounds – the belief that an increased birth rate would be temporary. After the first few years back-street abortions would cause it to decline again. Additionally, Soviet women would not consent to this suggestion (Holland, 1985).

Pronatalistic sentiments for family policy were reflected in Soviet debates about the population and the 'woman question' (Kaun, 1986). Profeminist demands and pressures came from women who organised the first feminist *zemustads* or underground women's groups (Mamanova, 1984). The Soviet regime, concerned about the falling birth rate, has surveyed women about the trend towards one child families. Their responses highlighted poor housing, insufficient childcare and low income as major disincentives. In short, the inadequacies of the Soviet welfare state have contributed to women having one child.

The divorce provisions of the 1920s liberated men leaving children in the care of women, rather than women (Rosenburg, 1989). The current increase in divorces reflects the high number of suits women are initiating as they voice their rejection of oppressive patriarchal familial obligations. Not having children frees women to pursue their own interests. Rejecting male standards for unsupported motherhood is also attributable to women's high participation in waged labour. Women can now survive independently without the dual career burden if they so choose.

The pronatalist line in Soviet birth control is also racist. The birth rate is below zero in western Russia which has a critical labour shortage. In the Islamic areas, and south Georgia, the birth rate is high. Attempts to increase the birth rate in Russia, the Ukraine, and the Baltic states while restraining it in Asia is racist. Such treatment parallels moves to control black women's fertility in Britain and the United States (see Mama, 1989; Lorde, 1984). Racism and eugenism are integral to pronatalist policies. Economic crises are also closely connected with a poorly distributed population. The Soviet economy's industrial base is in the west. Labour is abundant in the agricultural south and centre. Meanwhile, the minerals necessary to enhance production are located in the sparsely populated regions of northern Siberia. Also, 92 per cent of the urban population of working age is already in either production or school. The reserve army of labour has been plumbed to its depths, making increasing the birth rate attractive. However, the advantages are outweighed by disadvantages arising from the additional demands a substantially larger population makes on welfare services, employment provisions, consumer durables, and political structures in a stagnant economy.

STATE ASSISTANCE TO FAMILIES

Early considerations of the family examined the desirability of following bourgeois precedents promoting individualism or moving towards communalistic living arrangements. Discussions about sexual relations between men and women brought forward options varying from celibacy to the separation of loving relationships from sexual ones (Kollantai, 1971). However, attempts to impose gender equality in the 1920s floundered against: the opposition of both men and women (George and Manning, 1980); the inability of a poor country to sustain egalitarian relations; and limited attitudinal changes ensuring the survival of old relational forms. The nuclear family was ultimately accepted as most appropriate for realising socialism (Molyneaux, 1985) if its more oppressive elements were eradicated. This included enabling women to leave housework and enter waged work, making access to divorce easier, loosening the ties of responsibility binding family members together, allowing freer sexual relations to emerge, and providing public childcare facilities. Communal living experiments were conducted in urban communes during the 1920s where the need to get women into social production and resolve acute housing shortages were uppermost (Osborn, 1970; Parkins, 1953).

The absence of a material base fostering innovation in family relationships made it difficult to sustain these early developments and the liberal tenets of family policy were soon lost. In 1926, the Family Code was amended along traditional lines. Filial responsibility in providing for needy family members was strengthened and parental responsibilities tightened to reduce the numbers of deserted children roaming the streets (George and Manning, 1980). Traditional mores were firmly supported by Stalin who reinstated the family as the basic unit of Soviet society. Families were forced to stay together by making divorce more difficult to obtain. Parents could be prosecuted for neglecting their children. Abortion was made illegal. Against these 'coercive' measures, limited support became available. New allowances for expectant mothers and heads of large families were introduced in 1936 for mothers with seven or more children to increase the birth rate and subsequently the labour force. Women with ten or more offspring were accorded special status under the title of 'mother heroines'. These allowances made modest contributions to family incomes. After Stalin's death, industrialisation and concern with population growth diminished as a priority. This partly accounts for the government's failure to increase children's allowances in 1956 when other benefits went up.

The backbone of the current child allowances scheme formed in Stalin's time rests on small grants and monthly allowances weighted in favour of large families, payable only for the first five years of a child's life. The government has provided more support for single parent families to reduce family poverty. Unmarried mothers receive an additional allowance until a child's twelfth birthday. The allowance varies according to the number of children. Favouring larger families, the amount increases with each subsequent child beginning with the third. Prioritising large families when family size was declining had the greatest impact on low waged women workers facing financial difficulties (George and Manning, 1980). Women headed single parent families also receive income support through maintenance. Husbands are legally required to support former families despite relationship breakdown with one-quarter to one-third of their income, depending on the number of children left with their former wives, unless they obtain court orders to the contrary. The likelihood of having maintenance reduced by the courts if the man forms another relationship is high (George and Manning, 1980). Enforcing maintenance orders is easier than in capitalist countries because full employment is assured.

Additionally, women have access to maternity benefits. Regulations for the payment of maternity benefits to collective farmers and workers were relaxed in 1973, giving all working mothers irrespective of the length of their employment a maternity allowance on full wages eight weeks before and eight weeks after the birth thereby reducing income insecurity around childbirth. Women could also obtain unpaid leave until the child's first birthday for remaining at home to care for their children. Their doing so reduced demand on state provided childcare services. Unfortunately, this was not an easy option for women without recourse to additional incomes, and seriously disadvantaged single parent women. Low paid workers also received a small maternity grant payable on the birth of a child to help with the additional expenses incurred at this time.

Poverty continues to be a problem in the Soviet Union though exact figures are unavailable. The official poverty line is fifty roubles per person per month. McAuley (1977) uses this definition to estimate that 61 per cent of *kolhozniki* and 24–6 per cent of state employees are below the poverty line. Following official definitions of poverty in the 1960s, Matthews (1972) ascertained that one-third of the Soviet working class was poor by official Soviet standards, making material insecurity a reality for many families. A high number of the poor work, raising the question of the inadequacy of both wages and income maintenance policies. Poverty affects women headed single parent families disproportionately. Low waged incomes, low social security benefits and reduced opportunities for obtaining incomes from other sources make it difficult for women with children to enhance their living standards. Single parenthood, applying to one Soviet family in ten in 1970, is high (George and Manning, 1980, p. 59). The precarious economic situation of working single parent women is aggravated by the absence of substantial state assistance meeting their specific needs and position as unskilled and non-manual employees, for example cleaners and office workers, earning the lowest wages. Wage differentials within firms can be wide. For example, a male director in an industrial firm can earn eight times more than a woman cleaner (Yanowitch, 1977).

The Soviet government attempted to tackle family poverty by improving family allowances and encouraging more mothers with young children to join the labour force. This approach had a limited impact in that women's wages and children's allowances remained low. Additionally, increased childcare provisions failed to meet demand, particularly for younger children and babies for all mothers to opt to return to work immediately after giving birth (George and Manning, 1980). Further assistance for low paid families introduced in 1974 was the family income supplement payable for each child for eight years. Poverty in the Soviet Union, as in the West, is located largely among single parent families. Strategies for addressing it resemble those used in capitalist societies. That is, marginally redistributing income through the welfare state rather than eliminating the causes of poverty – low wages, inadequate benefits, the absence of a guaranteed income for individuals.

The family is central to the well-being of Soviet people. In this respect, the social organisation of this particular institution is similar to that prevailing in the West.

STATE INTERVENTION IN DAY CARE

Hyde (1974) suggests childcare services were developed during the struggle to develop healthier living conditions. A full picture of the situation is lacking as the relevant literature is scarce despite the provision of day care being a Soviet achievement (Heitlinger, 1979). Childcare remains women's responsibility whether collectivised or not. Women as mothers, grandmothers, and nursery nurses undertake this work in both the home and public facilities. Public childcare provisions are more highly developed than in the West as women constitute 52 per cent of waged workers. Day care for children under 7 expanded rapidly between 1928 and the late 1930s when Stalin needed women's labour to fuel industrialisation. Stalin's counter-revolution in family matters stopped this growth and provisions stagnated until the mid-1950s.

Eighty per cent of urban children needing day care currently have access to it twenty-four hours a day (Heitlinger, 1979). Crèches exist for peasant children during peak seasons. Maternity-leave and the private care of children at home have meant very few children under age one need day care. Nurseries are well-staffed with trained personnel interested in stimulating the development of children. Besides keeping them healthy, educational materials are used to develop cognitive skills and children are socialised into a socialist morality which includes self-discipline, politeness, acquiring skills, and helping others (Brofen-brenner, 1972). The demand for more nurseries and other support for the family is increasing as only 23 per cent of pre-school children actually receive day care. Grandparents are the mainstays in this arena, not institutional provisions. Only in cities like Moscow and Leningrad are levels of provision sufficient to meet demand (Rosenburg, 1989). Because of such shortages, traditional support through the extended family is more important to childrearing in the Soviet Union than in capitalist countries like Britain and America.

OLDER PEOPLE

By 1970 older people formed 16 per cent of the Soviet population. Permitted to work after retirement age, they have retained their role in the waged economy and can work in the domestic economy as childminders. Around 75 per cent of elders are women. Poverty strikes a substantial proportion of them because pensions are inadequate and not automatically increased when wages or prices rise. According to Madison (1973) half of Soviet pensioners exist on incomes below the officially defined poverty line. The situation is more dire for those with marginal roles in the waged economy because there are no national social assistance benefits although they may receive aid through schemes established by individual republics. A vast number of women do not qualify for pensions. These include: women entering employment late in life, women working part-time, disabled people unable to work, and former collective farmers with short work records (George and Manning, 1980).

Without occupational schemes, pension choices for working people are dependent primarily on state provisions. The average pension is 50 per cent of the average wage; the maximum 90 per cent (George and Manning, 1980). As families are obliged to care for their members, the state does not facilitate this role in the provisions it makes available. Allowances for adult dependants are very low for both widows and spouses. Widows must establish a right to their own pension to mitigate poverty in old age. Working women married to retired men must do likewise.

The Party attempted to respond to poverty among its elders in 1964 by abolishing the earnings rule for those working beyond retirement age. By 1975, half of those eligible for retirement remained at work (George and Manning, 1980). Low paid women benefited from this change because remaining at work longer increased the amount of their pension (Mandel, 1975; Dott, 1966). However, poverty in old age remains a fact of life for many Soviet women.

IN CONCLUSION

The impact of family policy in the Soviet Union is not significantly different from that evident in capitalist countries, regardless of whether they have an explicit family policy. This means that familial ideology which places women in a subordinate position is still reinforced while women struggle with their dual career burden. However, women's financial dependency on men is not so thoroughly assumed in Soviet social policy as it is in capitalist welfare states.

Chinese family policy

SHIFTING PATRIARCHAL RELATIONS: DEVELOPMENTS PRIOR TO THE REVOLUTION

Chinese women's liberation goes up and down with the forces of change emanating from: power struggles in the Communist Party; the unfolding of the class struggle; economic development; demographic changes; the ideological reconstruction of social relations, and the strength of women's organisations. Family policy therefore follows the see-saw principle, making the family both liberating and oppressive. It is liberating because its revitalisation has enabled women to enter the labour force, secure an income in their own right, and raise the status of women (Andors, 1983). The family is oppressive in that women still carry major responsibility for housework, ensuring that the dual career burden is a central feature of Chinese women's lives.

Before the revolution, women led a circumscribed existence defined by Confucian ideology in a society whose social relations were patrilocal, patrilineal and patriarchal. Women were always subject to male authority: as daughter, a woman was responsible to her father; as wife she answered to her husband; as widow she obeyed her eldest son. This situation was known as the Three Obediences (Croll, 1978). When married, a woman lived with her husband's family. Here she would be subject to further authority, this time a female one, her mother-in-law. Women's life was epitomised by the saying 'the frog in the well' (Croll, 1978). Because a woman left home when she married, her presence in her family of birth was considered transient. She was important as a source of labour, but a secondary one which would disappear before long as girls could be married without their consent at the age of 10 or 12. After marriage a woman's labour bolstered her husband's family fortunes. A married woman's standing was determined by the husband's work, not hers. Nonetheless, some recognition of the woman's contribution to her husband's family resources was made through the payment of a bridal price as compensation to her natal family for her lost labour. The temporary nature of women's position devalued the contribution of their labour made in both their natal families and husbands' families and advanced people's preference for male children as they contributed permanently to their family's welfare through their own work and that of their wives who would also provide additional labour by giving birth. Men were seen as adding to family income. Women were merely an expense. These dynamics were central to placing women in a subordinate position and keeping them there. Women were important in reproduction *as long as they bore male children* since these brought additional labour into the family. Female only children brought humiliation (Peng, 1987). In their personal behaviour, women were expected to follow the Four Virtues of knowing their place, not boring others by chatting and gossiping, being clean and attractive, and doing the housework. These defined women as passive beings obeying men.

Life was hard for women, regardless of their class though it was much tougher for poor peasant women bearing the burden of housework as well as heavy work in the fields, or other waged toil. They could be sold into bondage, concubinage, or child labour and physically abused. Croll (1978) has estimated that 60–70 per cent of women were routinely beaten. Infanticide was common and usually perpetrated on girls.

Women's sexual expression inside or outside marriage was tightly controlled. Women committing adultery could be killed. Chastity was a must for women. With such strong social sanction, men murdered women freely. Widows, as soiled goods, could not remarry (Lang, 1946; Peng, 1987). Footbinding prevailed.

Despite heavy penalties for insubordination, women did not blindly follow the Confucian world order. Throughout Chinese history, they struggled for women's liberation (Croll, 1978; Broyelle, 1977). Their activities in the White Lotus Rebellion, Taiping Rebellion, 1898 Reform Movement, Boxer Rebellion, 1911 Revolution, May Fourth Movement of 1919 were milestones in pre-Maoist China. Feminists argued for women's social and property rights and against compulsory marriages and footbinding. Other women resisted individually rather than politically by committing suicide in desperate attempts to change their families' behaviour towards them (Lang, 1946; Peng, 1987).

Changing women's position through family reform was an urgent aim of the Chinese Communist Party. Though initially developing its own approach to establishing equality between men and women, it drew on the experiences of the Soviet Union and Kollantai's writings (Broyelle, 1977). Its basic stance was the classical Marxist one of changing the economic base before women's position could be radically altered.

Between 1923 and 1927, women in the Communist Party worked jointly with the Women's Department in the Guomingtang which was led by the wives of leading Guomingtang men who had adopted some feminist demands following the arrests of leading feminists in 1913. Their main purpose was to glorify the family and channel women into education. Women in the Communist Party were demanding more far-reaching changes – free marriage, the equal right to work, education, own and inherit property, vote and hold office.

The Communist Party also used women to promote its ideas in the countryside and to serve in the army and rural areas where it formed local women's unions known as Women's Peasant Associations. Communist women, critical of the old ways and supporting peasant women in challenging these, proved problematic for the peasants, male and female. They thought the short-bobbed Communist women were prostituting themselves through their 'unladylike' behaviour (Croll, 1978). Additionally, men rejected the Women's Associations for encouraging divorce and free marriage and called it the Bureau of Divorce and Remarriage.

The demise of the alliance between the Guomingtang and the Communist Party enabled Chiang Kai Shek to launch a vicious attack on women and close down the women's unions. Leading feminists and women with bobbed hair were raped and/or killed (Croll, 1978). The Guomingtang redefined women's emancipation to encompass femininity, domesticity, and professional employment in areas considered 'women's work' such as teaching. This attack split the feminist movement, dividing middle class women from working class women. The Communist Party responded to this assault on women by separating feminism from socialism and pushing women out of politics (Croll, 1978), justifying its action as a compromise between the forces of tradition and the call for modernity.

The Guomingtang enacted the 1931 Civil Code enshrining patriarchal and patrilineal principles and conceding some feminist demands by giving men and women equal property rights, the right to choose their own marriage partners, and sanctioning divorce. The regulation of personal life in accordance with patriarchal principles continued, especially in sexual matters. The New Penal Law, still on the statute books, demanded chastity of unwed men and women. Concessions to modernity granted patriarchal relations a new lease of life. Women supported the New Life Movement of 1934, breathing new ideological life into Confucian views of the family, despite their increased entry to educational establishments and paid employment. Women's vulnerability in waged work was particularly poignant during recessions when they faced dismissal before men (Croll, 1978).

Leading feminists attacking the restricted view of womanhood promoted by the New Life Movement argued for economic independence for women and respect for their lives. The war against the Japanese and the Chinese Civil War enabled Chinese women to develop collective forums through which to challenge traditional definitions of their conditions. Their active involvement in the war effort meant that they were increasingly drawn into public life (Hinton, 1966).

Meanwhile, the Chinese Communist Party criticised the feminist movement for being dominated by petty bourgeois intellectuals seeking equality before the law as the basis for women's liberation and argued against women having an independent line and organising separately because that enabled the Guomingtang to incorporate the women's movement (Croll, 1978). The Communist Party also feared feminist isolation from the class struggle would distort socialist development and leave women as second class citizens which men continued to dominate. However, the Communist Party recognised that women had an additional oppression as women, even though they shared class oppression with men (Croll, 1978). It therefore mobilised women for both military and political struggle and drew both peasant and working class women into it.

A COMMUNIST ALTERNATIVE

The first Chinese Soviet Republic established in Kiangsi in 1929 redefined the Party's approach to working with women and led it to guarantee their emancipation. Women's departments were established in all Chinese Communist Party organisations, and the local women's congress elected representatives to them. The 1931 Marriage Code or Plan for Work Among Women attempted to unite both economic and political issues by encouraging women to participate in class organisations in a bid to end the separatism between feminism and socialism. A quota whereby two-fifths of the leaders in the Soviet had to be women was established. And by 1934, 25 per cent of deputies in Kiangsi Soviet were women (Croll, 1978). Unfortunately for women, this structure was destroyed by male hostility, particularly to the idea of free marriages being promoted by women and the Civil War with the Guomingtang. Divisions between men and women assumed second place in the liberation struggle as they united to fight for their physical and economic survival under the onslaught of Chiang Kai Shek and his supporters from the West.

Following the Long March involving fifty women, the Chinese Communist Party established Shianxi Soviet where the Party and women leaders constructed a women's movement involving the peasants and forming solidarity groups with them. The women soldiers tackling poverty and Confucian norms were initially rejected by both peasant and gentry women. To counter their perceptions and get women interested in emancipation, Communist women initiated consciousness raising groups to examine their experiences of oppression as women, adopted peasant clothes, babysat and worked with peasants. Their overtures were successful and rural women began to think of themselves in active roles. They initiated 'speak bitterness' meetings in which they could share ideas, experiences, support one another's struggle for new rights and form Women's Associations to meet their special needs.

The Communist Party feared this development would split it, undermine land reforms and prevent its appropriating women's labour to work in the fields in a part of China where women were not traditionally involved in agriculture. Assuring women's involvement in production became a major task of the women's movement. Women's Associations also set up women's spinning co-operatives, created a guerrilla corps for the Eighth Army, and started a women's university in Hunan. Despite this progress older women and men continued opposing Women's Associations. In 1946, the Communist Party limited its objectives on women's liberation to maintain its unity and channel women's energies into fighting Japan. It promised to attend to the 'women's question' after defeating Japan. The subordination of women's liberation to economic and military objectives, featured strongly in the Party's initial approaches to the 'woman's question'.

Measures fostering women's equality were enacted in 1947 when the Agrarian Reform Law gave men and women land certificates, and the Women's Association promised to mobilise women behind the revolution.

DEVELOPMENTS AFTER THE REVOLUTION

The all China Democratic Women's Federation (Women's Federation), established in 1949 on a group membership basis, became the central organising organ of the women's movement. Supported by the main Communist Party, its ventures sought to balance women's demands for liberation with those of the socialist revolution (Croll, 1978). Its primary aims and objectives included redefining the division of labour, promoting equality between women and men, prohibiting concubinage, and allowing divorce if mediation failed when either one or both parties desired it. This last point was crucial for women formed 76.6 per cent of plaintiffs filing for divorce (Croll, 1978). The Women's Federation also supported women exercising their rights, for example getting violent men to stop abusing them. It used consciousness-raising techniques to promote the idea that individual women's well-being was a group responsibility and help women acquire skills they lacked, for example literacy (Hinton, 1966).

In 1950, pressure from the Women's Federation and the Party's commitment to the 'Woman's Question' prioritised the Family Revolution in governmental planning and facilitated the passage of the 1950 Marriage Law drafted by the Women's Federation to foster equality between men and women and increase women's participation in social production (Andors, 1983).

Success in getting the Marriage Law on the statutes increased Chinese women's respect for and encouraged participation in the Women's Federation activities, particularly those dealing with practical problems. In Shanghai, for example, 22 per cent of women had joined the Women's Federation by 1951 (Croll, 1978). The Communist Party was keen to encourage the Women's Federation in reaching out to women to secure their endorsement of its land reform and industrialisation programmes (Broyelle, 1977; Andors, 1983). Women were asked to farm land, form women's co-operatives, undertake light industrial work, and create mutual aid teams. Yet, the Chinese Communist Party was not prepared to give women a right to an independent income. Instead, income earned by individuals was aggregated as the family's income. Economic exigencies informed the Party's response to women's demands despite the ideological and practical challenges they prompted. Meanwhile the dual career burden women carried increased as they worked outside and inside the home.

Unfortunately, the patchy implementation of the Marriage Law contributed to its failure in altering people's attitudes as anticipated. Party cadres ignored the circulars relating to its provisions and turned a blind eye to violations of it. Male hostility to women's increased rights continued, especially in the rural areas where male children were preferred, and arranged marriages based on the exchange of women for a bridal price continued (Johnson, 1983). Consequently, the murder of women, and their suicide rate remained high. Worried about this state of affairs, the Women's Federation convinced the Communist Party to launch a campaign to publicise the Marriage Law in 1953 (Croll, 1978). During this campaign, trained representatives from the Women's Associations, Peasant Associations, the Chinese Communist Party, and the Young Communist League, called public meetings in villages, held small group discussions, and spoke to individuals to explain the value of the Marriage Law in supporting family life and enhancing relationships between men and women, thereby minimising its threatening potential. Despite these efforts, resistance to the Marriage Law continued. It was dubbed the Women's Law for giving women too much freedom. Peasant men worried that granting women equal rights to work and own property undermined their ability to fulfil their roles as male providers (Johnson, 1984). The recent Land Reform giving them access to the land enabling them to meet family responsibilities as men for the first time in their lives was being subverted by the Women's Law. They were prepared to have none of it (Johnson, 1983). The Party feared that supporting feminist aims would initiate a backlash endangering the unity essential in maintaining the class struggle and continuing the Revolution. Consequently, ending women's oppression became of secondary importance.

While this campaign was proceeding, the Communist Party was safeguarding women's interests as workers and mothers rather than looking after their interests as women. For example, in 1951, the Labour Insurance Law included provisions for maternity leave guaranteeing working mothers fifty-six days of leave on full pay. These were generous for their time and exceeded provisions available to women in the West. Additionally, this legislation authorised light work for pregnant and nursing women, and established a network of ante-natal, pre-natal, and post-natal care. Midwives were trained to provide this care and ensure hygiene. Sanitation measures and inoculations against disease, especially tetanus, reduced infant mortality by one-third (Croll, 1978).

Further initiatives were forthcoming as the Communist Party drew more heavily on women's labour to modernise the Chinese economy and ensure that demographic and economic growth worked in tandem with each other. In 1954, heterosexual monogamous marriage was endorsed at age 18 for women and 20 for men to integrate women more effectively in social production. Birth Control Campaigns were also mounted under the aegis of the Women's Federation to encourage women to marry later, plan their pregnancies, and improve their physical health. While not engaging directly with issues around women's sexual expression, it addressed the problems of raising children in conditions of extreme poverty and the state's desire to control population growth.

In 1955, contraceptive advice and family planning were combined to establish birth control clinics. The ban on abortion was relaxed to eliminate unwanted children, rather than provide another contraceptive measure (Croll, 1978). Sterilisation was available to consenting couples. Both moves were consistent with including abortion and sterilisation in a population control policy. Women were encouraged to take good care of their offspring to ensure a fit and healthy workforce. Counselling and advice on childcare was made accessible to pregnant women. Nursery places and nursery rooms blossomed as collective childcare became popular. The Women's Federation trained nursery nurses on a short-term basis. Working mainly with women, its activities failed to undermine the prevailing sexist division of labour. Men were not interested in joining activities clearly considered 'women's work' (Andors, 1983). Gains for women were limited. Many nurseries in rural areas opened seasonally during peak harvest periods, suggesting that economic priorities were ascendant over the needs of women and children. Crèches, staffed by older and younger women, were formed following group discussions in which women considered their operation in detail, but had limited opening periods. Childcare was receiving collective attention, but the solutions proffered reinforced women's position as primary caregivers and maintained the sexist division of labour, keeping men out of caring work.

As these changes did not reverse patriarchal definitions of men's and women's roles, women's domestic duties became entrenched and their burden increased considerably between 1953 and 1957. However, women were not working solely in the home as the economy demanded their labour outside it. Domesticity was also reinforced through the Five Good Movement encouraging housewives to plan their household budget, help their husbands and children, study and co-operate with other women. However, matters were becoming critical. Women being crippled by the demands made of them prompted the Women's Federation to criticise government action at the Eighth Party Congress in 1956. It complained the government had overlooked women's house-hold duties and physical needs, demanded social services to ease women's domestic burden and sought help in encouraging recalcitrant men to co-operate in domestic chores. It also pointed out that women were underrepresented in the Communist Party, the Young Communist League and trade union decision-making structures and discriminated against in promotions at work.

Encouraging women to participate in public life was an important dimension of Party policy towards women. During the early days of the Revolution, women's political activities increased substantially. In 1953, 84 per cent of women voted, formed 20 per cent of the representatives in the Central People's Government, and constituted 12 per cent of the Deputies in the National People's Congress. On the local level, women elected to street committees comprised 48 per cent of their representatives (Croll, 1978). Women's tradition of activism in the workplace continued through liaison committees the Women's Federation formed to develop links with the trade unions. Women met separately from male trade unionists to consider their welfare needs and improvements in the workplace. In 1952, 70 per cent of women industrial workers belonged to trade unions. Trade unions involved in the technological and political education of women established workplace welfare activities and improved working conditions for them.

THE PERIOD OF THE GREAT LEAP FORWARD

The rural co-operative movement encouraged five million women into the workforce. However, economic developments requiring women's labour on a massive scale prompted the Communist Party to develop other initiatives to draw more women into the labour market and ease the labour shortage. Aimed to expand the economy and increase rural production, these were implemented during the Great Leap Forward of 1957-8. The rural commune was created as the lynchpin of the ensuing reforms. It was intended to influence collective living and social production on a grand scale by forming new institutions collectivising household chores and freeing women's labour time. The Great Leap Forward established 26,000 communes at its height. Though this compared poorly to the 700,000 co-operatives formed during the Socialist High Tide of 1956 (Howard, 1988), the commune movement was audacious for the scope of the transformation it was trying to achieve.

Communes were formed by joining several co-operatives into units varying in size from 10,000 to 20,000 households, located mainly in rural areas. Meanwhile, the dual career burden on women increased. Most housework was done by hand as families lacked resources to purchase household gadgets. Although their work was socially relevant and benefited others, it was not recognised as such. Women slept less to fit in the domestic and production work heaped on their shoulders, thereby meeting their social obligations by living a poorer quality of life. While economic considerations took precedence in the activities of the communes, the Chinese attempted to achieve common ownership in more than agricultural production by collectivising social reproduction during the struggle to shift women's domestic responsibilities. The Women's Federation became involved in socialising household chores to alleviate women's excessive workloads by setting up community dining rooms, nursery rooms, day nurseries, kindergartens, neighbourhood service centres, and maternity hospitals. Self-help, self-sufficiency and learning from the experiences of others were key features of this movement. Commune cadres were enjoined to fight for the common good by channelling people's talents and resources into collective endeavours.

By 1959, 4.98 million nurseries and 3.6 million dining rooms had placed some of women's private domestic burden in the public arena. However, domestic work whether paid or not, remained a 'menial' occupation unattractive to men, for example waitressing. This included domestic labour requiring training when collectivised, for example nursery staff.

The collectivisation of housework facilitated the entry of one hundred million women into the labour force performing a variety of jobs primarily in workteams drawing on their talents for small scale production (Croll, 1978). In cities, women entered neighbourhood factories, built their own workshops and worked collectively while training each other (Andors, 1983; Howard, 1988). Women were paid in their own right, thereby ending the aggregation of family incomes. However, women still received fewer workpoints than men (Andors, 1983). Equal pay for equal work was also resisted and men doing heavy skilled agricultural work received more workpoints than women doing the same tasks (Andors, 1983). Women team leaders were responsible for taking up women's issues and discussing them with women and the authorities. Women cadres presented women with poor role models in challenging the sexist division of labour as they performed 'women's work'. Special attention was given to women's needs during menstruation, pregnancy, childbirth, and breastfeeding.

Responding to women's needs on this basis locked them more firmly into biological roles, giving credence to the view that women undertook less than their fair share of the work (Andors, 1983; Chan et al., 1984). Such attitudes legitimated communes paying women workers fewer workpoints than men. Additionally, women performing domestic work justified the view that women could be different and remain men's equals (Andors, 1983). However, as differences between men and women were not placed on an egalitarian footing, these became another vehicle for reinforcing women's subordinate position. Housework done by women was considered unproductive and not socially recognised through the workpoint system. This belittled the value of women's contribution to social production through the domestic economy and reinforced inequality between working women and men. For example, women had to take time off waged communal work to do unwaged domestic work.

Collectivised housework was problematic in other respects. Food preparation required skills staff lacked. Many women employees were illiterate and could not perform the duties expected of them without prior training which was not forthcoming, for example bookkeeping and accounting. Socialising domestic work also required material resources on a scale impossible when extreme scarcity in consumer durables prevailed. Poor quality canteen food was rejected by better off members of the commune who cooked meals on their own *kang* (brick stove). This introduced disparities among commune members and deprived the commune and workteams of time and resources required to cook private meals. In the urban areas, only the main meal was eaten in communal canteens.

Patriarchal forces remained powerful despite the development of the commune with its collective and egalitarian thrust (Stacey, 1983). Women continued most of the caring work, much of it as socialised labour. Thus, within the: 'context of simultaneous increase of production and expansion of social services, there emerged a clear pattern that tended to perpetuate *relative* (sic) inequalities between men and women' (Andors, 1983, p. 71). Familial living arrangements altered little in recognition of people's affection for each other. Children were identified as independent persons, subject to parental discipline. Parents remained responsible for their children, though their upbringing was shared more with others.

By the end of the collectivisation process, 80 per cent of urban women and 90 per cent of rural women were in social production. Individuals no longer depended on private households for economic support and social services. Women ceased being considered economic burdens and found satisfaction working outside the home. Women formed groups to engage in economic activity, although they desisted from becoming active in communal politics (Andors, 1983; Chan *et al.*, 1984).

The Great Leap Forward revealed that altering the economic base does not necessarily liberate women (Andors, 1983; Stacey, 1982). Structural economic changes must be accompanied by political and ideological ones for men's and women's roles to be redefined. This includes challenging the sexist division of labour in both the workplace and home, and moving men into areas of women's work and vice versa. Family relationships have to be transformed during this process as men and women change their attitudes and refrain from colluding with male supremacy.

Some of these issues were addressed in 1962 when consciousness raising grappled with building women's confidence and shifting their attitudes about feeling inferior through separate study groups. Personal life histories were linked to women's collective history to depict the social nature of women's personal oppression (Andors, 1983). Women were praised for doing housework and waged labour and encouraged to enjoy both waged work and their children. While commendable, these activities placed the responsibility for change on women's shoulders. Little direct work on these matters was done with men. The second Birth Control Campaign was mounted to reduce the size of the population and in individual women's lives. Issues thrown up by sexual politics and women controlling their sexuality remained mute.

The Cultural Revolution of 1966–8 exacerbated divisions between the needs of women's liberation and the economy (Andors, 1983; Croll, 1978). Claiming bourgeois feminism stifled the socialist revolution, the Communist Party suspended the Women's Federation in 1967. The Communist Youth League and trade unions were disbanded at the same time. The banning of these active social movements caused feminist issues to recede further from the public agenda, subordinated women's liberation to class struggle and denied feminists the opportunity to influence policy. Lin Piao's campaign praising family life proceeded without interference from mass organisations and urged women to emulate men and get fully involved in social production. Meanwhile, women's engagement in economic life was glorified. The state remained inactive on transforming the domestic front at this time. Firmly placing the responsibility for women's predicament on them, Lin Piao acknowledged women had problems arising from the Confucian past and their reproductive role, but ignored men's contribution to their disadvantaged status. The birth control campaign was also abandoned. Youthful marriages increased as restrictions were relaxed. Having lost most of its productive functions, the family operated as a unit of consumption. Initiatives assisting women to join the Communist Party meant 27 per cent of the six million new Party members enrolling between 1966 and 1973 were women (Croll, 1978). However, women held lowly positions in the central Party organisation.

In 1973–4, the Party initiated a campaign to improve women's positions as workers and family members by breaking down traditional roles and reinstating the Women's Federation under Party tutelage rather than as an autonomous organisation. Subservient to Party policies, the Women's Federation was given a role in furthering women's development by destroying Five Old Ideas and setting up Five New Ideas. Its guiding principles included destroying:

1. The idea that women were useless.
2. The feudal mentality oppressing women and limiting them to motherhood.
3. Women's dependence on and subordination to men.
4. Bourgeois concepts of 'the good life'.
5. Narrow family self-interest (Andors, 1983).

Then these are replaced with:

1. Women 'hold up half the sky'.
2. Women as 'revolutionary proletarians'.
3. Women's independence from men.
4. Proletarian ideals.
5. The nation as the family (Andors, 1983).

The belief that women are useless except as wives and mothers was to be abolished and replaced with the commitment to women as proletarian revolutionaries. Women were to be involved in national politics, and given time to study while men did the housework. These ideas informed the Anti-Lin Piao and Anti-Confucian Campaigns. During the 1973 elections of higher administrative cadres, the Women's Federation ensured men did not monopolise and manipulate ideological resources. The Third Birth Control Campaign was initiated and later marriages were promoted again.

These measures had a limited impact. People still preferred sons over daughters, especially in rural areas where traditional attitudes were reinforced by the sexist division of labour retained when allocating work in private plots. Some communes, however, had considerable success in shifting patriarchal attitudes and developing new modes of behaviour. The showpiece brigade of Dazhai believed that women's interests would be subsumed by 'class struggle' and their position would remain oppressive under socialism unless women instigated changes. It therefore promoted social relations favouring women's liberation by eliminating private plots and encouraging matrilocal marriage.

THE POST-MAO PERIOD

The death of Mao Tse Tung in 1976 and the downfall of the Gang of Four which included Mao's widow Chiang Ch'ing led to a resurgence of the right wing of the Party under Deng. Women's demands for liberation were downgraded in favour of economic development through the *Four Modernisations* in developing industry, agriculture, science and technology, and the military. People were encouraged to engage in sideline activities to maximise personal incomes. Pressures challenging collective responsibilities for welfare were building up because poor economic performance inhibited communal developments. People were getting impatient for a better life and resented having those working hard receive the same benefit as those doing little work (Howard, 1988; Chan et al., 1984). The growth of private plots, selling surpluses in the private market exacerbated women's subordinate position since women were responsible for developing sidelines as part of their domestic workload (Croll, 1983).

In 1978, Deng Xiao Ping introduced the Responsibility System to resolve the conflict between those supporting collective welfare provisions and those wanting welfare devolved onto the family. The Responsibility System picked up on feelings against equality – the hard working refusing to carry the lazy, and promised to destroy the 'iron rice bowl' system (Howard, 1988), indicating the rise of neo-conservative forces in the East. However, material assistance through safety net provisions was a right guaranteed by the state to all in need during old age, illness, and disability. Men are entitled to pension benefits after working twenty years and women fifteen at ages 60 and 55 respectively. These regulations exclude women who have spent the bulk of their lives in unwaged work.

The New Marriage Law of 1981 strengthened the family. Stressing equality between men and women, the patriarchal familial basis remains. Parents are responsible for caring for their children. Mothers and grandmothers act as childminders whenever collective provisions are unavailable. Children are obliged to take care of their parents (Bonavia, 1982). Free marriage has been upheld, but 75 per cent of marriages are still arranged. Men are having difficulties providing the bridal price as expensive consumer durables and houses have become wedding currency. This is curbing marriages and population growth to some extent. Making divorce available only when mediation fails or the couple are completely alienated from each other enforces family stability, a major objective of family policy.

Women's sexuality remains addressed as a reproductive issue checking population growth before it outstrips economic growth. The government has been pushing a strict population control policy, the One-Child Policy, linked to other policies since 1979 (Andors, 1983; Croll, 1983). Having formulated this policy, the Women's Federation has a central role in its day-to-day implementation. Its efforts have concentrated on convincing women to marry later and adhere to the One-Child Policy. This policy allows each couple one offspring except in rural areas where resistance has been modified it to two (Peng, 1987). Adherents to the policy are rewarded with additional workpoints, grain rations, housing allocations, educational privileges, and community approval (Andors, 1983; Croll, 1983). Parents breaking the one child norm face stiff penalties and the burden of raising the extra child(ren) falls on them. Penalties are incurred if a family has more than two children having a four year age gap between them. These include: the revocation of all extra welfare benefits obtained for the first child; reductions in pay; no promotions at work; loss of maternity benefit; buying grain at higher prices; paying for educational and housing provisions for the extra child(ren) and community disapproval. Despite such punishment and the Women's Federation efforts in enforcing the strictures of this policy, it is broken often, especially in the rural areas. Croll (1983) maintains the One-Child Policy is rejected because children are a major source of additional family labour. Moreover, she argues the One-Child Policy is being undermined by the Responsibility System as additional labour is essential in cultivating private plots. Relaxing inhibitions on private production has intensified pressures on women to bear more children to increase the family's disposable labour power and accumulate private wealth (Croll, 1983).

The family's significance as an agent of socialist socialisation and control is becoming more crucial as social relations are being ruptured by the unemployment attending Deng's incursions into the marketplace. The family is being compelled to mop up social problems coming as a by-product of the declining 'iron rice bowl' welfare system and decreasing opportunities for waged employment. Young people's unemployment is serious as the state has failed to develop an urban based substitute for the *xia xiang* policy under which urban youths obtained jobs in the countryside (Andors, 1983). It is being slowly dismantled following parental protests. The family is being asked to provide for its unemployed young by using them in private enterprises and keeping them out of trouble. But the family is proving unable to meet these expectations. Crime is increasing; the neglect of elders is rising. The calls being made on the family have reinforced women's prime responsibilities as mothers though fathers are being encouraged to do domestic work.

Citing the Soviet Union and China, Molyneaux (1985) argues socialist societies use equality to redefine relations between the sexes when removing women from kinship control by allowing free marriages, and giving women rights as childbearers and rearers. These moves politicise personal relations, ensure institutional support for change, and convince men and women to assume different gender identities (Molyneaux, 1985). Although family structures have changed, equality remains elusive. Molyneaux (1985) postulates two phases through which family structures change in socialist societies. During the first phase, women are emancipated from the traditional social order. In the second phase, women fulfil traditional roles in both social and domestic spheres. In China, phase one occurred soon after the Communists seized power. The second phase began during the 'Socialist High Tide'. Molyneux (1985) maintains these phases enable economic developmental needs to supercede those of women's liberation. The restructured heterosexual nuclear family advancing traditional male and female roles becomes prominent because it makes economic change easier. Women's emancipation in socialist societies is, therefore, measured in terms of their increased participation in the labour force, the improved quality and skills of women's labour, the altered structure of rural society, increased political support for the state, and family stability in socialising people in socialist directions (Molyneux, 1985). By not focusing on women's specific interests as women, socialist societies neatly avoid evoking women's liberation as women and addressing the conflict of interests which may arise between women's liberation and economic growth.

While this analysis has some validity, it is deterministic and functionalist. The two phases of family restructuring have always co-existed in China rather than unlinearly following one another as state directives prioritising one phase over the other were not always followed by large segments of the Chinese population. Additionally, the development of women's labour in social production was dependent on what happened in their domestic work. Conversely, changing domestic arrangements depended on developments in waged labour. Also, the state's control over women's reproductive capacity was not always effective. States lack the monolithic powers suggested by Molyneux. For example, women in the Soviet Union in the 1930s failed to reproduce as the state required. Chinese women currently give birth more often than the state wishes. Moreover, by focusing on the family's socialising roles, the state ignores other equally important ones, particularly those concerning emotional fulfilment and security. Men and women have been loath to concede these aspects of their lives despite state dictates. The continued preference of male children in China is largely due to older people's need for security, and younger women fulfilling themselves in the expected manner (Andors, 1983). Finally, the family's key role in consumption can undermine the state's commitment to industrial production. This tension has been evident in the Soviet Union in people's demands for consumer durables to ease life at home since Khrushchev's days (George and Manning, 1980; Gorbachev, 1986), and among Chinese people since 1978 in the popularity of private income earnings schemes for purchasing recreational facilities and household gadgets (Howard, 1988). Stacey's (1983) analysis of enduring patriarchal relations in China suggests these have persisted because the peasantry supported the Chinese Revolution to acquire the land which would enable them to fulfil traditional male and female roles for the first time in their lives. Gaining peasants' allegiance and commitment to fighting for the Communist cause compelled the Chinese Communist Party to compromise its radical stance on the 'woman's question'. In the course of achieving this, socialist aspirations were as much determined by patriarchal relations as challenging them. The net effect of the interplay between them produced new family farms both supporting socialism and constraining its development when it threatened to undermine patriarchal relations (Stacey, 1983).

IN CONCLUSION

The family remains a central element in Chinese social policy reinforcing patriarchal relations and subordinating women's interests as women. Although Chinese women's liberation remains a goal for fulfilment, they have gained considerably more status and control over their lives under the Communist regime than they had before the revolution. The subordination of women's interests to gendered economic and military exigencies has been crucial in marginalising feminist priorities in the formation of social policy. From a feminist perspective, moving feminist concerns centre stage requires that women's needs as women be addressed directly. This means that changing oppressive gender relationships has to take on board the complex interdependence between social production and domestic production and tackle power relationships between men and women in their personal as well as public lives.

CONCLUSIONS

Whether implicit or explicit, family policies in the countries examined have similarities and differences between them. Though developed in different circumstances and assuming different forms, key features occurring in both capitalist and socialist systems are:

1. Endorsing various social divisions including age, race, gender, sexual orientation and through these, oppressive social relations.
2. Subordinating family policy to economic exigencies.
3. The political subordination of women's interests to those of men, children and the economy.
4. Reinforcing gender based inequality in both social and domestic production.

5. Changing women's behaviour rather than men's.
6. The limited state resources assigned to improving women's position.
7. Formulating policies for women without extensively involving women.
8. The primacy of the heterosexual nuclear family.
9. The existence of family poverty.
10. The impact of all social policy on family policy.
11. Aggregating the incomes of family members.

The main differences which can be identified are:

1. The different social, political and economic circumstances within which these similarities are embedded.
2. The varying priorities accorded to women's interests in the different countries.
3. The variation in the detailed specifics of policies such as maternity leave, ante-natal care, etc.
4. The more comprehensive provisions supporting families in command economies than free market ones.
5. The limited periods of policy experimentation with less oppressive forms of family life in socialist societies and its absence in capitalist societies.
6. The different levels at which women collectively organise to promote their interests as women.

From a feminist perspective, family policy needs to underpin the expression of a variety of family forms, none of which can be accorded priority over others in the formation of social policy. Nor can social policy be subordinated to economic needs (Walker, 1984; Coote, 1981). To foster egalitarian relationships in both personal life and workplace relations, economic policy and social policy have to be considered together, taking into account the impact of one on the other. This means dualistic concepts currently informing family policy such as work–home, public–private, state–market, individual–collective, must be replaced with those focusing on the interconnections between these dualisms and complex reality encompassing all issues. Eliminating dualism is central to developing sensitive policies that do not subject different aspects of an issue to a hierarchy of domination and subordination thereby subverting the use of family policy in fostering egalitarian relations and the well-being of individuals, families and communities.

4

Health policy

THE DESTRUCTIVE POTENTIAL OF HIGH TECHNOLOGY 'SCIENTIFIC' MEDICINE

The health systems of the countries under study are in crisis. The burden of providing high quality medical care for those needing it is becoming a strain on economic development, causing each country to consider curtailing demand. In Britain and Canada, bureaucratic mechanisms cutting down waste and claimant numbers are being developed. Both nations have introduced user fees to reduce service costs. Some of these affect clients at an acute stage in their illness, for example prescription charges in Britain and hospital food charges in Canada. Others undermine preventative work by hitting consumers prior to treatment, for example eye test and dental check up charges in Britain. The United States has shelved plans for developing a national health service, despite the proven inadequacy of existing provisions. Meanwhile, in the public sector, Medicare and Medicaid costs have escalated alarmingly, despite public expenditure cuts. In the private sector, doctors are worried that the costs of litigation insurance premiums will force them out of business. The Swedish state has expressed concern about the ever increasing costs of health care. The Soviet Union and China are trying to hold down costs so that economic development on consumer durables and the industrial infrastructure can take place.

The response of consumers in these countries has been interesting. In Britain, the United States, Canada and Sweden, alternative medicine based on low technology, non-pharmaceutical products is gaining ground as patients express disillusionment with the care offered by traditional western high technology medicine. Individuals have developed self-help health provisions which meet their needs more appropriately, for example women's self-examination clinics. Determined

to save scarce resources, the Chinese government has for decades encouraged its consumers to use Western medicine as a last resort, relying
instead on traditional herbal medicine and acupuncture for their
treatment.

The power of the medical profession, pharmaceutical companies and
hospital suppliers is being increasingly scrutinised in the West as this has
been shown to work to the detriment of customers in both the developed
world (Silvers, 1976) and developing world (Doyal, 1979). These
analyses reveal a convergence between the interests of consumers and
those controlling public expenditure. In China, eroding the power of the
medics provided a major impetus in creating the 'barefoot' doctor health
care system. Besides bringing control over health matters closer to the
people, this system ensured a wider distribution of scarce health
resources. The Bolsheviks also curbed the power of doctors in the early
days of the Revolution to counter their resistance to innovation
(Lampton, 1977). Both China and the Soviet Union succeeded in
drawing large numbers of women into the medical profession, but failed
to eradicate its sexist segregation of labour. Women doctors are located
primarily in the lower echelons of the system. Their low status in
socialist countries mirrors that found in the Western countries studied.
This chapter examines the health care systems of America, Canada,
Britain, Sweden, the Soviet Union and China; identifies the points at
which the power of the medical profession, pharmaceutical companies,
and research interests define the types of health provisions available;
considers the extent of consumer involvement in each system and
consumers' ability to challenge the power of the medics and their allies in
developing health services; and focuses on the division of labour in each
health care system, highlighting the significance of gender and 'race'.

HEALTH CARE IN CAPITALIST COUNTRIES

The American health system

The basic tenet in American health care provisions is minimal state
involvement. The market is responsible for providing a range of health
and medical services attracting customers. In the absence of state
provisions, individuals purchase services directly, or through a third
party such as an insurance company which can pool risks and by
introducing economies of scale hold premiums to levels lower than those
necessary if only a few people participated in health schemes. This

ensures more people can afford to buy into them. The guiding principle of the marketplace in health matters is profit (Silver, 1976). Inequalities in health can arise because some types of provision are unprofitable and unlikely to be provided, for example long-term facilities for chronically ill elders, and facilities in poorer parts of the country. Within the framework of the market, state provisions are primarily residual ones easing access to medical services for the 'deserving' poor. The state system also serves the market by subsidising its activities, infrastructure, and service delivery. The 'residual sector' for the individual may well generate substantial profits for capital.

SERVICE PROVISION

The United States does not have a publicly funded comprehensive national health system as do Britain and Canada. Rather, it has a conglomeration of services forming part of the welfare state mosaic. These are:

1. Private insurance provisions.
2. Publicly subsidised services for the 'deserving poor'.
3. Self-help provisions.
4. Family care provided mainly by women.

Despite the official view that combined private insurance and public safety net provisions adequately provide health care for all Americans, a substantial proportion *do not* have formal health care coverage. Estimates of those excluded vary between twenty-five and forty million people (Sidel, 1986; Kotelchuck, 1976).

The component parts of the formal provisions are:

1. Private:
   (a) non-profit insurance companies, for example Blue Cross, Blue Shield;
   (b) profit-making insurance companies, for example workplace schemes.
2. Public federally subsidised schemes:
   (a) Medicare for older people;
   (b) Medicaid for poor people.

PRIVATE NON-PROFIT MAKING INSURANCE COMPANIES

Blue Cross, established in Texas during the Depression to help hospitals collect outstanding payments, covering eighty million people, provides hospital insurance nationwide. Additionally, it administers benefits for a further thirty-two million people under Medicaid and Medicare. Blue Cross offers limited coverage, paying only 75 per cent of hospital stays, or 41 per cent of consumer expenditure on health.

Blue Cross is powerful because it is large, acts as a political lobby and provides health care information nationally. Blue Cross also sets health policy by having representatives sit on hospital boards and government advisory committees. It also contracts with employers and so is supported by unions. Blue Cross also contains a progressive element, the community rating, through which all those seeking insurance are charged the same premiums. However, escalating costs are making Blue Cross rethink this policy in favour of premiums set according to the services covered. Blue Cross controls neither the quality nor costs of provisions and so contributes to inflation. Fraud has also been exposed in the scheme (Silver, 1976; Kotelchuck, 1976). Blue Shield, similar to Blue Cross, provides insurance for doctors' visits and encompasses all its shortcomings (Silver, 1976; Kotelchuck, 1976).

PRIVATE PROFIT-MAKING INSURANCE COMPANIES

These schemes are purchased in the market individually or collectively through workplace bargaining. Occupational schemes made available by employers and trade unions may be extended by individuals. Schemes vary considerably in their coverage, treatment of dependants, and costs of premiums. Occupational welfare schemes formed an important aspect of Reagan's policy of having corporate rather than state welfare assume major responsibility for people's well-being (Lesemann, 1988).

FEDERALLY SUBSIDISED PROVISIONS

Medicare and Medicaid formed under Johnson's plans for a 'Great Society' are the major federal schemes. Other state funded health care initiatives include maternal health and childcare programmes, family planning, community mental health, and neighbourhood health centres.

Medicare covering twenty-one million elders was established through Title XVIII of the Social Security Act in 1965. It consists of: Part A, the universal hospital insurance element; and Part B, the optional premium covering ambulatory services and doctors' visits. Medicare is problematic. Providing only partial coverage, it does not meet the health needs of older people. Additionally, health care costs have increased dramatically for consumers. Premiums rose from $250 in 1966 to $520 by 1987. Besides this, Medicare patients paid a $75 deductible and 29 per cent of the actual costs of treatment provided under Part B of the scheme (Lesemann, 1988). Medicare expenditures fuelled inflation as its budget could rise by 25 per cent in one year. Treatment was expensive, often involving older people in unnecessary hospitalisation and using services where supply exceeded demand, for example nursing homes.

Medicaid provides means-tested care for sixteen million poor including many on AFDC (Lesemann, 1988). Losing eligibility to AFDC can mean the loss of Medicaid coverage, as the poor removed from the welfare rolls under Reagan's budget cuts have discovered. Medicaid, financed by the federal government, is run by the states, enabling each state to set different eligibility criteria and benefits. Medicaid was passed quietly alongside Medicare under Title XIX of the Social Security Act of 1965. Medicaid is also problematic. It has contributed to inflation by being two times more expensive than other forms of health care. The delivery of a poor service to patients has been institutionalised through the 'fee for service' system which has routinised 'pingponging' – the referral of patients from one doctor or agency to another and back, and created 'Medicaid Mills', clinics run by several practitioners offering a variety of services through which Medicaid patients pass whether they need these or not (Silver, 1976; Kotelchuck, 1976). While not offering patients the services they need, these clinics are profitable because doctors are paid every time a 'service' is rendered (Silver, 1976). Medicaid can only impose limited controls over doctors as the hospitals in the scheme choose whether task it is to check, authorise and audit the scheme's finances. Inadequate controls on the growth of Medicaid have fuelled its expansion as new buildings, staff, equipment and technology are directed into this sector.

FORCES SHAPING THE AMERICAN HEALTH SYSTEM

Political, economic and ideological forces have shaped the American health system in contradictory ways. Forces opposing today's developments can become tomorrow's allies. The dominant ideology supported the idea that individuals should procure health coverage through private insurance companies by paying either a premium or a payroll tax. Nonetheless, a considerable segment of the population favoured a national health insurance scheme. A national health plan supported by the Bull Moose Party and the unions, and later Franklin D. Roosevelt, was on Teddy Roosevelt's platform in 1912. Implementation of this proposal was thwarted by the advent of the First World War, the growth of anti-Bolshevik hysteria, the defeat of the Democrats by the Republicans in the 1920s and the entrenched opposition of the American Medical Association, big business, and medical professionals.

Medical interests rejected a public health service on the grounds that profitability was more likely to be assured by market provisions (Silver, 1976). Comprehensive, publicly funded schemes were obstructed by drug companies, hospital equipment suppliers, and private insurance companies safeguarding their profit margins. For example, drugs provided twice the profits in the private sector than in the public one. However, businessmen reversed their opposition once they grasped the opportunities for making money in the public sector. Their change of heart followed their gaining control over government health care subsidies and acquiring government guarantees for their investments and income, thus offsetting the vagaries of the market. The Hill Burton Act of 1946 authorising federal subsidies on hospital construction was crucial in changing their minds by substantially expanding hospital facilities at public expense. Similarly, Medicare and Medicaid were accepted by big business when the government conceded control of the system to the medical experts and agreed a 'fee for service' payment scheme.

The medical profession grew as a scientific activity organised by men after the Flexner Report of 1912 gave the American Medical Association the right to establish medical schools and license doctors. Professional interests gained sway through the American Medical Association's control of licensing provisions which defined the criteria under which licenses were granted and the basis of teaching in medical schools. Flexner's proposals brought medical schools, research stations, and hospitals under academic control. This arrangement fostered: 1. An emphasis on research rather than services; 2. High technology provisions; and 3. Male domination of the system (Ruzek, 1978). Professional medical opinion dominated discussions on state funded health care and was influential in convincing the public to oppose it.

The American Medical Association's hostility to a comprehensive, publicly funded system was consistently voiced in its responses to: the 1912 plans for socialised medicine; F. D. Roosevelt's proposals under the 1935 Social Security Act; bills introduced by Senator Wagner; and in 1952, the Truman Commission proposals on the health needs of America. The American Medical Association rejected these propositions for proposing to cover both the poor and the well-off, potentially increasing demand beyond the capacity of the system to cope; failing to distinguish between the 'deserving' and 'undeserving' poor; and setting a precedent for socialised medicine. It was so determined to see the Truman Commission's proposals for health care as a right fail that it imposed a levy of $25 on each doctor to campaign against them (Silver, 1976; Sidel and Sidel, 1977). The American Medical Association's rejection of a national scheme forced the government to opt for limited public provisions for the 'deserving poor' like older people. This liberal compromise enabled the Association to accept Medicare in the 1960s. It currently opposes cuts in both Medicaid and Medicare because servicing them provides fee revenue and research grants for its members (Silver, 1976). Finally, supporting existing public provisions enables the American Medical Association to retain power when its control is being challenged by hospital boards, drug companies, insurance companies, government quangos, and consumers critical of medical offerings (Navarro, 1975b).

The weakness of the trade union movement and its emphasis on occupational welfare has limited its impact on the development of state funded provisions. Although service workers are more unionised, the rate among the American workforce generally is low, declining from 35 per cent in 1954 to 17 per cent in 1987 (Lesemann, 1988). Trade unions have preferred to handle health issues through the local collective bargaining process, supporting community based health initiatives through workplace insurance schemes linking into Health Maintenance Organisations, for example the Kaiser Foundation Health Plan. Occasionally, unions have favoured initiatives for a national publicly funded health care system, for example the Knights of Labour, the Congress of Industrial Organisations (CIO). Their attempts to promote such schemes in 1919 and the 1930s floundered against weak inter-union organisation and the poor bargaining position of health sector employees. Attempts to organise strikes in 1919 failed miserably. Few health workers joined unions during the Great Depression. Health care workers' right to organise was withdrawn in 1947 when hospitals were exempted from the 1935 Wagner Act on the grounds that public health would be endangered. It was not restored until 1962 when John F. Kennedy passed a law granting federal employees, including hospital workers, the right to strike. Since then, health workers have been unionised to a substantial degree and are keen to establish social issues on their agenda (Silver, 1976; Navarro, 1975b).

Feminists have also shaped health care provisions by contesting medical practitioners' handling of women's health issues and developing a health movement outside of the medical profession's auspices and control (Ruzek, 1978). Feminists tackled issues which exposed the poor quality of care provided, the authoritarian nature of the doctor–patient relationship, the importance of the profit motive in the allocation of resources to services, and the hypocrisy of a profession opposing abortion for women until it was legalised. Doctors realising what enormous profits could be made by meeting the needs of desperate women rushed to open private clinics, organising them in ways denying women control over the processes and treatment to which they were subjected (Frankfort, 1972; Worcester and Whatley, 1988). Feminists developed self-help initiatives to secure alternative provisions focusing on the quality of care women received and giving women control over the service. These were small local ventures using resources, knowledge and skills women already possessed to address primarily gynaecological and related matters, for example cervical smears. The feminist challenge did not undermine existing health systems although it threatened the power of the medical profession to determine which provisions were available. Doctors responded to this threat by taking feminists to court for illegally practising medicine as feminist self-help groups were neither licensed by the American Medical Association nor trained in the appropriate medical schools (Ruzek, 1978). Although incapable of upsetting the prevailing distribution of health resources and the medical profession's hold over the system, feminist alternatives have successfully enabled women to opt out of existing provisions (Ruzek, 1978).

GOVERNMENT AND THE PUBLIC EXPENDITURE CUTS

The financial turnover and number of employees make health care one of America's largest industries (Kotelchuck, 1976). The government's responses to funding health care have varied over time, depending on the state of the economy, the party in power, and political pressures on it to take action during crises. Successful federally funded proposals included subsidising hospital building in the 1950s and extending coverage for poor people and elders. In the 1970s, budget deficits introduced cuts in expenditure. This trend has continued in the 1980s. Although America has no publicly funded national comprehensive health service like the British National Health Service, government expenditure on health is higher than in countries having one. For example, in 1976, the United States spent 8.6 per cent of its GNP on health, compared to 5.5 per cent in Britain and 6 per cent in the Soviet Union (OECD, 1977).

Government intervention in health care initially provided economic stability for the system and encouraged expansion. The lack of public control over the American Medical Association, doctors, and 'medical–industrial complex' (Silver, 1976) and the spread of deficit financing have produced a crisis in the system. Inflation and escalating costs have virtually bankrupted Medicaid and Medicare. The government has responded to the fiscal crises by enforcing cuts and reorganising services following paths taken by other capitalist countries, for example Britain and Canada.

RESTRUCTURING AMERICAN HEALTH CARE PROVISIONS

The rising costs of Medicare and Medicaid during the 1970s have caused the federal government to rethink its interventions and take counter action. Nixon initiated restructuring measures by supporting the Health Maintenance Organisations which he expected to deal with the crisis by efficiently co-ordinating services, reducing costs and waste by eliminating duplication and accumulating capital by collecting annual premiums to cover doctors' visits and hospital treatment in advance, and giving consumers a choice of doctor. By 1985, more than fifteen million people were covered by Health Maintenance Organisations (Lesemann, 1988, p. 154). The American Federation of Labour–Congress of Industrial Organisations (AFL–CIO) favoured such organisations for their consumer orientation. Insurance companies liked them because they provided a windfall at the beginning of the year and flexibility in organising their resources. These are the reasons that Thatcher favoured their introduction in Britain.

Reality is different. Health Maintenance Organisations are unable to fulfil their promises. They provide fragmented care and are seen as ineffective by consumers. They are not popular in rural areas and inner cities where premiums are too high for the poor. Insurance companies favouring middle class suburbs have neglected the countryside and ghettos because the risks of ill health and costs are higher in such communities. Finally, the organisations are under-resourced as the average payments people make are insufficient for the services required and the schemes do not attract sufficient subscribers (Sidel, 1986).

Nixon also attempted to introduce the Professional Standards Review Organisation to control the quality of service and examine doctors' claims for treating Medicaid and Medicare patients. This organisation was successfully opposed by the American Medical Association, particularly its representatives on local health boards, as serious government interference in doctors' affairs. The Comprehensive Health Programme (CHP) was a parallel move aimed at planning and regulating new hospital construction.

The Comprehensive Insurance Plan proposed by Nixon in 1974 aimed to reduce government health care subsidies by forcing everyone to buy tax deductible private insurance and attract contributions from employers and employees. It formed part of Nixon's 'New Federalism' which provided a revenue sharing formula limiting the federal government's contribution to block grants, reducing expenditure on research and training, and making health care self-financing.

The Democrats put forward an alternative plan called the Kennedy–Mills proposal which was later endorsed by Carter. Under its provisions, federal funds would help working people buy private health insurance, an option less expensive than having tax deductible premiums. Insurance companies were responsible for reviewing costs although the government would keep an eye on its subsidies. However, Carter was unable to steer this scheme through Congress; increasing deficits over existing health care services undermined his position while strengthening the opposition's.

Reagan continued the 'cuts', imposing them disproportionately on Medicaid (Sidel, 1986; Lesemann, 1988). Aiming to reduce federal subsidies and push the burden of care onto the states, his actions exacerbated existing regional disparities and made the poor defer treatment (Lesemann, 1988). The poor are more sick when seeking care and more expensive to treat as hospitals become their first port of call.

Hospitals demanding payment before treatment has increased the number of property liens desperate patients offer as security despite the illegality of such action. Reagan's initiatives altered the state's role as mediator between capital and labour to being pro-capital by easing the welfare burden borne by employers while increasing the caring responsibilities women had to adopt at home. Despite Reagan's 'cuts' health expenditure continued to rise. By 1981, there were forty-eight million Americans on Medicaid and Medicare, costing the state $76 billion (Chapman, 1979). Additionally, his moves pushed the Left into defensive positions on health care.

THE PROBLEMATIC NATURE OF THE AMERICAN HEALTH CARE SYSTEM

Notwithstanding the large sums expended on health care privately and publicly, the majority of Americans have a poor experience of it. Service organisation and delivery are riddled with inequality. This includes unequal access according to region, income levels, gender and 'race'. The disparity of provisions across regional boundaries increases inequality in service delivery. The system is bedevilled by social divisions which are reflected throughout the process of service delivery and in the make up of the health care workforce. The fiscal crisis seems intractable unless health care is subsidised through general taxation and preventative care intensified (Sidel, 1986). The lack of control exercised over the professionals and poor quality of care contributes to high consumer dissatisfaction. Control of services and the workforce is in the hands of white middle class males. Black people receive the most inadequate services and have least access to its provisions. American health care is experienced as classist, sexist, and racist (Sidel, 1986; Ruzek, 1978). Silver (1976) suggests the American health system's key problem is serving the interests of the 'medical–industrial complex' or being profit rather than needs-oriented.

Geographical disparities are also expressed through class and 'race'. Middle class suburbs receive the best medical services and have proportionately more doctors than other areas. For example, in 1976, Iowa had one doctor per 999 people; Vermont had one doctor per 565 people. In 1976, across the United States, 748 villages had no doctors and forty-six states had towns with no doctors. Similarly, the distribution of nurses is uneven. In the Southern states there is one nurse for every 500 people, compared to one for every 200 in New England (Silver, 1976). Since class is racially structured (Mama, 1989), it means that class cleavages reinforce racial discrimination. The poorest provisions are in poor working class areas, for example rural Appalachia, inhabited by poor whites and inner cities where blacks live (Sidel and Sidel, 1977). White male doctors at the top of the health care labour hierarchy earn four times more than 50 per cent of the American population (Kotelchuck, 1976; Navarro, 1975a). Most doctors and nurses are drawn from the white middle classes. Black people are in low paid jobs. Black doctors are compelled to serve in inner city areas where practice is difficult and poorly resourced. As 98 per cent of medical doctors are white, few black people reach this position. Black people are also underrepresented in nursing where 92 per cent of nurses, 86 per cent of practical nurses and 86 per cent of nurses' aides are white. Black people are more likely to be located in those occupations which are of low status and do not attract white people (Sidel, 1986; Silver, 1976), making the division of labour in the health care system racist.

White people, especially men, are in control of service delivery and determine the options available for treatment. Black people, particularly Afro-Caribbeans, Puerto Ricans and Hispanics, receive low quality services and fewer preventative services (Sidel, 1986). According to Silver (1976), poverty and illness go together, affecting black people more. Lower incomes, poorer housing, more unemployment, less access to education, more divided families, and the daily stress of racism have a detrimental impact on black people's physical and mental health (Maas, 1972). Black people have the shortest life expectancy in America and the highest infant mortality rate (Sidel, 1986). Black people are more likely to be admitted into mental hospitals because white psychiatrists pass negative judgments on and make racist interpretations of their behaviour (Brown, Willis and Cramer, 1972). Once in treatment, white therapists' ignorance of and ambivalence about black people make them react inappropriately to them; they will be oversympathetic, indulgent, patronising or hostile (Maas, 1972). Black people are also more likely to receive electro-convulsive therapy and custodial care while in psychiatric treatment (Maas, 1972). Black people cannot afford to visit doctors during the early stages of illness, thus their treatment is more expensive when they finally receive attention. The poor are considered a burden on hospital services because coming in when very sick lengthens their hospital stay.

Reagan's 'cuts' have decreased service availability to the poor, particularly the unemployed, as county hospitals no longer take charity cases. As only 50 per cent of those earning less than $5,000 per year are insured, forty million Americans including adults working at low wages and the large number of women working part-time fall outside safety net provisions. A large number of Americans are inadequately insured because they cannot afford to pay the extremely high hospital insurance premiums. Only 75 per cent of the under-65s have hospital insurance, 35 per cent are insured for doctor's visits, and 11 per cent have dental insurance. Underinsurance and non-insurance affect poorer Americans primarily and contribute to the classist nature of health services. Reagan's insistence that able-bodied people pay for their health care has exacerbated this, making health care another site reinforcing labour discipline.

Sexism became particularly evident following the masculine takeover of traditional medicine, the dominance of high technology scientific medicine and the emphasis on curing rather than preventing ill health (Ehrenreich and English, 1979; Ruzek, 1978). Employment practices follow a sexual division of labour reinforcing sexism. Women are found in low status, poorly paid work. Of the five million employees in the health care system, 2.5 million are in nursing services: 98 per cent of nurses and 96 per cent of practical nurses are women. Pay is also unequal. Women nurses get 10 per cent less pay than men and work part-time. 'Race' and gender divisions interact with each other, giving black women the lowest pay. Gynaecology and geriatric services meeting primarily the health needs of women, are low priority areas. Treatment of women patients shows lack of respect for their real needs. A woman is 60 per cent more likely to get a hysterectomy in the United States than in Britain. Most of these hysterectomies are unnecessary (Ruzek, 1978). Women are also more likely to be prescribed tranquillisers and diagnosed as mentally ill. Black women have experienced profound racism in health service delivery. Abortions, sterilisations and unsafe contraceptives such as Depro Provera have been forced upon them (Sidel, 1986; Davis, 1989). These practices have continued despite regulations enacted in 1974 to curb such abuse following public protests and a court case black people filed against the Department of Health, Education and Welfare.

Finally, women's access to private health care insurance is more limited than men's because it relies on working for employers who have developed adequate health care benefits under trade union pressure. Women in waged work are often in poorly unionised firms where welfare benefits are absent. However, women may be registered for health care as dependants of working male partners. Women working at home lack access to health insurance coverage in their own right. Lack of adequate coverage for women is paralleled by inadequate provisions for children. Children's vulnerability is intensified by poverty. The numbers of unprotected children rose following the 'cuts' Reagan imposed on Medicare, causing 2.2 million children previously covered by Medicare to lose their benefit (Sidel, 1986, p. 154). In 1985, nine million children had no medical coverage, and eighteen million lacked dental care (Children's Defense Fund, 1985).

Complaints about the poor quality of state subsidised health care have come from consumer groups, feminists, black activists, and government. These have revolved around: the lack of consumer and governmental control over services; fragmented nature of doctor-patient relationships, especially for the poor; bureaucracy interjecting intermediary institutions between patients and the services they require; delays in receiving reimbursements; and demands for monthly re-registration of the poor. Yet, little has been done to improve Medicaid and Medicare. Private sector customers are also dissatisfied with the low levels of reimbursement of medical expenses, larger deductibles substantially increasing pre-treatment costs, and rising coinsurance costs to cover the remaining treatment. Consumers are having to heavily subsidise their health care as government and insurance schemes combined cover only two-thirds of the costs of treatment (Silver, 1976).

Consumers have also received unnecessary treatment to safeguard the interests of doctors or protect medics' incomes (Silver, 1976). For example, numerous tests are carried out to protect doctors in litigation; 15 per cent of surgical operations are unnecessary, but generate substantial fees; and profit-making drugs are overprescribed, for example 66 per cent of antibiotics prescriptions are unnecessary (Silver, 1976). Patchy provisions and difficulties in purchasing coverage have made the hospital's emergency department a primary care centre. With the exclusion of informal domestic health care, only self-help groups provide alternatives to the market or the state. Yet, such provisions are rare, under-resourced and reach few people, although feminists and black activists have sought extended contact with their constituent groups.

Consumer dissatisfaction, insurance company unease, and the medical profession's fears converge in the rising number of malpractice suits. Malpractice suits are the only form of intervention conventionally available to patients. However, litigation can only occur after the fact and is not preventative. Consumers are limited to demanding payment for misery caused rather than actively promoting improvements in services. Lawyers taking malpractice cases demand increased payments to maximise their incomes. Insurance companies charge higher premiums to meet larger awards. Doctors may lose their reputations or be driven out of practice by the high insurance premiums without tackling the underlying issues around poor quality care. Additionally, industrial relations in the health system are poor. Disputes are increasing as technicians and nurses demand a say in health provisions. The main dissatisfaction with the American health system from the consumer's point of view is the treatment of patients as commodities from whom profits are extracted by doctors, insurance companies and pharmaceutical companies (Silver, 1976).

IN CONCLUSION

The American health system is dominated by the 'medical–industrial complex' (Silver, 1976). It provides the poor, elders, women and black people with inadequate services despite the large sums of money spent on health care. Poor service, medics' lack of accountability, and escalating costs have caused consumer dissatisfaction and federal and state government unease. High technology orthodox medicine exacerbates the lack of access experienced by low income groups, but is increasingly being challenged by alternative provisions developed by feminists and others.

The Canadian health care system

Unlike the United States, Canada has a publicly funded national health scheme established in 1968. The federal government shares the costs of provision with the provinces. Because health care is a provincial responsibility, there are provincial variations in services covered and charges to patients within a national framework. Extensions to provincial provisions can be obtained through occupational health schemes and self-help provisions. Feminist groups in particular have established alternative services offering low cost provisions under consumer control. Additionally, free domestic services are provided by women caring for children and dependent relatives.

FORCES SHAPING THE CANADIAN HEALTH CARE SYSTEM

Health care in Canada became a provincial matter, under Section 92 of the 1867 British North America Act and the 1982 Constitution. The federal government can only intervene by persuading provinces to adopt its views and offering funding to move them in its direction. Other factors having a significant impact on the development of health care in Canada include:

1. Market forces operating at both individual and collective levels.
2. Government austerity programmes.
3. Federal–provincial government disagreements on sharing costs.
4. Parliamentary opposition to government proposals orchestrated by the New Democratic Party, the former Co-operative Commonwealth Federation.
5. The medical profession retaining its power and privilege through the fee-for-service system.
6. The demands of the organised labour movement.
7. Pressure groups, including those belonging to the poverty lobby, women's movement, and Native People's organisations.

Before the Second World War, individuals were responsible for their own and their family's health care provisions which they either purchased privately in the market or obtained through workplace agreements. Doctors were paid on a fee-for-service basis. Medical care for the poor was provided by charitable agencies which established charity wards in hospitals and paid doctors' fees. Government intervention was limited as provinces unable to fund medical services confined their activities primarily to public health campaigns around sanitation, and fighting infectious diseases such as cholera, smallpox and typhoid. Poor diets, a major cause of disease, were cause for concern. In 1939, 33 per cent of Canadians could not afford an adequate diet because their wages were too low (Guest, 1980). A number of ad hoc collective provisions had been proposed following public concern for sanitation and control of epidemics. These programmes became co-ordinated in 1919 when the federal government created the Department of Health. In the provinces, British Columbia had established a Royal Commission to examine health care insurance in 1919. Alberta, Saskatchewan and Manitoba had formed 'municipal doctor' services in the 1930s whereby the provincial governments paid for medical care. Demands for collective provisions increased as socialists mobilised around health issues during the Depression.

Meanwhile, the doctors organised to promote their interests. In 1934 they indicated their willingness to accept state financed health insurance if the medical profession controlled crucial aspects of it, namely:

1. Method of remuneration.
2. Fee schedules.
3. Eligibility criteria.
4. Majority representation on local health insurance commissions.

These demands were part of a strategy aimed at restricting public health schemes to the poor unable to purchase expensive hospital treatment. In British Columbia, for example, the relief workers, the One Big Union and the Co-operative Commonwealth Federation put pressure on provincial premier Pattullo to investigate the issue and come out in favour of state funded health services in 1936. However, his proposed Health Insurance Act floundered against the opposition of the medical profession. Alberta advocated a public health scheme in 1937. This initiative also failed to reach the statute books because it was opposed by doctors. The powerful Medical Association reiterated the medics' demands when accepting the formation of health commissions according organised medicine a majority on their governing bodies, payment according to fees established by doctors controlling the fee schedule, and the restriction of public provisions to low income people.

The medical profession also commenced its own voluntary group medical hospital plans. The Associated Medical Services of Ontario, created in 1937, was its most successful example. Older people, chronically ill people, labourers, unskilled workers and itinerants received no coverage. Women were poorly served by these schemes because they were strongly represented among older and chronically ill people. Additionally, the inability of large families to meet health care costs from their own resources continued to be an obstacle which the doctors' proposals could not surmount. Public sentiments were reflected in the Reports the federal government commissioned on the issue. Marsh and Heagerty went beyond the medics' suggestions and argued for a comprehensive service to cover public health, sickness benefit, pensions, services required for the chronically ill, and provisions for the permanently disabled.

Marsh, prompted by the growing recognition of the need for a state funded comprehensive health care system, highlighted high infant mortality rates and malnutrition among children and the working poor as chief causes of concern. Unfortunately, the recommendations of the Marsh Report were opposed by the Social Services Council under Charlotte Whitton. It favoured a residual system of medical care covering most poor people. Provincial governments rejected Marsh's Report because its implementation would strengthen the hand of central government. Some trade unionists also opposed its suggestions. In the face of such hostility, the federal government ignored the Marsh proposals.

However, the issue did not go away. Demand for institutional provisions increased and became more acute when Canada was shown to have the highest infant mortality rate in the white Commonwealth. Poverty was shown to bar people from providing for themselves. Opposition parties capitalised on these sentiments. The Co-operative Commonwealth Federation, standing on a platform favouring publicly funded health care, gained substantially in provincial elections, particularly in Ontario where it threatened to overtake the Liberals.

These pressures forced the federal government to commission a report on the health needs of the nation in 1941. This produced the Health Insurance or Heagerty Report in 1943. Heagerty recommended a full range of services – medical, dental, hospital, drugs, nursing, be provided through a federally funded two stage initiative. In the first stage, people saw a general practitioner (GP). The GP refered patients to the second stage of specialist services. Heagerty proposed a federally funded, but provincially administered scheme. Federal grants in aid were sought to ensure national standards. The insured were expected to contribute to their care through an annual insurance premium and a health insurance tax ranging between 3 and 5 per cent.

Heagerty's Report was accepted by the Canadian Congress of Labour, the Trades and Labour Congress, the Canadian Medical Association, the Canadian Dental Association, and the Canadian Life Insurance Officers Association. However, his plans floundered against federal–provincial antagonisms. During the Dominion–Provincial Conference on Reconstruction in 1945, the provinces, particularly Ontario and Quebec, could not agree to the fiscal arrangements offered by the federal government. In 1947, the Co-operative Commonwealth Federation government in Saskatchewan introduced the first provincial universal hospital scheme and medical insurance plan. Frustrated by the lack of progress nationally by 1948, the medical profession led by Dr Penfield, threatened to emigrate to the United States. This put pressure on the Liberal federal government which agreed to make available national health grants for hospital construction, medical training and research.

The first national universal hospital insurance scheme came into existence in 1957 when the Hospital and Diagnostic Services Act was passed. It became operative in 1958 with 50 per cent federal funding of inpatient acute and chronic care. Mental health, tuberculosis, and nursing were excluded from the Act. Additionally, patients were expected to pay a daily user charge. By 1961, 99 per cent of Canadians received hospital coverage under these provisions (Guest, 1980). The new Act also spelt the demise of charity based hospital care. By 1963, for example, it no longer existed in British Columbia. Medical coverage continued to be purchased through private insurance schemes.

The first attempt to extend publicly funded schemes beyond hospital care took place in Saskatchewan in 1959 where the Co-operative Commonwealth Federation under the premiership of Tommy Douglas introduced a medicare plan. The proposal was vehemently opposed by the Canadian and American Medical Associations which successfully thwarted plans to make doctors salaried employees and abolish the fee-for-service basis of payment. Legislation taking account of doctors' views was passed in 1961. Saskatchewan's Medicare went into effect in 1962. Meanwhile, doctors' professional associations organised 'Keep Our Doctors Committees' to enlist patient support against the measure. Doctors also went on strike for three weeks. Doctors consented to Medicare when they secured the right to opt out and bill patients directly according to a schedule which they agreed with the provinces. The Co-operative Commonwealth Federation considered this compromise undesirable because it established a two tier system supporting the status quo. However, it accepted the doctors' solution because it brought health care within the financial reach of the average Saskatchewan family.

In 1961, the Canadian Medical Association asked for a Royal Commission to re-examine health care needs. Diefenbaker, heading the

Conservative federal government established the Hall Commission. It reported in 1964 when the Liberals were in power. Discovering that 7.5 million Canadians were not covered by medical insurance, the Hall Commission recommended a universal non-means-tested comprehensive health service favouring preventative care. Suggesting 50 per cent federal funding, Hall argued health care was a right of citizenship that should be publicly administered and paid for through taxation. His recommendations were rejected by the medical profession, insurance companies, financial interests, and the Canadian Chamber of Commerce on the grounds that it would deny individuals the freedom to choose their own care. Ontario and Quebec also threw out the Hall Report.

Hall's proposals commanded massive grassroots support among women, the organised labour movement, and the New Democratic Party. Accepting the Hall Report, the Liberals passed the 1966 Medical Care Act. Doctors threatened strikes in a last ditch attempt at reversing the government's position (Black Report). Nonetheless, the Medicare Act providing a comprehensive medical plan with portability from province to province, equal availability to all citizens, and unfettered access to a doctor, came into effect in 1968.

By 1971, all provinces had joined the scheme. Physicians were paid on a fee-for-service basis, could opt out of the scheme, and extra-bill patients, ensuring medical services remained firmly in the control of the medical profession. Provincial funding arrangements vary. Quebec remains uncommitted to compensating patients if doctors opt out. Seven provinces fund the scheme through general taxation. Ontario, British Columbia and Alberta, rely on premiums. Though assistance in paying these is available, they are disincentives to low income groups, especially older women deeming aid charitable handouts. Accessibility to services thus varies according to region, income, and ideology. Medicare's structure is problematic. The arrangement with the doctors facilitates the expansion of high technology based care for patients and high bills for government. However, Medicare has eased the financial burden carried by families.

Ideological factors are important in curtailing services involving women's reproductive capacities, as happens with abortions, and are therefore particularly pertinent to women. Nova Scotia has refused to fund abortions through Medicare since 1988. Other problems include the exclusion of drugs and dental services, although provinces can cover these if they wish. The New Democratic Party extended benefits while in power in the provinces of Manitoba, Saskatchewan, and British Columbia. These provisions were precarious as British Columbians discovered when high costs and a changing political complexion in Victoria led to the withdrawal of publicly funded dental care except for those on welfare. Despite these weaknesses, the Medicare Act established health care as a right in Canada.

THE PUBLIC EXPENDITURE CUTS

The growing federal budget deficit, the recession of the mid-1970s and the accompanying government austerity programme when the federal government abandoned its cost-sharing formula and introduced block funding affected health services. Its Established Program Financing has also considerably reduced federal grants to provinces. New provincial taxation powers were introduced in 1977 to cover the deficit. Fiscal restraint was introduced while the rate of expenditure on health care services was expanding uncontrollably following rocketing high costs in technology health care and increased demands for services. Restraint has failed to contain costs. During the 1980s, inflation in the health service compounded matters by being twice the general rate (Banting, 1989). In Ontario, for example, health costs accounting for one-third of provincial spending in the 1980s compared to one-quarter in the 1970s restricted growth in other welfare areas, particularly education (Banting, 1989). Financial constraints curtailed the provincial governments' plans to improve coverage of dental services and introduce free drugs. Individuals must pay a portion of their drugs bill before the province will intervene. Deterrent fees, user fees, and extra-billing were all introduced at various times to cushion the impact of austerity. The working poor were most affected by the cuts in services and resources, as workplace negotiations succeeded in extending medical coverage for better organised and more highly paid workers. Women, working in less well-organised industries, benefited least from such agreements.

Public resistance to the erosion of Medicare particularly from the labour movement, feminist groups, anti-poverty lobby and New Democratic Party has so far prevented the decimation of the health care system as a public institution in Canada. The battle over extra-billing and the Canada Health Act of 1984 have helped prevent increased health costs from being totally passed onto the consumer by either doctors or provinces (Armitage, 1989). Limitations on its powers have forced the medical profession to examine its practices and identify areas where savings could be made without detracting from the quality of patient care. These factors have helped avoid a major restructuring of the service although criticism of the fee-for-service payment system, and the power of the medical profession in determining provisions continues to be voiced.

The future of Medicare is far from assured. According to the National Federation of Nurses Unions, Canada's Free Trade Agreement with the United States threatens to undermine public health care by having state funded health care declared as a subsidy to industry and not allowed under the agreement because public subsidies are deemed to provide an unfair competitive advantage to Canadian firms by reducing their costs. If sustained, a challenge of this nature could open the door for private health care provisions. Market based providers such as American insurance companies and Health Maintenance Organisations are entering the country to offer their wares and prepare themselves for any opportunities which might arise.

The power of the medical profession in determining the direction of the system, particularly its curative slant, continues to be problematic. Confrontation between the provincial governments and the medical profession emerged in 1980–1 when doctors demanded increases in their fee-for-service schedules. Doctors opted out of Medicare, threatened emigration to the United States, and proposed to strike if their demands for higher fees were not conceded (Black, 1981). Their failure to secure the increase they desired meant higher charges were passed on to patients. Approximately 20 per cent of doctors extra-bill patients to recover that portion of fees which the state refuses to accept.

Despite their reluctance to join Medicare, doctors have benefited considerably from its existence. They have acquired a guaranteed income with earnings substantially higher than other workers and the assured payment of bills. However, doctors deem themselves professionals having a right to a continuously increasing income to maintain their position over other workers (Black, 1981). Cuts in public expenditure have yielded a relative decline in their income. Changes in their labour processes have occurred as provinces demand doctors justify continual referrals of patients. At the same time, patients are becoming more critical of the services offered. As Black (1981) says: 'the proletarianisation of doctors paralleled growing demands by consumers for more say in the *type* of health services offered'. The growth of larger clinics to maximise the use of medical resources and create greater profitability has contributed substantially to this process. As in Britain and America, the growth of the women's health movement and increased popularity of alternative low technology holistic medicine have challenged doctors' prerogatives over what constitutes *health* care. Along with organised labour, these movements have expressed concern over the impact of the erosion of the health service on poorer members of society. Increasingly militant unionised health care workers, the majority of which were women, added their voice to the demand for better health care. Some sections of the organised labour movement, for example the Manitoba Federation of Labour, and some segments of the women's movement have demanded the nationalisation of medical facilities and the establishment of community clinics responding more appropriately to people's health needs by focusing on both preventative and curative medical care.

The debate over service provision and curtailing costs led the federal government to appoint Hall to study the health service and evaluate its programmes in 1979. In their submissions to the Hall Commission, community groups, organised labour, and women's groups called for more preventative services and the removal of monetary incentives for doctors to overservice patients, for example the endless tests and visits required to establish treatment. Protesters complained about geographical disparities between regions, and between cities and rural areas. These were intensified by doctors choosing to work in urban areas and towns. Despite a 50 per cent increase in the number of doctors between 1975 and 1988, rural areas did not get their share (Banting, 1989). The grassroots opposition also demanded a joint organisation of consumers, workers and doctors to determine the development of health services and their payment. Hall's proposals, delivered in 1980, stopped short of approving these demands. He suggested remuneration adequate to maintain doctors' position in the pay league through the fee-for-service system; arbitration over the setting of fee schedules; and phasing out premiums in British Columbia and Alberta. Although conceding many of the doctors' points, Hall rejected extra-billing as he felt this would destroy Medicare as a national system.

Following Hall's recommendations, the federal government passed the 1984 Canada Health Act outlawing extra-billing and user fees. Several provinces have ignored this legislation. The federal government, fearing legal action over these violations could destroy Canada's comprehensive, national health service, found handling of this law problematic. The limited options at its disposal made blunt fiscal measures including withholding money provinces collected from user fees from its block funding the main weapon in its fightback. However, these penalties have backfired. The number of hospital beds has been reduced, leading to longer waiting lists and increased suffering among patients. Provinces have increased user fees and introduced other financial measures to make good the deficit. For example, British Columbia introduced a health tax of 8 per cent to recoup user fee money lost from the federal block grant. In the end, this controversy has penalised poorer Canadians by increasing their health care costs. The problem of redefining the nature of the system and of ensuring adequate funding for it remains.

IN CONCLUSION

The Canadian health service has retained its public orientation in the 1980s without being penetrated by market provisions to the same extent as the British or American health care services. In this respect at least, it is more like the Swedish model. However, unlike Sweden, a commercial sector is not flourishing alongside the public one. Change is likely to take place in Canada during the 1990s as continued fiscal restraints and the flowering of the Free Trade Agreement have further impact. This may well lead to increased market-based provisions in which low income groups including women, particularly single parent and older women, will lose out.

The British National Health Service

The British National Health Service (NHS) based on the social insurance principle was created in 1948 by a Labour government committed to health care free to all at the point of need. Heralded as a socialist measure, it aimed to deal with the major health problems of the time, including tuberculosis, childhood mortality from infectious diseases like diphtheria and measles, and provide acute care. It acquired a three-tiered structure – a general practitioner service, a hospital service, and a local authority based administrative structure. A private medical sector remains for those who can afford to pay for services directly or obtain private insurance. The continuation of a private sector was a compromise reached between doctors and government to appease medics vehemently opposing the formation of the NHS.

The humanitarian and universal values espoused in the NHS were undermined by the sexist and racist ideology underpinning the Beveridge Report which framed it (Williams, 1989; Manchester Law Centre, 1983). It incorporated eugenist principles suggesting that social progress and societal health is based on breeding the best of a 'race'. The Manchester Law Centre (1983) argues the NHS was created to deal with the disease of 'idleness' rather than being constructed as an essentially caring institution. Access to the NHS is facilitated by the lack of direct charges for everything but drugs and appliances, and as of 1989, dental and eye checks. However, long waiting lists deny access to those awaiting surgical care. Those who can afford it buy themselves out of such waits by opting for private medicine.

Great variations in health, whether measured by mortality rates, incidence of using medical facilities, or health status, exist between women of different classes and ethnic groups (Doyal, 1986; Littlewood and Lipsedge, 1982). Regional and local inequalities in the distribution of services result in London being better provided than most other areas. Facilities for women outside London are worse than those in it. Regional and local inequalities in the distribution of services also exist, with London being served better than most other areas. Services to working class people, women and black people reinforce class, gender and 'race' inequalities. Sexual and racial discrimination and stratification are also apparent among NHS workers.

Before 1948, health care could be purchased through the private market, extracted from women as domestic health care, and obtained from limited public provisions. The 1911 National Insurance Act made primary health care available to working class men and waged working women. Children received state care through schools and infant welfare clinics. This left married women as a large group fending for themselves except for local authority care available to them during pregnancy. Poor housing conditions, overwork, and poor nutrition contributed to women's ill health (Doyal, 1986). Lack of access to birth control information and devices and the illegality of abortions made unwanted pregnancies a serious problem for them.

Women's health issues have occupied feminists throughout this century. Despite considerable opposition, Marie Stopes founded a clinic providing women with contraceptive aids and advice in London in 1921. Local authorities following her lead allowed maternity and child welfare clinics to provide married women with contraceptive advice in 1930. But it was the 1970s before further feminist pressure succeeded in making contraceptives widely available to all women using the NHS. Assistance in giving birth became more accessible to women from 1939 onwards as professionally trained midwives became more prevalent. However, their power diminished as obstetrics became a field increasingly controlled by male doctors. By the mid-1980s, hospital deliveries as the dominant mode of giving birth left community midwives with a limited role in the birth process. Childbirth has become highly medicalised and taken out of the control of women having children. The struggle for women to control this process reached apotheosis in a London hospital in the struggle to reinstate Wendy Savage, dismissed for promoting women's involvement in giving birth (Savage, 1986). Well Women Clinics have only partially challenged the lack of control women patients experience (Marshall, 1985, p. 39).

Teenage pregnancies number 90,000 a year in Britain, 30,000 of these end in abortion (Doyal, 1986, p. 8). The struggle over who determines young women's access to information about fertility control has been a difficult one with parents trying to oust professionals in this arena. The Gillick ruling in 1985 tilted the balance towards parents until the House of Lords overturned the decision. Doctors were given the power to prescribe for girls under sixteen without having to inform parents of their action following opposition from the medical profession and feminist groups. Neither of these options leaves the decision in the hands of the young woman herself. Moreover, medicalising the issue is inappropriate. As Campbell (1984) discovered, young working class women are deliberately choosing motherhood to acquire identity and purpose in the economically declining areas.

Women's fertility in general continues to be outside of women's control with the medical profession's unwillingness to place women's interests foremost in dealing with this issue. For example, unnecessary caesarean sections, sterilisations, hysterectomies and mastectomies have been performed on women. Despite the advent of family planning clinics, access to contraceptive devices is not easy, though some groups find it more difficult than others. Such facilities are grossly under-resourced and located in areas which discourage women from attending them. Despite the considerable health risks it carries, Depro Provera has been used more frequently on working class and black women in London, reflecting modern eugenic attitudes among medical professionals (Doyal, 1986). Also, such behaviour symbolises the contempt with which medics view women patients.

Introduced by a male Liberal MP after much heated debate and extensive campaigning by feminists, the 1967 Abortion Act gave doctors more freedom in performing abortions by including social health grounds. This liberalised attitudes towards abortions and led to an increase in the number of women having legal abortions. Abortions are performed primarily in the voluntary/private sector. The NHS undertook only 47 per cent of all abortions in Britain in 1980 (Doyal, 1986). Doctors' hostility to abortions has made it extremely difficult for women to get NHS abortions. For example, in the West Midlands in 1984, only 17.4 per cent of abortions occurred in NHS hospitals. This situation is particularly detrimental to women lacking the finances to pay for voluntary or commercial services. But it indicates the NHS' lack of commitment to women having control over their own fertility. Women outside London are more likely to have to go to voluntary or private agencies to get abortions.

THE PUBLIC EXPENDITURE CUTS

Funding of the NHS has always been inadequate for the demands placed on it. The Conservatives deliberately held costs in the 1950s low by pegging NHS expenditure at 5 per cent of GNP, a policy maintained by subsequent governments (Iliffe, 1985). In the early 1970s, the NHS consumed about 5 per cent of GNP and employed about one million people, giving the NHS one of the lowest costs for health care in the Western world. Canada, the United States and Sweden, for example, spend considerably more on their health care services (Office of Health Economics, 1979). Much of the capital investment in the NHS goes on hospitals which receive 60 per cent of expenditure, leaving proportionately less for the larger community based sector. Moreover, the proportion of the health budget going to hospital services has increased whereas that allocated to general practice has fallen. The growth in high technology medicine, hospital services, and health care staff has caused hospital expenditures to rise. This skewing of health care resources has raised questions about priorities in service provision and delivery, pitting the interests of high cost patients, for example those requiring renal dialysis or heart transplants, against those of low cost patients with illnesses not requiring intensive technological hospital care. Services for low priority groups, for example the chronically sick, mentally ill or handicapped, have been neglected. The nature and length of their illnesses have made their care high cost with little prestige attached to working in them.

The policy of under-resourcing the NHS was made possible by drawing on external resources located in private medicine, charities, voluntary workers, and the unpaid labour of women at home. Cost cutting initiatives within the NHS have focused on: limiting health authority budgets, thereby controlling capital spending and operating expenses; streamlining administrative structures; increasing labour efficiency; transferring costs to the family via 'community care', and imposing tighter financial controls on services contracted out, enabling the government to make substantial savings. Iliffe (1985, p. 59) shows that while demographic and technological pressures on hospital expenditure in 1984–5 increased by 7.7 per cent, current spending on hospital and community health services went up by only 5.7 per cent, giving a 2 per cent cut. Using different years and taking the higher inflation rate operating in respect of medical supplies, the National Union of Public Employees (NUPE) calculated that between 1979 and 1985, the Conservatives increased health expenditure by 0.6 per cent. However, this coincided with a 10 per cent increase in the number of patients being treated (NUPE, 1985). These cuts have reduced the capacity of health authorities to finance new developments and caused the closure of many hospitals, thereby shedding staff and reducing hospital bed numbers. This has rendered the service less responsive to patient demand and greatly increased the length of waiting lists and misery endured by individual patients requiring treatment.

Preventative services are an important part of the NHS, particularly with regards to immunisation, clean air and family planning services. Such provisions are expected to play a major role in reducing the burden sickness imposes on state finances and lost work. Preventative measures relying on individuals taking action on their behalf, such as asking for screening tests, stopping smoking, and eating nutritionally, have become important parts of the programme. However, major factors causing ill health in modern society, for example poor housing, work hazards and pollution, are outside the scope of the NHS (Doyal, 1979). Preventative measures have failed to substantially reduce health care costs.

Health care costs were rising substantially, faster than GNP in the late 1960s (Klein, 1973, p. 4). The NHS administrative and financial structures were incapable of meeting the emerging new priorities and demands for health care perpetrated regional inequalities. Britain's demographic makeup has shifted considerably since its inception resulting in larger numbers of older people, mainly women, requiring more health services to deal with chronic diseases. Staffing has increased rapidly, adding to costs. According to the Treasury, economies were needed (Draper and Smart, 1974). A severely underfinanced NHS was reorganised in 1974. Economic pressures forced this reorganisation upon a Conservative government reluctant to meet the ever rising costs of NHS care.

Central government's commitment to restructuring local government by 1974 would have affected the health service, so its reorganisation at the same time seemed desirable. The 1974 reorganisation transferred control of the NHS to regional and area health authorities, sought to integrate services and introduce managerial changes to increase effectiveness. Later reorganisations of the NHS included the 'Patients First' initiatives of 1980–2, and the Griffiths proposals of 1984.

'Patients First' attempted to streamline the three-tier administrative system of the NHS. Both hospital networks and family practitioner services were to retain their autonomous organisational structures outside of local government control, ensuring primary care and secondary care remained separate from each other and consensus management continued. These proposals were aimed at retaining the hospital orientation of the health system instead of furthering multidisciplinary and community-directed efforts; shifting the costs of the service elsewhere; reducing the impact of lay people on the service; increasing the power of the professionals at the expense of consumers; minimising public planning; and fostering a commercial orientation in state health care (Iliffe, 1985). 'Patients First' drawn up largely by men, exacerbated gender division in health care. Men dominated its implementation at managerial level while women were most affected at the point of service delivery. Women's nursing workloads would have increased both in the number of patients under their care, but also in the range of activities they would have to undertake. Women ancillary workers found their wages and hours lowered as services were contracted out to the private sector to reduce costs. As the main consumers of health services, women, especially older women, had to face even longer waiting lists. Women in their homes were charged with caring for patients discharged from hospitals earlier to free hospital beds for others and those refused admittance or waiting their turn.

The Griffiths proposals grappled directly with the problem of consensus management which was considered a drag on decision-making and on the quick introduction of change in the NHS. Flexibility in management was necessary if the private sector was going to be drawn more closely into the NHS structure. Griffiths suggested the replacement of consensus management with powerful general managers and a strategic policy-making leadership. This structure drew heavily on Griffiths' experience of managing supermarkets in the private sector. It failed to grasp differences of material interest in NHS provision, including the importance of safeguarding patient interests in the face of rapid technological and pharmaceutical developments in medical care. But it provided a solution to the difficulties of day-to-day budgeting and staff management (Iliffe, 1985). These measures were useful in promoting the major concern of the government — cost containment. Griffiths' commercial ideology was also evident in the proposals that NHS property be handled as business propositions. In practice, this meant asset stripping as property was sold to make up for lost government revenues (Iliffe, 1985). Griffiths suggested that industrial relations be re-examined in light of NHS needs in the different economic environment of the 1980s. Performance evaluation of staff and dismissal of less productive members was also recommended. Iliffe (1985, p. 66) argues that the Griffiths proposals were likely to reduce the NHS to a 'public administration co-ordinating the work of commercial subcontractors, on the style of Family Practitioner Committees'. Nonetheless, cost-cutting measures have ensured that the relative proportion of the nation's wealth spent on public sector health services has declined since the early 1960s (NUPE, 1985).

Griffiths also put forward community care, particularly for older people, mentally handicapped and mentally ill people. Despite studies indicating that properly resourced, it would not constitute a cheap option to institutional care, Griffiths argued community care would cost less and be of better quality. He assumed a net contribution to the care of individuals by their families and relatives, without any assessment of its cost, the availability of such support in the form of women being willing to undertake this additional work, or the existence of the material resources necessary for the care required. The government promoted the joint financing of community care with local authorities. Unfortunately, restricted social services budgets limited their participation in joint ventures, making it impossible for them to cover the decline in institutional provisions. Services to mentally ill and mentally handicapped people have fared better than services for older people, excluding day care provisions (Iliffe, 1985). Voluntary agencies were drawn into making up this shortfall when the Department of Health and Social Security (DHSS) provided £10.5 million to facilitate their involvement in community care initiatives.

Other cost-cutting measures have included: deregulating and privatising services, ending monopoly practices, for example opticians dispensing optical prescriptions, increasing the costs of prescription drugs and dental care borne by patients, limiting spending by general practitioners, especially on drugs and commercial deputising services, and improving the management of general practice. Moreover, the Tories have imposed these measures on doctors, despite opposition from the British Medical Association (BMA) and the British pharmaceutical industries.

The privatisation of the health service is on the cards more than ever. In 1989, the Conservatives put forward proposals allowing GPs to administer their own budgets and hospitals to opt out of the NHS. Opposition through the BMA and popular support for a publicly funded NHS are hindering the implementation of these proposals. Such initiatives are likely to increase regional variations, provide poorer access to those without either funding or the skills to negotiate their way through the complexity of services on offer and the bureaucracies servicing them, make the NHS less accountable to the consumer, and increase the overall sums the nation spends on health care.

The NHS has succeeded in containing payments to professionals. Having low paid black people and women staff has provided one way of controlling labour costs. Other methods include paying general practitioners a capitation fee which limits their salaries in a way unknown in Canada and the United States where fee-for-service schemes have made doctors very affluent workers. Many British doctors emigrate to Canada and the United States to take advantage of this. Nurses receive low pay. The sexual segregation in the division of labour in the medical hierarchy has given women nurses jobs with low status and salaries to accompany them. Nurses have become increasingly militant about inadequate services, poor working conditions, and their low pay and status. Health sector strikes occurred several times during Margaret Thatcher's leadership as her governments attempted to reshape the NHS. However, nurses have opted to support a publicly funded health service free at the point of need rather than endorse commercially provided services. The government has tried limiting the NHS 'monopoly' in health care while quietly ignoring the private medical sector co-existing alongside the NHS, exploiting its resources in the process. Private contractors undertaking profitable hospital services such as meal preparation, laundry and cleaning already operate on a considerable scale (Labour Research, 1983; 1987).

Despite containing costs, the New Right is convinced that privatising the NHS would make it cheaper and more effective. Unfortunately, the country used to build such a case, the United States, has failed to demonstrate this. As a nation, it spends more on health care to cover a smaller percentage of people, and provide services of questionable quality (Griffiths, 1987, p. 17). This has not deterred the government from attempting to introduce commercialism into the NHS and to propose new structures, for example Health Maintenance Organisations to challenge the NHS monopoly and blow fresh air into its corridors. Although freedom of choice is often vaunted as a desirable objective achievable under a mixed economy of welfare provisions, the extent to which the market can provide this is overestimated. Real choice exists only for those with the financial resources to buy the best care. Low-income groups and unwaged people remain outside its ambit. Women, as the largest group of low income earners and unwaged individuals in Britain have more to lose if the NHS were to be seriously dismantled. Although women can demonstrate their health needs are not being met at many points, their position would deteriorate if private practitioners were to become the major providers of health care.

THE PROBLEMATIC NATURE OF THE NHS

The NHS has had limited impact in reducing relative inequalities in health identified in the little publicised Black Report (1980). Class, gender and 'race' based inequality is particularly evident. Medical services to women have been criticised for their failure to meet the needs of women (Doyal, 1979). Women are seldom found in significant numbers at the higher decision-making levels of the NHS, or within the medical profession. In Britain, as in other Western capitalist countries, the majority of doctors are male, the majority of nurses are female. The dominance of the male gender has affected service provision. The 'Cinderella services' are those concerned mainly with women's health – geriatrics, gynaecology, psychiatry. Women patients are more likely to be treated with disdain and diagnosed as having mental illnesses than men. This is particularly evident in the medicalisation of childbirth which has taken the birth process out of the control of women (Mitchell and Oakley, 1976).

Feminist groups have picked up on gender inequalities and used their existence as the basis for developing self-help initiatives under women's control, for example Well-Women Clinics, screening for cervical and breast cancer, and feminist therapy. Some of these have been incorporated into mainstream NHS services. Feminist self-help initiatives are grounded in women's experience of oppression and staffed by women. The services which feminists have developed promote women's sense of control over what happens, respect for their person, egalitarian relationships between the carer and the woman being cared for, and encourage the sharing of skills and knowledge among women (Barker, 1986). Like their counterparts in the United States, feminist groups have tried to improve mainstream services, although their efforts remain small local provisions, incapable of challenging the power of the medical establishment outright.

'Race' based inequality affects black people settled in Britain and those intending to make their homes there as 'immigration status' has been linked to access to welfare state provisions. Ill health has been defined as a 'burden on the state' and used to exclude black people from acquiring settler status (Manchester Law Centre, 1983). Under the 1982 Immigration Rules, 'medical undesirability' constitutes grounds for refusing people entry. The rationale for this is that such individuals are unfit to enter the job market. Moreover, mental illness in immigrants can lead to their repatriation. Conduct disorders, such as alcoholism, drug addiction, and abnormal sexuality can be considered mentally unsuitable conditions for immigration purposes and form the basis on which entry can be denied (MLC, 1983). If admitted, immigrants may be required to report to a Medical Officer in the Environmental Health Department in their town of residence to ensure that they acquire health care without resorting to the NHS. Failure to report as required is a criminal offence. These measures have increased the internal surveillance of black people and make the health service party to the internal control of immigration. Foreigners are allowed into Britain to receive *private* medical treatment, a condition of entry which is enforced. Deterioration in health can also be grounds for repatriation. This becomes pertinent to fiancé(e)s admitted on time-limited visas. They may fall ill once in Britain and risk losing their visa or have an application for resident status rejected for having broken their conditions of entry by having 'recourse to public funds' if they use NHS facilities.

Patterns of disease vary according to class and ethnicity. Rickets is more common in children of Asian origin, sickle-cell anaemia in people of Afro-Caribbean descent (HEC, 1987, p. 30). Asian people are more likely to die of tuberculosis than other ethnic groups. While some TB is contracted abroad, their poor living conditions in overcrowded, low quality British housing contributes to their ill health (Doyal, 1986). The NHS' failure to address black women's health needs has resulted in their having poorer maternal health, less access to ante-natal and post-natal provisions and higher infant mortality rates (HEC, 1987).

The Black Report (1980) claimed the major factors accounting for these differences are material deprivation, income inequalities, and environmental factors. Yet, the medical profession has used cultural explanations to 'culturise' diseases such as rickets and assert black people's diets and lifestyles cause them (see De Lobo, 1976; Patton, 1990). White people, particularly the young and older people, are also at risk from these diseases. The prevalence of rickets among these groups was established before the Second World War and led to the fortification of various foods including margarine with vitamin D (Torkington, 1985). Similar solutions compatible with black people's diets have been rejected by the government (Doyal, 1986).

Black people have also provided the wealth and labour power on which the NHS is based. India has lost $144 million in trained doctors who emigrated to Britain to staff the NHS; Caribbean countries provided nurses and ancillary workers (*New Society*, 1982). The transfer of trained professionals from Third World countries to Britain has saved the British welfare state the costs of training them and providing for their health, housing, and educational needs. Black doctors are located in the busy inner city hospitals, practising medicine in the Cinderella areas of geriatrics, gynaecology, and psychiatry. Black nurses are also at the bottom of the hierarchy, usually as State Enrolled Nurses rather than State Registered Nurses and unable to reach the upper echelons of their profession (Littlewood and Lipsedge, 1982). Interestingly, the mythologies of black people being a 'burden on the state' and/or 'diseased' arose as they demanded to become consumers of health services rather than providers of them. This myth has drawn on racist stereotypes and contributed to the media portrayal of black people as 'abusing' rather than 'using' the NHS (*The Times*, 1958).

Class inequalities are also evident. Mortality rates for people in social class v are higher than those in social class I (Labour Research, 1987). Infant mortality rates are also higher in the lower classes than in the upper classes (Black, 1980). The Black Report suggested alleviating material deprivation was central to improving the health of partly skilled and unskilled manual workers, as was the promotion of healthier lifestyles among all groups (Townsend, 1989). The gap between social classes is widening (Whitehead, 1987). Britain is doing less well in eliminating such inequality than other countries. Inadequate income in old age and among families with young children contributes substantially to poor health among these groups. Poor health caused by inadequate income has been exacerbated since 1969. The Family Expenditure Survey (1984) has shown that the incomes of the richest 25 per cent of the population have increased substantially while those of the poorest 25 per cent have declined. Analysing class differences on their own masks gender and racial inequalities in health.

The Black Report (1980) suggests addressing material and environmental circumstances by prioritising the needs of children to give them a better chance in life, promoting disabled people's interests to improve their quality of life and retain their independence, and encouraging good health through preventative and educational services.

With regards to children's health, the Black Report recommended resources be shifted from the NHS and social services to community care, particularly ante-natal, post-natal and child health services. These included making child health clinics and ante-natal clinics more accessible, expanding nursery and day care provisions, and providing a revitalised school health service. The Black Report also recommended that the quality of disabled people's lives be improved by supporting their remaining in their own home. Unfortunately, community care for these groups remains under-resourced – a private matter between the carer and those receiving care. The state's role has been to shut institutional provisions and dump their inmates in the laps of women working in isolation at home and assuming this additional care at the expense of developing their own lives and interests. In contrast, private nursing homes and residential establishments are expanding rapidly, receiving £500 million in government funds in 1986. The government has ignored the contents of the Black Report and tried suppressing its impact by printing and distributing very few copies. The 1982 reorganisation of the NHS went against some of the Black Report's recommendations. For example, removing the posts of the area medical and nursing officers responsible for child health.

Some district health authorities have taken action on health inequalities in their strategic ten year plans by prioritising low pay and identifying one parent families, the unemployed, the overcrowded, the disabled, ethnic minorities and lone pensioners as high priority groups. The impact of their intentions has been blunted by the limited funds at their disposal.

IN CONCLUSION

The British NHS is currently at the crossroads. It will either be restructured in accordance with market principles or the resistance of the British populace will convince the government that investing public resources in the NHS and using these to eradicate class, gender and 'race' based inequalities is the way forward. The prognosis at the time of writing is pessimistic, for the Queen's speech opening Parliament in November 1989 forecast the implementation of measures radically altering the NHS and moving it closer to market provisions.

HEALTH CARE IN SOCIAL DEMOCRATIC COUNTRIES

The Swedish health care system

The Swedish national health service has combined state provisions with individual responsibility in meeting health needs. Government priorities, economic constraints, business interests, the labour movement and traditional provisions contributed towards shaping the current system of health and medical care in Sweden. Health care in Sweden is provided primarily by local government, particularly the county councils, and the national health insurance system. Unlike the British NHS, neither comprehensive care nor a free service at the point of delivery is guaranteed. Moreover, except for maternity care, preventative medicine is not part of the national insurance system. It focuses largely on curative medicine. Until national health insurance legislation was passed and national health insurance became compulsory in 1955, Swedish people relied on the private market, occupational schemes, and trade union initiatives for health services (Wilson, 1979). These arrangements fostered inequality of access to care because most private provisions were located in urban areas, occupational schemes excluded unemployed and unwaged workers and trade union provisions were unavailable to non-unionised workers. Women, as a small proportion of the workforce at that time, and as poorly unionised workers, had limited access to health care provisions in their own right.

FORCES SHAPING THE SWEDISH HEALTH CARE SYSTEM

The sickness benefit societies established in the workplace by employers or trade unions provided uneven coverage for different occupational groups (Wilson, 1979). As membership of trade union schemes was voluntary, these failed to encompass all workers in a particular occupational grouping. Some areas of risk, for example industrial injury and sickness, were too expensive for trade union schemes to cover, and so became among the first areas in which state provisions were developed. The Swedish government made employers responsible for industrial injury in 1901. However, this requirement applied only to dangerous occupations such as mining. Demands to rationalise and systematise coverage across occupational groups were made as early as 1918 (Uhr, 1966), but opposition from the medical profession, county councils, and voluntary societies prevented enabling legislation from reaching the statute books until 1947.

The initiation of compulsory health insurance continued to be strongly opposed by the medical profession which feared a decline in doctors' incomes. Doctors' opposition was spearheaded by the Swedish Medical Association which had a long legacy of protecting its members' interests. In the 1930s, the Association had restricted entry to medical schools to protect doctors' living standards. This produced a shortage of doctors which became highly visible later when compulsory health insurance was introduced and contributed to the uneven distribution of doctors throughout the country. In the 1950s, most doctors were practising in the newer county hospitals in urban areas, leaving services in rural areas under-resourced.

The government finally overcame professional opposition to its plans in 1955 when compulsory national health insurance provided Swedes with sickness benefits and reimbursed the medical expenses incurred. The legislation, amended in 1962, required counties to provide hospital services, out-patient medical care, and some preventative measures for mothers and children. Health insurance and the supply of medical care are separately administered and financed in Sweden. Except for certain life-saving drugs, patients are expected to pay for medicines. Excluding pensioners who receive only 365 days of free in-patient care, hospital treatment is free of charge.

The 1955 legislation also fostered the growth of a centralised service supervised by the National Board of Health and Welfare. Yet, the dominant local providers were the county councils (Sidel, 1986). Compulsory health insurance caused health care provisions to expand, substantially increasing costs. Expanding at twice the rate of the GNP, health care became the fastest growing area of public spending. The local government health expenditure index rose from 100 in 1950 to 1394 in 1975 (Heidenheimer et al., 1980), forcing the government to restrain expansion in the late 1960s to protect tax revenues from being eroded by escalating health costs, making the National Board halt hospital building for a time.

Maternal and child health have been accorded high priority in the Swedish health care system. The comprehensive provisions include pre-natal care; parenting training for mothers and fathers; preparing parents for childbirth; advising on contraception; well-baby care; medical care for pre-school children and chronically ill and disabled children; and parental training for the care of pre-school children.

Family planning services are also readily available. By 1975, legalised abortion and family planning reduced unwanted pregnancies among all women of childbearing age (Sidel, 1986). This trend is particularly noticeable in substantially reduced teenage pregnancies. Sidel (1986) credits the free family planning service and the ease with which Swedish women can get abortions for this shift, which in her opinion contrasts markedly with the situation in the United States, where the reverse is the case.

'CUTS' IN SERVICE PROVISIONS

Health spending amounting to one-third of social expenditure has risen faster than that of social services (Wilson, 1979, p. 56). As a proportion of GNP, Sweden spends more on health services than most countries. Sweden spent 10.2 per cent of GDP on health care in 1975 compared to 5.2 per cent in Britain and 3.5 per cent in the United States. Hospitals, funded through county council taxes on private and corporate incomes consume the largest proportion of health expenditure – 50 per cent (Wilson, 1979, p. 56). This system of funding differs from Britain's where general taxation provides about 90 per cent of the finances required by the health service overall.

Excluding hospital care and public health services, health care provisions are funded largely through insurance contributions employers have paid since 1975 when employees' contributions were abolished. Employers' payroll tax covers 80 per cent of the costs of health care, thus freeing the government from having a major interest in health care financing. High health costs have worried employers who fear these made Swedish goods highly uncompetitive internationally. By 1978, the employers' health insurance contribution had risen to 9.6 per cent of their total payroll (Wilson, 1979, p. 57). As in the other Western countries considered, businessmen's economic priorities influenced their reaction to social policy and called for an easing of their tax burden. Increasing health expenditures alongside other social and public expenditure contributed to the high rate of inflation Sweden experienced during the 1970s (Wilson, 1979, p. 57). Balancing these disadvantages were the advantages accruing to individual users through the higher benefit levels and wider range of services made available. The Lansorganisation was committed to retaining these advantages for its members. Increased expenditure also substantially improved the doctor–patient ratio from 800 in 1968 to 600 in 1975. The number of hospital beds increased by 30 per cent between 1955 and 1975 (Wilson, 1979, p. 60).

People's aspirations to healthier lives and increased expectations about access to medical care means that Sweden, like other Western countries, is facing rising demand for health services, and attempting to restrain this (Lindgren, 1970, p. 23). The Swedish county councils imposed limits on tax increases in the early 1970s, though these have risen as coverage has improved through the introduction of a national dental insurance scheme and enhanced sickness benefits. In contrast, cash limits and user charges have been imposed on the health service in Britain, the United States and Canada.

The Swedish Social Democratic Party's victory under Olaf Palme in 1969 produced another round in the state's power struggle with the doctors. Partial curbs on private practice were introduced by compelling doctors to serve in both sectors. However, this change encouraged doctors to use public facilities for treating private patients. This anomaly ended in 1970 when legislation making doctors full salaried employees of the county councils was passed. Nicknamed the 'Seven Kroner Reform', this legislation obliged doctors to opt for either public or private practice. These reforms were opposed by the older members of the Swedish Medical Association who called a strike which was broken through legislation in 1971. Doctors who became county council employees were remunerated entirely from public funds. Patients consulting them paid their fees directly to the hospital concerned. Private patients paid the doctors direct, but doctors had to operate from their own private premises. Despite more stringent government controls on private practice, it has remained an attractive option for patients who can afford it because they can freely choose their own doctor and receive speedier treatment (Wilson, 1979). However, private practice located in the larger urban areas contributes to geographical inequalities in the distribution of medical services.

Further innovation took place in 1971, when the Swedish Social Democratic Party's government nationalised retail pharmacies and turned pharmacists into salaried employees. The state already owned three large pharmaceutical companies which produced one-fifth of Sweden's drugs (Wilson, 1979, p. 52) and had imposed controls on the sales of drugs and the profits pharmacists made. Drug advertisements and the range of drugs doctors prescribe are strictly controlled. These restrictions notwithstanding, drug expenditures rose faster than any other medical item and the number of prescriptions dispensed doubled between 1955 and 1975 (Wilson, 1979, p. 52). Cutting costs has encouraged policy makers to prefer home care with medication over expensive hospitalisation (Wilson, 1979). This position ignores the costs women bear in making home care possible.

Dentists supported by the Dentists Association objected to dental practice being placed under a national insurance scheme in 1974 because it made them salaried public servants. The government pushed the relevant legislation through, but allowed dentists over 65 to continue working privately. Patients pay a portion of the dentist's fees while the remainder is covered by the Social Insurance Office out of funds raised through a payroll tax on employers. Employers dislike this form of funding for increasing labour costs and reducing the competitiveness of Sweden's commodities in the international market.

Sickness benefit payments were increased to 90 per cent of employees' previous salary in 1974. These are paid out of the Health Insurance Scheme by social insurance officers instead of the National Insurance Contributions as is the case in Britain. Sickness benefits are taxable and count as income for graduated pension purposes. A medical certificate is required only from those whose sick leave is longer than eight days. In addition, a flat-rate sickness benefit is payable to either parent caring for a child under the age of 16 at home. This sum may be topped up through the acquisition of an additional voluntary insurance. This measure was introduced to raise the status of household duties and to encourage parents to share childcare (Wilson, 1979, p. 54). In practice, this helps women financially, but reinforces their role as carers. Employers pay for three-quarters of these provisions, the government contributes one-quarter. Employee contributions ended in 1975 following trade union pressure for a lighter tax burden on workers. Self-employed people opting out of sickness coverage must have their spouse's agreement. The main disadvantage for those exercising this option is their exclusion from the earnings-related pension scheme. As a result, 90 per cent of self-employed persons take out sickness insurance (Wilson, 1979, p. 54).

The number of days lost through work has been substantial in Sweden as in other European countries, including Britain. These have risen sharply since the introduction of superior sickness benefits, giving Sweden one of the highest rates in Europe. Between 1955 and 1977, the average annual number of days for which sickness pay was drawn rose from 11.3 to 23.5 (Wilson, 1979). Swedish trade unions dispute the view that more generous provisions have caused workers to 'malinger' through sick leave. They claim the figures cannot be attributable solely to improved benefit levels for salaried workers whose employers make up their salaries in full have a lower incidence of illness than manual workers. Demographic features such as an ageing working population, more married women joining the labour force, and more stressful working conditions are other factors contributing to this increase.

Protection against injury arising out of one's employment is the oldest branch of Swedish social security. Though administered separately, the Swedish national health insurance scheme covers victims of industrial accident and disease. The scheme provides generous benefits and operates as a pace-setter determining other benefit levels (Kaim-Caudle, 1973, p. 65). Workers incapacitated at work are exempted from medical charges and receive a wide range of free benefits including dental and

ophthalmic treatment. Since 1977, victims of industrial accidents and diseases have received 100 per cent of their earnings for the first ninety days off work. Thereafter, an indexed disability pension is used to bring payments up to full earnings.

High levels of spending on health care have not made the Swedish population more healthy if the yardstick is the number of working days lost through sickness. However, increased life expectancy and a considerable decrease in the number of infant deaths suggest the population is healthier. Average life expectancy rose to 73.04 years for men and 79.4 for women by 1982. Infant mortality rates dropped from 21.0 per thousand live births per year in 1950 to 6.8 by 1982 (Sidel, 1986, p. 83). These improvements cannot be attributed solely to improved health care. Better nutrition, sanitation, housing and environmental conditions have contributed substantially to making these gains possible.

THE PROBLEMATIC NATURE OF THE SYSTEM

Though less marked than inequalities in the health care systems of other Western countries, Sweden's health services have also failed to eradicate class, gender, 'race' and regional disparities. The health reforms of the 1970s did not solve the problem of encouraging doctors to practise in remote rural areas. Doctors are attracted to urban areas by better facilities and prospects for advancement. Hospital based work is more interesting and rewarding than community based medical practice (Wilson, 1979, p. 60). Additionally, the reforms have failed to tackle discontinuity of care arising from group practice which is becoming increasingly popular amongst doctors. Neither did they reduce doctors' reluctance to undertake home visits. The proportion of doctors in general practice in Sweden was 35 per cent compared to 48 per cent in Britain and 23 per cent in the United States (Anderson, 1972). The Cinderella areas of medicine in Sweden are like those of other Western countries – geriatric services, provisions for the chronically ill, and psychiatric medicine. These are also areas in which women patients predominate and standards of care are lower than those evident in the prestigious areas of medicine. In this respect, Swedish health care reflects the position of women patients in other Western countries. Additional resources would have to be directed into the lower status areas of medicine and new doctor–patient relationships would have to be created for these forms of inequality to be eliminated.

The shortage of doctors and the poor deployment of scarce resources have contributed to inequality of access in service provisions. In 1962, there were 203 doctors per 100,000 population in Sweden's three largest cities compared to 151 in other cities and towns, and twenty-six in the rural districts housing 48 per cent of the population (Wilson, 1979, p.

60). The Swedish government has placed priority on reducing the urban–rural divide by encouraging some of the newly qualified doctors to practise in the rural areas. This measure is enforced through the National Board of Health and Welfare which has the legal right to control the number of doctors given posts in hospitals and clinics. The National Board has collaborated with the county councils and the Swedish Medical Association in planning the distribution of training posts between the different specialisations and location of newly qualified doctors. This restriction on individual doctors' choice is considered compatible with protecting the long-term needs of the population and interests of the health service. The Board's interventions have not produced the anticipated results (Wilson, 1979).

Social inequalities persist. Although the fees patients pay cover only a quarter of the costs, they discourage people on very low incomes from receiving treatment (Andersen, 1970). Means-tested social assistance and exemption schemes operated by county councils target those requiring financial help. These provisions have not eliminated the problem and disparities in the use made of the service are evident among different income groups. Research carried out by the Nordic School of Public Health has exposed 'race' inequality and established that immigrants have worse health problems than the rest of the population (quoted in Sidel, 1986, p. 183).

Access to the health service is also affected by class status. The Low Incomes Commission of the late 1960s found that low-income families with large numbers of children, older people, and the chronically sick experienced hardship through the charges they were expected to pay and consequently were using health services less often than affluent groups. Andersen (1967) substantiated this by finding low income groups did not visit their physicians as frequently as higher income groups. Class differences were also apparent in relation to dental care. However, Rosenthal (1967, p. 46) claims that charges discomfort people, but do not pose serious financial hardship. Rein (1970) maintains lower income groups in Britain make more intensive use of GPs and hospital facilities and receive the same quality of care as higher income groups. His findings have been challenged by the Black Report (1980). In the United States, the availability of medical care and income status were strongly correlated (Sidel, 1986; Navarro, 1975a).

Gender issues have received more direct government attention in Sweden than in the other Western countries examined, but this has not eradicated gender inequality. More women have joined the ranks of the medical profession, but men predominate in its higher reaches and control the direction of the service. Women still dominate the nurses ranks. One element promoting gender equality is the policy of allowing both parents to share the care of sick children. However, it presupposes a man and woman couple, in reality absent from the lives of single parent households and lesbian or gay families. Also, women are more likely to take it than men. Nonetheless, it challenges the idea that caring is solely 'women's work'.

Samuelsson (1969, p. 252) suggests the major sources of dissatisfaction with Swedish health care are not user charges, but: the quality of services; long waits for medical appointments; lengthy queues for non-urgent hospital treatment; doctors' reluctance to make home visits; lack of continuity in group practices; and impersonal care in hospitals. This list of consumer dissatisfaction is similar to complaints made of health care provisions in Britain, Canada and the United States. Swedish middle class people, as their counterparts in other Western countries, buy themselves out of these inconveniences through private care. Another area of public concern was the over-concentration of medical resources in urban hospitals at the expense of community medicine which provided 90 per cent of medical care (Anderson, 1972). This also mirrors the position in other Western countries and socialist ones.

IN CONCLUSION

The Swedish health care system was expanding benefits during the 1970s when the economic difficulties in free market countries like the United States were forcing cutbacks. Sweden also faced a declining revenue base as the 'oil crisis', high taxes and worker activism threatened economic development and in consequence, welfare provisions. The Swedish government chose to handle this situation by expanding services and the tax burden for employers while reducing employees' taxes. Although economic concerns are at the front of the Swedish government's mind, market forces were tempered with more compassion and concern for human well-being than elsewhere.

SOCIALIST HEALTH CARE

The Soviet health care system

THE SERVICES AVAILABLE

There are essentially two separate health systems in the Soviet Union: a rural one and an urban one. In the urban system, health care delivery is based on the place of work. Here, a local physician ministers to the needs of the sick on both a curative and preventative basis. Workplace provisions were introduced by Stalin to integrate medical services into the social control mechanisms enforcing labour discipline. It is also the point at which industrial workers obtain access to superior facilities. The next stage is the polyclinic where primary care services and specialist doctors are located. The polyclinic is responsible for providing care for people living in the microdistrict (*uchastok*). Eighty per cent of *uchastok* physicians are women. From here, referral is to the district hospital, followed by the regional hospital, and finally the republic hospital.

In the rural areas, people are cared for by the *feldsher* and midwife in health stations. Patients are referred to the *uchastok* physician if the *feldsher* is unable to deal with them. *Feldshers* forming 22 per cent of all medical staff are mainly male, often perform midwifery duties, play an important role in lowering infant mortality and undertake preventative sanitary work. Unlike the Chinese *barefoot doctors*, they do not undertake non-medical productive work while practising medicine. If no other doctor is attached to their station, *feldshers* supervise the other medical workers and cover the practice's administrative work. *Feldshers* have minimal medical training and report directly to a district physician. Often making basic diagnostic errors *feldshers'* clinical effectiveness is in doubt. Although required to refer patients to specialists for advanced care, they often fail to do so.

The next level is the hospital housing specialist services. Rural hospitals are of three types: intercollective farm hospitals, district hospitals and regional hospitals. *Uchastok* physicians refer patients to the district hospital if they are unable to help. From here, patients can progress to the regional hospital or the republic hospital.

The political élite enjoy special provisions administered by the 'Fourth' division of the Ministry of Health (Deacon, 1983; George and Manning, 1980). These include a separate hospital network called the *Kremlouka*, polyclinics, and pharmaceutical suppliers. The operation of these facilities is not open to public scrutiny. They represent a private service as access depends on holding membership of a special club, the Communist Party. In this respect, the Soviet health system mirrors the Chinese one. The presence of such privileges was an element of the widespread corruption of Party officials identified and condemned by students in Beijing's Pro-Democracy Movement.

Except for prescription charges for some groups, health treatment in the Soviet Union is free at the point of need. However, bribing and tipping are common as workers try to gain speedier access to services, entry to better facilities, or admission to provisions from which they are excluded.

The Soviet health care system illustrates the development of a health service subordinated to economic exigencies through determined political intervention. The linking of health care initiatives to the economy was particularly evident during Stalin's strategy of enforced rapid industrialisation, a decision backed by the Fifteenth Congress of the Communist Party in December 1928. It eventually produced a health system featuring the following characteristics:

1. Providing Soviet people with free health care when needed.
2. Operating a centrally planned state-run system integrated into the planned economy.
3. Achieving the highest ratio of trained physicians and health personnel to population in the world.
4. Preventing infectious diseases, and meeting workers' occupational health needs by developing preventative care.
5. Prioritising services benefiting mothers, children and industrial workers (Sidel and Sidel, 1977).

Interestingly, 70 per cent of doctors are women. But, women enjoy neither high status nor high salaries in the medical profession. Encouraged as a pragmatic response when men's labour was diverted to heavy industry, women entering the medical profession reinforced a sexist division of labour enabling men to occupy the higher echelons of the medical hierarchy in teaching, research and practice. Prestigious specialism, hospital administration, and research work are dominated by men earning higher salaries than their practitioner women colleagues. Most nurses are women who are underpaid and overworked (M. Walker, 1988). Their training takes place under the direct auspices of a medical profession treating nurses and their contribution to health care as secondary. Anti-private practice measures introduced by Stalin have restricted developments in private health care (George and Manning, 1980). However, the private sector may begin to influence the form of the Soviet health service as a result of Gorbachev's initiatives under *peristroika* (rebuilding) (Roberts, 1990).

PRE-REVOLUTIONARY HEALTH CARE

Health care in pre-revolutionary Russia consisted of a two tier system reinforcing regional disparities and class inequality. The urban system containing most doctors and medical facilities catered for wealthier classes. In the rural areas, physicians ministered to the needs of the nobility while peasants sought a *feldsher*, or semi-trained assistant doctor. Navarro (1977) claims class snobbery was rife. He quotes Mistskevitch as saying: 'The peasant is not accustomed to and does not need specific medical assistance; his diseases are "simple" and for this a feldsher is enough – a physician treats the masters, and a peasant is treated by a feldsher' (Navarro, 1977).

The growth of the *feldsher* system occurred as a result of the 1864 reorganisation of rural local authorities into *zemstvos*. The *zemstvos* provided two parallel health services – a 'touring' system and a stationary one. The 'touring' health personnel travelled from village to village within the *zemstvo's* jurisdiction and attended to sick people *en route*. The 'stationary' system provided basic primary care and facilitated the creation of local dispensaries staffed by district doctors. At least, that was the intention. In practice, fiscal restraints compelled the *zemstvos* to employ cheaper *feldshers* rather than expensive doctors. In time, *feldshers* and midwives became the crucial health personnel in the *zemstvo* system of medical care. The system legitimated a tradition of publicly salaried medical personnel and established an extensive national network of medical care which the Bolsheviks drew upon after the Revolution. Despite these measures, the Russian population's health was jeopardised by high levels of infectious diseases, epidemics, famines, and disparities in the distribution of medical resources. Most qualified doctors lived in urban areas treating wealthy nobles and middle class people rather than peasants and workers. Health problems loomed large in pre-revolutionary Russia. Hyde (1974) estimates 25 per cent of the people were suffering from typhoid, typhus and smallpox in 1914. Crude death rates were high at 30 deaths per 1000 of the population. Infant mortality rates at 250 per 1000 live births were also appalling compared with other European countries.

THE EXPERIMENTAL DAYS

Despite the lack of adequate resources, the need to deal urgently with widespread disease and epidemics caused Lenin to attempt the speedy development of Soviet health services. A decree calling for comprehensive health care was issued on 13 November 1917. The principles guiding it were elaborated during the Congress of Medical–Sanitary Departments of Soviets of Workers', Peasants' and Soldiers' Deputies in June 1918. These declared the Soviet health care system was to be:

1. A comprehensive qualified medical service.
2. Available to all the people.
3. Free at the point of need.
4. A single unified service provided by the state.
5. Preventative in orientation, aiming to create a healthy population.
6. Fully run by workers.

A medical–sanitary committee of Bolshevik physicians was assigned the task of organising medical services for workers and soldiers and encouraging grassroots participation in medical matters through the local Soviets. In the early days, the unions played a substantial role in health matters, including bringing the medical profession to heel. The implementation of an ideal health system was thwarted by the diversion of resources to fighting the Civil War, the lack of an adequate health care infrastructure; and the opposition of the medical profession which objected to the standards the Bolsheviks were setting, particularly those according peasants, workers, and soldiers priority treatment and lowering doctors' status. Measures enacted to quickly tame doctors included dissolving their powerful medical association, the Pirogov Soviety, and creating a People's Commissariat of Health, with Dr N.A. Semashko as Commissar in 1918. These changes produced a single body to orchestrate the nation's medical services and health care networks.

Under war communism, infectious diseases, malnutrition, and fatalities from the Civil War, were extensive. But creating a comprehensive health service had to wait until the 1930s. During war communism, health care, pragmatically adapted to the prevailing circumstances of chronic shortages of food, medicine, hospitals and doctors, followed the principles of:

1. Dealing with epidemics decimating one-quarter of the people.
2. Ensuring the health of the Red Army fighting the Civil War.
3. Using the *zemstvo* model to develop a health care system providing health care for everyone in the long run. This meant staffing urban hospitals and clinics with doctors and rural ones with roving paramedical *feldshers* and midwives.
4. Emphasising health care for mothers and children through 'consultation clinics' though few were built.
5. Taming the medical profession by disbanding the Pirogov Society and creating a People's Commissariat of Health to fight for a Bolshevik service responding to grassroots pressure (Field, 1989).

Lenin's comment that 'Either the lice defeat socialism or socialism defeats the lice' was taken to heart during the Eighth Party Congress in Moscow implementing initiatives emphasising public health; combating social diseases such as tuberculosis, venereal disease; guaranteeing medical services to all without charge; protecting the health of mothers and children; and opening new medical schools to train medical personnel recruited from the peasants and working class. The powers of the Centralised Commissariat of Health were also increased at the expense of the Soviets and trade unions.

HEALTH CARE UNDER THE NEW ECONOMIC POLICY
The strategy of a single service was shortlived when market provisions became available under the New Economic Policy. Preventative care

emphasising public health measures to fight epidemics was strengthened. Doctors could choose to work for either the public or private sector. Following personal choices, doctors re-established private practice. It flourished, private hospitals were built, pharmacies were denationalised and returned to their former owners. Public provisions favouring industrial and agricultural production restricted services to insured workers. Centralised power in the hands of the Commissariat became entrenched as trade unions were subordinated to the Party. The gap between the country and the towns increased despite improvements in rural provisions and an upsurge in the number of trained doctors. Qualified doctors tended to practise in the cities; the *feldshers* in the countryside.

HEALTH CARE UNDER STALIN

The subordination of the medical and health services to economic objectives was most marked during the Stalinist period when the needs of the health system were subordinated to the industrialisation process, particularly the development of heavy industry such as mineral extraction, and the enforced collectivisation of agriculture. Stalin divided the economy into productive and non-productive sectors. Male industrial workers occupied the former. Peasants and women worked in the latter. This made a gendered division of labour an integral feature of his industrial strategy. The health service, staffed largely by women, formed part of the non-productive sector. As men were increasingly drawn into industrial production, women's involvement in the service sector and medicine rose. Consequently, the number of women physicians climbed from 10 per cent of the total in 1917 to 60 per cent in 1940 (Sidel and Sidel, 1977, p. 172). This trend increased when Stalin lowered the profession's status further by removing medical schools from the university. The health care system became increasingly hierarchical: specialists became more powerful than generalists; doctors more important than nurses and *feldshers*; technical research and academic pursuits more prestigious than practice. Physicians' incomes followed the decline in the status of their profession, falling to three-quarters of the average wage during the 1920s (Kaser, 1976). Additionally, the fabric of the health service deteriorated through disinvestment. Peasants were especially hard hit by Stalin's dictates because he classified them as unproductive and responsible for their own health care. Stalin justified his stance by saying, 'Peasants are required to pay a tribute to the rest of society' (Field, 1989, p. 64).

Subjecting health care to industrial priorities gave it targets consistent with the first Five Year Plan. Regions such as the Urals having minerals such as coal and iron essential for Russian industrialisation were accorded preferential treatment. Industrial workers and collective farmers received priority allocation in provisions and the health service was integrated into the drive maintaining labour discipline. Stalin established Medical Sanitary Units in factories to promote preventative care and reduce absenteeism attributable to illness. Brigades of doctors were also sent into the countryside, especially at harvest time to ensure that agricultural workers attended to their duties. These measures contributed to making the medical profession enforce work discipline and succumb to Party tutelage. Vladiminsky, Stalin's Commissar of Health enhanced doctors' role in controlling the workforce. Believing workers were frustrating production plans, he demanded absenteeism be policed and the issuing of medical certificates strictly curtailed. This reduced absenteeism, jeopardised the health of workers compelled to work even when sick. However, the system was dogged by difficulties in meeting its objectives. In December 1929, the Party criticised the Health Ministry for failing to meet its goals in providing medical care to workers and peasants.

Vladiminsky's second priority, the health of women and children, was calculated to encourage women to enter the workforce in large numbers thereby reducing the critical shortage of labour ensuring from the expansion in industrial production and the loss of men during the War. Crèches and kindergartens became more readily available and placed under the auspices of the health authorities. Children as future workers were also central to the production process. Subordinating women's interests as women to other priorities, Stalin aimed to increase the birth rate. This intensified women's domestic role. Women, not men, were given state grants to take time off work to nurse sick children. Despite the high demands placed on the health service, investment in it lagged behind that of industry and charges for prescriptions were introduced. Nevertheless, considerable improvements in service provisions were evident if one took account of the low levels of resourcing. Stalin's Health Commissar also waged an ideological battle on two fronts. One was against 'Right opportunists' demanding health care based on insurance contributions. The other was against Menshevik idealists arguing industrialisation should not be pursued if detrimental to people's health. They maintained socialism needed to safeguard workers' health as did capitalism. Stalin's rejoinder focused on everyone making sacrifices to create a communist society (George and Manning, 1980). Many Mensheviks were shot during Stalin's purges including Kaminsky, the Health Commissar, in 1937.

Medical training was expanded under Stalin and firmly controlled by the state issuing certificates enabling doctors to practise. Degrees are still not awarded to Soviet medical practitioners. Navarro (1977) argues removing medical schools from universities and dividing medical studies into three branches – general clinical and industrial medicine; maternity and child care; and public health – in 1938 was consistent with slanting medical care towards serving industrial needs and enforcing labour discipline. Navarro (1977) suggests the first sector serviced and maintained a productive workforce; the second reproduced labour power; and the third prevented illness which might reduce a scarce labour supply.

Under Stalin, the health system became highly centralised, a feature facilitating its reorientation towards a war economy when the Soviet Union became embroiled in the Second World War. The terrible lessons of the First World War and preventing epidemics were uppermost in Soviet people's minds as they went to fight. Stalin successfully prevented a reoccurrence of this dire scenario. The number of medical sanitary units in key factories, particularly those servicing the armaments industry, was substantially extended. Drafting large numbers of women to train as doctors freed men to fight and work in the war industries. After the war, medical priorities shifted to servicing mothers and children to encourage population growth and replace the estimated twenty to forty million people lost during the war.

From 1950 onwards, Soviet medical care followed the hierarchical 'materialist' principles of Pavlovian medicine. Responding to people on a physiological basis, it fostered a manipulative physiology affirming that people, like Pavlov's dogs, could be controlled and disciplined through appropriate incentives. Stalin branded critics of this position bourgeois idealists.

THE POST-STALINIST PERIOD

The situation eased slightly after Stalin's death (Ryan, 1978). Health care became less influenced by Pavlovian principles, less centralised and less dogmatic as responsibility for maintaining it devolved onto republics. Primary care preventing illness was emphasised although the hospital system controlled its development. In 1956, public health stations were placed under hospital auspices. Polytechnics had been placed under its authority in 1947. Medical care became more highly technological, specialised and hierarchical. Very few people in either prestigious specialist services or in medical administration were women. Medical priorities established by Stalin were confirmed by the 1969 Public Health Act and health care legislation in 1977. Incentives attracting doctors to rural areas were improved. These included higher salaries than urban doctors, the opportunity to buy a car, the purchase of food direct from state farms and a free flat. Health care expenditure increased under Khrushchev, without consuming a growing proportion of GDP as in the West (Ryan, 1978). The Soviet Union spends less of its GDP on health care than other countries. In 1968, it was 2.8 per cent (Deacon, 1983, p. 71). Capital expenditure was also low. In 1970, 5 per cent of Soviet health care expenditure was used for this purpose compared to 10 per cent in Britain (Deacon, 1983, p. 71). Doctors' salaries are also comparatively lower. By 1984, the Soviet Union spent 4.0 per cent of GDP on health, compared to 5.9 per cent in Britain, 9.4 per cent in Sweden and 10.4 per cent in the United States (Lear, 1989, p. 165). The massive expenditure on armaments and aerospace developments as part of the Soviet Union's struggle to maintain the balance of power in the Cold War left limited room for increased social expenditure (Rosenberg, 1989). Nonetheless, resources devoted to health care are substantial. For example, 25 per cent, or 800,000 of the world's doctors practise there. Most of these are women (George and Manning, 1980; Navarro, 1977).

THE PROBLEMATIC NATURE OF THE SYSTEM

Lack of data makes examining the problematic nature of the Soviet health system difficult (George and Manning, 1980). Details highlighting class and 'race' based inequality are sketchy. They are less so for gender and urban–rural divisions.

Despite a large centralised state bureaucracy administering the system, coverage is patchy; its objective of universal accessibility remains to be realised. Rural areas are under-provided, regardless of policy initiatives directing doctors to work in specified districts for a given period. The continued urban bias can be traced to Stalin's priorities favouring industrialisation and doctors' resistance to working in rural areas. Doctors' enforced period in the rural areas is short – three years. Turnover in medical staff is rapid as doctors return to the cities offering cultural pursuits and favourable career opportunities. The government's target of having one qualified doctor for every area by 1980 has not been achieved in the countryside. Many rural districts have emergency treatment facilities with only the *feldsher* available. In 1972, Moscow had seventy-six physicians per 10,000 people compared to 28.3 for the country as a whole (Navarro, 1977, p. 76). The expectation that the more accessible *feldshers* could cover the gap in rural areas has not been met (George and Manning, 1980).

Geographical variations intensify the urban–rural split and are particularly marked between the Asian and European regions. This reflects the division of the Soviet Union into an industrial European part and an agricultural Asian one. Services in Asian Republics, particularly Tajikastan and Uzbekastan are inferior to those available in the Ukraine. This smacks of racism. Racism in the Asian Republics is exacerbated by there being a white Russian ruling élite with access to better medical provisions available to Party *apparatchiks* (Lear, 1989).

Universal accessibility has been deliberately reduced by state action prioritising industrialisation and the health needs of industrial workers and granting the ruling élite preferential treatment. Key industrial groups receiving more health resources because they are essential to the economy or defence of the country include miners and railway workers on the Trans-Siberian line. Railway workers, crucial to the Soviet defence system, have access to 6,000 health care institutions employing 126,000 staff members (34,000 doctors). Additionally, trade unions provide facilities for members. Prime among these are the Black Sea sanitoria and high quality hospitals to which non-members try to gain access by bribing officials.

In contrast to industrial workers, dissidents are poorly served by the health system. Service provision is appalling; abuse of certain facilities, especially psychiatric ones, is common. Orderlies working in psychiatric hospitals for dissenters are ex-prisoners and doctors addressing their needs lack qualifications in psychiatry. Low status groups like the mentally handicapped also have very poor provisions. Services for older people and mentally handicapped patients are even poorer than the Cinderella services meted out to such groups in Britain (George and Manning, 1980).

Preventative medicine, given high priority in the system as a whole, is implemented more readily for essential workers. Annual health checks are required of all Soviet citizens. But their take up is higher among factory employees having medical services at work. Groups not economically active, for example women caring for children in the home, retired people, have a lower take up rate, but their non-attendance is not followed up (Sidel and Sidel, 1977).

Medicine has a female image. The specialist basis of the system perpetuates gender inequality. Walker (1988) uses women's oppression to argue that the comprehensive Soviet health system has been made possible by exploiting women's labour. Women occupy the lower levels of the profession, despite entrance examinations setting lower standards for men. In 1975, only 20 per cent of surgeons were women; they formed 80 per cent of primary care doctors. No Republic had a woman Minister of Health. Medical personnel, particularly physicians and nurses, are poorly paid.

Soviet health care controls workers rather than being controlled by them. Patients are treated as objects rather than subjects of medical attention. Workers' lack of control over the service, its direction, formation and administration reveals another form of élitism. The health system fits the needs of the élite and the priorities they identify rather than the people's. In denying egalitarianism, it does not constitute a fully socialist system. Ryan (1978) argues the ruling élite has gained the upper hand in the Soviet system because professionals including general practitioners do not mitigate social control as they do in Britain.

The Soviet health care system is in crisis (Lear, 1989). Questions are increasingly raised about its overall performance and lack of accountability. High technology care is becoming more unpopular. The failure of the system's preventative services to reduce infant mortality and raise life expectancy has been highlighted internally and externally.

External research on infant mortality carried out by Davis and Feshback, two American epidemiologists, reveals that infant mortality rates rose from twenty-three per thousand in 1970 to thirty-one per thousand by 1975/6. Questioning the value of preventative work which fails to produce infant mortality rates transcending those of Third World countries, they posit a health crisis. Moreover, racism underpins these figures. Infant mortality was higher in Soviet Asia than in Soviet Europe. Davis and Feshback (1980) linked their findings to the ineffective medical intervention of rural *feldshers*, and parents' reluctance to use ante-natal and post-natal facilities. They also suggest these trends have been exacerbated by the liberalisation of the system during the 1970s. Women stayed at home rather than contacting professionals. From a feminist perspective, this analysis is unacceptable because it blames women for the problem without addressing the structural inequalities inherent in the system. Since then, infant mortality rates have improved in Soviet Europe (Lear, 1989). The general pattern of ill health approximates that of the West. Improvements in mortality rates have slowed down considerably because environmentally induced and industrial diseases such as cancer and cardiovascular diseases feature prominently, lowering anticipated life expectancy rates. In 1984, it was 65 years for men and 74 years for women compared to 71 and 77 years for British men and women respectively (Lear, 1989, p. 165).

The uneven development of the Soviet health service and its failure to follow socialist principles have been variously interpreted depending on writers' political philosophy and views on Soviet socialism. Szymanski (1982) considers the Soviet Union socialist and suggests the significance of health statistics has been exaggerated. He regards the high infant mortality rate a temporary problem arising from the later industrialisation of Soviet Asia, problems in health service delivery, and the poor implementation of 'scientific' principles in childcare. His comments fail to address the central issue of why development has proceeded on a differential basis. Even if Soviet Asia industrialised after Soviet Europe, why should services be poorer? Surely, improvements should have followed if the lessons learnt in the European part had been applied to Soviet Asia and the necessary resources made available. Szymanski (1982) favours conspiracy theory analyses for he draws attention to Davis and Feshback's publishers, the American Bureau of Census, and suggests their prime purpose was spreading 'disinformation' about the Soviet Union for the purposes of American Cold War propaganda.

Szymanski's interpretation is disputed by Cooper and Schatzkin (1982) who argue the emergence of similar patterns of disease, a preferential system for the élite and the crisis in health care signals the capitalist orientation of the Soviet state. Cooper and Schatzkin (1982) fail to account for the crisis in the health services of other Communist countries such as China, which have not been considered capitalist states. Cooper and Schatzkin (1982) also ignore the concern Soviet officials have expressed over the health system's failure to meet their stated objectives. Soviet newspapers have drawn attention to the existence of a two tier system (*The Guardian*, 1984), widespread negligence and mistakes, professionals' indifference about the quality of service provided, bureaucratic inertia, and heavy administrative loads impeding the overall performance and efficient operation of the system. Consumers have voiced dissatisfaction regarding the unhygienic hospital conditions and poor quality food fed to patients. Food is so unpalatable friends and relatives bring patients meals, augmenting the domestic load women carry during the working day.

Ryan (1978) criticises Soviet health care from a social democratic position for underplaying the doctor–client relationship. Those examining the Soviet health care system from a radical left perspective, concede the benefits which have accrued to the Soviet people as a whole following the expansion of provisions since the 1950s, but reject its authoritarian and centralised basis, for example Navarro (1977), Deacon (1983), and Sidel and Sidel (1977). They condemn the system for being hierarchical, without popular control, mainly curative in focus, inegalitarian in service delivery between rural and urban areas, and preoccupied with the social control of the workforce rather than meeting human needs.

Much of the demoralisation with service provision and delivery can be attributed to the low professional standing of doctors, their low pay, and the inordinate amount of overtime required to complete their work. The low status accorded medical practice is partly due to the gendered division of labour sustaining the edifice and the low prestige accorded to service work as opposed to industrial work. The profession's low standing has deterred young people from joining its ranks. This picture is markedly different from the high status and salaries enjoyed by Western doctors regardless of whether they work for the state on a fee-for-service basis as in Britain, or as private entrepreneurs as in the United States.

IN CONCLUSION

The Soviet health care system is impressive for being freely available when needed. Some element of consumer control is present in so far as patients can change physicians at will, though few exercise this option (Sidel and Sidel, 1977). Other positive features include integrating curative and preventative medicine, and emphasising occupational health care. The weighting accorded to these is greater than that prevailing in Britain. The development of the Soviet health care system confirms the convergence hypothesis insofar as economic exigencies have influenced its development. The model of care which has emerged approximates that evident in the West. Similar patterns of ill health also prevail. However, it contradicts convergence theory in that its organisation and financing are very different from those prevailing in Western capitalist countries. Finally, convergence theorists have underestimated the significant role played by the Soviet political élite in forming the system and women in maintaining it.

Health care in China

Before the Revolution, with 12,000 doctors for 500 million people, medical care in China was the prerogative of the rich. Infectious diseases, particularly cholera, tuberculosis, typhoid, and venereal disease were rampant; malnutrition and starvation widespread (Horn, 1966). The health service in China today comprises of three levels. The lowest level is the health centre or clinic staffed by *barefoot doctors* in rural areas and *worker doctors* in urban areas. The second tier is based on county hospitals having from thirty to 300 beds covering all branches of medicine including dentistry and gynaecology. These have outpatient services and act as the final referral points for the rural population. The third tier is made up of large, well-equipped hospitals in cities serving as medical centres or comprehensive hospitals for the district. The standard of Chinese health care has improved beyond recognition from its pre-Revolution levels, and in many instances rivals the best care available in the West.

Infant mortality rates and life expectancy are close to those prevailing in developed countries. For example, the infant mortality rate in Shanghai is 12.6 per thousand live births. This compares to 18.1 per thousand white babies and 27.1 per thousand black babies in New York (Sidel and Sidel, 1977). The average life span is around 70 years. The high birth rate and increased longevity have produced demographic stresses which the Chinese economy is struggling to handle (Croll, 1983). As in the West people's health has been advanced through better health care, improved nutrition, proper sanitation and higher living standards. Even the top three diseases causing death in China resemble those of the industrialised West – cancer, stroke and heart disease. These impressive statistics have been achieved by a poor country with one-thirtieth the GNP of the United States (Sidel and Sidel, 1977). Like Western health systems, the Chinese one also follows a sexist division of labour, although women have entered the lower levels of the medical profession in larger numbers.

Health services geared specifically towards women revolve around women's reproductive capacities, for example birth control. Contraceptives are freely available, though they may be crude, for example paper saturated with steroid contraceptives. Abortion on demand has been possible since 1963. Early abortions are preferred as these can be easily carried out through vacuum aspiration. Tubal ligations and sterilisation are options for women with two or more children. The countryside continues to have a higher birth rate than the urban areas. Women workers get three days sick leave each month for menstrual difficulties. They are offered lighter work if they are pregnant and receive fifty-six days of maternity leave on full pay after the birth of the child. This is increased to seventy days for women having difficult deliveries or twins. Women can take their babies to work as crèches are usually available and mothers given time off to nurse them.

POST-REVOLUTIONARY IDEALS

After 1949, new national health care priorities aiming to conserve limited economic resources and maximise the value extracted from existing health care facilities were set at the National Health Congress in Beijing (Lampton, 1977). This meant replacing high technology, élitist medical services with socialised ones and proclaiming the following priorities:

1. Preventing disease rather than curing the symptoms.
2. Serving the health needs of workers and peasants.
3. Achieving a 'unity' between Western medicine and traditional Chinese medicine.
4. Involving the Chinese people in creating their health services (Sidel and Sidel, 1977).

These principles owed much to the precedents set during the revolutionary struggles in Jiangsi and Shaanxi provinces. These mobilised people to educate themselves while collectively and individually providing their own health care and medical services (Horn, 1966).

Preventing disease and developing the health service within community structures became the main planks of Party activities in this field. Focusing on these priorities meant that the health service had to develop within community structures. Everyone was involved in providing health services to develop a sense of collective responsibility for one another's health and effectively use the limited resources at their disposal. These priorities required the Chinese Communist Party to: redistribute health resources; curtail the medical profession's power to define health care and treatment of diseases; relegating Western medicine to the realms of last resort; and relying on low technology traditional Chinese medicine like herbalism and acupuncture to maximise the use of resources (Lampton, 1977). Achieving these goals successfully required establishing a unity between traditional medicine and Western medicine to prevent traditional medicine from becoming second class medicine. Also, the Chinese people as a whole had to participate in defining illness and creating structures through which it would be treated. Knowledge of the social causes of disease and individuals' responsibility in caring for their health needed popularising for the elimination of illness to be tackled collectively. This led the Communist Party to identify ways of combining these aims and objectives effectively and meant:

1. State control of large and medium sized hospitals.
2. Grouping clinics into health co-operatives.
3. Decentralising care and fostering local decision-making.
4. Increasing consumer participation in health care.

Mass campaigns provided the method for securing health policy objectives. These drew on the 'mass line', that is, 'the conviction that ordinary people possess great strength and wisdom and that when their initiative is given full play, they can accomplish miracles' (Horn, 1966). Mass campaigns were launched immediately after liberation to train doctors in all forms of medicine, maintain the unity principle, and eliminate diseases, especially infectious ones. A key purpose of mass campaigns was educating people to gain awareness of the social causes of illness and disease and control the environment instead of becoming its victims. Mass campaigns involved everyone, young, old, medical personnel and lay people. As a result of the mass campaigns, the Chinese trained 200,000 doctors in Western medicine between 1949 and 1965 (Sidel and Sidel, 1977). By 1953, they had brought smallpox, cholera, malaria, and snail fever under control, and eliminated venereal disease and opium addiction.

A brief consideration of some of these campaigns gives an idea of how the Communist Party's objectives held together. The anti-venereal disease campaign combined an analysis of the social and economic causes of prostitution with free medical treatment of prostitutes and their clients. To overcome the financial forces pushing women into prostitution, women were given vocational training and jobs. To get rid of opium addiction, opium fields were burnt and crops planted instead.

Pushers were jailed, rehabilitated and found jobs in the community. The Patriotic Health Movement of the 1950s consisted of short, locally based campaigns of short duration. It initially aimed to destroy four pests: flies, mosquitoes, rats, and sparrows. Later, bedbugs were targeted. The campaigns educated people individually about hygienic food preparation and collectively ensured sanitary conditions in homes, streets, and the environment more generally. Larger environmental concerns were tackled subsequently. For example, the campaign to Clean Up Huangpu River and Suzhou Creek in 1968; the Spring Patriotic Sanitation Movement in 1970. Organised by local revolutionary committees, the latter sought to rid homes, farms, and factories of litter and pests, and collect reusable waste for recycling. In all these campaigns, people studied the problem and identified its causes, co-operated with others to work out the treatment, organised the funding for the work that needed doing, and set about improving their environment, and through that their health. Preventative work was thereby instilled into people's minds and actions.

Between 1949 and 1965 the medical professionals and the Chinese Medical Association controlled the health service and gave it an urban bias (Lampton, 1977). Medical graduates were attracted to the Curative Centres established primarily in the cities and large towns. In the rural areas, maternal care was the main state funded health provision until 1958. State trained public health workers had the limited remit of working in epidemic prevention centres, providing information on contagious diseases, and administering mass immunisation campaigns. This organisation of provisions created a growing disparity between facilities in urban and rural areas.

HEALTH SERVICES AND THE GREAT LEAP FORWARD

The Great Leap Forward tried to redress the urban–rural imbalance by opening more medical schools and training more doctors, especially in Western medicine. Results produced by this method were slow. Training took a minimum of six years and was expensive. Doctors could refuse employment in rural areas on graduation. Rural health care, particularly pre-natal and post-natal care, birth control and women's sexual rights remained neglected. With the majority of doctors and medical facilities in the cities, traditional herbalists and practitioners provided medical care in the rural areas prior to the reorganisation creating barefoot doctors.

Until 1960, the Women's Federation, a lone voice pressing for reform in rural health care, criticised the neglect of peasant diseases in general and women's health issues in particular. Emphasising women's health needs when they were nursing, menstruating, pregnant, or giving birth, reinforced traditional prejudices against women and demeaned their continuation in social production. Despite these demands, when women 'substituted for men' in the fields, they undertook all the tasks required of them (Andors, 1983). However, traditionalist attitudes enabled male brigade leaders to avoid acknowledging they were prioritising production needs over health ones by not providing for women's health and continue allocating resources to meet set production quotas. The downgrading of women workers' health needs was shortsighted in the long run because as healthy workers women could contribute more to production. The Great Leap Forward brought women's health issues to the fore, highlighting how essential health is to their contributing fully to social production, continuing with domestic work and giving birth. Although the Great Leap Forward demonstrated the necessity of providing adequate health care, the issue was not directly addressed until 1965 when Mao criticised the Ministry of Health. Specific action on rural health was not taken until the Cultural Revolution when the commune provided the network for rural health services and a co-operative medical insurance system (Howard, 1988).

Discrimination against women's labour in the workpoint allocation system and its failure to take domestic work into account militated against women while the allocation of income on an individual household basis increased the pressures on women to have large families (Croll, 1978). The Birth Control Programme during the Great Leap Forward exposed the tension between drawing women into the waged (workpoint) workforce and demanding they meet their domestic responsibilities including giving birth and caring for children. The need to bring population growth into line with economic growth resumed urgency in the recession following the Great Leap Forward and revived the campaign for later marriages and birth control, particularly using the 'coil' in 1962. Women were the chief targets of this campaign as birth control was considered their responsibility. This enabled men to escape assuming a direct interest in the issue and became another avenue through which the health service reinforced traditional concepts of masculinity and femininity.

The development of the commune and socialisation of domestic labour began unravelling resistance to women assuming key roles in both social and domestic production. The implementation of socialised domestic services was limited by the lack of resources available for this purpose. The national government could not be approached for funds, raw materials, machines or buildings. Neither could communes poach workers from state industries. These restrictions meant only affluent communes could provide a full range of health services including sick leave and maternity pay. But even these were hard pressed during 1959 and 1962 when production failed and natural disasters including flooding played havoc with the economy.

HEALTH SERVICES AND THE CULTURAL REVOLUTION

Mao had to curb the power of the medical profession to increase peasant and worker accessibility to its ranks and influence its education and training processes. Mao opened the power struggle between the Communist Party and doctors in 1965 by criticising the Ministry of Health for devoting too much time and resources to the needs of urban areas. The Party then issued the June 26th Directive aiming to change medical education, medical research, and medical practice. The specifics of these changes were implemented during the Cultural Revolution. Medical schools were closed down and reopened to facilitate peasants' access to them. This included altering entrance requirements to favour an individual's work history and political attitudes rather than academic achievements and shortening the training period to two years. Those recruited and trained under these criteria lacked knowledge and skills to competently handle many cases referred to them, lowered the quality of services provided and caused costly and fatal mistakes. The ascendancy of the rightwing of the Communist Party in 1978 reversed this process and reintroduced the six year training period.

The Ministry of Health was closed down during the Cultural Revolution between 1967 and 1971 to revolutionise health care at all levels. The vehicles used during this move were Three-in-One Combination Revolutionary Committees having representatives from the People's Liberation Army, the Party cadres, and the masses, usually doctors or health workers making decisions about local health services. The military has considerable power of its own in the health field for the army runs its own hospitals and militia organisation providing first aid training.

When the National Ministry of Public Health was reopened in 1971, the central state resumed a controlling role in developing health services. It assumed responsibility for: epidemic prevention, parasitic disease control, medical education, medical treatment and education, traditional medicine, maternal and child health care, pharmaceutical control, medical equipment production, supervision of the People's Health Press, and overseeing the work of the Physical, Cultural and Sports Commission. It also provides national control and direction for medical research carried out in fourteen institutes through the Chinese Academy of Medical Services. Women remain excluded from top levels of research work in the Ministry.

Eliminating the gap in medical provisions between the rural and urban areas was a major concern of the Cultural Revolution. It sought to ensure that people in the countryside acquired routine access to medical services by developing the barefoot doctor health system in which preventative measures became the responsibility of communities and individuals. Revitalising rural health care required the decentralisation of health services, an expansion in services by increasing the number of medical personnel, and a closer integration between Western and traditional medicine to achieve greater complementarity between them. The development of the barefoot doctor system marked a period which introduced radical changes in Chinese health service organisation and delivery and in the control and autonomy exercised by the medical profession (Lampton, 1977). It also introduced large numbers of women into the service, albeit at the lower levels of the medical hierarchy (Sidel and Sidel, 1977). Recruiting *xia-xiang* students into this initiative resulted in half of the barefoot doctors being female students (Andors, 1983).

In the countryside, the barefoot doctor was a part-time doctor and a part-time agricultural worker. They were paid in workpoints for both their medical and agricultural work. This marked an attempt to integrate mental and manual labour and ensure that doctors did not become too far removed from those they served. Drawing women into this position was advantageous in fostering the rational and extensive use of women's labour. Women barefoot doctors also offered young women positive role models to follow although people continued to consider this an extension of women's traditional caring work and role in medicine. It also locked women into the lower echelons of the medical profession, practising at its most impoverished points.

To do their work, barefoot doctors were given a short period of training ranging from three to six months. They were able to treat simple illness. Beyond that they referred people to a fully trained doctor who supervised their work. Thus, they provided primary health care, including environmental sanitation, health education, immunisation, and simple personal medical care. Immunisations were carried out with *Red Health Workers* helping them. Red Health Workers were usually women who had received a shorter period of training (Sidel and Sidel, 1977). This system meant that educational and training costs were substantially reduced and accessibility to medical personnel was considerably increased. Moreover, barefoot doctors controlled drug costs by using herbal medicine.

A parallel system was developed for the urban areas. The worker doctor was based in the factory and undertook part-time industrial work and part-time medical work. Payment for both types of activity was in workpoints. Worker doctors received short periods of training with monthly refresher courses. Their work was supplemented by the Red Medical Workers. Red Medical Workers given a one month training course carried out immunisations and provided basic information in their neighbourhoods. These were usually housewives receiving *no work-points* for their domestic chores. The practice of ignoring women's economic contribution through domestic labour perpetuated inequality between men and women and reinforced the invisibility of housework. The irony of the situation was that women's homemaker role facilitated their participation in health service provision and the use of their labour in expanding the service. Once again, the fruits of the Revolution were wrested from women's shoulders.

In 1965, Mobile Teams integrating urban doctors into the countryside and linking medical services at different levels were formed to live, work, eat and study among peasants and supplement rural medical provisions. Each mobile team had fifteen to twenty members divided into groups treating individual patients and training midwives and barefoot doctors. Each doctor remained in a Mobile Team from one to three months although in 1967, some Mobile Teams were permanently resettled in the countryside. About 165,000 urban doctors went into the countryside to train barefoot doctors, supplement their services, and help develop rural health care services (Sidel, 1977). Urban doctors were spread around the countryside by having one-third on the move all the time. In 1971, the government sent 330,000 urban medical workers into the countryside to augment Mobile Teams and make health care more accessible at local level (Sidel and Sidel, 1977).

Changes introduced during the Cultural Revolution were significant: accessibility to rural medical services improved substantially; health care delivery was better; the gap between urban and rural areas was reduced; the power of the high technology medical professionals was curtailed; and the masses had a greater say in determining local services. By 1973, there was one fully trained doctor for every 5,000 people and one barefoot doctor for every 7,000 people. The number of barefoot doctors reached 1.8 million by 1978 (Croll, 1983).

DEVELOPMENTS IN HEALTH CARE POST-MAO

The post-Mao shift in policy towards industrialisation and modernisation has had serious repercussions for Chinese health care, though the picture that is emerging is far from clear. It appears that the *Four Modernisations* and the *Responsibility System* have contributed to a decline in collective provisions. As Howard expresses it:

the 'three freedoms' which include the right to till private plots, sell goods in rural markets, and for communes to manage their operations independently with responsibility for their own profits and losses has revitalised the rural economy at the expense of collective provisions including clinics. (Howard, 1988)

In some instances, smaller contributions to the brigades' accumulation funds (5 to 7 per cent) and welfare funds (2 to 3 per cent) have already seriously depleted co-operative medical care systems. Consequently, the number of brigades with co-operative medical care systems declined from 80 per cent in the 1970s to 58 per cent in 1981 (Parish, 1985, p. 21). Howard (1988) found that communal health care provisions have largely disappeared in the grasslands. This is cause for concern because the diversion of funds to increase industrial production means collective care is not being replaced. The depletion of commune welfare funds and services under the Responsibility System may be less disastrous than it sounds because the changes appearing now parallel those occurring earlier when Liu Shao Chi introduced the 60 Articles whose disruptive effects on collective care were temporary (Howard, 1988).

The loss in collective provisions may be compensated through private provision. Howard (1988) discovered barefoot doctors leaving the co-operative medical system had either opened up private practices and pharmacies or given up medicine and returned to full-time farming. Doctors are also providing private hospital practice on a fee-for-service basis. Some have even concluded agreements enabling them to receive 20 per cent of the hospital's income on drug sales (Howard, 1988). These changes follow economic dislocation and foreshadow a Chinese version of privatising the health care system. If these trends intensify and are increasingly adopted by individuals, rural–urban disparities will resurface with greater vigour. Also, having a sector with better services purchased by richer people may precipitate the creation of a publicly funded residual health care system for the poor and resurgence of a powerful medical profession. The ruling élite already enjoys access to superior provisions (Sidel and Sidel, 1977).

Not all communes are following the road to the marketplace. Some brigades, for example the Five Cassia Tree Brigade in Sichuan province, have distributed only 60 per cent of earnings as personal incomes. The remainder has been split equally to expand production and finance welfare services including day care centres, schools, and the co-operative medical system (Howard, 1988).

THE PROBLEMATIC NATURE OF THE SYSTEM

The lack of concrete data makes commenting with certainty on the problematic nature of the Chinese health care system difficult. This is particularly evident in the impact of racism on service delivery in a society in which 80 per cent of the population belongs to the Han ethnic group. The localised nature of service delivery and the requirement that it be self-sufficient can exacerbate existing social divisions. Gender differentiation is a key feature of the health system, but women do not enjoy the prestigious posts and incomes to which their male colleagues have access. Forming a substantial proportion of the health care workforce, women comprise: all the health workers dealing with women around issues of birth control; an overwhelming majority of medical workers and nurses; 50 per cent of medical students; 50 per cent of barefoot doctors; and 30–40 per cent of physicians. The lower down the labour hierarchy and the more one gets into low priority fields of medicine, the more likely one is to find women working.

Demanding local areas provide their own health services reinforces regional and urban–rural inequalities for poor communes cannot obtain central state funding. Enforced self-sufficiency also exacerbates the trend towards privatised health care. Government expenditure and subsidies on the Chinese health service are low. In 1966, it amounted to 4 per cent of general government expenditure. Payment for medical services varies according to the workplace. Government employees, industrial workers, miners, university and college students, and national ethnic minorities receive free medical care paid for by the state. Factory workers have their health care costs paid for by their factory or trade union. Factory schemes also pay half the costs of medical care for a worker's dependants. State and factory schemes cover about 20 per cent of the population. Peasants, forming the remainder of the population, rely on the commune for their health care. Each family pays an annual premium and nominal registration fee for each member to the collective. These payments are low and are not barriers to care (Sidel and Sidel, 1977). Communes aim to dispense with them as soon as resources permit (Sidel and Sidel, 1977). The privatisation of services may drastically alter this picture.

IN CONCLUSION

Until recently, the Chinese health service has attempted to redistribute resources to those classes having the least. It has emphasised prevention of illness rather than curative services and encouraged self-sufficiency and mutual help individually and collectively. It has fostered consumer participation in service delivery and curbed the medical profession's powers. Health provisions nonetheless remain problematic. Urban services are technically superior and more accessible than their rural counterparts. The shortage of skilled medical personnel in the country-side remains while patients demand a higher quality of service than that provided by barefoot doctors with limited training. Moreover, physicians still carry a higher status than other doctors and are more centrally involved in making health care decisions. The integration of Chinese and

Western medicine is far from complete. A sexist division of labour continues to exist. And, the privatisation of medical care entering via the side door threatens the entire edifice.

CONCLUSIONS

Regardless of their political complexion, the health care systems in the countries examined are in crisis. Health care costs have risen to levels exceeding the resources of either individuals or states. The emphasis on high technology, curative care has contributed to escalating costs, but so too have people's demands for increasing access to medical services, a wider variety of provisions, and greater consumer control over these. Countries emphasising preventative care like Sweden, the Soviet Union and China, also experience these pressures, though their resolution of the problem differs from the cost-cutting measures initiated in Canada, Britain and America. Ironically, all the countries studied have developed services compatible with economic priorities being pursued politically, making the subordination of health care provisions to economic exigencies occur within politically set economic limitations. These political decisions were made through the interplay of ideological factors and political forces at the local and national levels.

Women have entered the medical profession in increasing numbers in all the countries considered, though their highest profile is in the Soviet Union and China, where a gendered division of labour placing women in its lower echelons also prevails. Interestingly, women have been recruited as doctors when the status of the profession was diminishing. In the Soviet Union, this took place to free men for more prestigious industrial work. In China, women became active in medicine during a drive to increase the accessibility of rural services when men were needed for the more important task of raising industrial production and carrying out the technological industrial revolution. Housewives, the major reservoir of untapped labour available, were drawn into the ranks of the barefoot and worker doctors in a clearly subordinate position to fully qualified (male) doctors. But they did have status within the communities they served.

Consumer dissatisfaction with service provision is high in all the countries covered. In the West and the Soviet Union, health care users are unhappy about both the nature of the services on offer and the quality of the doctor-patient relationship. Chinese people are less dissatisfied with this relationship because health services are locally determined and people have a closer connection with the 'doctor' who is one of them. But, demand for Western style medicine is higher than resourcing allows.

The desire of people in all these countries to lead healthier lives is common, though the possibility of this being realised is more uncertain. Resources are tight, the political will to release further resources is in some doubt, environmental pollution and the stress of industrial life are eroding earlier gains in health in all the countries studied. Meanwhile women, particularly those in Britain, Canada and the USA, have taken their health in their hands and developed feminist alternatives capable of responding more appropriately to their needs and providing them with greater control over the treatment and services available to them.

5

Conclusions

NEW MODELS OF WELFARE: FEMINIST PREFIGURATIVE FORMS

Social policy in the countries we have examined, whether capitalist, social democratic or socialist has not unambiguously fostered the well-being of women, children or men. Subservience to economic exigencies whether to maintain labour discipline, as in the case of Britain, Canada and the United States, sustain full employment as in Sweden, or launch extensive industrialisation and modernisation programmes as in the Soviet Union and China, has ensured that social policy never seriously threatened patriarchal relations.

The absence of a strong autonomous feminist movement capable of defending women's rights in China and the Soviet Union has meant that the contradictions between women's liberation and socialist develop-ment were resolved in favour of socialist developments furthering the interests of a male dominated society, for example China during the Great Leap Forward (Stacey, 1983), the Bolshevik Revolution in its early days (Kollantai, 1971). The incorporation of the women's movement into the social policy negotiating machinery favouring trade union, employer and state interests in social democratic Sweden resulted in women's equality being defined through the imperatives of waged work, limiting the gains women could make as women with responsibility for undertaking both waged and unwaged work.

The presence of an active feminist movement in each of the capitalist countries of Britain, America and Canada, has successfully kept women's issues high on the political agenda. Women's relative power-lessness compared to other interest groups seeking to influence social policy has contributed to the subordination of feminist demands despite resistance by feminists and their supporters. The impact of Western feminism has not been limited to shaping state policy. Feminists have also established alternative welfare resources based on their critique of existing state provisions for women. These embody feminist principles of theory in practice and prefigure or attempt to create now the transformed social relations feminists aim to establish more generally in society. Feminist services are rooted in an understanding of women's oppressed position in society, the desire to eliminate oppression, and the commitment to creating non-oppressive relationships between men and women, adults and children.

In this chapter, I examine the theory and practice informing feminist welfare initiatives. I also consider the contribution insights garnered from feminist criticisms and experiences of existing welfare provisions and the development of feminist alternatives can make to the creation of an anti-racist feminist social policy. Particularly relevant in the context of this book are feminist achievements in the areas of income maintenance, family policy and health care in the countries under study, and evaluating the extent to which these can become the basis of public provisions. I will argue that welfare services in both capitalist and socialist societies can benefit from the extension of feminist prefigurative forms. Under the impact of feminist intervention, state welfare services can be made: more amenable to people's needs; less remote; more responsive to consumer control; less hierarchical by reducing the impact of professionalism in decision-making; and more health oriented by giving preventative care the same status as curative care. In this way, human need rather than economic and political exigencies can become the basis of welfare provisions and the life chances of women, children and men enhanced.

FEMINIST WELFARE THEORY AND PRACTICE

From a feminist perspective, the welfare state has failed to meet women's aspirations in both capitalist and socialist countries, in income maintenance provisions, services to lessen women's caring burden in the home, institutionally provided personal social services, health care, or employment opportunities. The women of America, Canada, Britain, Sweden, the Soviet Union and China are expected to work in the labour market by contributing both waged labour and unwaged domestic labour to meet the needs of their families and the economy. In the context of a world economy in which waged labour and capitalist principles of organisation dominate the marketplace (Wallerstein, 1974), unpaid domestic labour and waged labour are both active agents in it. Their existence in that arena means they interact with one another, shaping each other through that interaction. They are constantly in the process of forming and transforming themselves and each other. The main differences between them is that waged labour is visible and classified as a factor of production, while domestic labour is invisible and omitted from the costs of production equation. *But, although unquantified, domestic labour is there nonetheless.* Were it not, the costs of producing the goods and services presently being produced and consumed by humankind would be immeasurably higher.

The presence of domestic labour in the labour market helps lower the costs of production. This includes both men's and women's wages, and will remain so until the costs of domestic labour are made visible. For women, excluding domestic labour from the costs of production equation has meant denigrating the value of both this work and their waged work, for this draws on the skills of domestic labour, although these have been catapulted into the waged labour arena. Such dynamics have furthered the creation of a welfare state which has tapped women's labour on these premises and built welfare services on the cheap. Thus, women's employment in state welfare is at the bottom of the labour hierarchy in positions subordinate to those occupied by men and earning lower incomes. Additionally, defining womanhood in terms of domestic labour confines women to the private arena while men dominate the public one where acknowledged power and authority reside. Keeping these two spheres separate is essential in maintaining relations of subordination and domination.

Women have not meekly accepted their subservient role in society. They have struggled against it in a myriad of ways – collectively by organising as women in either feminist or woman-centred organisations which may have formed alliances with male dominated groups to achieve specific goals, and individually in acts of defiance woven into the fabric of everyday life, for example the exhausted mother, waged worker and housewife who feigns illness in explaining why she feels unable to respond to her husband's insistence that they go out together that evening. By rationalising her behaviour in acceptable terms she avoids a confrontation with her partner and gives the appearance of accepting her situation while resisting it. However, this approach does not ameliorate her position because the problem of her excessive workload remains mystified and unaddressed. But it is an active survival strategy in a situation in which she can exercise little social power. Similarly, women are driven to suicide to escape oppressive situations, as they did, for example, in large numbers in pre-Communist China (Croll, 1978). They too were resisting their subordinate status, however ineffectual this may have been in securing changes in women's condition for either themselves or others.

None of the regimes we examined has come to terms with these dynamics in women's existence, despite their centrality in the relationships these states have mediated with women living within their borders. The expectation that a socialist formation would disentangle patriarchal dynamics has not been realised.

The experience of both Chinese and Soviet women reveals that socialism (accepting these countries' own definitions of themselves) does not in and of itself emancipate women. Rather, it may re-entrench patriarchal relationships by reorganising them in ways compatible with socialist economic developments (Molyneaux, 1985; Stacey, 1983; Johnson, 1983). At the same time, patriarchal relationships define the terms within which socialism develops. Stacey (1983) argues that the socialist revolution in China succeeded in achieving a family revolution which established the 'new democratic patriarchal family' consolidating men's privileges on a sounder economic footing through land reform. This made it possible for *male* peasants to acquire land, facilitated their ability to get married and acquire wives which they could support, and fulfilled an earlier impossible ambition. Meanwhile, the egalitarian thrust of land reforms legitimated the use of women's labour in agricultural production, increasing women's contribution to family incomes.

Stacey (1983) declares peasants supported the Communists precisely because they promised to satisfy their hunger for land which to the peasantry, male and female, was the key to realising their dreams for a better family life. She suggests the Communist Party 'democratised' the availability of women and retreated from supporting feminists' views on the family because this provided them with the opportunity of consolidating and strengthening their economic security on the basis of male kinship bonds, thereby reinforcing the patriarchal family economy. This process turned the new democratic patriarchal family into the patriarchal socialist one. Stacey (1983) attributes the failure of the Great Leap Forward to male peasant resistance to both the full integration of women into social production and the socialisation of domestic labour because these measures threatened to radically undermine the patriarchal socialist family established by the co-operative movement. Peasant women, especially older women, resisted these measures because their traditional status and power over their sons' wives had declined as they were drawn more heavily in to domestic labour and made responsible for childminding in to free daughters-in-law for more active roles in social production (Stacey, 1983).

Stacey (1983) goes on to say that the commitment to the Revolution. Stacey (1983) 'historic compromise' reached between the Communist Party and the masses early in the revolutionary struggle later acted as a brake on the development of socialism. Stacey (1983) maintains, peasants endorsed the collectivisation movement grouping families into co-operatives because doing so would have jeopardised male peasants' commitment to the Revolution.

Stacey (1983) highlights contradictions in the accommodation the Chinese Communist Party made with the peasantry, although she is unclear about how these might have been resolved. These contradictions are strikingly evident in the *Four Modernisations* Programme aiming to revitalise the economy and contain population growth. Stacey (1983) and Croll (1983) suggest economic developments will strengthen the patriarchal family by encouraging the growth of private family production exploiting women's labour. At the same time, Stacey (1983) believes the population control policy will undermine the preference for sons and thereby threaten male power. Unfortunately, events since Stacey's book was written have revealed that the One Child Family is being strongly resisted, particularly in rural areas where the preference for sons is as strong as ever (Peng, 1987). Meanwhile, private production has undermined collective welfare provision, increased pressures for private solutions to income insecurity and drawn women more firmly into productive activity through the family production system (Howard, 1988).

The Chinese revolution offers us an excellent example of how patriarchal relations are reconstructed in the absence of a powerful autonomous feminist movement. It also reveals the importance of viewing social change as a dialectical process in which every part of the social system interacts with every other part in the process of being acted upon itself. Social change is not a linear process, but a convoluted one in which the social relations being acted upon act on those acting upon them. Thus, the transformer is being transformed while it is transforming others. This suggests a wholistic interdependence between one part of the social system and all the other parts. Applying this understanding to oppression implies that social change aimed at eliminating one form of oppression must tackle all forms of oppression simultaneously if it is to achieve its goal. This both requires and leads to the transformation of society in all respects as feminists have argued. The problem is how to achieve this in practice. Do feminist prefigurative forms provide a way forward?

Feminist analysts have identified the significance of rejecting dualist thought in advancing feminist praxis. They have also suggested that achieving women's liberation means overcoming the subordination of social policy to economic policy and integrating them on an equal footing (Coote, 1981). Freeing women from oppression also requires social change to occur in both domestic production and social production simultaneously (Segal, 1987). It must transform social relations between men and women, adults and children. It has to proceed along egalitarian lines and eliminate all forms of oppression as they are encountered. In other words, although feminists begin tackling gender oppression by focusing on and working with women, their work undermines the edifice which bolsters patriarchy, revealing the suffering men and children endure in the process and pointing to the necessity of addressing their well-being as well as women's if the welfare of all is to be assured (Dominelli and McLeod, 1989). Anti-sexist men have begun to disentangle themselves from the alleged privileges patriarchy brings by taking the cue from feminists and examining patriarchal masculinity. Having embarked on this process, they have found it wanting and begun redefining it for themselves (Bowl, 1985).

Feminist critiques of existing provisions have led to the creation of woman-centred alternatives prefiguring those that would exist in a feminist society. Variety and controversy have been their keynotes as there is neither a single feminist blueprint nor only one feminist perspective which is dogmatically applied in all situations (Dominelli and McLeod, 1989; Marchant and Wearing, 1986; Banks, 1981). However, there is a set of common principles within which different forms of practice are elaborated (Adamson et al., 1988). A central one is integrating theory and practice and developing one from the other. Feminist principles and practice are constantly evolving and changing as a result of insights gained in practice, giving feminist work a persistent unfinished quality that avoids both the rigidity inherent in dualistic constructs and the hierarchical ordering of thought which accords conceptual work a higher status than practical work, and ensures that egalitarianism, another key feature of feminism, permeates both intellectual and practical activities. The ends, means, processes, actions of those involved and relationships between them have equality and democracy pervading them. Additionally, feminist theory and practice advance through collective action whereby women support each other, share skills with and learn from one another, gain confidence in their talents, develop feminist consciousness and change their material reality.

Feminists' preoccupation with social change to eradicate oppression gives feminism its dynamism, orients it in progressive directions and places it at odds with the status quo. This is not to say feminists do not reinforce sexist, racist, disablist, heterosexist or ageist values and norms, for they too are products of a society riven by social divisions (Dominelli and McLeod, 1989). But there is an explicit commitment to eliminating these, however imperfectly in the short run, from feminist theory and practice. Feminists' willingness to listen to criticisms of their work is evident in white feminists' attempts to explicated by other women is evident in white feminists' attempts to counter racism following critiques of their theory and practice by black feminists (see Barrett and McIntosh, 1985), middle class feminists reaching out to working class feminists (Lewycka, 1986; McCrindle and Rowbotham, 1986), heterosexual feminists examining their homophobia once lesbian feminists highlighted it (Perverse Politics, 1990).

Radical

Liberal

Socialist

The major feminist perspectives in current feminist thought have been identified as radical feminism, liberal/bourgeois feminism, socialist feminism, black feminism (Davies, 1989). These have different sets of assumptions about the origins and nature of patriarchy which influence their practice with women and the development of alternative welfare provisions. Radical feminists focusing on 'men' as the enemy eschewed alliances with them. They have opted for a separatist vision of the world in which women work with other women to provide services meeting their needs and avoid becoming entangled in masculinist dynamics in which women are losers. Some of feminism's most creative theories and practices have been formulated by radical feminists, for example work on male violence and pornography (Dworkin, 1976). Radical feminists' initial insights on these issues have been adopted by other feminists and reworked in a number of directions, producing services appealing to a wide range of women, for example Rape Crisis Centres in which feminists of varied persuasions offer their services (Brennan, 1989).

Liberal/bourgeois feminism locked in struggle within existing social structures to improve women's position is almost a contradiction in terms. Many of women's social, political and economic rights have been gained through the efforts of liberal/bourgeois feminists. Although they are more interested in gaining equality for women than transforming society, this label should not trivialise the contribution they have made and are making to improving women's status in society. Women's rights to vote, equal pay, family allowances, and other state welfare provisions can be traced back to liberal/bourgeois feminist struggles (Dale and Foster, 1986). Struggle is the operative word, for many of their chief objectives have yet to be realised even in societies formally accepting their demands.

Socialist feminists have included both patriarchy and capitalism in their analysis and action. Their concern with class perspectives enables them to see men as being oppressed under capitalism while they oppress women. Socialist feminists' appreciation of the unliberated position of men enables them to form alliances with men and/or work within mixed organisations to tackle problems, for example working relations in the workplace. Socialist feminist criticism of male comrades' behaviour has not been particularly effective in persuading men to examine their own behaviour and the ways in which they individually, collectively and through the use of institutionalised power oppress women, although some of this work is bearing fruit, for example men in trade unions responding to feminist demands for eliminating sexual harassment in the workplace.

Black feminists have had to tackle class, race and gender oppression simultaneously. Their critique of white feminists' racism has been crucial in breaking down racist stereotypes emerging in the 'feminist' movement. Challenging white women's presumption of sisterhood, black women have drawn attention to how racism structures their experiences of gender differently from white women's. They have also highlighted how white women's racism is as oppressive as white men's and stated clearly sisterhood is something that is earned, not assumed (Hooks, 1984). Black feminists have questioned white feminists' intellectual concepts as well as their practice. Feminist refusal to order different forms of oppression hierarchically can be attributed to black feminists' resistance to the subordination of race oppression to class and gender. Also, the development of the concept of equality based on difference owes much to black feminist work exposing the colourblind nature of 'universal' provisions and the systematic exclusion of black people from such resources (see Lorde, 1984). Black feminists have also promoted the idea that oppressed people struggle within existing institutions to ensure the human spirit triumphs over structural adversity and demonstrate that people actively both accept and reject their oppressed status and that resistance can occur within the 'normal' range of human interaction. For example, identifying black families as sites where racism and sexism are resisted, individuals strengthened and provided with a 'safe' arena (Carby, 1982; Mama, 1989; Bryan et al., 1985).

A further cleavage among women occurs when the boundaries between feminist approaches and women-centred ones are blurred. While feminists are women-centred, being woman-centred does not make one feminist. Though often fighting for similar causes, a crucial difference between them is that woman-centred women take women's interests further within the limits prescribed by society while feminists aim to transcend these by transforming society.

Feminists have used their pluralistic diversity as a strength to promote their understanding of the complexity of women's lives and provide a basis for eschewing either monocausal explanations of women's oppression or monolithic solutions for its elimination. Feminists have been inspired by other progressive movements – liberation struggles of various kinds and worked, albeit at times inadequately, to support them (Foster, 1989).

The absence of feminists holding positions of stature among the political élites in the countries examined, has blunted their impact within the corridors of power. Alexandra Kollantai was a major exception. But during her short ministerial term even she was assigned the task of working with women and dealing with their issues – matters which her male colleagues considered of secondary importance to the 'real' work of the Bolshevik Revolution. Her initial success rapidly disappeared in competition with other demands for resources and political power. The vulnerability of Kollantai's gains highlight the importance of having feminism infuse the whole of society for feminist achievements to endure. Ironically, women's position in Britain deteriorated while a woman, Margaret Thatcher, held the country's highest political office. She is neither feminist nor woman-centred, although she frequently used woman's role as mother, housekeeper and wife in her public pronouncements to bring the nation into people's living rooms and make her seem approachable.

FEMINIST PREFIGURATIVE FORMS

Feminists have sought to shape social policy in several ways. They have mounted critiques of existing welfare provisions and demonstrated how poorly they serve women's interests as either consumers or workers. Feminists have shown that welfare state provisions have been distorted by serving objectives other than those concerned with improving people's well-being. Economic imperatives such as enforcing labour discipline and rationing scarce public resources negate the provision of services enhancing people's welfare needs. Feminists have revealed that welfare state provisions and professionals reinforce women's domesticity and oppression (Brook and Davis, 1985; Marchant and Wearing, 1986; Hale, 1983; Dominelli and McLeod, 1989). They have exposed the welfare state's relationship with children as one structuring children's dependency on adults and denying them specific rights to independent incomes, a violence-free existence, and a variety of kinship and social relations in forming close relationships with adults. Feminists in Britain, Canada, the United States and Sweden have taken welfare as a major arena of struggle. They have been involved in forming the welfare state and creating services catering for women's specific needs as women whether homemakers, wage-earners, or both (Dale and Foster, 1986; Pascall, 1986). They have developed a variety of resources through feminist campaigns and networks, group activities and individual initiatives. These include: health care provisions such as Feminist Therapy Centres, Refuges for Battered Women, Incest Survivor Groups, Rape Crisis Centres, Well-Women Clinics; Women's Resource Centres; and feminist scholarship. Feminists have created services available to women at the point of need, operating in non-stigmatised, non-hierarchical ways and involving women fully in gaining skills and expertise themselves.

Although feminists have developed an enormous range of services and benefits for women, they have done so with minimal resources and often amid great hostility. This suggests that if public resources currently allocated to the welfare state followed feminist principles of organisation and service, they could be used more effectively and productively. Through their work, feminists have redefined the arena encompassed by social policy and brought into it previously neglected issues of major concern to women and children, for example child sexual abuse. Feminist campaigns and networks have been influential in challenging existing definitions of family policy, income maintenance systems, and health care systems, heightening public consciousness of these issues, supporting individual women and groups of women seeking to eradicate women's oppression and establishing alternative provisions espousing feminist principles and practice drawing primarily on women's own resources of self-help. At the same time, feminists have penetrated various levels of government and used their positions to further shape social policy and welfare practice. We shall now consider some of their initiatives.

Income maintenance

A major feminist demand has been women's *individual* right to an income rather than as family members to ensure women's right to an independent income and in a form which neither presupposes nor reproduces women's inequality (Weir and McIntosh, 1982). In the 1970s in Britain, this demand was publicly articulated through the Working Women's Charter calling for the abolition of income inequality in the workplace, and the provision of public day care facilities, and the 'Disaggregation Now' campaign demanding the abolition of the 'family wage', women's right to an independent income, and equality in social security and social assistance benefits and taxation law. The state has compromised in this direction, but feminist principles and practice do not infuse these provisions. Though feminists in America, Canada and Sweden have wrung more concessions from their governments than their British counterparts, the white heterosexual nuclear family remains the basic paradigm within which social policy and legislation are formulated. We have also seen that 'the family' in a somewhat more extended form is the cornerstone of Soviet and Chinese social policies. Feminist income maintenance policy supported by the state remains an objective requiring further feminist action for its realisation.

Feminist struggles over the income maintenance system have elaborated a critique of existing systems and identified principles which should inform non-oppressive ones. Existing systems could be ameliorated by being collectively underwritten, meeting needs highlighted by those using the service and working in it and rejecting considerations of social control. The system endorses participation based on feminist principles ensuring equality in the relationships between those involved, regardless of their status and provide unstigmatised public services available to all when needed. Moreover, connections between taxation and income maintenance systems would be made explicit to avoid hidden welfare subsidies to higher income groups. In the longer run, a feminist income maintenance system would be underwritten by a feminist society and would not resemble any of the income maintenance systems we know today. Its shape would be formed through the struggle involved in transforming those that currently exist in feminist directions.

Meanwhile, feminists have implemented their ideals regarding earned incomes in various commercial feminist collectives, for example feminist publications, and in non-commercial activities, for example refuges. Women have had equal wages policies to ensure that wage differentials did not thwart the establishment of egalitarian relationships amongst them (Binney *et al.*, 1981). Unfortunately, many feminist ventures have operated on shoestring budgets. Wages available for distribution in these collectives have been limited, often falling below the already inadequate market rate for such work, making women working collectively receive equal shares of financial impoverishment. Some feminist projects have sought to resolve their financial crises by seeking state funding. Such funding is invariably inadequate and usually constrained to funding full- or part-time posts, for example feminists in Women's Aid Refuges discovered much to their chagrin that funding established a distinction between paid workers and unpaid volunteers. They had to expend considerable energies in ensuring such distinctions did not block the creation of egalitarian relationships between paid workers, unpaid volunteers and women seeking refuge. Fully involving all these groups in running the refuge, determining its policies and developing its practices was central to achieving this objective. Participation on this basis was also intended to empower women and ensure that it was abused women rather than professionals speaking about their experiences, identifying their needs and finding ways of meeting them. Sharing power gave the real experts in the situation – the abused women a voice (National Women's Aid Federation, 1980).

These experiences have relevance for state provisions. Current welfare states could initiate policies guaranteeing each individual a basic income high enough to lead a dignified life. Inducements encouraging people to work could be initiated outside the welfare system. Models of practice could foster both user and worker participation and egalitarian relationships between service users and providers. The professional's task would then become one of empowering consumers rather than imposing their dictates on them. Welfare workers could be paid salaries reflecting the value of their work rather than the gender of those doing it. Income differentials could be reduced to eliminate internal hierarchies within the workforce. In other words, equality of access would have to be balanced with equality of outcome. Governments could introduce these policies but the likelihood is that they will not unless it is either in their interests to do so, or women organise to make it happen.

Family policy

Feminist critiques of family policy have highlighted the inadequacies of the white nuclear heterosexual family as *the basis* for policy formulation. It neither represents the living situation of many women and children, nor provides a safe environment for them as countless feminist accounts of male physical and sexual assault on women and children testify (see Armstrong, 1988; Kelly, 1988). Feminist practice on this front has endorsed diversity in family structures, including accepting the legitimacy of a single life, single parenthood, married couples with or without children, communal living, extended social kinship relationships, lesbian motherhood, gay fatherhood. Feminists have combined their tolerance for a variety of family forms with sexual rights for all women – women with disabilities, older women, young women in care, lesbian women and heterosexual women. Sexual rights follow the view that women have the right to determine whether, how, and with whom they will express their sexuality. The right to control their fertility on their own terms also forms part of women's reproductive rights. Family forms in keeping with feminist principles have equality as a central feature and reject violence. For heterosexual women, equality requires challenging traditional definitions of fatherhood and motherhood as men and women equally share childcare, housework, household expenditures, and incomes. However, heterosexual feminists have yet to achieve their aims, and resolve conflicts in their intimate relationships with men. Equality for lesbian women has involved sharing households, childcare, domestic work, expenditures and incomes with women lovers. Their households have often had to deal with the fierce hostility of homophobic lay people and professionals (Hanscombe and Forster, 1982). Despite their flaws, feminist relationships have shown 'loving' relationships between people are not inevitably structured around relations of subordination and domination. And, they have demonstrated the feasibility of alternative family forms which are more in tune with women's needs.

Family policy can be informed by these experiences and move in less oppressive directions. This requires social policy to refrain from reinforcing the patriarchal nuclear family, labelling other family arrangements deviant and reproducing women's domesticity. Policy could support a variety of family forms by providing publicly funded day care, guaranteeing women's reproductive rights, and endorsing women's and children's rights to financial independence. Family policy could also be formulated more democratically by involving women and children directly in its creation. Additionally, the state could underwrite women's and children's rights, giving men the clear message that neither women nor children are their possessions. The extent to which a state would incorporate these principles in its provisions depends on how powerfully women, children and men organise to make it so.

Feminist family policy would also make connections between women's work at home and in waged labour. Facilitating women's involvement in waged work on a non-oppressive basis requires changes in the organisation of both waged and domestic work and the redefinition of work. Redefining work would affect the whole basis of the interaction between men and women – their perceptions of themselves as people, their legitimate roles in society and the division of labour at home. Acknowledging the interconnectedness and interdependency between them holds the promise of divesting masculinity and femininity of their oppressive dimensions.

British local authorities led by Labour, especially in London, Sheffield, Leeds, Birmingham, have attempted to implement feminist ideas on family policy when they incorporated Women's Committees in local authority decision-making structures. Their initiatives were particularly important in lending generalised support to feminist attempts to reach a wide variety of women in the early to mid-1980s before the Thatcher government prematurely ended much of their experimentation by abolishing the Greater London Council and metropolitan counties and rate-capping others. The success of Women's Committees in reaching groups of women not normally served by local authorities partially caused their undoing by giving anti-feminist neo-conservatives targets for their hostility. For example, by drawing upon an extensive range of feminist networks to promote their work, London boroughs like Camden were highly innovative in getting services out to women who had been doubly marginalised by the political process. Their initiatives included supporting lesbian and gay rights to employment and family life; providing more appropriate services to black families, particularly in childcare by accepting black foster parents, supporting them in their work and developing other forms of anti-racist social work practice; enabling older and disabled women to use more public facilities; and creating more relevant day care and nursery provisions for all children.

The Tories mounted a legal and financial onslaught against their anti-sexist and anti-racist initiatives by alleging misuse of public funds (Campbell and Jacques, 1986; Livingstone, 1987). Feminist organisations and their few active supporters within the local state and labour movement were not powerful enough to withstand this attack.

Health policy

Feminist critiques of existing medical and health care systems have led them to develop alternative self-help provisions. These have been developed as part of a collective struggle aiming to subvert the power of male medical professionals, define the types of treatment appropriate for women, and demonstrate that women could responsibly provide their own medical and health care. Feminist health struggles provide well-documented feminist initiatives. Their variety is extensive for feminist activity in this field in Sweden, Britain, Canada, and America has flowered. However, I will focus on Well Women's Clinics in Britain because these illustrate relatively well known and researched feminist health praxis.

Feminists have criticised medical care for elevating doctors' negative subjective opinions of women patients to scientific status, using its knowledge and skills to control women and tying them firmly to domesticity (Ruzek, 1978; Foster, 1989). Women's unsatisfactory experience of health care caused feminists to create alternatives according women dignity and meeting their needs. Feminists' varying philosophies and political positions have made developing these provisions controversial. Radical feminists rejecting the involvement of male doctors, emphasise the creation of women-only alternatives. Liberal/bourgeois feminists and socialist feminists are committed to increasing women's employment opportunities in medicine and extending choice for women by having women doctors easily available to them. Whatever their persuasion, feminists have five principles guiding the health services they create. These are:

1. Sharing medical knowledge and experience to increase women's control over their well-being.
2. Sharing power between users and providers of services to foster egalitarian and democratic ways of working.
3. Providing a holistic service based on listening to women and their perceptions of their needs.
4. Having doctors sharing themselves, their expertise and their empathy when responding to women.

5. Having provisions acceptable to all women, regardless of their 'race', class, sexual orientation, age, or disability (Foster, 1989).

These principles have informed feminist practice in Well Women Clinics but are similar to those adopted in other feminist welfare provisions. In Britain, Well Women Clinics were established as bases of feminist practice in a vast NHS desert. Well Women Clinics have been formed both outside and inside the NHS, depending on the extent of local support or hostility generated when feminists put forward proposals. Staff teams are made up of doctors, nurses, and volunteers working together in less hierarchical ways. Their efforts are not always successful as users may respond to a volunteer's advice less readily than a doctor's, making volunteers experience a devaluing of their status (Foster, 1989).

As part of the holistic approach, women are given as much time as they need to talk through their concerns and have both their physical and emotional states taken into consideration. Listening validates women's own definition of their health needs and furthers preventative work. Preventative and listening strategies have reduced reliance on drugs or operations in resolving women's health problems. Throughout their interaction with women, workers are expected to be sensitive, caring, and show their own vulnerability and emotions, thereby challenging the neutral, uninvolved stance adopted in traditional professional approaches to clients and redefining the professional role. Working in this manner requires practitioners to take care of themselves, otherwise their vulnerability leads to exhaustion. Foster (1989) reports one Well Women Clinic which closed down after two years because workers had 'burnt out'.

Well Women Clinics aim to reach women not normally using medical facilities. However, lack of resources has meant poor progress on this front. The numbers of working class and black women using these facilities are small. Well Women Clinics have attempted to tackle these problems by seeking urban aid funding (Foster, 1989). Besides being limited, such funding is precarious. Outstanding amounts can be withdrawn at short notice. Funding is dependent on women obtaining support from both local and central states. Gaining such approval can be difficult as projects deemed to have 'political aims' are usually rejected. Urban aid funded posts are outside mainstream career grades. Black women appointed to them find their work marginalised while they are subjected to racist practices (Dominelli, 1988a).

Well Women Clinics have a tenuous hand-to-mouth existence as marginal provisions, whether inside or outside the NHS. For example, the first Well Women Clinic opening in Manchester had one session per week because it was all doctors could spare. Other Well Women Clinics open for restricted periods. This manages scarce resources but reduces their accessibility to women. If Well Women Clinics are located within GPs' surgeries, they may receive state funding only for cervical smears taken from women aged over 35 once every three to five years rather than all the services they provide (Foster, 1989). Within hospital settings, feminists practising on an individual basis may become extremely vulnerable, as Wendy Savage discovered. Although an established obstetrician with senior lecturer status, her practice of giving pregnant women control over their treatment antagonised her male colleagues who succeeded in dismissing her for incompetence in April 1985 (Savage, 1986). She was only reinstated in July 1986 after an enquiry and extensive campaign feminists mounted in her defence. Few Well Women Clinics exist. In 1987, 100 area health authorities claimed Well Women Clinics (Foster, 1989, p. 345). This overestimates their number because the Well Women Clinic name has been appropriated by some authorities and misused to describe family planning clinics staffed by women not practising according to feminist principles (Foster, 1989).

Well Women Clinics expose both the strengths and weaknesses of self-help approaches operating within the confines of a dominant medical model antagonistic to their existence. As separate provisions, Well Women Clinics are easily accessible because they are located in the community they serve. Practitioners within them have a fair degree of autonomy from external interference in running their affairs. But, their very smallness means workers' time and energies are consumed by activities needed just to keep them going (Foster, 1989), leaving no time for either further developmental or outreach work. Their limited resourcing also restricts the numbers of women receiving their services. Waiting lists for feminist provisions can be lengthy (McLeod, 1987). The services Well Women Clinics offer are constrained by their being prevented from referring women to other facilities in the way GPs can. Well Women Clinics can be abused by unsupportive NHS doctors who pass 'difficult' women onto them (Foster, 1989). As a marginalised activity, Well Women Clinics are unlikely to threaten established interests in the NHS. They have had a limited effect on the dominant mode of service delivery and labour organisation in the NHS. Their local impact is more positive. Well Women Clinics offer women a service not otherwise available, giving women more choice when seeking medical attention in their locality. Moreover, women are enthusiastic about the services Well Women Clinics proffer (Foster, 1989). Finally, Well Women Clinics stand as examples of good medical practice that does not rely on glorifying high technology medicine which makes patients feel power-less and alienated from what is happening to them (Doyal, 1986).

In theory, the presence of feminist self-help provisions should make the market more responsive to women's needs. In practice, at least in the United States, feminists have argued the opposite is the case. Medical service providers, especially large health care corporations, have cynically used information gathered in feminist health ventures to: provide more high technology and drug based provisions for women, for example progesterone therapy for premenstrual syndrome; attract healthy women to use their facilities by promising them more fulfilling lives; and cater to women in the higher income brackets (Dreifus, 1973; Ruzek, 1986; Worcester and Whatley, 1988). Future developments in Britain depend largely on whether the Tories dismantle the NHS for market provisions or more consumer oriented democratic reforms take place. If opposition to the Tories' plans to dismember the NHS succeeds, reforms in keeping with the latter possibility might occur. These could take the form of curbing doctors' powers, making them salaried state employees instead of independent contractors (Iliffe, 1985). However, the mere fact of doctors becoming state workers will not guarantee their working in ways which will empower consumers. The present welfare state stands as witness to how far removed from their clients state employees can be. Also, research has revealed that employment in the welfare services can make workers less rather than more sensitive (Maynard et al., 1986). In the final analysis, change conducive to people's welfare will only take place if either the ruling élite promotes it in this direction, or grassroots activity can force its rulers to act in those terms. However, changes endorsing feminism will only endure if they are underwritten by the infusion of feminist principles in theory and practice at both central and local state levels and in society more generally (Dominelli and McLeod, 1989).

PRINCIPLES GUIDING FEMINIST SOCIAL ACTION ON SOCIAL POLICY AND WELFARE ISSUES

In concluding, I will identify the principles located at the heart of feminist theory and practice fostering the well-being of women, children and men. These are founded on the belief that relationships are socially constructed through interactions between people and can, therefore, be changed. This change is geared to the formation of a collectively organised, democratic new world order, not the substitution of one ruling élite (male) by another (female). According to Segal (1987), achieving it would require a major transformation of existing social relations:

A vision of a world free from sexual hierarchy would require a very different economic system from any we have yet seen. It would be a world where work, pleasure, creativity and caring were no longer separated off and posed against each other, and no longer sex-linked, therefore a world no longer seriously damaging to the autonomy, authority, creativity, health and happiness of women. (Segal, 1987, p. xiii)

The feminist principles which would guide this transformation include:

1. Organising society to foster the well-being of all its members, irrespective of their social status, including class, 'race', gender, sexual orientation, age, or physical and mental capacities.

2. Making caring a collective responsibility undertaken by both men and women.

3. The right of all people to have a decent standard of living guaranteed by the state.

4. The right of all individuals to welfare.

5. Personal taxation as an issue of social policy which is an individual, not a 'family' responsibility.

6. Fiscal transfers to corporate bodies defined as matters of social policy and subjected to public scrutiny and accountability.

7. Egalitarian relations permeating all social institutions and social interaction between people.

8. The right of women, children and men to live full and creative lives.

9. The transformation of society and its social relations in non-oppressive, egalitarian directions.

10. Making explicit connections between private and public life; production and reproduction, home, community and workplace.

11. Asserting control over production and directing it towards meeting social needs.

12. Individuals' right to control their lives and work co-operatively with others.

13. Individuals' right to develop personal, familial and community relationships.

14. Equal recognition of work carried out at home and in the marketplace.

15. Work providing people with choices about what they are doing, how they are doing it, and why they are doing it.

16. Enhancing men's and women's nurturing capacities by committing public resources to this purpose.

17. Popular planning for social need.

18. Elevating the status of social policy and highlighting the links between economic policy and social policy.

19. Equality of status, pay, and humane conditions of work for men and women, whatever their status.

20. Eliminating all hierarchies in the division of labour.

21. Forming alliances with others seeking to eliminate social injustice.

22. Redefining masculinity and femininity.

23. Redefining familial ideology.

24. Shifting priorities in health care in preventative directions and dealing with the social causes of illness.

25. Making the state fully participative.

If these principles were to be adopted by the state and implemented, then we would have what Ruth Sidel (1986) described as a 'humane environment in which people can work, thrive and raise children'. Working to bring that about wherever we work, whatever our status, is a cause to which we should be devoting our energies. This means working to eliminate oppression in our personal relationships at home with our children, partners, relatives, and friends; in our workplaces with colleagues and consumers; and our political institutions at both local and central state levels (Dominelli and McLeod, 1989). Getting feminist theory and practice to infuse all these social relations would radically alter our world and provide for more satisfying relationships between people. These principles also provide the basis for developing comparative analyses which take women out of the margins of social policy and bring them centre stage.

Bibliography

Abella, I. (1974) On Strike, Toronto: James Lewis and Samuel Publishers.

Abel-Smith, B. (1976) Value for Money in the Health Services, London: Heinemann.

Abel-Smith, B. and Titmuss, R. (eds.) (1974) Social Policy: An introduction, London: George Allen and Unwin.

Abbot, E. and Bompas, K. (1943) The Woman Citizen and Social Security, London: Katherine Bompas.

Abramovitz, M. (1986) 'The Privatisation of the Welfare State: A Review', Social Work, July–Aug., pp. 257–64.

Ackerman, F. (1982) Reagonomics: Rhetoric versus reality, Boston: Southend Press.

Adams, C. and Winston, K. T. (1980) Mothers at Work: Public policies in the United States, Sweden and China, London: Longman.

Adams, I., Cameron, W., Hill, B. and Penz P. (1971) The Real Poverty Report, Edmonton: M. G. Hurtig.

Adamson, M. and Borgos, S. (1985) This Mighty Dream: Social protest movements in the United States, London: Routledge and Kegan Paul.

Adamson, N., Briskin, L. and McPhail, M. (1988) Feminist Organizing for Change: The contemporary women's movement in Canada, Toronto: Oxford University Press.

Adler, M. and Asquith, S. (eds.) (1981) Discretion and Welfare, London: Heinemann.

Ahmed, S. (1977) 'Population myths and realities', Race and Class, vol. 19, no. 2, pp. 19–28.

Ahmed, S. (1978) 'Asian girls and cultural conflicts', Social Work Today, August.

Ahmed, S., Cheetham, J. and Small, J. (1987) Social Work with Black Children and their Families, London: Batsford.

Aitken-Swan, S. (1977) Fertility Control and the Medical Profession, London: Croom Helm.

Albrecht, G. L. (1979) Health, Illness and Medicine, Chicago: Rand McNalley Publishing.

Alcaly, R. and Mermelstein, I. (1977) The Fiscal Crisis of American Cities: Essays on the political economy of urban America with special reference to New York, New York: Vintage Books.

Alford, R. (1975) *Health Care Politics: Ideological and interest group barriers to reform*, Chicago: University of Chicago Press.

Allen, I., Wicks, M., Finch, J. and Leat, D. (1987) *Informal Care Tomorrow*, London: Policy Studies Institute.

Anderson, O. W. (1972) *Health Care: Can there be Equity? The United States, Sweden and Britain*, New York: Wiley.

Anderson, O. W. (1972) *Uneasy Equilibrium: 1875–1965: Private and public financing of health services in the United States*, New Haven, Conn.: New College University Press.

Anderson, R. (1967) *A Decade of Health Services: A Social Survey of Trends in Use and Expenditure*, Chicago: University of Chicago.

Andors, P. (1983) *The Unfinished Liberation of Chinese Women: 1949–80*, Bloomington: Indiana University Press/Wheatsheaf Books.

Andrews, M. (1977) 'Attitudes in Canadian women's history', *Journal of Canadian Studies*, Summer, p. 69.

Armitage, A. (1975) *Social Welfare in Canada: Ideals and realities*, Toronto: McClelland and Stewart Ltd.

Armitage, A. (1988) *Social Welfare in Canada: Ideals and realities, revised edition*, Toronto: McClelland and Stewart Ltd.

Armstrong, J. (1985) 'Community Work', paper presented to Leicester Community Work Unit.

Armstrong, P. (1984) *Labour Pains: Women's work in crisis*, Toronto: Women's Press.

Aronowitz, S. (1973) *False Promises: The shaping of American working class consciousness*, New York: McGraw-Hill.

Ascher, I. (1976) *China's Social Policy*, London: The Anglo-Chinese Educational Institute.

Ashford, D. E. (1978) *Comparing Public Policies: New concepts and methods*, London: Sage.

Ashford, D. E. (1988) *The Emergence of Welfare States*, Oxford: Blackwell.

Ashworth, G. and Bonnerjea, L. (1985) *The Invisible Decade*, Aldershot: Gower.

Atkinson, D., Dallin, P. and Lapidus, G. (eds.) (1978) *Women in Russia*, Brighton: Harvester Press.

Atwood, D. (1980) *Social Policy*, London: Routledge and Kegan Paul.

Avery, D. and Neary, P. (1977) 'Laurier, Borden and a white British Columbia', *Journal of Canadian Studies*, vol. 12, no. 4, p. 24.

Bader, M. (1976) 'Breast feeding and the multi-nationals', *Journal of International Health Services*, vol. 6, no. 4, pp. 609–26.

Badgley, R. R. and Wolfe, S. (1967) *Doctors' Strike: Medical care and conflict in Saskatchewan*, Toronto: Macmillan.

Badgley, R. F. and Smith, D. A. (1979) *User Charges for the Health Services*, Toronto: Ontario Council of Health.

Bahro, H. (1978) *The Alternative in Eastern Europe*, London: New Left Books.

Bailey, R. and Brake, M. (1975) *Radical Social Work*, London: Edward Arnold.

Baker, H. (1965) *Chinese Family and Kinship*, New York: Columbia University Press.

Banting, K. (1982) *The Welfare State and Federalism*, Toronto: The University of Toronto Press.

Banting, K. (1985) 'Institutional conservatism: Federal and pension reform', *Canadian Social Welfare Policy*, edited by J. Ismael, Edmonton: University of Alberta Press, pp. 48–74.

Banting, K. (1989) 'Looking Back: The political economy of social policy in the 1980s', paper presented at the 4th National Conference on Social Welfare Policy, October 24–7, Toronto, Canada.

Banting, K. and Critchley, D. (1972) 'Two poverty reports', *Canadian Welfare*, vol. 48, pp. 1–30.

Banks, O. (1981) *Faces of Feminism*, Oxford: Martin Robinson.

Barber, C. L. (1972) *Welfare in Manitoba*, Winnipeg: Province of Manitoba.

Barker, D. L. and Allen, S. (eds.) (1976) *Sexual Divisions and Society: Process and change*, London: Tavistock.

Barker, H. (1986) 'Recapturing sisterhood: A critical look at "process" in feminist organising and community work', *Critical Social Policy*, no. 16, pp. 80–90.

Barker, J. (1984) *Black and Asian Old People in Britain*, London: Age Concern.

Barker, M. (1981) *The New Racism: Conservatives and the Ideology of the Tribe*. London: Junction Books.

Barratt Brown, M. (1983) *The Economics of Imperialism*, Harmondsworth: Penguin.

Barratt Brown, M. (1984) *Models in Political Economy*, Harmondsworth: Penguin.

Barratt Brown, M. (1985) *The Politics of Aid*, Harmondsworth: Penguin.

Barrett, M. (1981) *Women's Oppression Today*, London: Verso.

Barrett, M. S. (1989) 'Women and income: generating projects in developing countries: social and psychological effects', *Affilia*, vol. 4, no. 2, pp. 46–59.

Barrett, M. and McIntosh, M. (1980) 'The family wage: Some problems for socialists and feminists', *Capital and Class*, no. 11, pp. 51–71.

Barrett, M. and McIntosh, M. (1982) *The Anti-social Family*, London: Verso.

Barrett, M. and McIntosh, M. (1982) 'Narcissism and the family', *New Left Review*, no. 135, pp. 35–48.

Barrett, M. and McIntosh, M. (1985) 'Ethnocentrism and socialist feminist theory', *Feminist Review*, no. 20, pp. 23–48.

Baxandall, R., Gordon, L. and Reverby, S. (eds.) (1976) *America's Working Women*, New York: Vintage Books.

Belden, J. (1970) *China Shakes the World*, New York: Monthly Review Press.

Bell, D. (1960) *The End of Ideology*, New York: The Free Press.

Bennett, F. (1983) 'The state, welfare and women's dependence', *What is to be done about the Family?* edited by L. Segal, Harmondsworth: Penguin.

Benyoussef, A., Christian, B. and Tamahashi, H. (1977) 'Health and socio-economic development: An intersectoral model', *Social Science and Medicine*, vol. 11, no. 2, pp. 63–70.

Berer (1984) *Abortion*, London: Virago.

Beresford, P. and Croft, S. (1984) 'Welfare pluralism: The new face of Fabianism', *Critical Social Policy*, issue 9, pp. 19–40.

Berfenstam, R. (1974) *Early Child Care in Sweden*, New York: Gordon and Breach.

Besemeres, J. (1980) *Socialist Population Politics: The political implications of demographic trends in the USSR and Eastern Europe*, New York: M. E. Sharpe.

Beveridge, Sir William (1942) *Social Insurance and Allied Services*, Cmnd. 6404, London: HMSO.

Bhalla, A. and Blakemore, K. *Elders of the Ethnic Minority Groups*, Birmingham: All Friends for One Race.

Bhavnani, K. and Coulson, M. (1986) 'Transforming socialist feminism: The challenge of racism', *Feminist Review*, no. 23, pp. 81–92.

Billingsley, A. and Giovannoni, J. M. (1972) *Children of the Storm: Black Children and American Child Welfare*, New York: Harcourt Brace Jovanovich.

Binney, V. (1981) 'Domestic violence: battered women in Britain in the 1970's', *Women in Society: Interdisciplinary essays*, edited by Cambridge Women's Studies Group, London: Virago.

Binney, V., Harkell, G. and Nixon, J. (1981) *Leaving Violent Men: A study of refuges and housing for battered women*, London: Women's Aid Federation.

Black, Sir D. (1980) *Inequalities in Health*, London: Department of Health and Social Services.

Black, E. (1981) 'Dealing with the Doctors', *Monthly Review*, vol. 33, no. 4, pp. 27–35.

Bland, L. (1985) *Nationalism and Imperialism*, London: ZED Press.

Blanpain, J. (1978) *National Health Insurance and Health Resources: The European experience*, Brighton: Harvester Press.

Blaxter, M. (1981) *Health of Children: A review of research on the place of health in cycles of disadvantage*, London: Heinemann.

Blecher, M. (1989) 'China's struggle for a new hegemony', *Socialist Review*, vol. 89, no. 2, pp. 5–36.

Boles, J. (1980) 'The politics of child care', *Social Services Review*, vol. 54, no. 3, pp. 344–62.

Bolger, S., Corrigan, P., Dorking, J. and Frost, N. (1981) *Towards a Socialist Welfare Practice*, London: Macmillan.

Bonavia, D. (1982) *The Chinese: A portrait*, Harmondsworth: Penguin.

Bookman, A. and Morgan, S. (1989) *Women and the Politics of Empowerment*, Philadelphia: Temple University Press.

Bosanquet, N. (1983) *After the New Right*, London: Heinemann.

Boserup, E. (1970) *Women's Role in Economic Development*, London: Allen and Unwin.

Boskin, M. (ed.) (1978) *The Crisis in Social Security: The problems and prospects*, San Francisco: Institute for Contemporary Studies.

Bowl, R. (1985) *Changing the Nature of Masculinity – A Task for Social Work*, Norwich: University of East Anglia Monography.

Boxer, M. and Quataert, J. (1978) *Socialist Women: European socialist feminism in the nineteenth and early twentieth centuries*, New York: Elsevier.

Bradshaw, J. and Piachaud, D. (1980) *Child Support in the European Community*, London: Bedford Square Press.

Braeger, G. and Purcell, F. (1967) *Community Action Against Poverty*, New York: New Haven College and University Press.

Brandes, S. (1976) *American Welfare Capitalism: 1880–1920*, Chicago: University of Chicago.

Brazier, C. (1987) 'Changing the guard: The new face of China', *New Internationalist*, no. 170, April, pp. 4–25.

Bremner, R. H. (1956) *From the Depths: The discovery of poverty in the United States*, New York: New York University Press.

Bremner, R. (1960) *American Philanthropy*, Chicago: University of Chicago Press.

Bremner, R. (1986) *American Choices: Social dilemmas and public policy since 1960*, Columbus, Ohio: Ohio State University Press.

Brennan, T. (ed.) (1989) *Between Feminism and Psychoanalysis*, London: Routledge.

Brent Community Health Council (1981) *Black People and the Health Service*, London: Brent Community Health Council.

Bridenthal, R. (1977) *Becoming Visible: Women in European history*, Boston: Houghton Mifflin.

Briggs, A. (1961) 'The welfare state in historical perspective', *The European Journal of Sociology*, vol. 2, no. 2, pp. 221–58.

Brinkerhodd, M. and Lupri, E. (1978) 'Theoretical and methodological issues in the use of decision-making as an indicator of conjugal power: Some Canadian observations', *Canadian Journal of Sociology*, vol. 3, no. 1, p. 1.

British Committee on Family Research (1982) *Families in Britain*, edited by Rapoport, R. N., Fogarty, M. P. and Rapoport, R., London: Routledge.

Brittan, A. and Maynard, M. (1984) *Sexism, Racism and Oppression*, Oxford: Basil Blackwell.

Bromley, D. and Longino, C. F. (1972) *White Racism and Black Americans*, Cambridge, Mass.: Schenkman.

Bronfenbrenner, U. (1972) *Two Worlds of Childhood*, New York: Simon and Schuster.

Bronfenbrenner, U. (1977) 'The calamitous decline of the American family', *The Washington Post*, 2 January.

Brook, E. and Davis, A. (1985) *Women, The Family and Social Work*, London: Tavistock.

Brown, A. and Kaser, M. (1975) *The Soviet Union Since the Fall of Khruschev*, London: Macmillan.

Brown, A. and Kaser, M. (1982) *Soviet Policy for the 1980s*, London: Macmillan.

Brown, D. (ed.) (1968) *The Role and Status of Women in the Soviet Union: Mother Russia*, New York: Transaction Publications.

Brown, D. and Harrison, M. J. (1978) *A Sociology of Industrialisation*, London: Macmillan.

Brown, E. (1966) *Soviet Trade Unions and Labour Relations*, Cambridge, Mass.: Harvard University Press.

Brown, E. (1979) *Rockefeller Medicine Men: Medicine and capitalism in America*, Berkeley: University of California Press.

Brown, J. (1972) *An American Philosophy of Social Security: Evolution and issues*, Princeton, N.J.: Princeton University Press.

Brown, J. (1989) *Why don't they go back to Work? Mothers on Social Security*, HMSO: Social Security Advisory Committee.

Brown, D., Willis, F. and Cramer, S. (1972) *Racism and Mental Health*, New York: Prentice Hall.

Broyelle, C. (1977) *Women's Liberation in China*, Brighton: Harvester Press.

Broyelle, C. and Broyelle, J. and Tschirhart, E. (1980) *China: A second look*, Brighton: Harvester Press.

Bruce, C. (1978) 'The effect of young children on female labour force participation rates: An exploratory study', *Canadian Journal of Sociology*, vol. 3, no. 4, p. 431.

Bruegel, I. (1989) 'Sex and Race in the Labour Market' in *Feminist Review*, no. 32, Summer, pp. 49–68.

Brugger, B. (1978) *China: The impact of the cultural revolution*, London: Croom Helm.

Brugger, B. (1980) *China Since the Gang of Four*, London: Croom Helm.

Brugger, B. (1981a) *China: Liberation and transformation: 1942–62*, London: Croom Helm.

Brugger, B. (1981b) *China: Radicalism to revisionism: 1962–79*, London: Croom Helm.

Bryan, B., Dadzie, S. and Scafe, S. (1985) *The Heart of the Race*, London: Virago.

Buckley, M. (1981) 'Women in the Soviet Union' *Feminist Review*, no. 8, pp. 79–106.

Buhle, M. (1981) *Women and American Socialism: 1870–1920*, Chicago: University of Illinois Press.

Bull, D. and Wilding, P. (1983) *Thatcherism and the Poor*, London: Child Poverty Action Group.

Burchett, W. G. and Alley, R. (1976) *China: The quality of life*, Harmondsworth: Penguin.

Burden, D. S. and Gottlieb, N. (eds.) (1987) *The Woman Client: Providing human services in a changing world*, London: Tavistock.

Burke, V. J. and Burke, V. (1976) *Nixon's Good Deed*, New York: Columbia University Press.

Calamai, P. (1989) 'It's the surveillance society, vast computer files, lax rules', *The Vancouver Sun*, 15 November, p. A1.

Cameron, D. (1989) 'Who defines the social policy agenda? Consumers or capital', paper presented at the 4th National Conference on Social Welfare Policy, October 24–7, Toronto, Canada.

Campbell, B. (1984) *Wigan Pier Revisited: Poverty and politics in the 1980s*, London: Virago.

Campbell, B. and Jacques, M. (1986) 'Goodbye to the GLC', *Marxism Today*, vol. 30, no. 1, p. 6.

Campling, J. (ed.) (1981) *Images of Ourselves: Women with disabilities talking*, London: Routledge and Kegan Paul.

Canada, Committee on Unemployment (1986) *Report of the Commission of an Inquiry on Unemployment Insurance*, Ottawa: Queen's Printer.

Canada, Special Senate Committee on Poverty (1971) *Poverty in Canada*, Ottawa: Queen's Printer.

Carby, H. (1982) 'White women listen! Black feminism and the boundaries of sisterhood', *The Empire Strikes Back*, edited by Centre for Contemporary Cultural Studies, London: Hutchinson.

Carpenter, V. (1982) 'Working with girls', *Women in Collective Action*, edited by A. Curno, A. Lamming, A. Leach, J. Stiles, V. Ward, A. Wright and T. Zoff, London: Association of Community Workers.

Carr, E. H. (1964) *Socialism in One Country*, London: Macmillan.

Carr, E. H. (1966) *The Bolshevik Revolution 1917–23*, vols 1, 2, and 3, Harmondsworth: Penguin.

Carr, E. H. (1979) *The Russian Revolution from Lenin to Stalin: 1917–29*, London: Macmillan.

Carrier, J. and Kendall, I. (1977) 'Development of welfare states: The production of plausible accounts', *Journal of Social Policy*, vol. 6, pp. 271–90.

Carter, C. O. (1976) *Equalities and Inequalities in Health*, New York: Academic Press.

Cassidy, H. (1932) *Unemployment and Relief in Ontario*, Toronto: J. M. Dent and Sons.

Cassidy, H. (1945) *Social Security and Reconstruction in Canada*, Toronto: Ryerson Press.

Castles, F. (1978) *Social Democratic Images of Society: A study of the achievements and origins of Scandinavian social democracy in comparative perspective*, London: Routledge and Kegan Paul.

Castles, S. and Kosack, C. (1973) *Immigrant Workers and Class Structure in Western Europe*, Oxford: Institute of Race Relations/Oxford University Press.

Castles, F. and McKinlay, R. D. (1979) 'Public welfare provision: Scandinavia and the sheer futility of the sociological approach to politics', *The British Journal of Political Science*, vol. 9, pp. 157–72.

Cawson, A. (1982) *Corporatism and Welfare: Social Policy and State Intervention in Britain*, London: Heinemann.

Cell, C. (1977) *Revolution at Work: Mobilisation campaigns in China*, New York: Academic Press.

Centre for Contemporary Cultural Studies (CCCS) (1982) *The Empire Strikes Back*, London: Hutchinson.

Central Statistical Office (1984) *Social Trends: 1984*, London: HMSO.

Chafe, W. (1972) *The American Woman: Her changing social, economic and political roles*, New York: Oxford University Press.

Chambers-Brown, J. (1983) *Day Care*, London: Virago.

Champagne, A. and Harpham, E. (eds.) (1984) *The Attack on the Welfare State*, Prospect Heights, Ill.: Waveland Press, Inc.

Chan, A., Madsen, R. and Unger, J. (1984) *Chen Village: The recent history of a peasant community in China*, Los Angeles: University of California Press.

Chao, P. (1977) *Women Under Communism: Family in Russia and China*, New York: General Hall.

Chapman, J. (1963) *Real Wages in Soviet Russia since 1928*, Cambridge, Mass.: Harvard University Press.

Chapman, J. (1977) *Women into Wives: The legal and economic impact of marriage*, New York: Sage.

Chapman, J. and Yates, M. (ed.) (1978) *The Victimization of Women*, New York: Sage.

Chapman, P. (1979) *Unmet Needs and the Delivery of Care*, London: Bedford Square Press.

Chapman, P. (1989) *The Youth Training Scheme in the United Kingdom*, Aldershot: Avebury.

Chapman, R. and Rutherford, J. (eds.) (1988) *Unwrapping Masculinity*, London: Lawrence and Wishart.

Checkland, E. O. and Checkland, S. G. (eds.) (1974) *The Poor Law Report of 1834*, Harmondsworth: Penguin.

Chey, J. and Hunter, N. (1974) *China's New Society*, London: New Educational Press.

Children's Defense Fund (CDF) (1985) *A Children's Defense Budget: An analysis of the President's FY 1984 budget and children*. Washington, DC: Children's Defense Fund.

Childs, M. (1961) *Sweden: The middle way*, New Haven, Conn.: Yale University Press.

China (1988) 'China: Feeding her millions', *Food and Politics*, vol. 1.

Chinn, J. (1977) *Manipulating Soviet Population Resources*, Oxford: Martin Robertson.

Chodorow, N. (1978) *The Reproduction of Mothering*, London: University of California Press.

Chossudovsky, M. (1983) 'Underdevelopment and the political economy of malnutrition and ill health', *International Journal of Health Services*, vol. 13, no. 1, pp. 69–88.

Christian, W. and Campbell, C. (1974) *Political Parties and Ideologies in Canada*, Toronto: McGraw-Hill and Ryerson Press.

Clarke, S. (1988) *Keynesian Monetarism and the Crisis of the State*, Aldershot: Edward Elger Publications.

Clarke-Stewart, A. (1982) *Day Care*, London: Fontana.

Clements, B. (1979) *Bolshevik Feminist: The life of Alexandra Kollantai*, Bloomington, Ind.: Indiana University Press.

Cliffe, T. (1976) *State Capitalism in Russia*, London: Pluto Press.

Cloward, R. (1972) *The Politics of Turmoil*, New York: Prentice-Hall.

Coburn, D., Torrance, G. and Kaufert, J. (1983) 'Medical dominance in Canada in historical perspective: The rise and fall of medicine', *International Journal of Health Services*, vol. 13, no. 2, pp. 407–32.

Cockburn, C. (1977) *The Local State*, London: Pluto Press.

Cockburn, C. (1981) 'The material of male power', *Feminist Review*, no. 9, pp. 41–59.

Cockburn, C. (1983) *Brothers: Male dominance and technological change*, London: Pluto Press.

Cohen, C. (1970) 'Experiment in freedom: Women of China', *Sisterhood is Powerful*, edited by R. Morgan, New York: Vintage Books.

Cohen, C. (ed.) (1980) *The Soviet Union since Stalin*, Bloomington, Ind.: Indiana University Press.

Cohen, M. (1985) *The MacDonald Report and its Implications for Women*, Toronto: National Action Committee on the Status of Women.

Cohen, P. (1985) *The British System of Social Insurance*, London: Macmillan.

Cole, M. (1979) *Social Democratic Sweden*, London: Routledge and Kegan Paul.

Collard, D. (1980) *Income Redistribution: The limits to income distribution*, Bristol: Scientechnica.

Colletti, L. (1970) 'The question of Stalin', *New Left Review*, no. 61, pp. 61–83.

Comer, L. (1974) *Wedlocked Women*, Leeds: Feminist Books.

Commission for Racial Equality (CRE) (1985) *Immigration Control Procedures: Report of a formal investigation*, London: CRE.

Community Development Projects (CDP) (1977) *Gilding the Ghetto*, London: CDP.

Conkin, P. (1968) *The New Deal*, London: Routledge and Kegan Paul.

Cook, A. and Kirk, G. (1983) *Greenham Women Everywhere: Dreams, ideas and action from the women's peace movement*, London: Pluto Press.

Cooper, M. (1975) *Rationing Health Care*, London: Croom Helm.

Cooper, R. and Schatzkin, A. (1982) 'The patterns of mass disease in the USSR', *International Journal of Health Services*, vol. 12, no. 3, pp. 459–80.

Coote, A. and Gill, T. (1974) *Women's Rights: A practical guide*, Harmondsworth: Penguin.

Coote, A. (1981) 'The AES: A new starting point', *New Socialist*, November/December, pp. 4–7.

Coote, A. and Campbell, B. (1982) *Sweet Freedom: The struggle for women's liberation*, Oxford: Basil Blackwell.

Copp, T. (1974) *The Anatomy of Poverty: The condition of the working class in Montreal, 1897 to 1929*, Toronto: McClelland and Stewart.

Corrigan, P. (1977) 'The welfare state and class struggle', *Marxism Today*, March.

Corrigan, P. and Leonard, P. (1978) *Social Work under Capitalism*, London: Macmillan.

Coussins, and Coote, A. (1981) *The Family in the Firing Line: A discussion document on family policy*, Poverty Pamphlet No. 51, London: National Council for Civil Liberties/Child Poverty Action Group.

Costin, L. and Rapp, C. (1984) *Child Welfare: Policies and practice*, New York: McGraw-Hill.

Coward, R. (1983) *Patriarchal Precedents: Sexuality and social relations*, London: Routledge and Kegan Paul.

Cox, C. and Mead, A. (eds.) (1975) *Sociology of Medical Practice*, London: Collier-Macmillan.

Cox, T. (1987) 'The USSR under Gorbachev: The first two years', *Capital and Class*, no. 32, pp. 7–15.

Coyle, A. (1984) *Redundant Women*, London: The Women's Press.

Coyle, A. (1985) 'Going private: The implications of privatization for women's work', *Feminist Review*, no. 21, pp. 5–24.

Coyle, A. (1989) 'Women in management: A suitable case for treatment', *Feminist Review*, no. 31, pp. 117–25.

Coyle, A. and Skinner, J. (1988) *Women and Work: Positive action for change*, London: Macmillan.

Craig, G., Derricourt, N. and Loney, M. (eds.) *Community Work and the State*, London: Routledge and Kegan Paul with the Association of Community Workers.

Crean, S. (1988) *In the Name of Thy Fathers: The story behind child custody*, Toronto: Amanita Publications.

Croft, S. and Beresford, P. (1989) 'User-involvement, citizenship and social policy', *Critical Social Policy*, issue 26, pp. 5–18.

Croll, E. (1977) *The Women's Movement in China: A selection of readings, 1949–73*, London: Anglo–Chinese Educational Institute.

Croll, E. (1978) *Feminism and Socialism in China*, London: Routledge and Kegan Paul.

Croll, E. (1983) *Chinese Women since Mao*, London: ZED Books.

Cronin, J. E. and Radtke, T. G. (1987) 'The old and the new politics of taxation; Thatcher and Reagan in historical perspective', *The Socialist Register*, pp. 263–96.

Crosland, A. (1956) *The Future of Socialism*, London: Jonathan Cape.

Culhane, C. (1979) *Barred from Prison: A personal account*, Vancouver: Pulp Press.

Culver, A. J. (1976) *Need and the National Health Service*, Oxford: Martin Robertson.

Curno, A., Lamming, A., Leach, L., Stiles, J., Ward, V., Wright, A. and Zoff, T. (eds.) (1982) *Women in Collective Action*, London: Association of Community Workers.

Curtin, K. (1976) *Women in China*, New York: Pathfinder Press.

Curtin, K. (1979) 'Women and the Chinese Revolution', *International Socialist Review*, vol. 35, no. 3, pp. 8–40.

Curtis, J., Grabb, E., Guppy, N. and Gibert, S. (eds.) (1988) *Social Inequality in Canada. Patterns, Problems, Policies*, Scarborough, Ont.: Prentice-Hall.

Cutwright, P. (1965) 'Political structure, economic development and national social security programmes', *Social Welfare Institutions*, edited by M. Zald, New York: John Wiley and Sons.

Dale, J. and Foster, P. (1986) *Feminists and State Welfare*, London: Routledge and Kegan Paul.

Dale, J. and Taylor-Gooby, P. (1985) *Social Theory and Social Welfare*, London: Edward Arnold.

Dalheim Debate (1979) *Family Aid*, Stockholm: Family Aid Commission.

Daniel, W. (1980) *Maternity Rights: The experiences of women*, London: Policy Studies Institute.

David, M. (1978) 'Women caring for pre-school children in the United States', *International Journal of Urban and Regional Research*, vol. 2, pp. 440–62.

David, M. (1983) 'Sexual morality and the New Right', *Critical Social Policy*, vol. 2, no. 3, pp. 31–45.

David, M. and Land, H. (1983) 'Sex and social policy', *The Future of the Welfare State*, edited by H. Glennerster. London: Heinemann.

David, M. and New, C. (1985) *For the Children's Sake: Making childcare more than women's business*, London: Penguin.

Davin, A. (1978) 'Imperialism and Motherhood' in *History Workshop Journal*, Issue 5.

Davin, D. (1976) *Woman–Work: Women and the Party in Revolutionary China*, London: Clarendon Press.

Davis, A. (1981) *Women, Race and Class*, New York: Vintage.

Davis, A. (1989) *Women, Culture and Politics*, New York: Random House.

Davis, C. M. (1989) 'The Soviet Health System: A national health service in a socialist society', *Success and Crisis in National Health Systems*, edited by M. Field. London: Routledge.

Davis, C. M. and Feshback, M. (1980) *Rising Infant Mortality in the USSR in the 1970s*, Washington, DC: Bureau of the Census Report, series P–95, no. 74.

Davis, H. and Scase, R. (1985) *Western Capitalism and State Socialism: An introduction*, Oxford: Basil Blackwell.

Davis, K. and Schoen, C. (1978) *Health and the War on Poverty: A ten year appraisal*, Washington: Brookings Institute.

Davis, M. (1980a) 'Why is the American working class different', *New Left Review*, no. 123, pp. 3–46.

Davis, M. (1980b) 'The barren marriage of American labour and Democratic Party', *New Left Review*, no. 124, pp. 43–84.

Davis, M. (1981) 'The New Right's road to power', *New Left Review*, no. 128, pp. 28–49.

Davis, M. (ed.) (1987) *Towards a Rainbow Socialism: Essays on race, ethnicity, class and gender*, London: Verso.

Davis, M. (1988) *Reshaping the American Left: Popular Struggles in the 1980s*, London: Verso.

Davis, S. E. (1988) *Women Under Attack: Victories, Backlash and the Fight for Reproductive Freedom*, South End Press, Pamphlet No. 7, Boston: Southend Press.

Davies, E. (1943) *American Labour: The story of the American Trade Union Movement*, London: George Allen and Unwin and the Fabian Society.

Davies, M. (ed.) (1990) *The Sociology of Social Work*, London: Routledge.

Deacon, A. (1976) *In Search of the Scrounger, The Administration of Unemployment Insurance in Britain: 1920–31*, London: G. Bell.

Deacon, A. (1977) 'Concession and coercion: The politics of unemployment insurance in the 1920's', A. Briggs and J. Saville, *Essays in Labour History*, London: Croom Helm.

Deacon, A. (1982) 'An end to the means test? Social security and the Attlee Government', *Journal of Social Policy*, vol. 11, no. 3, pp. 289–306.

Deacon, A. and Bradshaw, J. (1983) *Reserved for the Poor: The means test in British social policy*, Oxford: Martin Robinson.

Deacon, B. (1983) *Social Policy and Socialism: The struggle for socialist relations of welfare*, London: Pluto Press.

Deacon, B. (1985) 'Strategies for welfare: East and West Europe', *Critical Social Policy*, no. 14, pp. 4–26.

Deacon, B. and Hyde, M. (1987) 'Working-class opinion and welfare strategies: Beyond the state and the market', *Critical Social Policy*, no. 18, pp. 15–31.

Deakin, N. (1987) *The Politics of Welfare*, London: Methuen.

Dean, H. (1989) 'Disciplinary partitioning and the privatisation of social security', *Critical Social Policy*, issue 24, pp. 74–82.

De Lobo, D. (1976) *Family Relationships and Disability*, London: Sage.

Dennis, M. and Fish, S. (1972) *Programmes in Search of Policy: Low income housing in Canada*, Toronto: Hakkert.

Department of Health and Social Security (DHSS) (1982) *The Social Security Handbook*, London: HMSO.

Desfosses, H. (ed.) (1981) *Soviet Population Policy: Conflicts and constraints*, London: Pergamon.

Deutscher, I. (1949) *Stalin: A political biography*, Oxford: Oxford University Press.

Deutscher, I. (1950) *Soviet Trade Unions and Their Place in Soviet Labour Policy*, Oxford: Oxford University Press.

Deutscher, I. (1953) *Russia After Stalin*, London: Hamish Hamilton.

Deutscher, I. (1954) *Trotsky, The Prophet Armed, 1879–1921*, Oxford: Oxford University Press.

Deutscher, I. (1960) *Trotsky, the Prophet Unarmed, 1921–29*, Oxford: Oxford University Press.

Deutscher, I. (1967) *The Unfinished Revolution: Russia 1917–67*, Oxford: Oxford University Press.

Diederichsen, F. (1982) 'Ideologies in the Swedish health sector today: the crisis in social democracy', *International Journal of Health Services*, vol. 12, no. 2, pp. 191–200.

Disney, R. (1982) 'Theorising the welfare state: Unemployment insurance in Britain', *Journal of Social Policy*, vol. 11, no. 3, pp. 33–59.

Dixon, J. and Schewell, R. P. (1989) *Social Welfare in Developed Market Countries*, London: Routledge.

Dixon, J. and Wyung, S. K. (eds.) (1985) *Social Welfare in Asia*, London: Croom Helm.

Doak Barnett, A. (1967) *Cadres, Bureaucracy and Political Power in Communist China*, New York: Columbia University Press.

Doak Barnett, A. (1969) *Chinese Communist Politics in Action*, Seattle: University of Washington Press.

Dobash, R. E. and Dobash, R. (1979) *Violence Against Wives: A case against the patriarchy*, New York: Free Press.

Dodge, J. S. (1969) *The Fieldworker in Immigrant Health*, New York: Staples Press.

Dodge, N. (1966) *Women in the Soviet Union*, Baltimore: John Hopkins University Press.

Doless, *et al.* (1987) *Family Policy*, London: Sage.

Dominelli, L. (1979) 'Racism: The challenge for social work education', *Social Work Today*, vol. 10, no. 25, pp. 27–9.

Dominelli, L. (1983) *Women in Focus: Community services orders and female offenders*, Coventry: Department of Applied Social Studies, University of Warwick.

Dominelli, L. (1984) *Working with Families: A feminist perspective*, unpublished: British Association of Social Workers Annual Conference at Nene College, Northampton, April.

Dominelli, L. (1986a) 'Father–Daughter Incest: Patriarchy's shameful secret', *Critical Social Policy*, no. 16, pp. 8–22.

Dominelli, L. (1986b) 'Women organising: An analysis of Greenham Women', paper presented at the International Association of Schools of Social Work Congress in Tokyo, August.

Dominelli, L. (1988a) *Anti-Racist Social Work*, London: Macmillan.

Dominelli, L. (1988b) 'Thatcher's attack on social security: Restructuring social control', *Critical Social Policy*, no. 23, pp. 46–61.

Dominelli, L. (1990) '"Race", gender and social work', *The Sociology of Social Work*, edited by M. Davies, London: Routledge.

Dominelli, L. (1986c) *Love and Wages*, Norwich: Novata Press.

Dominelli, L. (1986d) 'The Power of the Powerless: Prostitution and the reinforcement of submissive masculinity', *Sociological Review*, Spring, pp. 65–92.

Dominelli, L. and Jonsdottir, G. (1988) 'Feminist political organisation in Iceland', *Feminist Review*, no. 27, pp. 36–60.

Dominelli, L. and McLeod, E. (1989) *Feminist Social Work*, London: Macmillan.

Donovan, J. (1986) *We don't buy Illness, it just comes. Health, illness and health care in the lives of black people in London*, Aldershot: Gower.

Doress, P. B. and Siegal, D. L. (1987) *Ourselves Growing Older*, New York: Simon and Schuster.

Dossett-Davies, J. (1988) 'Where Glasnost has not yet arrived', *Community Care*, May, pp. 18–19.

Dott, I. (1966) *Health Care*, New York: Cape.

Douglas-Wilson, I. and MacLachlen, G. (1973) *Health Service Prospects: An international survey*, London: The Lancet and Nuffield Provincial Hospital Trust.

Doyal, L. (1979) *The Political Economy of Health*, London: Pluto Press.

Doyal, L. (1983) 'Women, health and the sexual division of labour: A case study of the women's health movement in Britain', *Critical Social Policy*, issue 7, pp. 21–33.

Doyal, L. (1986) 'Health priorities and health care', *Critical Social Policy*, issue 13, pp. 35–70.

Doyal, L. and Gough, I. (1984) 'A theory of human needs', *Critical Social Policy*, issue 10, pp. 6–38.

Doyal, L., Hunt, G. and Mellor, J. (1981) 'Your life in their hands', *Critical Social Policy*, vol. 1, no. 2, pp. 54–71.

Draper, C. and Smart, C. (1974) *Women and Work*, New York: Bantam.

Dreifus, C. (1973) *Woman's Fate: Raps from a feminist consciousness-raising group*, New York: Bantam Books.

Dreifus, C. (1977) 'Sterilising the poor', in *Seizing Our Bodies: The politics of women's health*, edited by C. Dreifus, New York: Vintage Books.

Drover, G. (ed.) (1988) *Free Trade and Social Policy*, Ottawa: Canadian Council on Social Development.

Duignan, P. and Rabuskha, A. (1980) *The US in the 1980s*, Stanford, Calif.: Stanford University Press.

Duncan, G. J. (1984) *Years of Poverty, Years of Plenty: The changing economic fortunes of American workers and families*, Ann Arbor: Institute for Social Research, University of Michigan.

Duncan, S. (1985) *Social Policy*, New York: Sage.

Dunning, E. and Hopper, E. (1966) 'Industrialisation and the problem of convergence', *Sociological Review*, vol. 14, no. 2.

Dworkin, A. (1976) *Against Our Will: Men, women and rape*, New York: Bantam Books.

Dyker, D. (1987) *The Soviet Union under Gorbachev: Prospects for reform*, London: Croom Helm.

Easlea, B. (1983) *Fathering the Unthinkable: Masculinity, science and the nuclear arms race*, London: Pluto Press.

Eberhard, W. (1971) *A History of China*, Berkeley: University of California Press.

Eberstadt, N. (1981) 'Health crisis in the USSR', *New York Review of Books*, 19 February.

Eckstein, A. (1975) *China's Economic Development*, Ann Arbor: University of Michigan Press.

Edholm, F. (1977) 'Conceptualising women', *Critique of Anthropology*, vol. 3, nos. 29 and 30.

Eekelaar, J. and Katz, S. N. (eds.) (1980) *Marriage and Cohabitation in Contemporary Society: Areas of legal, ethical and social change: an international and interdisciplinary study*, Toronto: Butterworth.

Ehrenreich, B. and Ehrenreich, E. J. (1971) *American Health Empires, Power, Profits and Politics*, New York: Vintage.

Ehrenreich, B. and English, D. (1973) *Complaints and Disorders: The sexual politics of sickness*, London: Writers and Readers Publishing Co-operative.

Ehrenreich, B. and English, D. (1979) *For Her Own Good*, London: Pluto Press.

Ehrenreich, J. (ed.) (1978) *Cultural Crisis of Modern Medicine*, New York: Monthly Review Press.

Eichler, M. (1981) 'The inadequacy of the monolithic model of the family', *Canadian Journal of Sociology*, vol. 6, no. 3, p. 373.

Eichler, M. (1983) *Families in Canada*, Toronto: Gage.

Eisenstadt, S. and Ahimeir, O. (eds.) (1985) *The Welfare State and its Aftermath*, London: Croom Helm.

Eisenstein, Z. (1987) 'Liberalism, feminism and the Reagan state: The neoconservative attack on (sexual) equality', *The Socialist Register*, pp. 236–61.

Elling, R. H. (1981) 'The capitalist world order and international health', *International Journal of Health Services*, vol. 11, no. 3.

Elliot, I. (1988) 'Gorbachev and Glasnost', *Survey: A Journal of East and West Studies*, vol. 30, no. 3, pp. 1–175.

Elvander, N. (1981) 'Barriers and opportunities to primary care delivery systems: A case study from the county council of Uppsala, Sweden', *Scandinavian Political Studies*, vol. 4, pp. 295–320.

Engels, F. (1972) *The Origin of the Family, Private Property and the State*, New York: Pathfinder Books.

Epstein, B. and Ellis, D. (1983) 'The Pro-family left in the US: Two comments', *Feminist Review*, no. 14, pp. 35–50.

Esam, P., Good, R. and Middleton, R. (1985) *Who's to Benefit? A Radical Review of the Social Security System*, London: Verso.

Esping-Anderson, G. (1979) 'Comparative social policy and political conflict in advanced welfare states: Denmark and Sweden', *International Journal of Health Services*, vol. 9, pp. 269–295.

Estes, C. (1979) *The Ageing Enterprise: A critical examination of social policy and services for the aged*, San Francisco: Jossey-Bass.

Estes, C. (1983) *Austerity and Ageing: Shifting government responsibility for the elderly*, London: Sage.

Evans, J. (1981) 'The Communist Party of the Soviet Union and the women's question: The case of the 1936 decree in defence of mother and child', *Journal of Contemporary History*, vol. 16, no. 4, pp. 757–76.

Evans, L. (1978) *China After Mao*, New York: Monad Press.

Fahey, W. (1986) 'Impressions of Soviet medicine', *Medicine and Society*, vol. 12, no. 2, pp. 45–8.

Family Aid Commission (1979) *A Debate Report on the Family Aid Commission: Day care*, Stockholm: The Family Aid Commission.

Family Expenditure Survey (1984) *The Family Expenditure Survey*, London: HMSO.

Family Policy Studies Centre (1984) *An Ageing Population*, London: Family Policy Studies Centre.

Family Policy Studies Centre (1986) *One-Parent Families*, London: Family Policy Studies Centre.

Family Policy Studies Centre (1987) *Inside The Family*, London: Family Policy Studies Centre.

Family Research Committee (1982) *British Committee on Family Research: Families in Britain*, London: Routledge.

Farnsworth, B. (1980) *Alexandra Kollantai: Socialism, feminism and the Bolshevik Revolution*, Stanford, Calif.: Stanford University Press.

Feagin, J. (1975) *Subordinating The Poor: Welfare and American beliefs*, New York: Prentice-Hall.

Feder, J. (1977) *Mediare: The politics of federal hospital insurance*, New York: Heath.

Feher, F., Heller, A. and Markus, G. (1983) *Dictatorship Over Needs*, New York: St Martin's Press.

Feshback, M. (1984) 'Soviet health problems', *Soviet Union in the 1980s*, vol. 35, no. 3, pp. 81–97.

Feminist Review Collective (1990) *Perverse Politics: Lesbian Issues*, special issue of *Feminist Review*, no. 34, Spring.

Festau, M. F. (1975) *The Male Machine*, New York: Delta Books.

Field, F. (1980) *Fair Shares for Families: The need for a family impact statement*, London: Study Commission on the Family.

Field, F. (1981) *Inequality in Britain: Freedom, welfare and the state*, London: Fontana.

Field, M. (1967) *Soviet Socialised Medicine*, New York: Free Press.

Field, M. (1989) *Success and Crisis in National Health Systems, A Comparative Approach*, London: Routledge.

Finch, J. (1984) 'Community care: Developing non-sexist alternatives', *Critical Social Policy*, issue 9, pp. 6–18.

Finch, J. (1987) 'Whose responsibility? Women and the future of family care', *Informal Care Tomorrow*, edited by I. Allen, M. Wicks, J. Finch and D. Leat, London: Policy Studies Institute.

Finch, J. and Groves, D. (1980) 'Community care and the family: A case for equal opportunities', *Journal of Social Policy*, vol. 9, no. 4, pp. 487–511.

Finch, J. and Groves, D. (1983) *A Labour of Love: Women, work and caring*, London: Routledge and Kegan Paul.

Finer, H. (1974) *The Finer Report on One Parent Families*, London: HMSO.

Fireside, H. (1979) *Soviet Psychoprisons*, New York: W. W. Norton.

Firestone, S. (1970) *The Dialectics Sex: The case for feminist revolution*, New York: Bantam Books.

Flora, P. (1981) *The Development of Welfare States in Europe and America*, London: Transaction Books.

Ford, A. B. (1976) *Urban Health in America*, Milton Keynes: Open University Press.

Foster, P. (1989) 'Improving the doctor–patient relationship: A feminist perspective', *Journal of Social Policy*, vol. 18, no. 3, pp. 337–62.

Francombe, C. (1984) *Abortion Freedom: A Worldwide Movement*, London: Unwin Hyman.

Frank, A. G. (1981) *Reflections on the World Economic Crisis*, New York: Monthly Review Press.

Franklin, G. (1978) *Day Care*, London: Sage.

Frankfort, I. (1972) *Vaginal Politics*, New York: Quadrangle Books.

Fraser, D. (1973) *Evolution of the British Welfare State*, London: Macmillan.

Freeberne, M. (1964) 'Birth control in China', *Population Studies*, vol. 18, no. 1, p. 13.

Freeman, G. and Adams, P. (1983) 'Ideology and analysis in American social security policy-making', *Journal of Social Policy*, vol. 12, no. 1, pp. 75–144.

Freeman, J. (1975) *The Politics of Women's Liberation: A case study of an emerging social movement and its relation to the policy process*, New York: David McKray.

Freeman, J. (ed.) (1984) *Women: A feminist perspective*, Palo Alto: Mayfield.

Friedland, J. (1987) 'Reagan's bleak legacy', *South World Business and Politics*, July, pp. 19–20.

Freidson, E. (1970) *Profession of Medicine*, New York: Donald Mead.

Freire, P. (1976) *The Pedagogy of the Oppressed*, Harmondsworth: Penguin.

Friedan, B. (1963) *The Feminine Mystique*, New York: Bell.

Friedman, M. (1962) *Capitalism and Freedom*, Chicago: The University of Chicago Press.

Fry, J. (1969) *Medicine in Three Societies: A comparison of medical care in the USSR, USA and UK*, Aylesbury: MTP.

Fry, J. (1979) *The Medical Limits of the Welfare State: Critical views on post-war Sweden*, Farnborough: Saxon House.

Furniss, N. (1977) *The Case for the Welfare State: From social security to social equality*, Bloomington, Ind.: Indiana University Press.

Galbraith, K. (1958) *The Affluent Society*, London: Penguin.

Gamble, A. and Walton, P. (1976) *Capitalism in Crisis: Inflation and the state*, London: Macmillan.

Garner, L. (1979) *The National Health Service: Your money or your life*, London: Pluto.

Geiger, H. K. (1968) *The Family in Soviet Russia*, Cambridge, Mass.: Harvard University Press.

Genovese, E. (1974) *Roll Jordan Roll: The world the slaves made*, New York: Pantheon Books.

George, D. (1986) *Challenge to the National Health Service*, London: Routledge.

George, S. (1976) *How the Other Half Dies: The real reasons for world hunger*, Harmondsworth: Penguin.

George, V. and Lawson, R. (eds.) (1980) *Poverty and Inequality in Common Market Countries*, London: Routledge and Kegan Paul.

George, V and Manning, N. (1980) *Socialism, Social Welfare and the Soviet Union*, London: Routledge and Kegan Paul.

George, V. and Wilding, P. (1976) *Ideology and State Welfare*, London: Routledge and Kegan Paul.

Gilbert, N. (1983) *Capitalism and the Welfare State: Dilemmas of social benevolence*, New Haven: Yale University Press.

Gilder, G. (1981) *Wealth and Poverty*, New York: Basic Books.

Gilroy, P. (1982) 'Steppin' out of Babylon: Race, class and autonomy', *The*

Empire Strikes Back, edited by Centre for Contemporary and Cultural Studies, London: Hutchinson.

Gilroy, P. (1987) *There Ain't No Black in The Union Jack*, London: Hutchinson.

Ginsburg, N. (1979) *Class, Capital and Social Policy*, London: Macmillan.

Ginzberg, E. (1977) *The Limits of Health Reform*, New York: Basic Books.

Giraldo, Z. (1980) *Public Policy and the Family: Wives and mothers in the labour force*, Lexington, Mass.: Lexington Books.

Gladstone, J. (1979) *Voluntary Action in a Changing World*, London: Bedford Square Press.

Glaser, W. (1980) *Paying the Hospital in Canada*, New York: Columbia University Press.

Glass, D. (1936) *The Struggle for Population*, London: Clarendon Press.

Glass, D. and Revelle, R. (eds.) (1972) *Population and Social Change*, London: Edward Arnold.

Glazer, N. (1988) *The Limits of Social Policy*, London: Harvard University Press.

Glazer, N. and Young, K. (1983) *Ethnic Pluralism and Public Policy: Achieving Equality in the US and Britain*, Aldershot: Gower.

Gleb, J. (1980) *Women and Public Polices*, London: Macmillan.

Glendinning, F. (ed.) (1979) *The Elders in Ethnic Minorities*, London: Beth Johnson Foundation.

Glendinning, J. and Millar, J. (eds.) (1987) *Women in Poverty in the UK*, Brighton: Wheatsheaf.

Glennerster, H. (ed.) (1983) *The Future of the Welfare State: Remaking social policy*, London: Heinemann.

Golding, P. and Middleton, S. (1982) *Images of Welfare: Press and public attitude to poverty*, Oxford: Martin Robertson.

Gonick, C. (1981) 'Lessons from Canada?', *Monthly Review*, vol. 32, no. 8, pp. 11–33.

Goode, W. (1963) *World Revolution and Family Patterns*, New York: Free Press.

Gorbachev, M. (1986) *Speeches and Writings*. Translated from Russian. Oxford: Pergamon.

Gordon, L. (1977) *Woman's Body, Woman's Right*, New York: Penguin.

Gordon, L. (1986) 'Feminism and social control: The case of the child abuse and neglect', *What is Feminism?*, edited by J. Mitchell and A. Oakley, Oxford: Basil Blackwell.

Gordon, P. (1983) 'Medicine, racism and immigration control', *Critical Social Policy*, issue 7, pp. 6–20.

Gordon, P. (1985) *Policing Immigration, Britain's Internal Control*, London: Pluto Press.

Gordon, P. (1986) 'Racism and social security', *Critical Social Policy*, issue 17, pp. 22–39.

Gordon, L. and Klopov, E. (1975) *Men After Work*, New York: Progress.

Gordon, P. and Newnham, A. (1985) *Passport to Benefits? Racism in Social Security*, London: Child Poverty Action Group and Runnymede Trust.

Gorz, A. (1982) *Farewell to the Working Class*, London: Pluto Press.

Gough, I. (1978) 'Theories of the welfare state', *International Journal of Health Services*, vol. 8 (1).

Gough, I. (1979) *The Political Economy of the Welfare State*, London: Macmillan.

Gottlieb, N. (ed.) (1980) *Alternative Social Services for Women*, New York: Columbia University Press.

Graham, H. (1983) 'Caring: A labour of love', *A Labour of Love: Women, work and caring*, edited by J. Finch and D. Groves, London: Routledge and Kegan Paul.

301

Graham, H. and Oakley, A. (1981) 'Competing ideologies of reproduction: Medical and maternal perspectives on pregnancy', *Women, Health and Reproduction*, edited by H. Roberts, London: Routledge and Kegan Paul.

Granquist, H. (1967) *The Red Guard*, London: Pall Mall.

Gray, J. and Gordon, W. (eds.) (1982) *China's New Development Strategy*, New York: Academic Press.

Grayson, J. P. (1980) *Class, State, Ideology and Change*, New York: Holt, Rinehart and Winston.

Grayson, R. (1985) 'America's doctors face up to an unwelcome revolution', *The Glasgow Herald*, 30 July.

Greater London Council (GLC) (1984) *Childcare Programme*, London: GLC.

Greater London Council (GLC/WEG) (1986) *London Women in the 1980s*, London: GLC.

Greenblatt, B. (1977) *Responsibility for Child Care: The changing role of the family and state in child development*, San Francisco: Jossey-Bass.

Greenwood, V. and Young, J. (1976) *Abortion in Demand*, London: Pluto.

Griffiths, R. (1988) *Community Care: Agenda for action*, London: HMSO.

Griffiths, S. (1987) *Women and Social Policy*, London: Macmillan.

Gronbjerg, K., Street, D. and Suttles, G. (1978) *Poverty and Social Change*, Chicago: University of Chicago Press.

Guardian, The 'Tower Hamlets Council declares Bangladeshi families intentionally homeless?', 28 April 1987.

Guest, D. (1986) *The Emergence of Social Security in Canada*, Vancouver: University of British Columbia Press.

Guillemerd, A. M. (1983) *Old Age and the Welfare State*, London: Sage.

Guisott, R. and Johannesen, S. (1982) *Women in China*, New York: Philo Press.

Guru, S. (1987) 'An Asian Women's Refuge' in *Social Work with Black Children and Their Families*, edited by Ahmed et al., London: Batsford.

Gyford, J. (1985) *The Politics of Local Socialism*, London: George Allen and Unwin.

Hadley, R. and Hatch, S. (1981) *Social Welfare and the Failure of the State: Centralised social services and participatory alternatives*, London: Allen and Unwin.

Haines, A. (1928) *Health Work in Soviet Russia*, New York: Vanguard Press.

Hale, J. (1983) 'Feminism and social work practice', *The Political Dimension of Social Work*, edited by W. Jordan and N. Parton, Oxford: Basil Blackwell, pp. 167–87.

Hall, P., Land, H., Parker, R. and Webb, A. (1981) *Chance, Choice and Conflict in Social Policy*, London: Heinemann.

Hall, S. (1983) 'The great moving right show', *The Politics of Thatcherism*, edited by S. Hall and M. Jacques, London: Lawrence and Wishart.

Hall, S. and Jacques, M. (eds.) (1983) *The Politics of Thatcherism*, London: Lawrence and Wishart.

Halpern, J. H. and Clemens, B. (1975) *Women in the Soviet Union: Mother Russia*, New York: Transaction Publications.

Halpern, S. (1986) 'HMOs: Maintenance or management', *The Health Service Journal*, 31 July, pp. 1018–19.

Hanscombe, G. and Forster, J. (1982) *Rocking the Cradle: Lesbian mothers*, London: Sheba Feminist Publishers.

Hanslohner, P. (1987) 'Gorbachev's social contract', *Soviet Economy*, vol. 3, no. 1, pp. 54–89.

Harman, H. (1988) 'No health care for working poor', *NUPE Journal*, no. 8, p. 3.

Harris, D. (1987) *Justifying State Welfare*, Oxford: Basil Blackwell.

Harrington, M. (1984) *The New American Poverty*, New York: Holt, Rinehart and Winston.

Harris, C. (1979) *The Sociology of the Family*, Newcastle Under Lyme: University of Keele Monograph.

Harris, N. (1978) *Mandate of Heaven: Marx and Mao in modern China*, New York: Quartet Books.

Harris, R. and Seldon, A. (1979) *Over-ruled on Welfare*, London: Institute for Economic Affairs.

Harris, R. and Seldon, A. (1987) *Welfare without the State: A quarter century of suppressed public choice*, London: Institute for Economic Affairs.

Hartmann, H. (1979) 'The unhappy marriage of Marxism and feminism', *Capital and Class*, no. 8, pp. 1–33.

Haskey, J. (1982) 'The proportion of marriages ending in divorce', *Population Trends*, vol. 27, pp. 4–8.

Haskey, J. (1983) 'Children of divorcing couples', *Population Trends*, vol. 31, pp. 20–26.

Hatch, S. and Mocroft, I. (1983) *Components of Welfare: Voluntary organisations, social services and politics in two local authorities*, London: Bedford Square Press.

Haveman, R. H. (ed.) (1977) *A Decade of Federal Anti-Poverty Programs: Achievements, failures, and lessons*, New York: Academic Press.

Hay, J. R. (1978) *The Development of the British Welfare State, 1880–1975*, London: Edward Arnold.

Hayek, F. (1949) *Individualism and Economic Order*, London: Routledge and Kegan Paul.

Hayek, F. (1972) *The Constitution of Liberty*, London: Routledge and Kegan Paul.

Hayek, F. (1976) *The Road to Serfdom*, London: Routledge and Kegan Paul.

Haynes, V. and Semyonova, O. (1979) *Workers Against the Gulag: The new opposition in the Soviet Union*, London: Pluto Press.

Hayter, T. (1971) *Aid as Imperialism*, Harmondsworth: Penguin.

Hayter, T. (1981) *The Creation of World Poverty*, London: Pluto.

Hayter, R. (1985) 'Aid: The West's false handout', *New Socialist*, no. 24, pp. 7–12.

Haywood, S. and Alaszewski, A. (1980) *Crisis in the National Health Service: The politics of management*, London: Croom Helm.

Hearn, J. (1987) *The Gender of Oppression: Men, masculinity, and the critique of Marxism*, Brighton: Wheatsheaf.

Heclo, H. (1974) *Modern Social Policy in Britain and Sweden*, New Haven, Conn.: Yale University Press.

Heer, D. (1971) 'Family allowances in the Soviet Union', *Soviet Studies*, vol. 22, no. 4.

Heidenheimer, A. and Elvander, N. (ed.) (1980) *The Shaping of the Swedish Health System*, London: Croom Helm.

Heidenheimer, A., Heclo, H. and Adams, C. T. (1983) *Comparative Public Policy: The politics of choice in Europe and America*, London: Macmillan.

Heinen, J. (1978) 'Kollantai and the history of women's oppression', *New Left Review*, no. 110, pp. 43–64.

Heitlinger, A. (1979) *Women and State Socialism*, London: Macmillan.

Heller, T. (1977) *Restructuring the Health Service*, London: Croom Helm.

Heller, T. (1977) *Poor Health, Rich Profits: Multinational drug companies and the Third World*, Nottingham: Spokesman Books.

Heller, T. and Elliott, C. (1977) *Health Care and Society: Readings in health care delivery and development*, University of East Anglia: School of Development Studies.

Henriques, U. R. (1979) *Before the Welfare State: Social administration in early industrial Britain*, London: Longman.

Henwood, M., Rimmer, L. and Wicks, M. (1987) *Inside the Family: The changing roles of men and women*, London: Family Policy Studies Centre.

Hepworth, H. P. (1985) 'Social welfare development in Alberta: The federal–provincial interplay', *Canadian Social Welfare Policy*, edited by J. Ismael, Montreal: McGill-Queen's University Press, pp. 139–72.

Higgins, J. (1978) *The Poverty Business: Britain and America*, Oxford: Basil Blackwell.

Higgins, J. (1981) *States of Welfare*, Oxford: Basil Blackwell and Martin Robinson.

Higgins, J. (1988) *The Business of Medicine: Private health care in Britain*, London: Macmillan.

Higgins, J. (1989) 'Caring for the carers', *Journal of Social Administration*, summer, pp. 382–98.

Hill, M. (1980) *Understanding Social Policy*, Oxford: Basil Blackwell.

Hill, R. (1972) 'The strengths of black families', *White Racism and Black Americans*, edited by O. Bromley and C. F. Longino, Cambridge, Mass.: Schenkman.

Hill, S. and Owen, D. (1982) *The New Religious Political Right in America*, Nashville, Tenn.: Abington.

Hillier, S. (1983) *Health Care and Traditional Medicine in China, 1980–82*, London: Routledge and Kegan Paul.

Hillier, S. (1988) 'Women and population control in China: Issues of sexuality, power and control', *Feminist Review*, vol. 29, pp. 101–13.

Himmelstrand, U. (1981) *Beyond Welfare Capitalism: Issues, actors and forces in social change*, London: Heinemann.

Hinton, J. (1983) *Labour and Socialism: A history of the British labour movement*, Brighton: Wheatsheaf.

Hinton, W. (1966) *Fanshen: A documentary of revolution in a Chinese village*, New York: Vintage.

Hirshfield, D. (1970) *The Lost Reform: The campaign for compulsory health insurance in the United States, 1932–43*, Cambridge, Mass.: Harvard University Press.

Hoar, V. (ed.) (1973) *Recollections of The 'On to Ottawa' Trek*, Toronto: McClelland and Stewart.

Hobart, C. W. (1981) 'Sources of egalitarianism in young married Canadians', *Canadian Journal of Sociology*, vol. 6, no. 3, p. 251.

Hole, J. and Levine, E. (1971) *The Rebirth of Feminism*, New York: Quadrangle.

Holland, B. (ed.) (1985) *Soviet Sisterhood*, Bloomington: Indiana University Press.

Holmes, L. (ed.) (1981) *The Withering Away of the State? Party and State under Communism*, London: Sage.

Holmes, L. (1986) *Politics in the Communist World*, Oxford: Clarendon.

Home Office, (1986) *Ethnic Minorities, Crime and Policing*, London: HMSO.

Hong, L. K. (1976) 'The role of women in the People's Republic of China', *Social Problems*, vol. 23, no. 5, p. 547.

Hooks, B. (1982) *Ain't I a Woman: Black women and feminism*, London: Pluto Press.

Hooks, B. (1984) *Feminist Theory: From margin to centre*, Boston, Mass.: South End Press.

Horder, W. (1988) 'The price of freedom', *Community Care*, 18 February, pp. 18–19.

Horgan, J. J., Cernik, J. A. (eds.) (1988) *The Reagan Years: Perspectives and assessments*, London: Institute for Policy Studies.

Horn, J. (1966) *Away With All Pests*, New York: Monthly Review Press.

Horn, M. (ed.) (1972) *The Dirty Thirties*, Toronto: Copp Clark.

Horn, M. (1976) 'The Great Depression: Past and present', *Journal of Canadian Studies*, vol. xi, no. 1, p. 41.

Horn, M. (1978) 'Academics and Canadian social and economic policy in the Depression and War Years', *Journal of Canadian Studies*, vol. 13, no. 4, p. 3.

Horowitz, I. L. (1977) *Equity, Income and Policy: Comparative studies in Three Worlds of Development*, New York: Praeger.

Hoskyns, C. (1985) 'Women's equality in the EEC', *Feminist Review*, no. 20, pp. 71–90.

Howard, P. (1988) *Breaking the Iron Rice Bowl: Prospects for socialism in China's countryside*, Armonk, New York: M. E. Sharpe.

Howe, C. (1973) *Wage Patterns and Wages Policy in China, 1919–72*, Cambridge: Cambridge University Press.

Howe, D. (1986) 'The segregation of women and their work in the personal social services', *Critical Social Policy*, no. 15, pp. 21–36.

Howe, D. (1987) *An Introduction to Social Work Theory*, Aldershot: Wildwood House.

Hughes, M., Mayall, B., Moss, P. and Petrie, P. (1980) *Nurseries Now*, Harmondsworth: Penguin.

Hufford, L. (1975) *Sweden: The myth of socialism*, Young Fabian Pamphlet, no. 33, The Fabian Society.

Hum, D. P. (1985a) 'Social security reform during the 1970s', *Canadian Social Welfare Policy*, edited by J. Ismael, Montreal: McGill-Queen's University Press, pp. 29–47.

Hum, D. (1985b) 'The working poor, the Canada Assistance Plan, and provincial response in income supplementation', *Canadian Social Welfare Policy*, edited by J. Ismael, Montreal: McGill-Queen's University Press, pp. 120–38.

Hunt, A. (1970) *The Home Help Service in England and Wales*, London: HMSO.

Hunt, A. (1978) *The Elderly at Home*, London: HMSO.

Hunter, A. A. (1988) 'The changing distribution of income', *Social Inequality in Canada*, edited by J. Curtis, E. Grabb, N. Guppy and S. Gibert, pp. 86–91.

Huntford, R. (1980) *The New Totalitarians*, London: Scarborough House.

Huws, U. (1985) 'Women and employment', *The Invisible Decade*, edited by G. Ashworth and L. Bonnerjea, Aldershot: Gower.

Huxley, C. (1979) 'The state, collective bargaining, and the shape of strikes in Canada', *Canadian Journal of Sociology*, vol. 4, no. 3, p. 223.

Hyde, G. (1974) *The Soviet Health Service*, London: Lawrence and Wishart.

Hyman, R. (1974) 'Inequality, ideology and industrial relations', *British Journal of Industrial Relations*, vol. 12.

Hyman, R. (1989) *Strikes*, London: Macmillan.

Iglitzin, L. and Ross, R. (1977) *Women in the World: A comparative study*, Santa Barbara, California: Clio Press.

Iliffe, S. (1985) 'The politics of health care: The NHS under Thatcher', *Critical Social Policy*, issue 14, pp. 57–72.

Ingleby, D. (ed.) (1981) *Critical Psychiatry: The politics of mental health*, Harmondsworth: Penguin.

Institute of Development Studies (IDS) (1981) 'Monetarism: Its effects on developing countries', *Institute of Development Studies Bulletin*, vol. 9, no. 2.

International Businessweek (1989) *The New America*, 25 September.

Irwin, I. (1971) *The Story of the Women's Party*, New York: Harcourt and Brace.

Ismael, J. (ed.) (1985a) *The Canadian Welfare State*, Montreal: McGill-Queen's University Press.

Ismael, J. (ed.) (1985b) *Canadian Social Welfare Policy. Federal and Provincial Dimensions*, Montreal: McGill-Queen's University Press.

Ismael, J. (ed.) (1987) *The Canadian Welfare State: Evolution and Transitions*, Edmonton: University of Alberta Press.

Jackman, R. (1975) *Politics and Social Equality: A comparative analysis*, New York: Wiley.

Jacoby, S. (1990) 'The Women's revolution', *Good Housekeeping*, March.

James, E. (1976) *America Against Poverty*, London: Routledge and Kegan Paul.

Jamieson, S. M. (1971) *Times of Trouble: Labour unrest and industrial conflict in Canada: 1900–60*, Ottawa: Information Canada.

Jenkins, P. (1963) 'Bevan's fight with the BMA', *The Age of Austerity*, edited by M. Sissons and P. French, London: Hodder and Stoughton.

Jenkins, S. (ed.) (1969) *Social Security in International Perspective*, New York: Columbia University Press.

Johnson, A. (1985) 'Restructuring family allowances: Good politics at no cost?', *Canadian Social Welfare Policy*, edited by J. Ismael, Montreal: McGill-Queen's University Press, pp. 106–19.

Johnson, B. and Waldman, E. (1983) 'Most women who maintain families receive poor labour market returns', *Monthly Labour Review*, vol. 106, no. 12, pp. 30–34.

Johnson, K. A. (1983) *Women, the Family and Peasant Revolution in China*, Chicago: University of Chicago Press.

Johnson, L. (1974) *Poverty in Wealth*, Toronto: University of Toronto Press.

Jones, L. (1983) *Keeping the Peace*, London: Women's Press.

Jordan, W. and Parton, N. (1983) *The Political Dimensions of Social Work*, Oxford: Basil Blackwell.

Jowell, R., Witherspoon, S. and Brooks, L. (1988) *British Social Attitudes: The 1987 report*, Aldershot: Gower.

Joyce, P., Corrigan, P. and Hayes, M. (1987) *Striking Out: Trade unionism in social work*, London: Macmillan.

Juviler, P. (1967) *Soviet Policy Making: Studies of communism in transition*, London: Pall Mall Press.

Kahn, A. and Kamerman, S. (1975) *Not for the Poor Alone: European social services*, Philadelphia: Temple University Press.

Kahn, A. and Kamerman, S. (1979) 'The day care debate: A wider view', *Public Interest*, no. 54, pp. 76–93.

Kahn, A. and Kamerman, S. (1988) *Child Support: From debt collection to social policy*, London: Sage.

Kaim-Caudle, P. (1973) *Comparative Social Policy and Social Security: A ten country study*, Oxford: Martin Robertson.

Kamerman, S. and Kahn, A. (1978) *Family Policy: Government and families in fourteen countries*, New York: Columbia University Press.

Kamerman, S. and Kahn, A. (1981) *Child Care, Family Benefits and Working Parents*, New York: Columbia University Press.

Kamerman, S. and Kahn, A. (1983) *Maternity Policies and Working Women*, New York: Columbia University Press.

Kanter, H. (1984) *Sweeping Statements*, London: Virago.

Karol, K. S. (1967) *China: The other communism*, New York: Hill and Wang.

Kaser, M. (1976) *Health Care in the Soviet Union and Eastern Europe*, London: Croom Helm.

Kaun, L. (1986) *Population Policy in the Soviet Union*, Boston: Beacon.

Katznelson, I. (1979) *The Politics of Power: A critical introduction to American government*, New York: Harcourt Brace Jovanovich.

Kealey, G. (1976) *Essays in Working Class History*, Toronto: McClelland and Stewart.

Kealey, L. (ed.) (1979) *A Not Unreasonable Claim: Women and reform in Canada: 1880s to 1920s*, Toronto: The Women's Press.

Kealey, L. (1989) 'Women in the Canadian socialist movement, 1904–14', *Beyond the Vote: Canadian women in politics*, edited by L. Kealey and J. Sangster, Toronto: Women's Press, pp. 171–95.

Kealey, L. and Sangster, J. (eds.) (1989) *Beyond the Vote: Canadian women in politics*, Toronto: Women's Press.

Kelly, L. (1988) *Surviving Sexual Violence*, Cambridge: Polity Press.

Keniston, K. (1977) *All Our Children: The American family under pressure*, New York: Harcourt, Brace and Jovanovich.

Kennedy, D. (1976) *Birth Control in America: The career of Margaret Sanger*, New Haven, Conn.: Yale University Press.

Kent, P. (ed.) (1976) *International Aspects of the Provision of Medical Care*, London: Oriel Press.

Kerr, C. (1962) *Industrialism and Industrial Man: The problems of labour and management in economic growth*, London: Heinemann.

Kessen, W. (ed.) (1975) *Childhood in China*, New Haven, Conn: Yale University Press.

Keyes, D. (1983) *Thatcher's Britain: A guide to the ruins*, London: Pluto Press.

Kincaid, J. (1973) *Poverty and Equality in Britain*, Harmondsworth: Penguin.

King, A. (1979) 'Ideas, institutions and the policies of governments: A comparative analysis: Parts I and II', *The British Journal of Political Science*, vol. 3, pp. 291–314.

Klass, A. (1975) 'There's Gold in Them Thar Pills', Harmondsworth: Penguin.

Klein, R. E. (1973) *Complaints Against Doctors: A study in professional accountability*, London: Knight.

Klein, R. E. and Steinberg, D. L. (1989) *Radical Voices: A decade of feminist resistance*, Oxford: Pergamon Press.

Koblik, S. (ed.) (1975) *Sweden's Development from Poverty to Affluence, 1750–1970*, Minneapolis: University of Minnesota Press.

Kolberg, J. E. (1978) 'Limits to welfare', *Acta Sociologica*, supplement, pp. 113–126.

Kolko, G. (1962) *Wealth and Power in America*, New York: Praeger.

Kolko, G. (1967) *The Triumph of Conservatism: 1900–16*, Chicago: Quadrangle Books.

Kollantai, A. M. (1971) *Communism and the Family*, London: Pluto Press.

Kollantai, A. M. (1977) *Alexandra Kollantai: Selected writings*, London: Allison and Busby.

Korpi, W. (1978) 'Democracy in welfare capitalism: Structural erosion, welfare backlash and incorporation', *Acta Sociologica*, vol. 3, pp. 97–112.

Korpi, W. (1978) *The Working Class in Welfare Capitalism: Work, unions and politics in Sweden*, London: Routledge and Kegan Paul.

Kotelchuck, D. (ed.) (1976) *Prognosis Negative: Crisis in the health care system*, New York: Random House.

Knaus, W. (1981) *Inside Soviet Medicine: An American doctor's firsthand report*, New York: Everest House.

Krause, E. A. (1977) *Power and Illness: The political sociology of health and medical care*, New York: Elsevier.

Krieger, J. (1987) 'Social policy in the age of Reagan and Thatcher', *The Socialist Register*, pp. 177–97.

Kristeva, J. (1977) *About Chinese Women*, London: Marion Boyars.

Krupskaya, N. (1930) *Memories of Lenin*, London: Martin Lawrence.

Kuhn, A. and Wolpe, A. M. (eds.) (1978) *Feminism and Materialism*, London: Routledge and Kegan Paul.

Labour Research (1983) 'Wandsworth Goes Private', London: Labour Research Department.

Labour Research (1987) 'Privatising Council Services', London: Labour Research Department.

Lagerstrom, L. (1983) *Social Insurance and Private Pensions in Sweden*, New York: Elsevier.

Lampton, D. (1974) 'Health policy during the Great Leap Forward', *China Quarterly*, vol. 60, p. 677.

Lampton, D. (1977) *The Politics of Medicine in China, 1947–77*, Folkestone, USA: Westview Press.

Land, H. (1975) 'The introduction of family allowances: An act of historic injustice?', *Change, Choice and Conflict in Social Policy*, edited by P. Hall, H. Land, R. Parker and A. Webb, London: Heinemann.

Land, H. (1976) 'Women: Supporters or supported?', *Sexual Divisions and Society*, edited by D. L. Barker and S. Allen. London: Tavistock.

Land, H. (1978) 'Who cares for the family?', *Journal of Social Policy*, vol. 7, no. 3, pp. 257–84.

Land, H. (1979) 'The boundary between the state and the family', *The Sociology of the Family*, edited by C. Harris. Newcastle upon Lyme: Keele University Monograph, pp. 141–59.

Land, H. (1980) 'The family wage', *Feminist Review*, no. 6, pp. 55–78.

Land, H. (1983) 'Who still cares for the family? Recent developments in income maintenance, taxation and family law', *Women's Welfare, Women's Rights*, edited by J. Lewis, London: Croom Helm.

Land, H. and Ward, S. (1986) *Women won't Benefit*, London: CPAG.

Landry, B. (1987) *The New Black Middle Class*, Berkeley, Calif.: University of California Press.

Lane, D. (1971) *The End of Social Inequality? Stratification under state socialism*, Harmondsworth: Penguin.

Lane, D. (1976) *The Socialist Industrial State: Towards a political sociology of state socialism*, London: Allen and Unwin.

Lane, D. (1978) *Politics and Society in the USSR*, Oxford: Martin Robertson.

Lane, D. (1982) *The End of Social Inequality? Class, status and power under state socialism*, London: Allen and Unwin.

Lane, D. (1984) *Soviet Economy and Society*, Oxford: Basil Blackwell.

Lane, D. (1985) *State and Politics in the USSR*, New York: New York University Press.

Lang, O. (1946) *Chinese Family and Society*, New Haven: Yale University Press.

Lapidus, G. (1978) *Women in Soviet Society: Equality, development and social change*, Berkeley, Calif.: University of California Press.

Lapidus, G. (1982) *Women, Work and the Family in the Soviet Union*, New York: M. E. Sharpe.

Lawson, R. and Read, L. (1975) *Social Security in the European Economic Community: Political and economic planning*, London: Sage.

LeGrand, J. and Robinson, R. (eds.) (1984) *Privatisation in the Welfare State*, London: George Allen and Unwin.

Leaper, R. and Read, L. (1980) *Health, Wealth and Housing*, Oxford: Basil Blackwell and Martin Robertson.

Lear, P. (1989) 'Caring for the 1990s in the USSR', *The Health Services Management*, August, pp. 16–8.

Leavitt, J. W. and Numbers, R. L. (1978) *Sickness and Health in America: Readings in the history of medicine and public health*, Madison: University of Wisconsin Press.

Lederer, K. M. (1972) *The Nature of Poverty: An interpretative review of poverty studies, with special reference to Canada*, Edmonton: Human Resources Research Council.

Lee, S. and Letha, A. (1989) 'Tensions between black women and white women: A study', *Affilia*, vol. 4, no. 2, pp. 31–45.

Leeds Social Security Cuts Campaign. (LSSC) (1986) *The Campaign against the Fowler Review*, Leeds: LSSC.

Leibman, M. (1981) *The Russian Revolution*, London: Sage.

Leiby, J. (1978) *History of Social Welfare and Social Work in the United States*, New York: Columbia University Press.

Leichter, H. (1979) *A Comparative Approach to Policy Analysis*, Cambridge: Cambridge University Press.

Leman, C. (1980) *The Collapse of Welfare Reform: Political institutions, policy and the poor in Canada and the United States*, Cambridge, Mass.: MIT Press.

Lenero-Otero, L. (ed.) (1977) *Beyond the Nuclear Family Model: Cross Cultural Perspectives*, London: Sage.

Lenin, V. I. (1965) *The Collected Works*, London: Lawrence and Wishart.

Leonard, P. (1984) *Personality and Ideology*, London: Macmillan.

Lerner, G. (1975) *Black Women in White America*, New York: Random House.

Lerner, M., Zoloth, L. and Riles, W. (1982) *Bringing It All Back Home: A strategy to deal with the right*, Oakland, Calif.: Friends of Families.

Lesemann, F. (1988) *La Politique Sociale Americain. Les Annees Reagan*, Paris: Edition Saint-Martin.

Leuchtenburg, W. (1963) *Roosevelt and the New Deal, 1932–40*. New York: Harper and Row.

Leuchtenburg, W. (1964) *Perils of Prosperity, 1914–32*. Chicago: Chicago University Press.

Leuchtenburg, W. (1968) *The New Deal*, New York: Harper and Row.

Leuchtenburg, W. (1989) *In the Shadow of FDR*, New York: Cornell University Press.

Levenson, J. (1958) *Confucian China and its Modern Fate*, Berkeley: University of California Press.

Levine, M. (1981) *The History and Politics of Community Mental Health*, New York: Oxford University Press.

Levitan, S. (1969a) *The Design of the Federal Anti-poverty Strategy*, Ann Arbor: Institute of Labour and Industrial Relations.

Levitan, S. (1969b) *The Great Society's Poor Law: A new approach to poverty*, Baltimore: John Hopkins University Press.

Levitas, R. (ed.) (1986a) *The Ideology of the New Right*, Cambridge: Polity Press.

Levitas, R. (1986b) 'Competition and compliance: The utopias of the new right', *The Ideology of the New Right*, edited by R. Levitas, Cambridge: Polity Press.

Levitt, K. and Wharf, B. (eds.) (1985) *The Challenge of Child Welfare*, Vancouver: University of British Columbia Press.

Levy, M. (1971) *The Family Revolution in Modern China*, New York: Octagon Books.

Lewin, G. and Olesen, V. (eds.) (1985) *Women, Health and Healing*, London: Tavistock.

Lewis, C. and O'Brien, M. (1987) *Reassessing Fatherhood*, London: Sage.

Lewis, J. (1982) *The Politics of Motherhood: Child and maternal welfare in England, 1900–39*, London: Croom Helm.

Lewis, J. (ed.) (1983) *Women's Welfare, Woman's Right*, London: Croom Helm.

Lewis, J. and Meredith, B. (1988) *Daughters Who Care: Daughters caring for mothers at home*, London: Routledge.

Lewis, J. and Meredith, B. (1988) 'Daughters caring for mothers: The experience of caring and its implications for professional helpers', *Ageing and Society*, no. 8, pp. 1–21.

Lewycka, M. (1986) 'The Way They Were' in *New Socialist*, 36 March.

Liljestrom, R., Mellstrom, G., and Liljestrom, G. (1975) *Sex Roles in Transition: A report on a pilot program in Sweden*, Stockholm: The Swedish Institute.

Liljestrom, R. (1975) *A Study of Abortion in Sweden*, in *Sex Roles in Transition: A report on a pilot program in Sweden*, Stockholm: The Swedish Institute.

Lindberg, L. (ed.) (1975) *Stress and Contradiction in Modern Capitalism: Public policy and the theory of the state*, Lexington, Mass.: Lexington Books.

Lindgren, H. (1970) *Men and Family Care*, Stockholm: The Swedish Institute.

Lindsey, A. (1962) *Socialised Medicine in England and Wales: The national health service 1948–61*, Chapel Hill, N.C.: North Carolina University Press.

Linton, M. (1985) *The Swedish Road to Socialism*, London: Fabian Society.

Lipman-Blumen, J. (1979) *Sex Roles and Social Policy: A complex social science equation*, London: Sage.

Lister, R. (1973) *As Man and Wife?* London: Poverty Research Series 2, CPAG.

Lister, R. (1987) 'Future insecure: Women and income maintenance under a Tory third term', *Feminist Review*, no. 27, pp. 9–16.

Littlewood, R. and Lipsedge, M. (1982) *The Aliens and the Alienists: Ethnic minorities and psychiatry*, Harmondsworth: Penguin.

Littlewood, T. (1977) *The Politics of Population Control*, Indiana: The University of Notre Dame.

Livingstone, K. (1987) *If Voting Changed Anything, They'd Abolish It.* London: Collins.

Lloyd, P. (1979) *Slums of Hope: Shanty towns in the third world*, London: Routledge and Kegan Paul.

Loach, L. (1987) 'Can feminism survive a third term?', *Feminist Review*, no. 27, pp. 23–35.

London Edinburgh Weekend Return Group (LEWRG) (1979) *In and Against the State*, London: Conference of Socialist Economists.

London Women's Liberation Campaign for Legal and Financial Independence and Rights of Women (LWLC) (1979) 'Disaggregation now!' *Feminist Review*, no. 2, pp. 19–31.

Loney, M. (1983) *Community Against Government: The British community development project, 1968–78*, London: Heinemann.

Loney, M. (1986) *The Politics of Greed: The New Right and the welfare state*, London: Pluto Press.

Loney, M. (1987) *The State or the Market*, London: Sage.

Loney, M., Boswell, D. and Clarke, J. (eds.) (1986) *Social Policy and Social Welfare*, Milton Keynes: Open University Press.

Lorde, A. (1984) *Sister Outsider: Essays and speeches*, New York: Crossing Press.

Lubove, R. (1963) 'The New Deal and National Health', *Current History*, vol. 22, p. 45.

Lucas, A. E. (1982) *Chinese Medical Modernisation: Comparative policy continuities, 1930–80*, New York: Praeger.

Luker, K. (1984) *Abortion and the Politics of Motherhood*, Berkeley: The University of California Press.

Luxton, M. (1988) 'The gendered division of labour in the home', *Social Inequality in Canada*, edited by J. Curtis, E. Grabb, N. Guppy and S. Gibert, Scarborough, Ont.: Prentice-Hall, pp. 274–86.

MacDonald, M. (The MacDonald Report) (1985) *The Report of the Royal Commission on the Economic Union and Development Prospects for Canada*, Ottawa: Supply and Services, Canada.

MacPherson, S. (1982) *Social Policy in the Third World: The social dilemmas of underdevelopment*, Brighton: Wheatsheaf.

McAuley, A. (1981) *Women's Work and Wages in the Soviet Union*, London: Unwin Hyman.

McAuley, M. (1977) *Politics and the Soviet Union*, Harmondsworth: Penguin.

McAuley, M. (1979) *Economic Welfare in the Soviet Union: Poverty, living standards and inequality*, Madison: University of Wisconsin Press.

McAuley, M. (1981) *The Soviet Union since 1917*, Harlow: Longman.

McAuley, M. (1987) *The Soviet Union under Gorbachev*, New York: St Martin.

McCrindle, J. and Rowbotham, S. (1986) 'More than Just a Memory', *Feminist Review*, no. 23, Summer, pp. 109–121.

McIntosh, M. (1978) 'The state and the oppression of women', *Feminism and Materialism*, edited by A. Kuhn and A. M. Wolpe, London: Routledge and Kegan Paul.

McKinlay, J. (ed.) (1984) *The Political Economy of Health Care*, London: Tavistock.

McLeod, E. (1987) 'Women's Experience of Love: The significance of feminist therapy', Research Project at the University of Warwick, Coventry.

McLeod, L. (1980) *Wife Battering in Canada: The vicious circle*, Ottawa: The Canadian Advisory Council on the Status of Women.

McNaught, K. (1969) *The Pelican History of Canada*, Toronto: Pelican.

Maas, S. (1972) 'Racism and Mental Health', *Radical America*, 84, pp. 76–92.

Mace, D. V. (1964) *The Soviet Family*, London: Hutchinson.

Macklin, E. and Rubin, R. (eds.) (1983) *Contemporary Families and Alternative Lifestyles*, Beverly Hills: Sage Publications.

Madison, B. (1968) *Social Welfare in the Soviet Union*, Stanford: Stanford University Press.

Madison, B. (1973) 'Soviet income maintenance policy for the 1970s', *Journal of Social Policy*, vol. 2, no. 2, pp. 30–48.

Madison, B. (1980) *The Meaning of Social Policy*, London: Croom Helm.

Maier, K. (1989) 'Pregnant women: Fetal containers or people with rights', *Afflia*, vol. 4, no. 2, pp. 8–20.

Malek, F. (1985) *Asian Women and Mental Health or Mental Ill Health: The myth of mental illness*, Southwark: Asian Women's Aid.

Mama, A. (1984) 'Black women, the economic crisis and the British state', *Feminist Review*, no. 17, pp. 21–36.

Mama, A. (1989) 'Violence against black women: Gender, race and state responses', *Feminist Review*, no. 32, pp. 30–48.

Mamanova, T. (ed.) (1984) *Women and Russia: Feminist writings from the Soviet Union*, Oxford: Basil Blackwell.

Manchester's Community Health Councils (1983) *National Guidelines for Well-Women Centres*, Manchester: Manchester Community Health Councils.

Manchester Law Centre (MLC) (1983) *The Thin Edge of the Wedge*, Manchester: MLC.

Mandel, B. (1975) *Welfare in America: Controlling the dangerous classes*, New York: Prentice-Hall.

Mandel, E. (1978) 'The nature of the Soviet State', *New Left Review*, no. 108, pp. 23–48.

Mandel, E. (1986) 'In Defence of Socialist Planning', *New Left Review*, no. 159, pp. 5–38.

Mandel, E. (1988) 'The myth of market socialism', *New Left Review*, no. 169, pp. 108–21.

Mandel, W. M. (1975) *Soviet Women*, New York: Anchor Books.

Manga, P. and Weller, G. R. (1980) 'The failure of the equity objective in health: A comparative analysis of Canada, Britain, and the United States', *Comparative Social Research*, vol. 3, pp. 229–67.

Manning, N. (1979) 'Health care policy in the Soviet Union', *Social Policy and Administration*, vol. 13, pp. 143–6.

Manning, N. (1984) 'Social policy in the USSR', *Critical Social Policy*, no. 11, pp. 74–88.

Manson, T. (1979) 'Health Policy and the Cuts', *Capital and Class*, no. 7, pp. 35–45.

Mao, Tse-Tung (1960) *Selected Works of Mao Tse-Tung*, Peking: Foreign Language Press.

Marchant, H. and Wearing, B. (eds.) (1986) *Gender Reclaimed*, Sydney: Hale Iremonger.

Marieskind, H. (1980) *Women in the Health System: Patients, providers and programmes*, St Louis: C. V. Mosby.

Marmor, T. (1970) *The Politics of Medicare*, London: Routledge and Kegan Paul.

Maroney, H. (1983) 'Feminism at work', *New Left Review*, no. 141, pp. 51–71.

Marris, P. (1974) *Dilemmas of Social Reform: Poverty and Community Action in the United States*, Harmondsworth: Penguin.

Marsh, L. (1943) *Report of Social Security for Canada*, Ottawa: King's Printer.

Marsh, L. (1975) *Social Planning for Canada*, Toronto: University of Toronto Press.

Marshall, J. (1985) 'Women and Child Care', *New Left Review*, vol. 95.

Marshall, T. (1949) 'Citizenship and Class', republished in *Sociology At The Crossroads* (1963), London: Heinemann.

Marshall, T. (1965) *Class, Citizenship and Social Development*, New York: Anchor Books.

Marshall, T. (1981) *The Right to Welfare and Other Essays*, London: Heinemann.

Martin, A. (1983) *The Politics of Economic Policy*, New York: Praeger.

Masters, D. C. (1950) *The Winnipeg General Strike*, Toronto: University of Toronto Press.

Matters, D. (1979) 'Public welfare Vancouver style, 1910–20', *Journal of Canadian Studies*, vol. 14, no. 1, p. 3.

Matthews, M. (1972) *Class and Society in Russia*, London: Allen Lane.

Matthews, M. (1978) *Privilege in the Soviet Union: A study of elite lifestyles under communism*, London: Allen and Unwin.

Matthews, M. (1987) *Poverty in the Soviet Union*, Cambridge: Cambridge University Press.

Maxwell, N. (ed.) (1979) *China's Road to Development*, Oxford: Pergamon.

Maxwell, R. (1975) *Health Care: The growing dilemma: Needs versus resources in Western Europe, the United States, and the Soviet Union*, New York: McKinsey and Co.

Mayall, B. and Petrie, P. (1977) *Minder, Mother and Child*, London: University of London Institute of Education.

Maynard, A. (1979) 'Pricing, insurance and the National Health Service', *Journal of Social Policy*, vol. 8, no. 2, pp. 157–72.

Maynard, A. (1975) *Health Care in the EEC*, London: Croom Helm.

Maynard, A. and Williams, A. (1984) 'Privatisation and the NHS', *Privatisation and the Welfare State*, edited by J. Le Grand and R. Robinson, London: George Allen and Unwin.

Maynard, A., Marinker, M. and Gray, D. P. (1986) 'The Doctor, the Patient and Their Contract. Alternative Contracts: Are They Viable?' in the *British Medical Journal*, vol. 292, pp. 1438–41.

Mayo, M. (1977) *Women in the Community*, London: Routledge and Kegan Paul.

Meade-King, M. (1988) 'Unpaid dues', *The Guardian*, 1 March.

Medvedev, Z. (1979) 'Russia under Brezhnev', *New Left Review*, no. 117, pp. 3–30.

Mencher, S. (1967) *Poor Law to Poverty Programme: Economic security policy in Britain and the United States*, Pittsburgh: University of Pittsburgh Press.

Merton, R. K. (1976) *Contemporary Social Problems*, New York: Harcourt, Brace and Jovanovich.

Merton, R. K. and King, R. (1968) *Social Theory and Social Structure*, New York: Free Press.

Miliband, R. (1973) 'Stalin and after', *Socialist Register*, pp. 377–97.

Millar, J. and Glendinning, C. (1989) 'Gender and poverty', *Journal of Social Policy*, vol. 18, no. 3, pp. 363–82.

Miller, S. M. (1979) 'Social Policy on the Defensive in Carter's America', *New Society*, 1 November, pp. 244–257.

Millett, K. (1972) *Sexual Politics*, London: Abacus/Sphere.

Mills, A. (1978) 'The Canadian Forum and socialism, 1920–34', *Journal of Canadian Studies*, vol. 13, no. 4, p. 11.

Milton, N. (1970) 'Women and revolution', *Socialist Revolution*, vol. 1, no. 6, pp. 139–44.

Minford, P. (1984) 'State expenditure: A study in waste', *Economic Affairs*, Special Supplement, vol. 1, no. 3, pp. i–xix.

Mirsky, J. (1988) 'China's little red station', *The Independent*, 9 August, p. 17.

Mirsky, J. (1989) 'Deng's bitter revenge', *The Observer*, 28 May, p. 25.

Mishra, R. (1976) 'Convergence theory and social change: The development of welfare in Britain and the Soviet Union', *Comparative Studies in Society and History*, vol. 18, pp. 25–56.

Mishra, R. (1977) *Society and Social Policy: Theoretical Perspectives on Welfare*, London: Macmillan.

Mishra, R. (1984) *The Welfare State in Crisis*, Brighton: Harvester Press.

Mishra, R. (1986b) 'The left and the welfare state: A critical analysis', *Critical Social Policy*, issue 15, pp. 4–20.

Mitchell, J, and Oakley, A. (1986) *What is Feminism?*, Oxford: Basil Blackwell.

Mohr, J. (1978) *Abortion in America: The origins and evolution of national policy, 1800–1900*, New York: Oxford University Press.

Mok, B. H. (1983) 'In the service of socialism: Social welfare in China', *Social Work*, July–Aug., pp. 267–72.

Molyneaux, M. (1981) 'Socialist societies old and new', *Feminist Review*, no. 8, pp. 1–34.

Molyneux, M. (1985) 'Family reform in socialist states: The hidden agenda', *Feminist Review*, no. 21, pp. 47–66.

Mommsen, W. (1981) *The Emergence of the Welfare State in Britain and Germany, 1850–1950*, London: Croom Helm.

Moraga, C. and Azaldna, G. (eds.) (1981) *This Bridge Called My Back: Writings by radical women of color*, Watertown, Mass.: Persephone Press.

Morgan, R. (1970) *Sisterhood is Powerful*, New York: Vintage.

Moroney, R. (1976) *The Family and the State: Considerations for social policy*, Harlow: Longman.

Moscovitch, A. and Albert, J. (1987) *The Benevolent State*, Toronto: Paramount Press.

Moscovitch, A. and Drover, G. (eds.) (1981) *Inequality: The political economy of social welfare in Canada*, Toronto: Toronto University Press.

Moss, P. and Fonda, N. (eds.) (1980) *Work and the Family*, London: Temple Smith.

Mount, F. (1982) *The Subversive Family: An alternative history of love and marriage*, New York: Jonathan Cape.

Moynihan, D. (1965) *The Negro Family: The case for national action*, Washington, DC: US Department of Labor.

Moynihan, D. (1969) *Maximum Feasible Misunderstanding*, New York: Free Press.

Moynihan, D. (1973) *The Politics of a Guaranteed Income*, New York: Random Press.

Mullard, C. (1973) *Black Britain*, London: Allen and Unwin.

Muller, M. (1982) *The Health of Nations: A north–south investigation*, New York: Faber and Faber.

Murray, C. (1984) *Losing Ground: American social policy 1950–80*, New York: Basic Books.

Myrdal, A. (1945) *Nation and Family: The Swedish experiment in democratic family and population policy*, London: Routledge and Kegan Paul.

Myrdal, A. and Klein, V. (1970) *Women's Two Roles: Home and work*, London: Routledge and Kegan Paul.

Myrdal, J. (1965) *Report from a Chinese village*, New York: New American Library.

Myrdal, J. and Kessle, G. (1979) *China: The revolution continued*, New York: Pantheon Books.

National Council of Welfare (NCW) (1975) *Poor Kids*, Ottawa: Minister of Supply and Services Canada.

National Council of Welfare (NCW) (1979a) *The Hidden Welfare System Revisited*, Ottawa: Minister of Supply and Services Canada.

National Council of Welfare (NCW) (1979b) *Women and Poverty*, Ottawa: Minister of Supply and Services Canada.

National Council of Welfare (NCW) (1981) *The Working Poor*, Ottawa: Minister of Supply and Services Canada.

National Council of Welfare (NCW) (1987) *Welfare in Canada: The tangled safety net*, Ottawa: Minister of Supply and Services Canada.

National Council of Welfare (NCW) (1988) 'Poverty in Canada', in *Social Inequality in Canada*, edited by J. Curtis, E. Grabb, N. Guppy and S. Gibert, Scarborough, Ont.: Prentice-Hall, pp. 97–101.

National Council of Welfare (NCW) (1989a) *The 1989 Budget and Social Policy*, Ottawa: Minister of Supply and Services Canada.

National Council of Welfare (NCW) (1989b) *A Pension Primer*, Ottawa: Minister of Supply and Services Canada.

National Women's Aid Federation (NWAF) (1978) *Half the Sky; and still no roof*, London: NWAF and Welsh Women's Aid.

National Women's Aid Federation (NWAF) (1980) *Annual Report 1979–80*, London: NWAF.

Navarro, V. (1975a) *Health and Medical Care in the United States: A critical analysis*, Farmingdale, NY: Baywood Publishing Company.

Navarro, V. (1975b) 'The political economy of medical care: An explanation of the composition, nature and functions of the present health sector in the United States', *International Journal of Health Services*, vol. 5, no. 1, pp. 65–94.

Navarro, V. (1977) *Social Security and Medicine in the USSR: A Marxist critique*, New York: Lexington Books.

Navarro, V. (1978) *Class Struggle, the State and Medicine: An historical and contemporary analysis of the medical sector in Great Britain*, Oxford: Martin Robertson.

Navarro, V. (1979) *Medicine under Capitalism*, London: Croom Helm.

Navarro, V. (1982) 'Crisis of the international capitalist order and its implications for the welfare state', *Critical Social Policy*, issue 2, no. 1, pp. 43–62.

Navarro, V. (1983) 'Radicalism, Marxism and medicine', *International Journal of Health Services*, vol. 13, no. 2, pp. 179–202.

Navarro, V. (1984) 'A critique of the ideological and political position of the Brant report and the Alma Ata declaration', *International Journal of Health Services*, vol. 14, no. 2, pp. 159–72.

Nett, E. (1981) 'Canadian families in social-historical perspective', *Canadian Journal of Sociology*, vol. 6, no. 3, p. 239.

Nett, E. (1982) *Women as Elders*, Toronto: Resources for Feminist Research.

Nettl, J. (1967) *The Soviet Achievement*, London: Thames and Hudson.

New Society (1982) 'Which way for the Welfare State?', 8 July, pp. 52–4.

News on Sunday (1987) 'Looney left takeover', 24 May, p. 13.

Newton, J. (1989) 'From wage slave to white slave: The prostitution controversy and early Canadian left', *Beyond the Vote: Canadian women in politics*, edited by L. Kealey and J. Sangster, Toronto: The Women's Press, pp. 217–38.

Nissel, M. (1980) 'The family and the welfare state', *New Society*, 7 August, pp. 25–62.

Nissel, M. and Bonnerjea, L. (1982) *Family Care and the Handicapped Elderly: Who pays?*, London: Policy Studies Institute.

Nove, A. (1972) *An Economic History of the USSR*, Harmondsworth: Penguin.

Nove, A. (1983) *Has Soviet Growth Ceased?*, Manchester: Manchester Statistical Society.

Nove, A. (1985) *The Economics of Feasible Socialism*, London: George Allen and Unwin.

O'Connor, J. (1973) *The Fiscal Crisis of the State*, New York: St James Press.

Offe, C. (1972) 'Advanced capitalism and the welfare state', *Politics and Society*, vol. 2, no. 4, pp. 479–88.

Offe, C. (1982) 'Contradictions of the modern welfare state', *Critical Social Policy*, vol. 2, no. 2, pp. 7–16.

Offe, C. (1984) *Contradictions of the Welfare State*, London: Hutchinson.

Office of Economic Cooperation and Development (OECD) (1976) *Public Expenditure on Income Maintenance Programmes*, Paris: OECD.

Office of Economic Cooperation and Development (OECD) (1977) *Unemployment Compensation and Related Employment Policy Measures: General report and country studies, Canada, France, Germany, Sweden, the United Kingdom, the United States*, Paris, OECD.

Office of Economic Cooperation and Development (OECD) (1979) *Public Expenditure on Health*, Paris: OECD.

Office of Health Economics (1979) *Compendium of Health Statistics*, London: OHE.

Office of Population Census and Statistics (OPCS) (1984) *Social Trends*, London: HMSO.

Office of Population Census and Statistics (OPCS) (1988) *The General Household Survey*, London: HMSO.

Oliker, S. (1981) 'Abortion and the left: The limits of "pro-family politics"', *Socialist Review*, no. 56, pp. 71–96.

Orleans, L. A. (1972) *Every Fifth Child: The population of China*, London: Eyre Methuen.

Osberg, L. (1981) *Economic Inequality in Canada*, Toronto: University of Toronto Press.

Osborn, R. (1970) *Soviet Social Policies*, Homewood, Ill.: Dorsey.

O'Sullivan, S. (1975) 'Sterilisation' in *Spare Rib*, no. 33, March, pp. 10–13.

Owen, D. (1971) *In Sickness and in Health*, London: Quartet Books.

Oyen, E. (ed.) (1986) *Comparing Welfare States and Their Futures*, Aldershot: Gower.

Pahl, J. (1980) 'Patterns of money management within marriage', *Journal of Social Policy*, vol. 9, pp. 313–35.

Pahl, J. (1985) *Private Violence and Public Policy*, London: Routledge and Kegan Paul.

Pal, L. (1985a) 'Federalism, social policy, and the constitution', in *Canadian Social Welfare Policy*, edited by J. Ismael, Montreal: McGill–Queen's University Press, pp. 1–20.

Pal, L. (1985b) 'Revision and retreat: Canadian unemployment insurance 1971–1981', in *Canadian Social Welfare Policy*, edited by J. Ismael, Montreal: McGill–Queen's University Press, pp. 75–104.

Panitch, L. (ed.) (1977) *The Canadian State: Political economy and political power*, Toronto: University of Toronto Press.

Papadakis, E. and Taylor-Gooby, P. (1987) *The Private Provision of Public Welfare*, Brighton: Wheatsheaf.

Parish, W. L. (1975) 'Socialism and the Chinese peasant family', *Journal of Asian Studies*, vol. 34, no. 3, p. 618.

Parish, W. (1985) *The Chinese Economy*, Chicago: University of Chicago Press.

Parish, W. L. and Whyte, M. F. (1978) *Village and Family in Contemporary China*, Chicago: University of Chicago Press.

Parkins, J. (1953) 'Care in the Community' *New Left Review*.

Parmar, P. (1982) 'Gender, race and class: Asian women, in resistance', in *The Empire Strikes Back*, edited by Centre for Contemporary and Cultural Studies, London: Hutchinson.

Parsons, T. (1954) *Essays in Sociological Theory*, New York: Free Press.

Partington, M. and Jowell, J. (1979) *Welfare Law and Policy: Studies in teaching, practice and research*, London: F. Pinter.

Pascall, G. (1986) *Social Policy: A Feminist Analysis*, London: Tavistock.

Patton, C. (1990) 'Aids' in *Feminist Review*, no. 33, Winter.

Patton, D. and Sawick, S. (1986) *Basic Methods of Policy Analysis and Planning*, Englewood Cliffs, N.J.: Prentice-Hall.

Penn, H. (1982) 'Who cares for the kids', *New Statesman*, vol. 103, no. 2651, pp. 6–8.

Peng, X. (1987) 'A women's story', presented in an International Women of Colour and Third World Women Film/Video Festival and Symposium, November 15–19, 1989, Vancouver, Canada.

Perry, N., Rustin, M. and Satyamurti, C. (1979) *Social Work, Welfare and The State*, London: Edward Arnold.

Petchesky, R. (1985) 'Abortion in the 1980s: Feminist morality and women's health', in *Women, Health and Healing* edited by G. Lewin and V. Olesen, London: Tavistock.

Petchey, R. (1986) 'The Griffiths reorganization of the National Health Service: Fowlerism by stealth?', *Critical Social Policy*, issue 17, pp. 87–103.

Peynstone, L. (1935) *Swedish Social Democracy*, London: Macmillan.

Phizacklea, A. (ed.) (1983) *One-Way Ticket: Women and migrant labour*, London: Routledge and Kegan Paul.

Piachaud, D. (1979) 'Diffusion of medical techniques to Third World countries', *International Journal of Health Services*, vol. 9, no. 4, pp. 629–44.

Piachaud, D. (1984) *Round about Fifty Hours a Week: The time costs of children*, London: CPAG.

Piachaud, D. (1987) 'The growth of poverty', in *The Growing Divide*, edited by A. Walker and C. Walker, London: CPAG.

Piachaud, D., Lewis, J. and Bulmer, M. (1989) *The Goals of Social Policy*, London: Unwin Hyman.

Pickard, T. (1982) *Jarrow March*, London: Allison and Busby.

Pincus, A. and Minahan, A. (1973) *Social Work Practice: Model and method*, Itasca, Ill.: F. E. Peacock Publishers.

Pinker, R. (1971) *Social Theory and Social Policy*, London: Heinemann.

Pinker, R. (1973) *The Welfare State: A comparative perspective*, Edinburgh: Department of Social Administration, Edinburgh University.

Phillips, A. (1984) *Hidden Hands: Women and economic policy*, London: Pluto.

Phillips, A. (1987) *Divided Loyalties: Dilemmas of sex and class*, London: Virago.

Phillips, A. (1987) *Feminism and Equality*, Oxford: Basil Blackwell.

Phillipson, C. (1982) *Capitalism and the Construction of Old Age*, London: Macmillan.

Phillipson, C. and Walker, A. (eds.) (1986) *Ageing and Social Policy: A critical assessment*, Aldershot: Gower.

Pinker, R. (1979) *The Idea of Welfare*, London: Heinemann.

Pinkney, A. (1984) *The Myth of Black Progress*, New York: Random House.

Piven, F. and Cloward, R. (1972) *Regulating the Poor: The function of public welfare*, London: Tavistock.

Piven, F. and Cloward, R. (1977) *Poor People's Movements: Why they succeed and how they fail*, New York: Pantheon Books.

Piven, F. and Cloward, R. (1982) *The New Class War: Reagan's attack on the welfare state and its consequences*, New York: Pantheon Books.

Plummer, J. (1978) *Divide and Deprive*, London: Joint Council for the Welfare of Immigrants.

Popay, J., Rimmer, L. and Rossiter, C. (1983) *One Parent Families*, London: Study Commission on the Family.

Popplestone, R. (1980) 'Top jobs for women: Are the cards stacked against them?', *Social Work Today*, vol. 12, no. 4, pp. 12–15.

Porket, J. L. (1979) 'OAP schemes in the Soviet Union and Eastern Europe', *Journal of Social Policy and Administration*, vol. 13, no. 1, pp. 22–36.

Porter, C. (1980) *Alexandra Kollantai: A biography*, London: Virago.

Porter, J. (1965) *The Vertical Mosaic*, Toronto: University of Toronto Press.

Poster, M. (1978) *Critical Theory of the Family*, London: Pluto Press.

Potts, M. (1977) *Abortion*, Cambridge: Cambridge University Press.

Pollock, S. and Sutton, J. (1989) 'Fathers' rights, women's losses', in *Radical Voices: A decade of feminist resistance*, edited by R. E. Klein and D. L. Steinberg, Oxford: Pergamon Press, pp. 132–42.

Prescod-Roberts, M. and Steele, N. (1980) *Black Women: Bringing it all back home*, Bristol: Falling Wall Press.

Provence, S. (1977) *The Challenge of Day Care*, New Haven, Mass.: Yale University Press.

Radical Statistics Health Group (RSHG) (1978) 'Whose priorities', *International Journal of Health Services*, vol. 8, no. 2, pp. 367–440.

Rainwater, L. (1960) *And the Poor Beget Children*, Chicago: Quadrangle Books.

Rainwater, L. and Yancey, W. (eds.) (1967) *The Moynihan Report and the Politics of Controversy*, Cambridge, Mass.: MIT Press.

Ransel, D. (1978) *The Family in Imperial Russia*, Chicago: University of Illinois Press.

Rawlings, C. (1981) *Social Work with Elderly People*, London: Allen and Unwin.

Rawlings, C. (1988) 'Raising standards with network meetings', *Social Work Today*, 17 March, p. 18.

Raynor, G. (1982) 'Reaganomics of welfare: The unfolding of the austerity programme', *Critical Social Policy*, vol. 2, no. 1, p. 46.

Raynor, G. (1983) 'Sick hospitals: The service crises of health care in New York City', *Critical Social Policy*, vol. 2, no. 3, pp. 90–98.

Rein, M. (1967) *Dilemmas of Social Reform: Poverty and Community Action in the United States*, London: Routledge and Kegan Paul.

Rein, M. (1970) *Social Policy: Issues of choice and change*, New York: Random House.

Rein, M. (1982) *Dilemmas of Welfare Policy: Why work strategies haven't worked*, New York: Praeger.

Rein, M., Esping-Anderson, G. and Rainwater, L. (eds.) (1987) *Stagnation and Renewal in Social Policy*, Armonk, NY: M. E. Sharpe, Inc.

Reindeau, R. (1979) 'A clash of interests: Dependency and the municipal problem in the Great Depression', *Journal of Canadian Studies*, Spring, p. 50.

Reinharz, S. (1989) 'Friends or Foes: Gerontological and feminist theory', in

Radical Voices: A decade of feminist resistance, edited by R. E. Klein and O. L. Steinberg, Oxford: Pergamon Press, pp. 222–42.

Reiss, S. (1986) 'China since Mao', *Newsweek*, 8 September, pp. 8–18.

Rendall, J. (1984) *The Origins of Modern Feminism: Women in three western societies: Britain, France and the United States, 1780–1860*, New York: Schoken.

Rhodes, M. (1986) *Ethical Dilemmas in Social Work Practice*, London: Routledge and Kegan Paul.

Rifkin, J. (1978) *The North Will Rise Again: Pensions, politics and power in the 1980s*, Boston: Beacon Press.

Righter, R. (1984) 'Sweden's welfare bonanza dubbed a "fool's paradise"', *The Sunday Times*, 24 June.

Rights of Women (ROW) (1979) *Women and Income Tax*, London: ROW.

Rights of Women (ROW) (1984) *Lesbian Mothers on Trial*, London: ROW.

Riley, D. (1983a) *War in the Nursery*, London: Virago.

Riley, D. (1983b) 'The serious burden of love? Some questions on child care, feminism, and socialism', *What is to be Done about the Family?*, edited by L. Segal. Harmondsworth: Penguin.

Rimlinger, G. (1971) *Welfare Policy and Industrialisation in Europe, America and Russia*, New York: Wiley.

Roberts, H. (ed.) (1981) *Women, Health and Reproduction*, London: Routledge and Kegan Paul.

Roberts, J. (1990) 'Winter in Leningrad', *The Health Service Journal*, 4 January, pp. 18–20.

Robertson, H. (1973) *Reservations Are For The Indians*, New York: James Lewis and Samuels.

Robinson, H. R. (1974) *Early Child Care in the United States of America*, New York: Gordon and Breach.

Rodgers, B. (1969) *The Battle Against Poverty*, London: Routledge and Kegan Paul.

Rodgers, B. (1979) *The Study of Social Policy: A comparative approach*, London: Allen and Unwin.

Rodwin, V. G. (1984) *The Health Planning Predicament: France, Quebec, England and the United States*, Berkeley, Calif.: The University of California Press.

Roelofs, S. (1989) 'In and against the state', *Spare Rib*, March, p. 46.

Roemer, M. (1969) *Organisation of Medical Care under Social Security. A study based on the experience of 8 countries*, Geneva: International Labour Office.

Roemer, M. (1971) 'Organised ambulatory care in international perspective', *International Journal for Health Services*, vol. 1, no. 4, pp. 354–61.

Roemer, M. (1977) *Comparative National Policies on Health Care*, New York: Marcel Dekker.

Room, G. (1986) *Cross National Innovation in Social Policy: European perspectives in the evaluation of action research*, London: Macmillan.

Roome, P. (1989) 'Amelia Turner and Calgary labour women, 1919–35', *Beyond the Vote: Canadian women in politics*, edited by L. Kealey and J. Sangster, Toronto: The Women's Press, pp. 89–117.

Rosa, J. J. (ed.) (1982) *The World Crisis in Social Security*, New York: ICS Press.

Rose, H. (1973) 'Up against the welfare state: The claimants union', *Socialist Register*, pp. 179–204.

Rose, H. (1981) 'Rereading Titmuss: The sexual division of welfare', *Journal of Social Policy*, issue 10, no. 4, pp. 477–502.

Rose, H. (1985) 'Women's refuges: Creating new forms of welfare?', *Women and Social Policy*, edited by C. Ungerson, London: Macmillan.

Rose, H. (1986) 'Women and the restructuring of the welfare state', *Comparing Welfare States and their Futures*, edited by E. Oyen, Aldershot: Gower.

Rose, H. and Rose, S. (1982) 'Moving right out of welfare – and the way back', *Critical Social Policy*, vol. 2, no. 1, pp. 55–61.

Rose, S. (1973) 'Science, racism and ideology', *Socialist Register*, pp. 235–60.

Rosenberg, A. (1989) *Women in the Soviet Union*, London: Sage.

Ross, D. (1981) *The Working Poor: Wage earners and the failure of income security policy*, Toronto: James Lorimer.

Rosser, S. (ed.) (1988) *Feminism within the Science and Health Care Professions: Overcoming resistance*, Oxford: Pergamon Press.

Rostow, W. (1971) *The Stages of Economic Growth: A non-communist manifesto*, Cambridge: Cambridge University Press.

Rothman, B. (1984) 'Women, health and medicine' in *Women: A feminist perspective*, edited by J. Freeman, Palo Alto: Mayfield.

Rothman, D. and Wheeler, S. (eds.) (1981) *Social History and Social Policy*, New York: Academic Press.

Rothman, S. (1978) *Women's Proper Place: A history of the changing ideals and practice, 1870 to the present day*, New York: Basic Books.

Rowbotham, S. (1972) 'The beginnings of women's liberation in Britain', in *The Body Politic*, edited by M. Wandor, London: Stage One.

Rowbotham, S. (1972) *Women, Resistance and Revolution*, London: Allen Lane.

Rowbotham, S. (1973) *Woman's Consciousness, Man's World*, Harmondsworth: Penguin.

Rowbotham, S. (1977) *Hidden from History: 300 Years of women's oppression and the fight against it*, London: Pluto Press.

Rowbotham, S. (1979) 'The women's movement and organising', in *Beyond the Fragments*, edited by S. Rowbotham, L. Segal and H. Wainwright, London: Merlin Press.

Rowbotham, S., Segal, L. and Wainwright, H. (1979) *Beyond the Fragments: Feminism and the making of socialism*, London: Merlin Press.

Royal Commission on the Status of Women (RCSW) (1977) *Royal Commission Report on the Status of Women in Canada*, Canadian Government Publishing Centre: Supply and Services, Canada.

Ruble, B. (1981) *Soviet Trade Unions: Their development in the 1970s*, Cambridge: Cambridge University Press.

Ruble, B. (1987) 'The social dimensions of perestroyka', *Soviet Economy*, vol. 3, no. 2, pp. 171–83.

Russell, L. (1978) 'The political economy of federal health programs', *International Journal of Health Services*, vol. 8, no. 4, p. 620.

Ruth, S. (1989) 'A feminist analysis of the new right', *Radical Voices: A decade of feminist resistance* edited by R. E. Klein and D. L. Steinberg, Oxford: Pergamon Press, pp. 93–106.

Rutter, M. (1986) *Maternal Deprivation Reassessed*, Harmondsworth: Penguin.

Ruzek, S. B. (1978) *The Women's Health Movement: Feminist alternatives to medical control*, New York: Praeger.

Ruzek, S. (1986) 'Feminist visions of health: An international perspective', *What is Feminist?*, edited by J. Mitchell and A. Oakley, Oxford: Basil Blackwell.

Ryan, T. M. (1978) *The Organisation of Soviet Medical Care*, Oxford: Basil Blackwell.

Ryan, W. (1976) *Blaming the Victim*, New York: Random House.

Sagmeister, N. (1987) 'In sickness and in health: Spousal benefits for gays and lesbians', *Our Times*, vol. 6, no. 6.

Salaff, J. and Merkle, J. (1970) 'Women and revolution: The lessons of the Soviet union and China', *Socialist Revolution*, vol. 1, no. 4, pp. 39–72.

Salamon, L. (1978) *Welfare: The Elusive consensus: Where we are, how we got there and what's ahead*, New York: Praeger.

Salkever, D. (1975) 'Economic class and differential access to health care. Comparisons amongst health care systems', *International Journal of Health Services*, vol. 5, p. 373.

Samuelsson, K. (1968) *From Great Power to Welfare State: 300 Years of Swedish Social Development*, London: Allen and Unwin.

Sandford, C., Pond, C. and Walker, R. (eds.) (1980) *Taxation and Social Policy*, London: Heinemann.

Saunders, E. (1988) 'Theoretical approaches to the study of women', *Social Inequality in Canada*, edited by J. Curtis, E. Grabb, N. Guppy and S. Gibert, Toronto: The Women's Press, pp. 248–63.

Sandqvist, K. (1987) 'Swedish family policy', *Reassessing Fatherhood*, edited by C. Lewis and M. O'Brien, London: Sage.

Sarvis, B. and Hyman, R. (1973) *The Abortion Controversy*, New York: Columbia University Press.

Sasson, A. S. (ed.) (1987) *Women and the State*, London: Hutchinson.

Saunders, P. (1988) *Home ownership and capital gains*, Brighton: University of Sussex.

Savage, W. and Leighton, J. (1986) *Savage Enquiry*, London: Virago.

Savitt, T. (1978) *Medicine and Slavery: The diseases and health care of blacks in Antebellum Virginia*, Chicago University of Illinois Press.

Scase, R. (1976) *Readings in Swedish Class Structure*, Oxford: Pergamon.

Scase, R. (ed.) (1980) *The State in Western Europe*, London: Croom Helm.

Schinnenkian (1979) *Soviet Social Planning*, Cambridge, Mass.: Harvard University Press.

Schneider, C. and Vinoskis (1980) *The Law, and the Politics of Abortion*, Lexington, Mass.: Lexington Books.

Schurmann, F. and Schell, O. (eds.) (1967) *The China Reader: Imperial China*, New York: Vintage Books.

Scott, H. (1982) *Sweden's Right to be Human: Sex role equality: The goal and the reality*, London: Allison and Busby.

Scott, H. (1974) *Does Socialism Liberate Women: Experiences from Eastern Europe*, Boston: Beacon Press.

Scott, H. (1976) *Women and Socialism: Experiences from Eastern Europe*, London: Allison and Busby.

Scott, H. (1984) *Working your Way to the Bottom: The feminisation of poverty*, London: Pandora Press.

Scruton, R. (1980) *The Meaning of Conservatism*, Harmondsworth: Penguin.

Scruton, R. (1983) 'Thinkers of the New Left', *The Observer*, May 22.

Scull, A. (1977) *Decarceration: Community treatment and the deviant: A radical view*, Englewood Cliffs, NJ: Prentice Hall.

Seddon, V. (1986) *The Cutting Edge: Women the pit strike*, London: Lawrence and Wishart.

Seebohm, Lord (1968) *Report of the Committee on Local Authority and Allied Personal Social Services*, Cmnd. 3703, HMSO.

Segal, L. (ed.) (1983) *What is to be Done about the Family?*, Harmondsworth: Penguin.

Segal, L. (1984) *The Family*, Harmondsworth: Penguin.

Segal, L. (1987) *Is the Future Female? Troubled thoughts on contemporary feminism*, London: Virago.

Seidel, G. (1986) 'Culture, nation and "race" in the British and French New Right' *The Ideology of the New Right*, edited by R. Levitas, Cambridge: Polity Press.

Selden, M. (1971) *The Yenan Way in Revolutionary China*, Cambridge, Mass.: Harvard University Press.

Selden, M. (1979) *The People's Republic of China: A documentary history of revolutionary change*, New York: Monthly Review Press.

Seldon, A. (1985) 'The idea of the welfare state and its consequences', *The Welfare State and its Aftermath*, edited by S. Eisenstadt and O. Ahimeir, London: Croom Helm.

Serebrennikov, G. (1973) *The Position of Women in the USSR*, London: Victor Gollancz.

Shaver, S. (1989) 'Gender class and the welfare state: The case of income security in Australia', *Feminist Review*, no. 32, pp. 90–110.

Sheffield Black Women's Group (1984) 'Black Women – What kind of health care can we expect in racist Britain?', *Sweeping Statements*, edited by H. Kanter, London: The Women's Press.

Shifrin, L. (1985) 'Income security: The rise and stall of the federal role', *Canadian Social Welfare Policy*, edited by J. Ismael, Montreal: McGill-Queen's University Press, pp. 21–8.

Shonfield, A. (1965) *Modern Capitalism*, Oxford: Oxford University Press.

Sidel, R. (1972) *Women and Child Care in China*, Baltimore: Penguin Books.

Sidel, R. (1974) *Families of Fengsheng: Urban life in China*, Harmondsworth: Penguin.

Sidel, R. (1986) *Women and Children Last: The plight of poor women in affluent America*, New York: Viking Books.

Sidel, R. and Sidel, V. (1977) *A Healthy State: An international perspective on the crisis in United States medical care*, New York: Pantheon Books.

Sidel, R. and Sidel, V. (1982) *The Health of China: Conflicts in medical and human services for 1 billion people*, Boston: Beacon Press.

Sigerist, H. (1937) *Socialised Medicine in the Soviet Union*, London: Gollancz.

Silver, G. (1976) *A Spy in the House of Medicine*, Germantown, Maryland: Aspen Systems Corporations.

Silverman, M., Lee, P. R. and Lydecker, M. (1982) 'The drugging of the Third World', *International Journal of Health Services*, vol. 12, no. 4, pp. 585–97.

Silverman, M. and Lee, P. R. (1974) *Pills, Profits and Politics*, Berkeley, Calif.: University of California Press.

Sinfield, A. (1981) *What Unemployment Means*, Oxford: Martin Robertson.

Singh Sethi, A. (1971) *Industrial Relations and Health Services*, Englewood Cliffs: Prentice-Hall.

Sissons, M. and French, P. (eds.) (1963) *The Age of Austerity*, London: Hodder and Stoughton.

Sivanandan, A. (1976) 'Race, class and the state: The black experience in Britain', *Race and Class*, vol. 17, no. 4, pp. 437–68.

Sivanandan, A. (1982) *A Different Hunger: Writings on black resistance*, London: Pluto Press.

Sivanandan, A. (1985) 'Race awareness training and the degradation of black struggle', *Race and Class*, no. XXVI, pp. 1–33.

Skerry, P. (1978) 'The class conflict over abortion', *Public Interest*, no. 52, pp. 69–84.

Skinner, R. J. (1976) 'Technological determinism: A critique of convergence theory', *Comparative Studies in Society and History*, vol. 18, pp. 271–5.

Small, J. (1984) 'The crisis in adoption', *International Journal of Social Psychiatry*, vol. 30, no. 1.

Smart, C. and Sevenhuijsen, S. (1989) *Child Custody and the Politics of Gender*, London: Routledge.

Smiley, D. (ed.) (1963) *The Rowell-Sirois Report*, Toronto: McClelland and Stewart.

Smith, H. (1976) *The Russians*, London: Sphere Books.

Smith, H. (ed.) (1980) *Public Policy and Administration in the Soviet Union*, New York: Praeger.

Snider, E. L. (1981) 'The role of kin in meeting the health care needs of the elderly', *Canadian Journal of Sociology*, vol. 6, no. 3, p. 325.

Snow, E. (1968) *Red Star over China*, New York: Grove Press.

Snow, H. (1967) *Women in Modern China*, The Hague: Houton and Co.

Sowell, T. (1981) *Markets and Minorities*, New York: Basic Books.

Spallone, P. and Steinberg, D. L. (eds.) (1987) *Made to Order: Myth of reproductive and genetic progress*, London: Pergamon.

Special Senate Committee on Retirement Age Policies (SSCRAP) (1979) *Retirement without Tears*, Canadian Government Publishing Centre: Supply and Services, Canada.

Spens, Lord (1979) 'House of Commons Debate' in *Hansard*, June.

Splan, R. (1965) *Social Welfare in Ontario: 1792–1893*, Toronto: University of Toronto Press.

Spring Rice, M. (1981) *Working Class Wives, their Health and Condition*, London: Virago.

Stacey, J. (1983) *Patriarchy and Socialist Revolution in China*, Berkeley, Calif.: University of California Press.

Stacey, M. and Price, M. (1981) *Women, Power and Politics*, London: Tavistock.

Stack, C. (1974) *All our Kin: Strategies for survival in a black community*, New York: Harper and Row.

Stallard, K., Ehrenreich, B. and Sklar, H. (1983) *Poverty in the American Dream: Women and children first*, Boston: South End Press.

Stanko, E. (1985) *Intimate Instructions: Women's experience of male violence*, London: Routledge and Kegan Paul.

Stanley, L. and Wise, S. (1983) *Breaking Out: Feminist consciousness and feminist research*, London: Routledge and Kegan Paul.

Staples, R. (ed.) (1971) *The Black Family: Essays and studies*, Belmont, Calif.: Wadsworth.

Stedman Jones, G. (1971) *Outcast London*, Oxford: Clarendon Press.

Stein, B. (1976) *Work and Welfare in Britain and the US*, London: Macmillan.

Stein, B. and Miller, S. M. (eds.) (1973) *Incentives and Planning in Social Policy*, Chicago: Aldine.

Steiner, G. (1966) *Social Insecurity: The politics of welfare*, Chicago: Rand McNally.

Steiner, G. (1971) *The State of Welfare*, Washington, DC: Brookings Institution.

Steiner, G. (1976) *The Children's Cause*, Washington, DC: Brookings Institution.

Steiner, G. (1981) *The Futility of Family Policy*, Washington DC: Brookings Institution.

Steinfels, M. (1973) *Who's Minding the Children: The history and politics of child care in America*, New York: Simon and Schuster.

Bibliography

Stephens, J. (1979) *The Transition from Capitalism to Socialism*, London: Macmillan.

Stevens, R. (1971) *American Medicine and the Public Interest*, New Haven, Conn.: Yale University Press.

Stevens, R. (1977) *In Sickness and in Wealth: American hospitals in the twentieth century*, New York: Basic Books.

Stevenson, J. (1984) *British Society 1914–45*, Harmondsworth: Penguin.

Stevenson, M. (1977) *Women in Canada*, Don Mills, Ont.: General Publishing.

Stewart, M. (1967) *Keynes and After*, Harmondsworth: Penguin.

Stewart, W. (1977) *Strikes*, Toronto: McClelland and Stewart.

Stites, R. (1978) *The Women's Liberation Movement in Russia: Feminism, Nihilism, and Bolshevism, 1860–1930*, Princeton, New Jersey: Princeton University Press.

Stoesz, D. (1981) 'A wake for the welfare state: The neo-Conservative challenge', *Social Services Review*, vol. 55, no. 3, pp. 398–411.

Stretton, S. (1978) *Elders*, London: Routledge and Kegan Paul.

Strong-Boag, V. (1977) 'Canadian feminism in the 1920s: The case of Nellie McClung', *Journal of Canadian Studies*, vol. 12, no. 4, p. 58.

Strong-Boag, V. (1979) 'Wages for housework: Mother's allowances and the beginnings of social security in Canada', *Journal of Canadian Studies*, vol. 14, no. 1, p. 24.

Struthers, J. (1979) 'Two depressions: Bennett, Trudeau and the unemployed', *Journal of Canadian Studies*, vol. 14, no. 1, p. 70.

Stuart, M. B. and Edmund, F. H. (1989) *A National Health System for America*, Washington, DC: Heritage Foundation.

Stubbs, P. (1985) 'The employment of black social workers: From "ethnic sensitivity" to anti-racism', *Critical Social Policy*, vol. 12, pp. 6–27.

Sundstrom, G. (1982) 'The elderly, women's work and social security costs', *Acta Sociologica*, vol. 25, pp. 21–38.

Su Yin, H. (1970) 'Family planning in China', *Japanese Quarterly*, vol. 17, no. 4, p. 436.

Swarup, S. (1966) *A Study of the Chinese Communist Movement*, Oxford: Clarendon Press.

Swedish Institute (SI) (1987) *Fact Sheets on Sweden*, Stockholm: SI.

Szymanski, A. (1974) *Is The Red Flag Flying? The political economy of the Soviet Union*, London: Pluto Press.

Szymanski, A. (1982) 'On the uses of disinformation to legitimize the revival of the cold war: Health in the USSR', *International Journal of Health Services*, vol. 12, no. 3, pp. 481–99.

Taylor, D. (1988/9) 'Liberal democracy and welfare theory: A way forward for critical social policy', *Critical Social Policy*, issue 24, pp. 91–112.

Taylor, J. (1979) '"Relief from Relief": the Cities' Answer to Depression Dependency', *Journal of Canadian Studies*, vol. 14, no. 1 p. 16.

Taylor-Gooby, P. and Dale, J. (1981) *Social Theory and Social Welfare*, London: Edward Arnold.

Taylor-Gooby, P. (1985) *Public Opinion, Ideology and State Welfare*, London: Routledge and Kegan Paul.

Thane, P. (ed.) (1978) *The Origins of Social Policy*, London: Croom Helm.

Thane, P. (1982) *Foundations of the Welfare State*, Harlow: Longman.

Thatcher, M. (1990) 'Interview on Radio 4's *Women's Hour*', February.

Therborn, G., Kjellberg, A., Marklund, S. and Ohlund, U. (1978) 'Sweden before and after social democracy: A first overview', *Acta Sociologica*, supplement, pp. 37–58.

Thorne, B. (1982) *Rethinking the Family: Some feminist questions*, New York: Longman.

Thunhurst, C. (1982) *It Makes You Sick: The politics of health*, London: Pluto Press.

Thursz, D. and Vigilante, J. (1976) *Meeting Human Needs: Additional perspectives from thirteen countries*, London: Sage.

Tilton, T. (1968) 'The Swedish road to socialism', *The American Journal of Political Science Review*, vol. 33.

Tindale, J. (1988) 'Income, pensions, and inequality in later life', *Social Inequality in Canada*, edited by J. Curtis, E. Grabb, N. Guppy and S. Gilbert, Toronto: The Women's Press, pp. 302–18.

Tipler, J. (1986) *Is Justice Colour Blind? A study of the impact of race in the juvenile justice system in Hackney*, London: Hackney Social Services Department.

Titmuss, R. (1950) *Problems of Social Policy*, London: HMSO.

Titmuss, R. (1958) *Essays on the Welfare State*, London: Allen and Unwin.

Titmuss, R. (1968) *Commitment to Welfare*, London: Allen and Unwin.

Titmuss, R. (1970) *The Gift Relationship*, London: Allen and Unwin.

Titmuss, R. (1971) 'Welfare rights, law and discretion', *Political Science Quarterly*, vol. 42, pp. 113–32.

Titmuss, R. (1974) *Social Policy: An introduction*, London: Allen and Unwin.

Titmuss, R. and Abel-Smith, B. (1956) *The Cost of the National Health Service in England and Wales*, Cambridge: Cambridge University Press.

Tizard, J. and Hughes, B. (1976) *All Our Children*, London: Temple Smith.

Tomasson, R. (1970) *Sweden: Prototype of a modern society*, New York: Random House.

Torkington, N. (1983) *The Racial Politics of Health*, Liverpool: Liverpool University.

Townsend, J. R. (1969) *Political Participation in Communist China*, Berkeley, Calif.: University of California Press.

Townsend, J. R. (1974) *Politics in China*, Boston: Little and Brown.

Townsend, P. (1962) *The Last Refuge*, London: Routledge and Kegan Paul.

Townsend, P. (1979) *Poverty in the United Kingdom*, Harmondsworth: Penguin.

Townsend, P. (1986) Foreword in *Excluding the Poor*, London: CPAG.

Townsend, P. and Bosanquet, N. (1989) *Labour and Inequality*, London: Heinemann.

Townsend, P., Bosanquet, N. and Parker, R. (1987) *Poverty and Labour in London*, London: London Low Pay Unit.

Townsend, P. and Davidson, N. (eds.) (1984) *Inequalities in Health*, Harmondsworth: Penguin.

Townsend, P., Phillimore, P. and Beattie, A. (1988) *Health and Deprivation: Inequality and the North*, London: Croom Helm.

Trevillian, S. (1988/9) 'Griffiths and Wagner: Which future for community care?', *Critical Social Policy*, issue 24, pp. 65–73.

Trivedi, P. (1984) 'To deny our fullness: Asian women in the making of history', *Feminist Review*, no. 17, pp. 37–52.

Trotsky, L. (1972) *The Revolution Betrayed*, New York: Pathfinder Press.

Trotsky, L. (1973) *Women and the Family*, New York: Pathfinder Press.

Twigg, J. (1989) 'Models of carers: How do social care agencies conceptualise their relationship with informal carers?', *Journal of Social Policy*, vol. 18, no. 1, pp. 53–66.

Uhr, C. G. (1966) *Sweden's Employment Security Programme and Its Impact on the Country's Economy*, Berkeley: California Institute of Technology.

Union for Radical Political Economics (URPE) (1981) *Crisis in the Public Sector: A reader*, New York: Monthly Review Press.

United Kingdom Home Office (1968) *Report of the Committee on Local Authority and Allied Personal Social Services*, London: HMSO.

Ungerson, C. (ed.) (1985) *Women and Social Policy. A Reader*, London: Macmillan.

Ungerson, C. (1987) *Policy is Personal: Sex, gender and informal care*, London: Tavistock.

Valentine, C. (1969) *Culture and Poverty: Critique and counter proposals*, Chicago: University of Chicago.

Vallieres, P. (1971) *White Niggers of America*, New York: Monthly Review Press.

Van der Tak, J. (1974) *Abortion, Fertility and Changing Legislation: An international review*, Lexington, Mass.: Lexington Books/D. C. Heath.

Van Langendonck, J. (1975) *Prelude to Harmony on a Community Theme: Health care insurance policies in the Six and Britain*, Oxford: Oxford University Press.

Van Stolk, M. (1973) *The Battered Child in Canada*, Toronto: McClelland and Stewart.

Vickers, J. (1989) 'Feminist approaches to women in politics', *Beyond The Vote: Canadian women in politics*, edited by L. Kealey and J. Sangster, Toronto: Women's Press, pp. 16–38.

Welsh Women's Aid Federation (WWAF) (1978) *Available for Work*, Cardiff: WWAF.

Walker, A. (ed.) (1982a) *Community Care: The family, the state and social policy*, Oxford: Basil Blackwell and Martin Robertson.

Walker, A. (ed.) (1982b) *Public Expenditure and Social Policy: An examination of social spending and social priorities*, London: Gower.

Walker, A. (1983a) 'Care for elderly people: A conflict between women and the state', *A Labour of Love: Women, work and caring*, edited by J. Finch and D. Groves, London: Routledge and Kegan Paul.

Walker, A. (1983b) 'Labour's social plans: The limits of welfare statism', *Critical Social Policy*, no. 8, pp. 45–65.

Walker, A. (1984) *Social Planning: A strategy for socialist welfare*, Oxford: Basil Blackwell.

Walker, A. (1988) 'Tendering care', *New Society*, 21 January.

Walker, A. and Walker, C. (1987) *The Growing Divide: A social audit, 1979–87*, London: CPAG.

Walker, H. and Beaumont, B. (1985) *Working With Offenders*, London: NASW/Macmillan.

Walker, M. (1988) 'Russian women exploited on the shop floor', *The Guardian*, 23 January, p. 7.

Waller, D. J. (1973) *The Government and Politics in the People's Republic of China*, London: Hutchinson.

Wallerstein, I. (1974) *The Modern World System: Capitalist agriculture and the origins of the European world-economy in the sixteenth century*, New York: Academic Press.

Wallsgrove, R. (1983) 'Greenham Common women's peace camp – so why do we still feel ambivalent?', *Trouble and Strife*, vol. 1, p. 4.

Walters, V. (1980) *Class Inequality and Health Care: Origins and impact of the National Health Service*, London: Croom Helm.

Walton, R. (1975) *Women in Social Work*, London: Routledge and Kegan Paul.

Wandor, M. (1972) *The Body Politic: Women's liberation in Britain 1969–72*, London: Stage One.

Watkin, B. (1978) *The NHS: The first phase, 1948–74 and after*, London: Allen and Unwin.

Watson, P. (1980) *Social Security Law of the European Communities*, London: Mansell Information Publishing.

Webb, S. and Webb, B. (1937) *Soviet Communism: A new civilisation at work*, London: Gollancz.

Wedderburn, D. (1965) 'Facts and theories of the welfare state', *The Socialist Register*, pp. 127–46.

Wedderburn, D. (ed.) (1974) *Poverty, Inequality and Class Structure*, Cambridge: Cambridge University Press.

Weinberg, I. (1969) 'The problems of the convergence of industrial societies: A critical look at the state of a theory', *Comparative Studies in Society and History*, vol. 11, pp. 1–16.

Weinstein, J. (1967) *The Decline of Socialism in the United States, 1912–25*, New York: Monthly Review Press.

Weinstein, J. (1975) *Ambiguous Legacy: The left in American politics*, New York: Franklin Watts.

Weinstein, J. (1981) *Corporate Ideal in the Liberal State: 1900–1918*, Westport, Conn.: Greenwood Press.

Weir, A. (1977) 'Battered women: Some perspectives and problems', *Women in the Community*, edited by M. Mayo, London: Routledge and Kegan Paul.

Weir, A. and McIntosh, M. (1982) 'Towards a wages strategy for women', *Feminist Review*, no. 10, pp. 55–72.

Weir, A. and Wilson, E. (1984) 'The British Women's Movement', *New Left Review*, vol. 148, pp. 74–103.

Weitzman, L. J. (1985) *The Divorce Revolution: The unexpected social and economic consequences for women and children in America*, New York: Free Press.

Wegman, M. (ed.) (1973) *Public Health in the People's Republic of China*, New York: Macy Foundation.

Wharf, B. (1988) *Towards First Nations Control of Child Welfare*, Victoria: University of Victoria Press.

Wheelwright, E. L. and McFarlane, B. (1970) *The Chinese Road to Socialism: The economics of the cultural revolution*, New York: Monthly Review Press.

Whitehead, M. (1987) *The Health Divide: Inequalities in health*, Harmondsworth: Penguin.

Whittington, M. S. and Williams, G. (eds.) (1981) *Canadian Politics in the 1980s*, Toronto: University of Toronto Press.

Widgery, D. (1979) *Health in Danger: The crisis in the National Health Service*, London: Macmillan.

Wigle, D. and Mao, Y. (1988) 'Income and life expectancy', *Social Inequality in Canada*, edited by J. Curtis, E. Grabb, N. Guppy and S. Gibert, Toronto: The Women's Press, pp. 439–44.

Wilensky, H. (1975) *Welfare State and Equality*, Berkeley, Calif.: University of California Press.

Wilensky, H. and Lebaux, C. (1965) *Industrial Society and Social Welfare*, New York: Macmillan.

Wiles, P. (1963) 'Will capitalism and communism spontaneously converge?', *Encounter*, vol. 20, no. 6.

Willcocks, A. (1967) *The Creation of the National Health Service: A study pressure groups and a major policy decision*, London: Routledge and Kegan Paul.

Williams, F. (1987) 'Racism and the discipline of social policy: a critique of welfare theory' in *Critical Social Policy*, Issue 20, Autumn, pp. 4–29.

Williams, F. (1989) *Social Policy: A critical introduction: Issues of race, gender and class*, Cambridge: Polity Press.

Willis, P. (1977) *Learning to Labour: How working class kids get working class jobs*, London: Saxon House.

Wilson, D. (1979) *The Welfare State in Sweden: A study in comparative social administration*, London: Heinemann.

Wilson, E. (1977) *Women and the Welfare State*, London: Tavistock.

Wilson, E. (1982) 'Feminism and social policy', *Social Policy and Social Welfare*, edited by M. Loney, D. Boswell and J. Clance, Milton Keynes: Open University Press.

Wilson, E. (1982) 'Women, the "community" and the "family"', *Community Care: The family, the state and social policy*, edited by A. Walker, Oxford: Basil Blackwell.

Wilson, E. (1987) 'Thatcherism and women: After seven years', *The Socialist Register*, pp. 199–235.

Wilson, E. with Weir, A. (1986) *Hidden Agendas: Theory, politics and experience in the women's movement*, London: Tavistock.

Wineman, S. (1984) *The Politics of Human Services: Radical alternatives to the welfare state*, Montreal: Black Rose Books.

Winn, C. (1988) 'The socio-economic attainment of visible minorities: Facts and policy implications', *Social Inequality in Canada*, edited by J. Curtis, E. Grabb, N. Guppy and S. Gibert, Toronto: The Women's Press, pp. 195–213.

Wise, S. (1985) *Becoming a Feminist Social Worker*, monograph in studies on sexual politics, Manchester: Manchester University Press.

Wistrand, B. (1981) *Swedish Women on the Move*, Stockholm: The Swedish Institute.

Withorn, A. (1984) 'For better and for worse: Social relations among women in the welfare state', *Radical America*, vol. 18, no. 4, pp. 37–47.

Witke, R. (1977) *Comrade Chiang Ch'ing*, London: Weidenfeld and Nicolson.

Wolf, M. and Witke, R. (eds.) (1976) *Women in Chinese Society*, Stanford: Stanford University Press.

Wolfe, A. (1981) 'Sociology, liberalism and the new right', *New Left Review*, vol. 128, pp. 3–27.

Wolfe, A. (1981) *America's Impasse: The rise and fall of the politics of growth*, New York: Pantheon Books.

Wolfenden, Lord J. (1979) *The Future of Voluntary Organisations (The Wolfenden Report)*, London: Croom Helm.

Wollstonecraft, M. (1978) *A Vindication of the Rights of Women (1792)*, Harmondsworth: Penguin.

Women in Eastern Europe Group (WEEG) (1980) *Women and Russia: The first feminist samizdat*, London: Sheba Feminist Publishers.

Woodsworth, D. (1977) *Social Security and National Policy: Sweden, Yugoslavia, and Japan*, Montreal: McGill-Queen's University Printer.

Worcester, N. and Whatley, M. (1988) 'The response of the healthcare system to the women's health movement: The selling of women's health centres' in *Feminism within the Science and Health Care Professions*, edited by S. Rosser, Oxford: Pergamon Press.

Wright, F. D. (1986) *Left To Care Alone*, London: Gower.

Yang, C. K. (1959) *Chinese Communist Society: The family and the village*, Cambridge, Mass.: MIT Press.

Yang, C. K. (1965) *The Chinese Family in the Communist Revolution*, Cambridge, Mass.: MIT Press.

Yanowitch, M. (1977) *Social and Economic Inequality in The Soviet Union*, Oxford: Martin Robertson.

Young, K. (ed.) (1984) *Of Marriage and the Market: Women's subordination internationally and its lessons*, London: Routledge, Chapman and Hall.

Young, M. (ed.) (1973) *Women in China: Studies in social change and feminism*, Ann Arbor: University of Michigan.

Yu, P. (1984) 'Black men, welfare and jobs', *New York Times*, 11 May.

Zakharov, M. and Tsivilyvov, R. (1978) *Social Security in the USSR*, Moscow: Progress Books.

Zald, M. (1965) *Social Welfare Institutions*, New York: Wiley.

Zaretsky, E. (1976) *Capitalism, The Family and Personal Life*, London: Pluto Press.

Zigler, E. and Valentine, J. (eds.) (1979) *Project Headstart: A legacy of the war on poverty*, New York: Collier–Macmillan.

Zinn, H. (1988) *People's History of the United States*, Harlow: Longman.

Author Index

Author Index

Author Index

Subject Index

Subject Index